# THE MAN WHO PRESUMED

Dad.

Merry Christmas & thanks for
the African trip!

Love Hugh

X-MAS '92

# The Man Who Presumed

## A BIOGRAPHY OF HENRY M. STANLEY

*By*

BYRON FARWELL

ILLUSTRATED WITH
PHOTOGRAPHS AND MAPS

W.W. NORTON AND COMPANY
NEW YORK, LONDON

Library of Congress Catalog Card Number: 57-6187

82751-0117

Printed in the United States of America

ISBN 0-393-30629-1

W. W. Norton & Company, Inc., 500 Fifth Avenue, New York, N.Y. 10110
W. W. Norton & Company Ltd., 37 Great Russell Street, London WC1B 3NU

1 2 3 4 5 6 7 8 9 0

TO

E. L. FARWELL,

MY FATHER

# *Preface*

"DR. LIVINGSTONE, I PRESUME?" said Stanley, and the world has been mimicking him ever since. He epitomizes for us the coolness and reserve of an Englishman in emotional circumstances. Yet, Henry Morton Stanley was not an Englishman, and, although he lived much of his early life in the United States and even fought on both sides in the Civil War, he was not an American either. In fact, his name was not even Stanley.

The name of Henry M. Stanley occupies a unique position in the American mind. Everyone knows that he found Livingstone somewhere in Africa and that he made that most inadequate of statements, "Dr. Livingstone, I presume?" Few people know more than this about the man. Yet, the finding of Livingstone was neither the first, the last, nor the greatest of the series of amazing exploits that made up his life. So incredible does it seem that one man could have done so much in a single lifetime that those to whom I have told the story have frequently asked if mine is not a fictionalized version. But there has been no need to invent or embroider; the facts are colorful enough.

When our grandfathers studied geography there was little that could be taught about Africa. Except for Egypt, the Cape colonies and a coastal town here and there, the map of the world's second largest continent was largely a blank. Many able and brave men devoted their energies and risked their lives to fill those vast empty spaces on the maps—and most of them lived and died within the last hundred years. But of all the great African explorers, two names stand out above the others: Livingstone and Stanley. They were very different men, but they were both obsessed with the spirit of Africa. Of the two, the most interesting was Stanley, the only newspaper reporter to found an empire. The story of his career is a picaresque novel come to life; it is the tale of an unloved bastard who became first an adventurer and finally a hero; it is the odyssey of a Ulysses without a Penelope or an Ithaca who, late in life and quite unexpectedly, found both.

This book tells of many travels and incidents, much movement, action of all sorts—parts of the story becoming, perforce, hardly more than a catalogue of personal happenings—for Stanley, although his gainful occupation was saying things, was essentially a man who did things. It is through his deeds that we must see the man, but, as in most lives, a man's history cannot be, and should not be, separated from his character and personality. The crammed incidents of Stanley's life are as diversified as they are romantic: he was a storekeeper, soldier, sailor, newspaper reporter, explorer, builder, statesman, author, politician, lecturer; he knew wars, famine, disease, brutality, poverty, wealth, and—eventually—love. Although going through much of his life almost friendless, he was a familiar of kings, pashas, slavers, slaves, statesmen, scientists, generals, African chiefs, and women. But this is more than a simple adventure story; the short, stocky man with the boyish eyes and perpetual frown hardly fits the conventional picture of the swashbuckling adventurer. His complex, restless personality with strong drives, unusual abilities, fierce ambition, and a strange attraction to and repulsion from love make of him an interesting psychological study of the man of action.

During Stanley's lifetime, from his sudden fame following the Livingstone expedition until his death thirty-three years later, many biographies and articles were written about him, but almost all of these contained incidents that could not have taken place. Stanley, for reasons of his own, did not discourage these false stories unless they were detrimental to his character. Thus, many of these fanciful tales were passed on long after the true facts were available to anyone who would take the trouble to find them out. But interest in Stanley waned after his death—possibly because the stories about him were too conflicting and complex—and all that remained of his fame (in this country, at least) were the first four words he spoke to Livingstone.

A fascinating personality who led an exciting and adventurous life, making at the same time a major contribution to the world's knowledge, should make an interesting story; I have tried to tell it with honesty. As far as can accurately be determined, all of the incidents reported here actually took place. Some of the translations of conversations in abstruse languages have been changed to more readable or appropriate English, but the sense has not been altered. For example, at one point Stanley reported his crew of Zanzibaris as complying with his orders by saying, "Aye, aye, sir!" Now whatever the original Swahili may have been, the "aye, ayes" have been changed to "yes." So, too, translations using "thee" and "thou" have been changed to "you." Also, in the interests of readability, but at the risk of being considered unscholarly, I have included only four footnotes. Major sources of information may be found in the bibliography.

A number of people and institutions have been helpful to me, but I am particularly grateful to Ruth Farwell, my patient and understanding wife.

BYRON FARWELL

*Birmingham, Michigan*
*May 2, 1957*

# *Acknowledgments*

I wish to thank Major Denzil Morton Stanley for his patience and fine cooperation, and Ian Anstruther for his assistance in providing me with useful material. In addition, I would like to express my gratitude to: Houghton Mifflin Co. for permission to quote from *The Autobiography of Henry M. Stanley*, edited by Dorothy Stanley, and for permission to use some of the photographs from the same book; Harper and Brothers for permission to quote from *Mark Twain's Speeches* and from the books by Stanley published by that house; Constable & Company for allowing me to quote from *Thirty Years Anglo-French Reminiscences* by Sir Thomas Barclay; Charles Scribner's Sons for the use of material from *A Voice from the Congo* by Herbert Ward; and The Bobbs-Merrill Company for special permission to use excerpts from *The James Gordon Bennetts* by Don C. Seitz, copyright, 1928, 1956.

# Contents

THE MAN WHO PRESUMED

CHAPTER I

# Boyhood and Early Adventures

IT WAS A DISGRACE to the family when, on January 28, 1841, Miss Elizabeth Parry gave birth to a son in her home town of Denbigh in northern Wales. The living symbol of her downfall was to become one of the world's greatest African explorers under the name of Henry Morton Stanley, but he was baptized John Rowlands, as this was believed to be the name of his father. Having no desire to remain where she would be pointed out by the neighbors and snickered at by the louts at the public house, she ran off to London, leaving her infant son in the hands of her father, Moses Parry. This old gentleman had once been fairly well-to-do, but now he was reduced to living with his two grown sons in a small cottage in the shadow of Denbigh Castle and earning a modest living by axing calves in the local slaughterhouse.

When John was four years old his grandfather died, and his care devolved upon his two uncles, Moses and John, who, unwilling to have the boy in their own household, boarded him out with an old couple named Price for half a crown (about thirty-five cents) a week. But the uncles grumbled at even this modest expenditure, and when John was six years old, they discontinued the arrangement. It was then that Dick Price, the son of the people who had been keeping him, took the boy by the hand and, under the pretense of taking him to see his Aunt Mary at Ffynnon Beuno, started out with him on a long walk.

It was a tiring trip for a little boy, but, although he frequently begged for rest, Dick urged him along with cajolings and false endearments. To John, the walk seemed interminable, but at last they arrived in front of a huge stone building surrounded by a massive iron fence. Passing through a heavy gate, Dick led his tired and puzzled charge to the door of the stone building and rang the bell. John could hear the hollow clanging as it echoed inside the building. The door was opened by a stony-faced stranger who, to John's astonishment and terror, seized him by the wrist and quickly drew him inside. Crying and pleading, he begged Dick to save him, but the young man only tried to soothe him with more lies: he would bring his Aunt Mary to see him here, he said quickly. Then the door slammed shut. John was left alone —terrified—with the grim man holding him in a manacle-like grip.

The stone building with the iron fence was the St. Asaph Union Workhouse, a sort of penitentiary to which impecunious old folk and superfluous children were confined in order, as Stanley later remarked, "to relieve the respectabilities of the obnoxious sight of extreme poverty." This dismal structure was to be John Rowlands' home for the next nine years.

It was some time before the young boy learned the unimportance of tears in a workhouse. In the prison-like routine, there was no time to be wasted on sympathy for a homeless, unwanted, frightened boy. Life in St. Asaph's was hard and grim for both its very old and its very young inmates. It was parish charity with a vengeance. At six in the morning, everyone was awakened; at eight o'clock in the evening, they were locked in their drab dormitories. In between there was only work and, for the children, lessons as well. The boys swept the grounds with oversized brooms, scrubbed the slate floors, and worked in the fields. In winter there was never enough heat in the building, and often they were sent into the fields to hoe the frozen ground, shivering in thin, inadequate clothes. Their diet consisted of bread, gruel, rice, and potatoes—all economically measured out. Every Saturday they were scrubbed, and every Sunday they submitted to two long sermons.

The workhouse education was intended to lead to apprenticeships in useful trades, but in practice much of it was simply the assignment of whole pages of texts to be memorized. The schoolmaster was a thirty-two-year-old ex-miner named James Francis who, having lost a hand in a mining accident, could find no better occupation. Soured by misfortune, he had both a vicious temper and a callous heart. He took a savage pleasure in pounding his small charges with fist, cane, boot, birch, and ruler, and little John Rowlands received his first flogging at his hands when he was unable to pronounce "Joseph" correctly in Bible class. This sadistic tyrant ended his days in a madhouse, but he was not removed soon enough to bring any comfort to the future African explorer and his unfortunate companions.

School was conducted in two rooms on the ground floor of the workhouse, one room for boys and one for girls. The curriculum was primitive. As the Board of Governors considered arithmetic and geography superfluous, slates and maps were not provided. The principal textbooks were the Bible, the Catechism and *Dr. Mavor's Spelling Primer,* the latter being fifty years out of date even then. Jellinger Symons, an inspector of schools who visited St. Asaph's during John's stay there, once noted that some of the children looked pale and spiritless, but he attributed this to a lack of sufficient occupation, being himself convinced that children should be worked ceaselessly from the moment they arose until bedtime.

There were about thirty boys in the institution most of the time, ranging in age from five to fifteen years. With their drab fustian clothes and close-mown hair, there was little to distinguish them. They looked what they were: outcast sons of Welsh peasants. But at one time there was a boy about John's age who stood out from the rest. He was strikingly handsome, with curly hair and a pale, delicately molded face. Some of the boys conjectured he must be the son of a lord. Willie Roberts was his name and, having a friendly disposition, he was a favorite of the other workhouse boys.

Then, one day, Willie disappeared, and it was rumored among the boys that he was dead. Discussing his fate in hushed voices, one of the boys whispered that at this very moment his corpse was probably in the "deadhouse," a little building near the infirmary. Another boy suggested that they go and see for themselves. So, with fast-beating hearts and sweating palms, John and two or three other boys crept silently across the yard and into the cold and gloomy morgue. Sure enough, there was a body stretched out on a black bier and covered with a white sheet. One of the boldest boys stepped forward and drew back the covering. John Rowlands was to see hundreds of dead men in his lifetime, but now he was awed and chilled as any other eleven-year-old boy seeing for the first time the waxen face and fixed stare of death. It was Willie Roberts. When the sheet was pulled back still more, what they saw made them gasp. Willie's naked, milk-white body was covered with dark bruises and deep gashes. One look was enough. Hastily covering the corpse, they fled, convinced that James Francis had murdered Willie Roberts. It was a terrifying thought.

During his years at St. Asaph John did not miss his mother. Indeed, he was twelve years old before he learned that every boy had a mother. One day in the winter of 1851, during the dinner hour when all of the inmates were assembled, Francis came up to him and, pointing out a tall woman with an oval face and a large coil of hair on the back of her head, asked John if he recognized her.

"No, sir," the boy replied.

"What," Francis sneered, "you don't know your own mother?"

John's face flushed as he looked up at her shyly. She returned his glance with a look of cool, critical scrutiny. His first gush of tenderness was immediately checked by her expression, and it was plain to the boy that she had no feeling for him. "Honor thy father and mother" he had been told, but this parent required neither love nor honor from him.

Elizabeth Parry, who had now married a man named Robert Jones, had brought with her a little boy named Robert and a girl, Emma—John's half brother and half sister. After a few weeks' stay, the mother departed, taking her little boy and leaving Emma. There was strict separation of the sexes at the workhouse—husbands were even separated from their wives—so although John occasionally saw his half sister in the halls, they never talked together and she remained a stranger. In the workhouse records she was listed as "a deserted bastard." In 1857, when she was fourteen years old, she left the workhouse to become a domestic servant in St. Asaph.

Distinction was difficult to achieve in the workhouse, but John did acquire a degree of local fame with his drawings. As his pictures were mostly copies of prints depicting cathedrals, they were shown to the bishop, who rewarded the boy's industry and talent by presenting him with a Bible autographed by himself. John stood out in other ways, too. On annual holidays he led the workhouse boys' choir, and one year he was even selected to attend the Eisteddfod, but he was unable to go because of a sudden attack of measles. Having an exceptionally good memory, he also did well in his lessons. The school inspector once pronounced him the most advanced pupil in St. Asaph.

A man named Hughes from Llandudno later remembered him as "a full-faced stubborn, self-willed, round headed, uncompromising fellow. . . . His temperament was unusually sensitive; he could stand no chaff, nor the least bit of humour. He was particularly strong in trunk, but not very smart or elegant about the legs, which were slightly disproportionately short."

John was fifteen years old when an incident occurred that drastically changed the course of his life. Speaking of it many years later he said, "But for the stupid and brutal scene that brought it about, I might eventually have been apprenticed to some trade or another, and would have mildewed in Wales."

A table had been scratched and Francis demanded to know who had done it. When no one confessed, he seized a birch rod and proclaimed that he would beat the entire school. Shouting at them to "unbutton," he started at the foot of the class. John, incensed by this injustice, refused to obey the order. When it came his turn and he was unprepared, Francis was in a frenzy.

"How is this?" he cried savagely. "Not ready yet? Strip, sir, this minute; I mean to stop this abominable and barefaced lying."

"I did not lie, sir. I know nothing of it."

"Silence, sir. Down with your clothes!"

"Never again!" the boy shouted.

The words were hardly out of his mouth when he found himself swung up in the air by the collar of his jacket and flung into a nerveless heap on a bench. Filled with brute passion, Francis pommeled him in the stomach until he gasped for breath. Again he was lifted and dashed against a bench with a shock that seemed to splinter his spine. What little sense was left in him after this treatment made him aware that he was being slapped on both cheeks.

Recovering his breath for an instant, John aimed a vigorous kick at the schoolmaster. His shoe crashed into Francis' face, breaking his glasses and temporarily blinding him. Starting back with a cry of pain, Francis fell over a bench and was knocked unconscious when his head struck the stone floor. John bounded up, seized the birch rod, and began to pound the prostrate schoolmaster. It was several minutes before he realized that the form he was beating was already senseless. Then reason returned, and fright and horror at what he had done swept over him. With the help of his classmates, he dragged Francis to his room and then fled over the school wall.

Outside the workhouse, he had imagined a world filled with smiling faces, cheery hearths, and hearty welcomes. He was soon disillusioned. Going first to his paternal grandfather, a prosperous Welsh farmer, he told him who he was and how he was now penniless and homeless. The old gentleman smoked his pipe and listened to the story in silence. Then pointing to the door with the stem of his pipe, he told his fourteen-year-old grandson to get out of the house and never come back.

The boy met with no better success in his visits to his uncles. At last, he went to a cousin, Moses Owen, a schoolmaster in the village of Brynford. After questioning him closely on the extent of his learning,

Moses agreed to give him board and lodging if he would work for him as a pupil-teacher. John quickly agreed. First, however, it was necessary that he be outfitted with proper clothes, and for this purpose Moses sent him to his mother, Mary Owen, who ran a combination farm, inn, and general store at Ffynnon Beuno, about four miles from Denbigh. This was the Aunt Mary whom he thought he was being taken to see when he was led to the workhouse nine years earlier.

Aunt Mary was thrifty, hard-working, and petulant. Although she fed him well and made him decent clothes, she did not hesitate to let him know that he was not wanted and that she thought her son had made a mistake by taking him into his school. She aired her feelings freely to every customer who came to the inn, and John squirmed as the tailor, the butcher, the gamekeeper, the farmers, and the navvies eyed him critically over their ale. To her own children, Mary Owen was a good and loving mother, but she had no affection to waste on this unwanted boy.

In a month, Aunt Mary had made his school clothes, and John was taken back to Moses' school to begin his new duties and his studies. Moses Owen was infatuated with books, and he infused this passion into his young charge. At first, all went well at the school; John liked his studies and he respected the intellectual qualities of his cousin. But it was not long before his schoolmates discovered his origins, and, like many schoolboys, they made great use of their knowledge and showed him no mercy. The effect of this treatment by his comrades was to drive him into his shell and to impress upon him that he was an outcast from normal society. Moses was no help to him, for he soon found his young cousin to be a financial burden. Instead of telling John to leave, however, he began a program of harassment, hoping perhaps that the boy would run away. But John had nowhere to run. So he remained to endure the insults of both students and teacher. Moses would push back his chair from the table and exclaim, "Your head must be full of mud instead of brains," or "You are good for nothing but to cobble paupers' boots." This life lasted for nine months before Moses sent him back to Ffynnon Beuno. He was never recalled to the school.

A few months later, Aunt Mary took him to Liverpool to turn him over to another aunt, Maria Morris. Like any country boy seeing a big city for the first time, John was amazed and frightened by the crowds and the hustle and bustle of Liverpool. He was comforted, though, by the kindliness of his Aunt Maria and more particularly by his Uncle Tom, who was robust, hearty, and full of good cheer—although somewhat rash in his promises. John had been taken to Liverpool because of his uncle's professed ability to secure a fine job for his nephew. At first, it did look as though Uncle Tom would obtain a position for him as a boy in an insurance office, but unfortunately Tom's hopes fell through. In the end, John was forced to find work for himself.

His first job was in a haberdashery where he had to be up before six and did not reach home until nine-thirty in the evening. His pay for working these hours six days out of every seven was five shillings —less than a dollar for a week's work. But this job lasted only two months. The haberdasher fired John and in his place hired an eighteen-year-old boy who was bigger and stronger.

John resumed his routine of walking the streets in search of a "Boy Wanted" sign. In a few days he found one in the window of a butcher's shop near the docks. He applied for the job and was hired. Here he carried fresh meat from the shop to the wharves, where he became fascinated by the tall ships from all over the world that sailed in and out of the harbor of Liverpool.

One day he was charged with carrying some provisions and a note to Captain David Harding of the packet ship *Windermere*. While the captain was reading the note, John looked around the cabin with admiring eyes. He gaped at the fine furniture, gilded mirrors, and glittering cornices. Suddenly, he became conscious that he was being scrutinized.

"I see that you admire my cabin," said the captain in a rich, strong voice. "Would you like to live in it?"

"Sir?" John answered, astonished.

"I say, how would you like to sail in this ship?"

"But I know nothing of the sea, sir."

"Sho! You will soon learn all that you have to do; and, in time, you may become a captain of as fine a ship. We skippers have all been boys, you know. Come, what do you say to going with me as cabin boy? I will give you five dollars a month, and an outfit. In three days we start for New Orleans, to the land of the free and the home of the brave."

Conditions at the Morris house had deteriorated. The family's poverty had even forced Aunt Maria to sell the school clothes that Aunt Mary had made. Three days later, on December 20, 1858, he found himself seasick and miserable in the hold of the *Windermere*.

For three days he was left to lie in lonely misery on his bunk, but on the fourth day out he was aroused by a stream of profanity from the second mate who hurried him out of the hold and set him to scrubbing the deck.

It was then he learned that his promised position as cabin boy was only a scheme of the captain's to obtain cheap deck hands. It was his practice to take on young boys, haze them to the point where they would jump ship at the next port, and then pocket their wages.

John was introduced to the ways of the ship by another boy named Harry, a veteran of one other voyage in the *Windermere*. Harry was not in the same situation as John. He had been taken on board by his father and had signed the ship's articles. If anything happened to him, Harry cheerfully explained, the captain would have to account to the authorities, but if John should be swept overboard or be beaten to death by the mates, the captain was accountable to no one. Although conceding that it was a rough life, Harry took great pride in his nautical knowledge and looked forward to being an able seaman.

John did not share Harry's enthusiasm for the sea, and his admiration for the "bucco sailor" soon vanished: "It is true," he said later, "the 'old salts' were loudest in their responses to the mate's commands, that they led the bowline song and the halyard chant, were cheerier with their 'Aye, ayes,' 'Belays,' 'Vast hauling,' and chorus; that they strove whose hands should be uppermost at the halyards and nearest to the tackles; but all this did not impress me so much as they might think it did. When the officers thundered out, 'All hands shorten sail,' 'Furl topgallant sails,' or 'Reef topsail,' the shell-backs appeared to delay under various shifty pretexts to climb the rigging, in order that being last they might occupy the safe position at the bunt of the sails; and when it was a four-man job, the way in which they noisily passed the word along, without offering to move, was most artful."

The voyage was one long nightmare for the young Welsh boy. Between the sea, the coarse sailors, and the bullying mates, he was caught in a crossfire of abuse. After six weeks on shipboard, he caught his first sight of America. The sights, sounds, and smells of the port of New Orleans as it appeared in 1857 thrilled the boy. The balmy air; the scents of coffee, pitch, and semibaked sugar mixed with the smell of rum and whisky drippings; the horses, mules, and the rumbling drays and carriages; the crowds of men—black, white, yellow, and red —milling about on the levee—all was strange and wonderful.

Excitedly, John followed the footsteps of his friend Harry, who promised to show him the town. After a good meal and a stroll through the streets, life began to look brighter, and the country boy from Wales felt that now he was seeing the world. After a while, Harry led him to a house where a gracious lady met them at the door and invited them both inside. They sat down in the parlor where, to John's surprise, they were presently joined by four gay young girls so scantily dressed that he was speechless with amazement. His ignorance of all women, to say nothing of prostitutes, was profound. He was in a strange country, however, and he surmised that foreign people must have different customs. He was willing to be instructed. But when the gay ladies began to get down to business, he jumped up and fled in embarrassment.

Harry ran down the street after him, calling for him to return. But John was adamant. Harry then led his uncooperative pupil into a bar, but John had taken the pledge early in life, and, proclaiming himself a member of the "Band of Hope," he refused to touch the liquor. Exasperated, Harry said, "Well, smoke then, do something like other fellows." In an effort to be a man in some respect, John lit a cigar. Even this failed. As he smoked, his head began to swim and tides of nausea swept over him. Contrite, repentant, and miserable, he crept back to the ship and crawled into his bunk. So ended his first night in the New World.

The following evening he put on his best clothes, stuffed the bishop's Bible into his pocket, and jumped ship. After spending the night behind some bales of cotton on the levee, he set out early the next morning to look for work. He did not find a "Boy Wanted" sign, but he did see a kindly-looking, middle-aged gentleman tilted back in his chair reading a newspaper in front of a store. The man's name was Henry Morton Stanley, a cultured, intelligent, and prosperous businessman. Mr. Stanley was happily married, but childless. If he could have had one wish granted him, he would have asked for a child, preferably a boy, who could grow up to succeed him in his business. Consequently, John's first question startled him.

"Do you want a boy, sir?"

"Eh?" he demanded with a start. "What did you say?"

"I want some work, sir. I asked if you wanted a boy," John explained.

"A boy," he repeated slowly.

Laying aside his newspaper, he began to question John about where he had come from and how much education he had received. Then he asked him to mark some coffee bags that were standing nearby.

Pleased with the results of his examination and with the boy's work, Mr. Stanley took him off to breakfast, followed by a haircut and a shoe-shine.

John was then taken back to the store and introduced to Mr. James Speake, the store's owner. He was soon engaged at five dollars a week and launched on his apprenticeship as a merchant. At first, he did only manual work—unloading and stacking merchandise or labeling and addressing various goods. In two weeks he learned the location of all the merchandise in the store, and he was able to keep track of the numbers of barrels, boxes, and sacks of each kind of goods. Naturally, a boy who could make himself a human current inventory was a good lad to have about. His pay was soon raised to twenty-five dollars a month, and he was given the rating of a junior clerk.

Meanwhile, John found lodgings in the attic of a boardinghouse on St. Thomas Street run by a kindly woman named Mrs. Williams. With a good job to pay his room and board and independent of relatives, masters, and mates, the young man was free for the first time in his life. With the extra coins in his pocket he indulged in that luxury he had tasted at his cousin Moses': books. His choice was on the heavy side and included Gibbon's *Decline and Fall*, Plutarch's *Lives*, a large volume on the history of the United States, Pope's *Iliad*, Dryden's *Odyssey*, Tasso's *Jerusalem Delivered*, and even that most formidable of tomes, Spenser's *Faerie Queene*.

With Mrs. Williams' help, he constructed bookcases for his room out of old packing boxes. Now he had his own possessions, purchased with his own money, in his own room. All of his free hours were spent here reading his books. He was blissfully content. It seemed incredible to him that only eighteen months before he had been a workhouse boy at the mercy of the sadistic Francis.

John's boyhood was over, but the treatment he had received as a boy left its mark on his personality. The beatings, cuffs, and kicks he had endured, his rejection by all his relatives from his cousin to his mother, and the complete absence of any affection had made an outcast of him. As a result, he was hypersensitive and uncertain in any social situation. He knew that he was alone in the world, and that he must learn to become self-sufficient. But there was more to learn than he realized, and sometimes life taught him in strange ways.

One day there came to Mrs. Williams' boardinghouse another young boy who, like himself, had shipped out as a cabin boy of a boat sailing from England, had been forced to work as a common sailor, and had deserted in New Orleans. His name was Dick Heaton, a slightly built, handsome lad with blue eyes and fair hair. Because he was English and had experienced adventures similar to his own, John consented to share his room with him.

The two were soon fast friends, and John enjoyed the companionship of his young roommate. There were several peculiar things about Dick, though. The boy was so modest that he would not retire except in the dark, and while in bed he would cling to the very edge, as far away from his bedfellow as possible. When John woke up the first morning, he was surprised to learn that his companion had not undressed. Dick explained this by saying that he had gotten into the habit of sleeping in his clothes while on board ship as he had been severely beaten early in the voyage for being slow to dress. He also told John how he used to pad his clothes to avoid the pain of the beatings given out by the mates.

A few days later it struck John that Dick had an "unusual forward inclination of the body, and a singular leanness of the shoulders." He chided him with walking more like a girl than a boy, but Dick laughingly retorted, "So do you."

One morning when John woke up, he noticed that Dick's shirt was open at the neck. On his chest he saw what he took to be two tumors, and his cry of surprise awakened his companion. Pointing to Dick's naked breast, he anxiously asked if the protuberances were not painful. Seeing his friend's embarrassment, it did not take him too long to come to the conclusion that his roommate was a girl.

It may seem incredible today that a young man of eighteen could be so innocent, but considering John's background and the age in which he lived it is not too surprising. He had never associated with young girls his own age, and his reading was severe enough certainly to keep him ignorant of the biological facts of life.

Alice Heaton—for that was her real name—had led an exciting life for a girl of sixteen. She had fled from a nagging grandmother in Liverpool and had managed to live the life of a sailor boy without being detected. What eventually happened to her is unknown. After the morning revelation—embarrassing for both of them—John had to leave for work. When he returned that evening, the girl was gone.

Writing of the event forty years later, he remarked, "She was never seen, or heard of, by me again; but I have hoped ever since that Fate was as propitious to her, as I think it was wise, in separating two young and simple creatures, who might have been led through excess of sentiment, into folly."

The first month he worked at Mr. Speake's store he did not see the man who had first befriended him and whom he regarded, even at this stage, as his benefactor. Henry Morton Stanley was a kind of broker in goods of all sorts, acting as a go-between for the New Orleans merchants and the planters and country store owners up the Mississippi River and its tributaries. When Mr. Stanley, who had been on business up the river, returned to New Orleans, however, he invited the young man to his house. There he was cordially received by Mrs. Stanley, who took an immediate liking to him.

As the months passed, John became a more and more frequent visitor to the comfortable Stanley house on St. Charles Street, and Mrs. Stanley, particularly, became quite attached to him. John responded to her kindness with openhearted devotion. One Sunday when he came to visit her—Mr. Stanley being in St. Louis on business at the time—he was met at the door by the Irish maid, who told him that Mrs. Stanley was seriously ill. John stayed at the house, sitting outside the sick woman's door day and night. Leaving his job at the store, he devoted every minute to the care of his patroness, the only woman who had ever shown him any real affection. He was by her bedside when she died after an illness of only a few days. Her last words were a blessing on him.

The next day, Mr. Stanley's brother, a ship's captain, arrived from Havana and took charge of the household and the funeral arrangements. There seemed nothing more that John could do in the Stanley house, so, feeling unneeded and unwanted, he set out to look for a new situation. Unable to find another position as a clerk, he worked at such odd jobs as, day to day, he could find. At last he obtained temporary employment as an attendant for a sick sea captain. This lasted several weeks, and when the captain recovered, he rewarded John quite handsomely for the care he had taken of him. With this money John took passage on the steamboat *Tuscarora* for St. Louis to search for Mr. Stanley. The trip up the Mississippi was filled with wonders for him: the churning steamers, heavily loaded barges, and countless river boats; the bustling plantations along the shores, the wagons piled high with cotton moving along the levees and the busy, growing towns—all combined to create an impression of prosperity and restless energy. America was a great country, and he longed to be a part of it.

When the *Tuscarora* docked in St. Louis, John made straight for

Planters' Hotel, where he had heard that Mr. Stanley was staying. To his disappointment he learned from the hotel clerk that Mr. Stanley had left for New Orleans only a few days before. For ten days he walked along the levee and up and down Broadway and the other principal streets looking for work. Tired and discouraged, he found himself one day sitting on a pile of lumber by the river. Around him were the great bearded rivermen who worked the boats. All at once he became aware of the conversation of two men standing near him. They were talking about the flatboat directly in front of him, and he heard them say that it would be leaving shortly for New Orleans. New Orleans! Mr. Stanley was on his way there now! He jumped up and ran down to the flatboat. The boss, a big man with a grizzled beard, unkempt hair, and filthy hands, had that independent air of natural dignity and gruff kindliness the Welsh boy found so characteristic of Americans. John's offer to work his passage down to New Orleans was accepted, and he was taken on as a general helper and cook's boy.

Floating down the broad river on a flatboat was an easy, quiet life except for those moments when all hands were called on to man the sweeps in order to avoid a collision with a sand bar or a steamboat. John saw the river in calm and in storm; he watched the currents, eddies, and whirlpools. Although he did not know it at the time, the knowledge of rivers and their humors was to be invaluable to him.

When the flatboat tied up at New Orleans, John ran straight to the Stanley home on St. Charles Street. There he found his benefactor at last, and he poured out for him the story of his troubles since they had parted. Mr. Stanley had heard from his Irish maid of the boy's devotion to his wife during her last days, and he had already resolved to search the town for him. John could hardly believe his senses when Mr. Stanley put his arms around him and announced that from now on he would take care of his future; there would be no more privation and loneliness. It was the first really tender action John Rowlands had ever known. Tears, which no amount of cruelty could wring from him, sprang to his eyes, and he broke down sobbing.

John spent that night in the Stanley home. The next morning, Mr. Stanley took him into his study and began to question him closely about every detail of his life up to this time. At last the older man said solemnly, "The long and the short of it is, as you are wholly unclaimed, without a parent, relation, or sponsor, I promise to take you for my son and to fit you for a mercantile career, and in the future you are to bear my name, Henry Stanley."

He then arose, dipped his hand in a basin of water, and made the sign of the cross on the boy's forehead. This strange sort of baptism, performed in all seriousness, ended with an exhortation to be worthy of his new name. The illegitimate child had found a father.

This was the beginning of what Stanley later described as "the golden period of my life." It lasted about two years and it was an important, if somewhat enigmatic, episode in his career. Although the elder Stanley did adopt the Welsh boy in the sense that he provided for him, gave him his name, attempted to educate him, and in almost every other way treated him as his real son, he did not go through the necessary legal procedure that would make the young man his son and heir in the eyes of the law. This omission was to prevent Henry from becoming the merchant his foster father intended him to be.

The day after his baptism, Henry was outfitted with new suits, collars, low-cut shoes, and all the other articles necessary to his new station in life—including his first toothbrush and his first nightshirt. What would stern Aunt Mary think if she could see him with all these store-bought clothes, he wondered? Table manners, frequent baths, and polite conversation were some of the other novelties with which he must now become familiar. The eighteen-year-old boy's education had begun.

Henry and his father spent much of their time traveling up and down the Mississippi and its lower tributaries, such as the Saline, Ouachita, and Arkansas rivers, visiting the larger cities of St. Louis, Cincinnati, and Louisville as well as the smaller towns of Harrisonburg, Arkadelphia, Little Rock, and Napoleon. Wherever they went they carried with them a portmanteau of books—essays, memoirs, biographies, and general literature, but no novels—which they constantly replenished. Henry was expected to read constantly—often aloud—and to discuss what he had read with his father. His reading was supplemented by frequent lectures from his father on morality, religion, thrift, business, and the ways of the world. Mr. Stanley had been trained for the ministry and even had been a preacher for a short time; now he used all of his eloquence to teach his son to live morally and think clearly. The elder Stanley would take advantage of everything worthy of notice—men, events, and situations—to impress upon Henry some practical or moral lesson and to warn him of things which he ought or ought not to do. Sometimes he would use the Socratic method, proposing some situation and asking Henry what he would do under such circumstances. He would then argue both sides of the question, perplexing his pupil, but at the same time teaching him to look at problems from all sides and making him reason for himself.

Young Henry was extremely anxious to please, and he rewarded the pains of his mentor-father by diligent study and a reverent devotion. His phenomenal memory also served as an auxiliary to his father's notebook. Once having seen a page, he could faithfully retain and recite almost word for word what he had read. Thus, he was able to keep in his head a record of shipments, purchases, and sales.

Mississippi river life around 1860 was colorful and exciting. Gamblers, planters, enterprising merchants, and adventurers of all sorts rode the steamboats and barges that filled the river and crowded the towns lining the river's banks. Mr. Stanley, who was familiar with the towns, the boats, and the people, did not neglect to teach his eager charge all he knew about the sorts and conditions of men and their gear, trades, and modes of life.

There are always places in the world which at certain times breed adventure, and throughout his life Henry Stanley seems to have been led to those places at the time when excitement and adventure were in the air. Certainly, the Mississippi River region in the years preceding the Civil War was such a place. No matter how engrossed the father and son were in their business and the pursuit of knowledge, they were bound to clash with the restless men and events swirling around them.

One night as they were traveling down the river on a steamboat, young Henry was standing on the deck when he saw a man listen at the door of his father's cabin and then stealthily enter. Henry ran after him. Inside he found his father struggling in the dark with the intruder. Henry sprang for the man, but he turned on him with a knife, stabbed at him, and then fled. Fortunately, neither of the Stanleys was injured, and the knife had only cut a gash in Henry's coat. The incident created considerable commotion on board the steamer, but they were unable to learn the identity of the would-be robber and murderer.

Naturally, not all of those who rode the river boats were of this sort. One of the men they met was a Major Ingham, a South Carolinian by birth who had moved to Saline County, Arkansas, and had built a large plantation there. He was pleasant and cultured, and it was not long before he and the Stanleys were quite friendly. Before they parted, Major Ingham extended an invitation to the younger man to visit him on his plantation. Mr. Stanley thought this would fit in very nicely with his plans for his son's future education. He had planned to take a trip to Havana to visit his brother, sending Henry to Cypress Bend, Arkansas, where he had made arrangements for the young man to work as a clerk in order to gain experience in retail trade. These plans were now altered slightly, and it was arranged that Henry would go with Major Ingham and spend a month on his plantation before going to Cypress Bend.

When the time came for Mr. Stanley to leave for Havana, Henry and Major Ingham went with him to the boat to see him off. The young man suddenly became painfully aware of how much his father meant to him. He wanted to beg his father not to leave him, but instead he said almost nothing and turned away, his throat tight. A half-hour later he watched the thin trail of the steamer's smoke disappear over the horizon.

Henry returned alone to the Stanley home. The only person in his life who had ever given him love, and the only person whom he had ever loved, was suddenly gone from him. There was no one else to fill the gap. Late in life Stanley wrote, "Nearly five and thirty years have passed since, and I have not experienced such wretchedness as I did that night following his departure." Yet, wandering about the empty house and catching sight of his own face in a mirror, he was amazed to find no trace of his torn feelings reflected there.

Stonelike, with fixed eyes and expressionless face, he sat in his father's study going over in his mind the details of hundreds of incidents they had shared together and countless words they had exchanged. He tormented himself with thoughts of his own unworthiness. He wished that he had been a better son, that he had tried harder to please his father, that he had loved him and valued him more. He was, indeed, a wretched young man.

Before leaving New Orleans with Major Ingham, Stanley received a letter (the first he had ever received) from his father in Cuba. He wrote of the fine commercial potential of the Arkansas River country, and of Stanley's future as a merchant. He also urged him to hold fast to his principles and to be "fearless in all manly things." But perhaps Stanley was most impressed by the signature, which had a peculiar flourish, or whip, just below it. Henry copied this bit of affectation, and in the long letter he wrote back to his father used the same flourish. He continued to use it for the rest of his life.

Soon Major Ingham was ready to return home, taking Henry with him. They boarded a stern-wheeler and headed up the Mississippi, turning off to go up the Red River, then up the Ouachita River, and at last turning off to go up the Saline River. Several miles up the Saline the boat landed on the right bank to put Henry and Major Ingham ashore. A well-worn buggy took them a few miles inland to the Major's plantation. The Ingham house was made of solid pine logs, roughly squared, with the chinks neatly filled with clay or plaster. The inside of the house was lined with planed boards, new and unpainted.

Henry was warmly welcomed by Mrs. Ingham, but the sumptuous evening meal she had prepared was spoiled for him by the presence of Major Ingham's overseer, a coarse, boisterous individual who disagreeably reminded him of the first mate of the *Windermere*. The young man and the overseer took an immediate dislike to each other. As the days went by, this dislike deepened into bitter hatred.

One day shortly after his arrival, young Stanley was helping the Major's Negro slaves clear land for cotton crops. He liked the work in the open air, the felling of the big pine trees, and the burning of the logs in huge bonfires, although his enthusiasm was dampened somewhat by the constant presence of the overseer with his long blacksnake whip. Then, as Stanley and some of the slaves were carrying a heavy log, the whip of the overseer suddenly whistled past his ear and landed on the bare shoulders of the Negro next to him. Both men dropped their pikes, and the log fell on the foot of another man. Incensed, Stanley upbraided the overseer and actually came close to fighting him, but the cries of the Negro whose foot had been crushed claimed his attention. Then, stomping back to the house, he found Major Ingham sitting in a rocking chair on the veranda. Indignantly, the young man poured out his story of the cruelties of the overseer, but the Major gave him an indulgent smile, told him that he did not understand these matters, and appeared highly unconcerned. Young Stanley promptly stormed into the house, packed his bag, and left the plantation.

He spent the night with a neighbor, and the next day started out for the Arkansas River, arriving at Cypress Bend (about fifty miles southeast of Little Rock, not far from South Bend) two days later. As the exact date of his expected arrival at the store was uncertain, there were no questions asked, and he immediately began his duties as a clerk. Although he got along well and enjoyed his work, it was not long before he was laid low by what was locally known as "Arkansas ague" and was probably malaria. During the remaining months he spent at Cypress Bend, he had attacks of fever on an average of three times a month.

His appearance at this time was not particularly striking. Normally stocky, short, dark-complexioned, his most distinguishing feature was his piercing, yet boyish, eyes. Growing into manhood now, he had already raised a mustache. As a very young boy he had been quite fat—in spite of the meager diet of the workhouse—but now he was reduced by his recurring fevers to a mere ninety-five pounds.

Meanwhile, a fever of a different sort was attacking the country as a whole. Secession and war were in the air. The Southern ports had been seized, and enlistments were being taken in an effort to raise a Southern army. The closing of the ports cut off communication between Stanley and his father.

Stanley had paid little attention to politics and was totally ignorant of the issues involved. Hearing only the Southern side of the argument and seeing all the people he knew enlisting to fight for the Southern cause, he naturally felt that the South must be in the right. Nevertheless, he had no desire to be a soldier and was not anxious to enlist.

One day he received a parcel addressed by a feminine hand. On opening it, he discovered a chemise and petticoat such as a lady's Negro maid might wear. Stanley had already noticed that while the men were certainly spoiling for a fight, the women were the greatest firebrands and were loudly calling on all men to defend the hearth and home. He had become infatuated with a young girl in the neighborhood, and he had reason to suspect that the package had come from her. Stung by the implication of cowardice, he decided to take immediate action. That afternoon the girl's father called on him, and when he asked if Henry did not intend to "join the valiant children of Arkansas" and fight for Dixie, Stanley answered, "Yes."

# CHAPTER II

# Soldiering in America

HARD AND DIFFICULT as his boyhood years had been, they were eclipsed by the hardships awaiting him in the next six years of his life. The tough human raw material, only slightly alloyed by his meager though excellent education at the hands of his foster father, was now about to be tempered by the furnaces of war. Looking back over these years in later life, Stanley regarded them as a long succession of blunders, beginning with his enlistment as a private in the Confederate Army.

In July, 1861, Stanley and the other volunteers from his district embarked on the Arkansas River in a steamboat bound for Little Rock. Lustily singing "Dixie," they steamed up the river. They had only gotten as far as Pine Bluff when a snag ripped open the bottom of the boat and held it fixed in the river while the water rushed in, filling the boat to the furnace doors. But before the boilers exploded, another steamer came to their rescue. Men and baggage were quickly transferred to the other ship, which took them the rest of the way to Little Rock. Debarking, they were sworn into the Confederate Army, issued flintlock muskets and accouterments, and formally enrolled in the 6th Arkansas Regiment of Volunteers, Colonel Lyons commanding. They were not given a physical examination, but each man was accepted upon his personal assurance that he was physically fit.

During the regiment's stay in the Arkansas capital, Stanley felt proud that he had enlisted to "live or die for Dixie." Patriotism was in the air, and those who wore the new gray uniforms were young gods. He bought a long Colt revolver and a Bowie knife and had his likeness taken with a stylish scowl. As he and his companions walked down the street, brass buttons shining, they caught the admiring eyes of young girls watching them and heard the gallant words of encouragement from old men.

In camp, they learned to march in step and to drill to the tune of fife and drum. So enthusiastic did they become that even off the parade ground they practiced their drill and called out commands— "Guide center!" "Right wheel!"—to each other when they walked around camp. They spent their spare time sharpening their bayonets to a razor edge, and at mess they discussed Southern chivalry, tactics, and the relative merits of Lee and Beauregard.

One sunny day they packed their knapsacks, shouldered their muskets, and marched through Little Rock to the Arkansas River where steamboats waited to ferry them across. The march to the riverside was a gay affair, and one that was repeated with little variation in many a town, both North and South, as green youths were marshaled for war. New uniforms, shining bayonets, regimental flags, and company guidons spanking the breeze; streets decorated with banners and lined with cheering men; ladies, overcome with emotion, weeping into their handkerchiefs—it was all so inspiring! When the soldiers broke into "Dixie," Stanley held his head high and sang with gusto. He was very proud.

Once across the river, however, they strapped on their knapsacks and canteens, shouldered their heavy muskets, and began their long march. At first, the untrained officers kept them marching in step and in strict formation, but as the heat of the afternoon sun and the unaccustomed weight of their packs began to smother their exuberance, they were allowed to march at ease. Sweat now stained their new uniforms and dust covered their bright buttons. As they covered mile after weary mile, the raw young soldiers began to drop by the wayside. It was a ragged column that finally wound its way into bivouac that night. With aching shoulders, blistered feet, and sweat-soaked, begrimed bodies, they threw themselves on the ground to seek relief from their pains in sleep.

The next morning, Stanley awoke stiff and aching for another day of marching. Before starting out, he wisely discarded half the contents of his pack, keeping as personal items only a daguerreotype of his foster father, a lock of his gray hair, and the Bible presented to him by the Welsh bishop. He had learned that most elementary rule of the infantryman: carry only what is absolutely necessary.

The Confederate commissariat in these early days of the war was primitive. Food was often scarce, and the men were frequently obliged to forage for themselves. Stanley soon became adept at the art of stealing food from farmers reputed to be "antisecessionists."

The monotony of the marches and the squalid conditions in camp were enough to make Stanley and his companions regret their willing abandonment of peaceful occupations. Added to their discomfort was the severity of military discipline. Stanley witnessed men hoisted up by their thumbs; horsed on triangular fence rails that were viciously jerked up to increase the pain; fettered with ball and chain. Military life soon lost its attraction.

In the first nine months of his military service, Stanley's regiment was shifted about the South. From Little Rock they marched to Columbus, Georgia, and from there they were taken by train to Cave City, Kentucky. In February of 1862, they were marched through the snow to Bowling Green and then to Nashville. From Nashville they tramped two hundred and fifty miles south through Murfreesboro, Tullahoma, and Athens to Decatur, Alabama. Here the regiment was put on a train and taken to Corinth, Mississippi, arriving on March 25, 1862.

On April 4, Stanley's regiment marched out of Corinth to take part in one of the bloodiest battles of the war: Shiloh. After two days of marching in the rain, with only cold rations to eat, they arrived at their battle position. Albert Sydney Johnston and Pierre Beauregard, the Confederate generals, intended to throw forty thousand tired troops against fifty thousand fresh Union soldiers under General Ulysses Grant.

Stanley, along with most of the Southern army, was armed with an old flintlock musket. The ammunition came wrapped in cartridge paper containing the powder, a round ball, and three buckshot. To load the musket it was necessary to tear the paper with the teeth, empty the powder into the pan, lock it, pour the remaining powder down the muzzle, press paper and ball down the barrel, and then ram it home. In contrast to these weapons—which even at this period were obsolete —the Union forces were equipped with Enfield and Minié rifles.

On April 6, 1862, a beautiful dawn found Stanley standing at ease in ranks waiting for the rest of the Confederate forces to move into position. He was in the center of a three-mile line of eager men waiting for the order to attack the Union troops opposite them and drive them into the Tennessee River. Next to him stood a seventeen-year-old boy named Henry Parker who pointed out some violets growing at their feet.

"It would be a good idea," said young Parker, "to put a few in my cap. Maybe the Yanks won't shoot me if they see me wearing them, for they're a sign of peace."

"Capital," said Stanley, "I'll do the same."

The men in the ranks began to laugh at the young men picking violets while waiting for the battle. Just then, an aide rode up to Stanley's brigadier and delivered a message. The officer called out an order, which was quickly passed down the line, and the gray ranks surged forward, shoulder to shoulder. They had gone about five hundred paces when they heard desultory firing ahead of them. At the sound, their pace became brisker, and an air of excitement pervaded the ranks. The sound of musketry increased in volume and intensity as they approached the skirmish line. It was not long before they heard a humming noise overhead. Stanley's company was moving through a woods now and the missiles flying above them brought down twigs and small branches on their heads.

"Those are bullets," young Parker said. "We are in for it now."

Two hundred yards farther and the firing had become an ear-filling roar. They passed out of the woods and through their own line of skirmishers. There was nothing in front of them now but the enemy. On they marched, trampling new grass and the buds of wild flowers under their boots.

"There they are!" someone shouted.

"Aim low," their captain called.

As they continued to advance, firing their muskets, Stanley tried hard to see at whom he was shooting. At last he saw a bluish line of men through the smoke. Just then he heard a series of fusillades, crashing one upon another with startling suddenness. He felt as though volcanoes were erupting under his feet. Looking around him, he noticed that his comrades were pale, solemn, and absorbed. Step by step they advanced, loading and firing their clumsy muskets in nervous haste. Then a sharp order rang out: "Fix bayonets! On the double quick!"

The gray lines bounded forward, the rebel yell in their throats. The battle cry relieved their suppressed emotion, and they sacrificed both reason and fear in the wild fury of a bayonet charge.

At first the Union line seemed inclined to await the attack; then suddenly it broke, and Stanley saw the blue figures running before him. An exhilarating thrill of victory surged through him as he arrived panting in the Federal camp. For a moment he had the impression that the battle was over. Actually, it had only begun; beyond this first camp were others, and it was not long before they were hotly engaged once more.

Now volley after deadly volley tore through the gray ranks. The attack slowed to a halt. Confused orders echoed among them. Stanley heard an order to lie down and continue firing, so he threw himself behind the trunk of a fallen tree along with a dozen other men. This respite gave him a chance to collect his thoughts, and he became aware of the terrible fire power that had been brought to bear on them. The air seemed full of humming bullets—he could hear the tattoo they made hitting the log that sheltered him and their pinging as they ricocheted. He did not see how anyone could live in such a deadly hail of lead. Where Stanley was lying there was a narrow strip of light between the fallen tree trunk and the ground, and some of the bullets found their way through this slit. The soldier next to him raised his chest as though to yawn, jostling Stanley. Turning to look at the man, he saw that a bullet had made a deep furrow through his face and buried itself in his chest.

"It's getting too warm, boys!" one man yelled, leaping to his feet. A bullet struck him square in the forehead and sent him sprawling. But the realization that they could not remain pinned down made the officers call out for a charge. Their shouts brought the men to their feet and, bent almost double, they ran forward.

Stanley heard a boy's voice cry out, "Oh, stop! Please stop! I've been hurt and can't move!"

Looking around, Stanley saw the tortured face of Henry Parker. He was standing on one leg; his other was smashed. The violets had not saved him. No one stopped. They were being pounded by cannon as well as small arms now, but a battery of Confederate field artillery was swinging into position to support their advance. They charged on, pausing only long enough to load their clumsy muskets. Again the blue line in front of them dissolved, and soon they were racing through the second line of Union tents.

Exhausted, his lungs aching from the long run, Stanley stopped for a moment to catch his breath. Just then, something struck his belt clasp a hard blow, knocking him to the ground. It was some minutes before he could recover his breath. On examination, he discovered that his belt clasp was bent and cracked, but that he was not hurt. By now it was ten o'clock in the morning, and he was hungry. Opening his haversack, he took out what food he could find and gulped it down.

Feeling invigorated, he got to his feet and followed in the wake of his regiment.

For the first time he became fully conscious of the desperate nature of the battle in which he was engaged. Around him the ground was littered with debris and the bodies of soldiers from both sides, lying singly and in grotesque, bloody piles. Of the dead, he saw many that he knew, lying face upward with staring eyes in the warm sun.

About one o'clock in the afternoon he caught up with his regiment, which was waiting in a woods while Confederate and Union artillery engaged in a duel. Soon they were moving forward once more; another wild charge, and again the enemy was sent flying in retreat. On and on they pressed, driving the Union forces back toward the Tennessee River. But their strength was waning; Stanley felt completely exhausted. He moved mechanically, feeling that he had no will of his own left. Powdery grime had gathered on his parched lips from opening the paper cartridges, and his canteen was empty.

Late in the afternoon, they captured a large Union camp and the officers ordered a halt. The tired soldiers listlessly fell to looting the tents of the enemy, but, although plunder was plentiful, the men were so exhausted they could do little more than idly turn over the bedding, clothing, equipment, and seeming luxuries that lay strewn about them. Finding a tin of biscuits and a jug of molasses, Stanley stuffed himself and then fell asleep in one of the tents. Although he slept soundly and fairly comfortably throughout the night, a torrential rain fell upon the tentless and the helpless wounded left in the open fields.

When Stanley fell in with his company at daybreak, there were only about fifty men left. But already scattered firing was heard, and they had no sooner started to move forward when their pickets were driven back upon them. Although in poor condition for further fighting, the men were deployed in skirmishing order and urged on by their officers. Stanley's company commander sarcastically called out, "Now Mr. Stanley, if you please, step briskly forward!"

Piqued by being singled out in this manner, Stanley stepped out more quickly than he should have. Presently, he found himself in an open field with no convenient tree or stump to crouch behind. Looking around, he saw a hollow about twenty yards ahead and made a dash for it. Assuming that his company was coming up in back of him, he became completely absorbed with the business of loading and firing his musket at the advancing blue forms in front. The enemy was approaching uncomfortably near when he stood up to discover that he was a lone Confederate soldier in a field swarming with Union troops. The next thing he knew, he was surrounded by Federal soldiers. One ordered, "Down with that gun, Secesh, or I'll drill a hole through you! Drop it quick!"

As his musket clattered to the ground, two men rushed forward and seized him. He was a prisoner! His captors proudly marched him to the rear. As they passed through the Union lines, the enemy soldiers cursed and reviled him. A number of men with German accents were particularly vituperative.

"Where are you taking that fellow to? Drive a bayonet into the son of a bitch!" one of them called.

Several soldiers lunged toward him with their bayonets, but his two captors saved him. Stanley saw that the faces surrounding him were wild-eyed with fury and hate. He looked at them with loathing and wished that he could return to the Confederate lines to tell his comrades what loutish beasts opposed them.

Once through the front lines, he was safe from the Union soldiers, but not from the shells of the Confederate artillery, which were dropping all around them. Hustled on by his guards, however, he was soon out of danger.

For twenty-one-year-old Henry Stanley the war was over—at least for the time being. The day after his capture, he was put on board a steamboat full of wretched-looking prisoners and sent to St. Louis. All they possessed were the thin, dirty, gray uniforms they were wearing, and all were dejected by their misfortune. Stanley wondered what would become of his knapsack with the bishop's Bible and the lock of his father's hair.

Reaching St. Louis, the prisoners were formed into a column and marched to a girls' school where they were kept penned up for four days. Then they were taken across the Mississippi, herded into boxcars and shipped to Camp Douglas, then a prison compound on the outskirts of Chicago.

Camp Douglas was little more than a great cattle pen where disease ran unchecked, and men were left to die lying in their own filth. The prison yard consisted of a large field surrounded by a high plank fence. About fifty feet from the base of the fence on the inside was a line of limewash. This was the "deadline." Any prisoner caught stepping over it was shot by the sentries, who were spaced in boxes about every sixty yards along the walls. The barracks for the prisoners consisted of twenty barnlike structures, each housing from two hundred to three hundred men.

A Mr. Shipman from Chicago handled the prisoners' commissary, and, at his suggestion, the prisoners made themselves up into companies, each with its captain who would draw their meager rations for them. Stanley was elected captain of his company, and it was not long before he and the commissary director were quite friendly. They had many conversations together about the war and the great issues that were involved. For the first time, Stanley heard the case for the Northern side. He was impressed by the arguments of Mr. Shipman, who spoke of the Union's cause with a great deal of reason and persuasion. Nevertheless, the thought of deserting the Southern cause, even though he now believed it wrong, deterred him at first from accepting the offer to change sides.

But conditions in the prison camp were demoralizing. The prisoners were denied both medical and spiritual aid, and even the simplest elements of hygiene were neglected. Vermin so permeated the barracks that even the piles of dust sweepings were alive with parasites.

The prisoners' latrines, consisting of open ditches, were in the rear of the barracks, and each trip Stanley made there was an ordeal. On the way he passed dozens of sick men who, having fallen from weakness, were crawling in their own and their companions' filth. Scores of men, more dead than alive from dysentery, hung over the gaping trenches or lay stretched out along the open sewers.

Inside the barracks conditions were little better. Debilitated men in rotting gray uniforms lay about, listlessly playing cards, picking off the lice and crushing them between their fingernails, or sitting, head in hands, staring at nothing. Many were too sick to move and lay praying or swearing on their straw beds. Some were delirious. Others prayed for death to relieve them of their pain. Dysentery and typhoid fever daily diminished the number of prisoners. Every morning Stanley helped to gather up the dead and stack them in carts to be carried away to an ignominious burial.

The life and the death that surrounded him, together with the reasoning of the kindly Mr. Shipman, at last persuaded Stanley to desert the Confederate Army, accept the terms of release, and enroll in the Union artillery. His life as a Union soldier was short, however, as only three days after his release from prison on June 4, 1862, he came down with dysentery. Sent to a hospital at Harper's Ferry, he lay there until June 22 when he was discharged.

His situation at this time could hardly have been worse. He was homeless, penniless, without friends or near relations, and he carried within him the seeds of the diseases he had contracted in prison. It took him a week to walk the twenty-four miles from Harper's Ferry to Hagerstown. There a farmer let him sleep in a corn silo. Covered with grime, hot with fever, and bleeding internally, he threw himself on some hay and lost consciousness. When he came to his senses several days later, he found himself on a mattress in a comfortable bedroom. To his surprise, he discovered that he was wearing a clean shirt, and his hands and face had been carefully washed.

The farmer had taken him in and cared for him. Under his care, and on a diet of fresh milk, he slowly mended, and his spirit and his will revived. In a few weeks he was able to help with the harvest and to join in the harvest supper. Stanley stayed with this good Samaritan until the middle of August when the farmer took him to the railroad station and paid his fare to Baltimore.

Although handicapped by recurring attacks of fever, Stanley worked on farms and once had a job on an oyster schooner. When he had saved a little money he signed on the *E. Sherman* for Liverpool. Arriving in November, 1862, he set out at once for Denbigh to find his mother. Although in poor health, without money, and dressed in shabby clothes, he wanted to show her how he had become a man, and perhaps make her believe that someday he would accomplish something in the world. But he hoped to rekindle an affection that had never existed.

Arriving at Denbigh and finding his mother's house, he knocked at the door. His mother, when she realized who he was, told him bluntly that he was disgrace to her in the eyes of her neighbors; that he must leave town at once—and he must not come back!

It was an embittering experience for the young man of twenty-one. Although his boyhood had been anything but sheltered, he still had not learned to protect himself against the hurts and disappointments that assailed him. There was something of the small child in his nature —a simplicity and a slight naïveté—that no amount of suffering had been able to dislodge. His mother's hostility left him in even deeper despair than her abandonment of him as a child.

Stanley now tried to find his foster father. Returning to America, he found a ship that would take him to Cuba, but once there he learned that his father had died nearly two years earlier. Now he had no one to whom he could turn. He was a man without friends, relatives, money, or even a country. But he had learned one lesson well: he would never again consciously seek or expect affection.

Abandoning the search for human warmth and comfort, Stanley fled to the world of action, shipping out as a common sailor on merchant ships. Considering his experiences aboard the *Windermere,* it is odd, in a way, that he should have chosen to go to sea again, but this life may have offered just the combination of drudgery and romance, monotony and danger, he needed to recover from the emotion-shattering experiences he had undergone. Sailing on first one ship and then another, he traveled to the West Indies, Italy, and Spain. In his sketchy diary from this period, a shipwreck is condensed into a two-line story: "Wrecked off Barcelona. Crew lost, in the night. Stripped naked, and swam to shore. Barrack of Carbineers . . . demanded my papers!"

Fate always seemed to give Stanley a final, bitter thrust when his fortunes or energies were lowest. On one occasion while boarding with a judge in Brooklyn in the winter of 1863, Stanley had to spend the night trying to keep the judge from killing his wife with a hatchet. The next morning, exhausted from his efforts, Stanley went into the parlor to smoke a cigar. The judge's wife, whom he had spent the night protecting, came storming down upon him, heaping abuse on the young man for daring to smoke in her house!

On July 19, 1864, Stanley enlisted in the United States Navy at the New York Naval Rendezvous for a term of three years. Naval records describe him as being five feet five inches in height, having hazel eyes, dark hair and complexion, with no marks or scars. He gave his residence as Kings County, New York, his birthplace as England, his occupation as clerk, and stated that he had had no previous naval experience. He was originally stationed on board the U.S.S. *North Carolina,* the Receiving Ship in New York at that time, but eleven days later he was transferred to the North Atlantic Blockading Squadron where he was attached to the U.S.S. *Minnesota.*

While on board the *Minnesota,* Stanley attained the rating of Ship's Writer, a petty officer who kept the log and various other ship's records. In this capacity he witnessed the exciting land and sea attacks of the Federal forces on Fort Fisher, North Carolina, defending the Confederacy's last open port. Probably it was while writing up his reports of this engagement for the ship's log that the idea occurred to him to send a firsthand account of the action to the newspapers in the North. At any rate, his stories of the battle, told in a clear and vigorous, if somewhat ornate, style, were accepted and used. This was the first writing he had ever done, but his powers of observation were acute, and they had been sharpened by his foster father who had encouraged him to be a close observer of men and events. Apparently, his success in this venture suggested journalism as a profession. In any case, it was one that he quickly adopted, and to the end of his life he remained an accurate reporter and skilled narrator of events.

But there was little chance to pursue journalism as a sailor in the United States Navy. Soon there would be no more battles to record— the Civil War was fast drawing to a close—and he still had two and a half years of his enlistment to serve out. But Stanley did not stay to serve out his time; instead, he took his fate into his own hands. Shortly after the capture of Fort Fisher, on January 15, 1865, the *Minnesota* sailed to Portsmouth, New Hampshire, to be decommissioned. It was there, on February 10, that Stanley, together with a young sailor named Louis Noe, deserted the navy.

Thus, before he was twenty-four years old, Stanley had established a long series of desertions: he had run away from his school, he had jumped his ship in New Orleans, he had become a traitor to the Confederate cause by changing sides, and he had deserted the United States Navy in time of war. It was a strange beginning for the man who was to establish his reputation as one who never quit, who carried out his assignments in the face of all odds and dangers.

# CHAPTER III

# *The Roving Reporter*

THE AMERICAN CIVIL WAR ended two months after Stanley's desertion from the navy, but by this time he was on his way west. Without ties or loyalties, he was free to indulge the wanderlust that possessed him. Exactly what he did or how he lived is not known, but apparently he was able to earn some money by writing stories for various newspapers. His diary gives only fleeting glimpses of place names and mnemonic words: "St. Joseph, Missouri—across the plains—Indians—Salt Lake City—Denver—Black Hawk—Omaha." He once said that his spirit at this period was so exuberant that when he saw a horse in his path, his impulse was not to go around the horse but to jump over it.

In Omaha, he became involved with some theatrical people. Following a benefit performance, which he had arranged, he and some of the performers went out on the town. He was particularly taken by one of the girls in the troupe, and perhaps her pretty face led the normally serious young man to excesses. At any rate, he forgot his pledge to the "Band of Hope" and got hopelessly drunk. Most of the night was spent roaming the streets of Omaha, singing and yelling. The next morning, full of repentance for this escapade, he vowed that he would never again go out on such a carousal. As far as is known, he never did.

In May of 1866, with a man named W. H. Cook, he went to Denver, built a flat-bottomed boat, loaded it with provisions and arms, and floated down the Platte River (then in the heart of Indian country) to Omaha. Although they had no trouble from the Indians, the boat overturned twice and the trip provided both excitement and, more important, escape from the world of civilized men. Stanley's appetite for this kind of life was whetted by this adventure, and he immediately laid plans for a grander expedition that would take him even further away from civilization for a longer period of time and would provide opportunities for even more exciting adventures. Leaving from Boston in July, 1866, Stanley and Cook, together with Louis Noe, the young sailor who had deserted the navy with Stanley, set sail for Smyrna (now Izmir) in Turkey. It is not known exactly what they had in mind, but apparently they planned to penetrate deep into Asia. Stanley was probably acting, at least partly, as a newspaper correspondent.

At first, all went well and Stanley was excited by his first glimpse of the Orient. But the Stanley-Cook expedition was soon to end in disaster. A few miles east of Smyrna, Noe started a fire that nearly destroyed a native village. Appeasing the Turkish villagers with difficulty, they struck out for the remote areas of the country. Unfortunately, they fell in with a treacherous guide who led them straight to a band of thieves. They were severely beaten, and all of their money (twelve hundred dollars), letters of credit, and their personal papers were taken from them. That final bit of ironic fate which always seemed to dog Stanley was not lacking. The thieves dragged them to the nearest village and had *them* arraigned as malefactors!

For five days they were hustled from place to place and subjected to indignity and abuse. The Turkish interior was a crude and semi-civilized region; justice was primitive. Finally, after being thrown into a particularly foul prison, they were saved by the intervention of a Mr. L. E. Pelesa, Agent of the Imperial Ottoman Bank. This kindly old gentleman set the facts before the Turkish governor and was able to secure their release.

Stanley wrote an account of their misadventure and it appeared in the *Levant Herald*, a newspaper published in English. Edward Joy Morris, the American Minister in Constantinople, read the account and arranged for their relief and protection. He gave Stanley a check for a hundred and fifty pounds and started suit for the recovery of their money and property. Morris did not ask for security, but simply loaned the young men the money. Nevertheless, Stanley gave him a worthless check which Morris did not attempt to cash. Later, after Stanley, Cook, and Noe had left Turkey, Morris recovered most of the money and compensation from the Turkish government, deducted the hundred and fifty pounds and sent the remainder of the money to Cook, who had borne the expense of the trip.

When he returned to the United States, Stanley obtained his first regular employment as a "special correspondent" for the Missouri

*Democrat.* He was not yet twenty-six years old when, in March, 1867, he was given the job of covering an expedition led by General Winfield Scott Hancock, of Civil War fame, into the Indian country.

In these years following the Civil War, immigrants by the thousands flocked to America's shores. Many of them headed straight for the West, and soon the lands west of the Mississippi were flooded by streams of settlers, goldseekers, adventurers of all sorts. The Union Pacific Railroad was being pushed forward at the rate of four miles a day, and new wagon roads were being made through the land where the Indians had been allowed to roam and hunt in peace. Settlers, roads, forts, and all the paraphernalia of civilization were ruining the red man's best hunting grounds. The Indians rebelled, and a series of outbreaks against the white men by the Comanches and Kiowas occurred in Nebraska and Kansas.

A sizable force under the command of General Hancock was sent out to deal with the Indians. It was widely believed that the expedition was a punitive one, and Stanley expected to see the Indians suffer for the atrocities they had committed. But he soon learned that Hancock's orders were quite different. He intended only to separate those who were guilty of violence from those who were still peaceful, to make treaties with all tribes whenever possible, and to reinforce troops stationed along certain military roads. In all this he was quite successful.

While Stanley did not see the action against the Indians he had expected, he did learn a great deal about the Indian problem. He was a witness to many palavers between the white men and the savages, and he sent back to his paper detailed accounts of these meetings. Some of the speeches of the Indian chiefs, as recorded by Stanley, were most moving. One of his reports quoted an old chief who said, "I love the land and the buffalo, and will not part with them. I don't want any of those medicine houses built in the country; I want the papooses brought up exactly as I am. I have word that you intend to settle us on a reservation near the mountains. I don't want to settle there. I love to roam over the wide prairie, and, when I do it, I feel free and happy; but, when we settle down, we grow pale and die."

But already Stanley was a staunch believer in the virtues and powers of civilization. He wrote that "few can read the speeches of the Indian chiefs without feeling deep sympathy for them; they move us by their pathos and mournful dignity. But they were asking the impossible.

The half of a continent could not be kept as a buffalo pasture and hunting ground."

Stanley's first dispatches to the Missouri *Democrat* are interesting because they show his amateurishness as a newspaper reporter as well as his ability to find and describe items of human interest. In his first letter he describes at some length his meeting with the commander of the expedition. "While jotting these notes down" he was called to Hancock's tent. The general told him, "You are welcome, sir," and that was all that really happened. He returned to his tent to "indite you this first letter."

In the last paragraph of the same dispatch, however, he hits that note of real human interest that eventually made him a reputation as a newspaper man: "Accompanying the expedition, under the special charge of the commanding General, is a little Indian boy, about five years old, the son of a chief who fell at the Sand Creek massacre. He is a boy of extraordinary intelligence, and shows the true spirit of the savage by drawing his jack-knife on anyone who attempts to correct him. He is called Wilson Graham, and was for a time with Wilson and Graham's circus, where he was exhibited as a curiosity. The Indians, before assenting to a meeting, expressly stipulated that this boy should be delivered up to them."

Accompanying the expedition were a number of Indian scouts, including the famous "Wild Bill" Hickok. Stanley described him as being thirty-eight years old, six feet one inch tall "in his moccasins" and "as handsome a specimen of a man as could be found." Stanley sought out the frontiersman for an interview:

"I say, Mr. Hickok, how many white men have you killed to your certain knowledge?"

After thinking for a moment, Wild Bill replied, "I suppose I have killed considerably over a hundred."

"What made you kill all those men? Did you kill them without cause or provocation?"

"No, by heaven! I never killed one man without good cause."

"How old were you when you killed your first white man?"

"I was twenty-eight years old when I killed the first white man, and if ever a man deserved killing he did."

Apparently, Hickok and the young reporter became friends, for once, when a man made an insulting remark to Stanley, Wild Bill reached out with his long arms, picked the man up, and threw him over a billiard table.

Stanley was impressed by the numbers and types of people who were moving westward. There were Mormons bound for Utah, and settlers with their wives, children, and all their worldly goods heading for Idaho and Montana. There were gamblers, adventurers, and wanton women who worked the saloons at night and walked the streets by day with fancy derringers strapped to their waists. There were immigrants who worked on the railroad, prospectors, miners, and freed slaves.

Although there were no battles with the Indians during the Hancock expedition, Stanley was able to satisfy his readers' thirst for blood by sending back a number of stories of people who had had close escapes from the red men. He saw one man who had been scalped and still lived to tell the tale. The brave had dropped the scalp in his excitement, and the unfortunate man had found it, picked it up, and carried it back with him in the hope that it could be sewn on again. To prove his story he had a sizable slice of skin missing from his head and the scalp itself, which he kept in a bucket of water.

When the Hancock expedition was over, Stanley stayed in the West to follow the dealings of a peace commission under General William Tecumseh Sherman. While waiting for the commission to arrive, he went to Colorado where fabulous amounts of gold, silver, and copper were then being found. He even took a little prospecting tour in the mountains himself, and excitedly returned with his pockets and a satchel filled with yellow ore. Sneaking up to his hotel room with his hoard, he emptied his pockets of all but one small piece. This he took downstairs with him. Sauntering up to a rough, bearded character who looked like a miner, he asked him as carelessly as he could manage what he thought of his nugget. The man pronounced it a "pretty nice specimen of pyrites of iron." Stanley was not the first man to mistake "fool's gold" for the real thing.

In September the peace commission arrived in Omaha and on October 21, 1867, at a place in Kansas called Medicine Lodge Creek, the commissioners signed a peace treaty with twenty Indian chiefs. All of the newspaper reporters covering the event, including Stanley, signed their names as witnesses.

Although only a spectator in these dealings with the Indians, Stanley learned a great deal about the ways in which primitive peoples must be handled. Sherman and the other commissioners were all experienced in talking with Indians, and their method of speaking to them both as great warriors and as children who must be taught and corrected served as a guide to the observant Stanley when he, too, was faced with the problems of negotiating with savage tribes in Africa.

Several years later, when in Paris after finding Livingstone, Stanley again met General Sherman.

"By the way, do you remember meeting me before?" Stanley asked the general.

"No," replied Sherman.

Stanley then began a speech of some length containing references to "fire water," "the great spirit," "our brother," "pale face," and a number of other subjects in which the Indian was supposed to be interested.

"Why, that's a speech I made some years ago to the Sioux Indians while out on the plains," Sherman exclaimed. "Were you there?"

"I was there," replied Stanley, "reporting it for the *Herald*, and, to tell you the truth, I have had occasion to repeat your speech almost verbatim more than once to the Negroes of Central Africa."

While he was the special correspondent of the Missouri *Democrat*, Stanley was also a contributor to a number of other papers, including the New York *Herald*, the New York *Times*, the Chicago *Republican*, and the Cincinnati *Commercial*. His salary from the Missouri *Democrat* was only fifteen dollars a week, but with the money he received from the other papers he was able to average ninety a week. Most of this he saved, and by January 1, 1868, he had accumulated three thousand dollars. He later recorded, "I practiced a rigid economy, punishing my appetites, and, little by little, the sums acquired through this abstinence began to impart a sense of security, and gave an independence to my bearing which, however I might try to conceal it, betrayed that I was delivered from the dependent state."

Covering peace commissions to the Indians was interesting, but it was not challenging enough; it offered no opportunities to prove himself, no chance to escape from the society of civilized men. Hearing of a British expedition to Abyssinia, Stanley determined to go there. Throwing up his job with the *Democrat* and the other papers, he set out for New York. There he stormed the office of the formidable James Gordon Bennett, famous publisher of the New York *Herald*. Bennett did not think the Abyssinian campaign would be interesting enough to Americans, but he asked Stanley about terms.

"Either as a special correspondent at a moderate salary, or by the letter," Stanley told him. "Of course, if you pay me by the letter, I should reserve the liberty to write occasional letters to other papers."

"We don't like to share our news that way," Bennett said, "but we would be willing to pay well for exclusive intelligence. Have you ever been abroad before?"

"Oh, yes. I've traveled in the East, and have been to Europe several times."

"Well, how would you like to do this on trial? Pay your own expenses to Abyssinia, and if your letters are up to the standard, and your intelligence is early and exclusive, you shall be paid by the letter, or at the rate by which we engage our European specials."

"Very well, sir. I am at your service, any way you like."

"When do you intend to start?"

"On the twenty-second, by the steamer *Hecla*."

"That is the day after tomorrow. Well, consider it arranged."

And so—if he paid his own expenses—he was hired. Two days later, he boarded the *Hecla* for London; from there he took the next ship to Egypt. On landing at Suez he made his way to the telegraph office, then the closest one to Abyssinia. There he made arrangements with the chief telegrapher to give his dispatches priority over the wires to London, promising him that he would be well rewarded for his trouble. This characteristic bit of foresight was to win him his first fame as a journalist.

He caught up with the British expeditionary force at the Red Sea port town of Zula, in what today is Eritrea. Although there were several British correspondents with the expedition, Stanley was the only American. As he marched from tent to tent presenting his credentials and drawing his gear, he felt the inconvenience of life in Central Africa for the first time: "The Major's tent was fully a mile from Captain Z——'s tent, and during the painful walk there, with the hot sand burning my shoes and the wind coming in hot fervid gusts in my face, I began to experience the discomforts of a tropical life." This was only the first of what were to be thousands of painful miles he would have to walk in Africa.

The now almost forgotten campaign that Stanley was about to witness was the result of a series of British diplomatic blunders. On the throne of Abyssinia was a man calling himself King Theodoro, or Theodore, who had made himself ruler of the country by the simple expedient of killing the former king, a man who had befriended him and raised him to a powerful position in the army. Theodore was well enough liked by his subjects when his iron-fisted rule brought some degree of order to the chaotic country, but his vanity, cruelty, and tyranny grew until many segments of his kingdom took up arms in rebellion. Theodore reacted by becoming more bitter and more cruel.

Following the instructions given him by his superiors, the British consul in Abyssinia, a man named Cameron, urged Theodore to write a letter to Queen Victoria in order to cement the relationship between the two nations and to bring Theodore into closer contact with the civilized world. At length, the Abyssinian king did write a letter in which he expressed a wish to have a treaty with England and requested Queen Victoria to make arrangements for him to send ambassadors to London. This letter was read by the English Prime Minister, thrown into a drawer, and forgotten.

As month after month passed and he did not receive an answer, Theodore began to smolder over what he considered a deliberate insult. About this time, Consul Cameron was ordered to make a trip into the Sudan. The Civil War in America, with the Union Navy's blockade of the Southern ports, had begun to cause a shortage of cotton in the British Isles, and Cameron was ordered to investigate the possibilities of raising and exporting cotton in the Sudan. As Theodore was continually plotting a war against the Egyptians for their encroachment on Abyssinian lands adjacent the Sudan, Cameron's visit to what he considered enemy territory only increased his suspicions and his hatred of the British.

When, at long last, in response to Cameron's repeated pleas, a letter from Queen Victoria was dispatched to the Abyssinian king it contained no reference to Theodore's previous letter nor to his request for permission to send ambassadors to England. Maddened by this slight, Theodore ordered Cameron's servant, together with two servants of an English missionary named Stern, to be beaten. Stern, who was forced to watch the beatings, clapped his hand over his mouth to suppress a cry of horror. This simple act was somehow interpreted by Theodore as a revengeful threat. He at once cried out, "Beat that man, beat him as you would a dog. Beat him, I say!"

Stern was pounded with sticks until he fainted. He and Cameron, along with several other missionaries and all their servants, were thrown into prison. Several months later, news of what had happened reached England, and there were indignant letters in the *Times*. Another letter was dispatched from Queen Victoria to King Theodore. It took over a year for this letter to be delivered to the Abyssinian Court. When at last it was presented to Theodore and he found that again the Queen had neglected to mention his previous letter, he threw the envoys who had brought it into prison.

Months turned into years while the English captives suffered the horrors of barbarian imprisonment. Cameron was tortured. He later told how "twenty Abyssinians tugged lustily on ropes tied to each limb until I fainted. My shoulder blades were made to meet each other. I was doubled up until my head appeared under my thighs, and while in this painful posture, I was beaten with a whip of hippopotamus hide on my bare back, until I was covered with weals, and while the blood dripped from my reeking back, I was rolled in the sand."

In 1866 the Conservative party came to power in England, and, after an unsuccessful attempt to ransom the prisoners, the government declared war on Theodore. In January, 1868, an expeditionary force, composed of twelve thousand troops of the Indian Army under Sir Robert Napier, was dispatched to Abyssinia. Half of the force was to hold the seacoast and form a base of operations while the other half made up the marching column that would attack Theodore's army. In addition to this fighting force, twenty thousand more men, principally from the Transport Service, were used to transport and supply the expedition.

By the time Stanley arrived in Abyssinia, the marching column had already started on its four-hundred-mile march to Theodore's stronghold at Magdala. Without even a tent, he hurried forward with only a buffalo robe to keep off the weather and an Arab servant named Ali to cook his meals. Passing through the wild, mountainous country full of giant crags and deep fissures, he at last reached the village of Senafe where part of the advance guard of the British Army was encamped. Having heard that the nights were cold, he went to the sumptuous marquee of the commanding general to ask for a tent. Speaking of this interview, he remarked that "it will be sufficient to say that I left him with 'good evening,' and an assurance that if I ever rested in his tent again it would be because he had sent for me."

Ordered out of the general's tent, Stanley found himself hospitably received by the expedition's most eccentric character, an officer nicknamed Captain Smelfungus, after a character in Laurence Sterne's *A Sentimental Journey*. The captain had never recovered from a severe wound on the head complicated by a sunstroke. He was famous for telling tall tales of his prowess in the arts of love and war, but he was generous. He shared his tent, his goodly store of provisions, and his five servants with Stanley for a good part of the campaign.

With the good-natured Smelfungus, Stanley set off ahead of the army for the village of Antalo, where an advanced group of engineers was engaged in constructing a camp. Here he was told that he must wait for the main body of the troops. While waiting, Stanley amused himself by riding at breakneck speed after jackals and hyenas, visiting villages in the vicinity, and buying items from the native market.

While out riding one day he encountered a young officer from a fashionable cavalry regiment. He called out, "Good morning!" but the young officer only screwed in his monocle, stared at him, and rode off without replying. To the aristocratic bluebloods who officered the crack regiments of the British Army Stanley, with his buffalo robe, was something one read about in the novels of James Fenimore Cooper but not one who should presume an equality with gentlemen.

These educated, proud, upper-class Englishmen were contemptuous of Americans. Stanley was perplexed by their rudeness and reserve. Once, a young cornet to whom Stanley spoke drew back several paces and demanded, "Whom have I the honor to address?" Even the English reporters with the expedition laughed at the correspondent from the scandalous New York *Herald* with his gauche American accent. Only the mad Captain Smelfungus was friendly.

The main body of the expeditionary force, led by General Napier, arrived at Antalo on March 3. It was a colorful sight, this nineteenth-century British army on campaign. There were English and Irish regiments filled with weather-beaten veterans in red coats, inured to life-long campaigns in India; colorful native regiments with red fezzes or green turbans; Punjabis and Beluchis; the 10th Native Regiment, composed of Sepoys; the sparkling Scinde Horse, in green uniforms and crimson turbans, riding on horses with green saddle-cloths; brilliantly dressed officers with silver helmets; a brigade of English sailors with rockets; horse-drawn artillery; elephants; camels; horses; thousands of mules; an archeologist from the British Museum, and one young officer sporting kid gloves and a green veil!

They remained at Antalo until March 14. The method of advance used by the army was to have the engineers construct a camp two marches away, then the main bulk of the troops would move to the new camp and wait for the engineers to build another. In this caterpillar fashion the Abyssinian Expeditionary Force arrived on April 9 before Magdala, stronghold capital of King Theodore.

Perched on top of a mountain of granite, Magdala seemed impregnable. But on April 10, undismayed by the formidable appearance of its objective, the British Army, each man dressed in his newest and best uniform, marched down into a ravine, crossed a river, and proceeded

to march up the mountain. Before the army could be arranged into a
fighting posture, Theodore disrupted Sir Robert Napier's plan of attack
by throwing thirty-five hundred well-armed warriors down the slopes
toward the advancing attackers. To meet this wild charge there were
only six companies of Bombay and Madras Indian sappers armed with
ancient muzzle-loaders. Directly behind them, sitting calmly on their
horses, were Sir Robert and his staff, armed only with dress sabers.
They did not move.

The Abyssinians were drawing dangerously close when an aide
dashed up to Napier: "Here it is, General! The Naval Brigade has
arrived!"

"Very good," said Napier calmly. "Let Captain Fellowes take position on that little knoll in front."

The sailors quickly moved into position. "Action front!" shouted the
naval captain.

"Action front!" repeated the lieutenant and the boatswain.

Just in time, the rockets of the naval brigade swished through the
air and exploded in the ranks of the charging Abyssinians. Stunned by
the onslaught of these strange weapons, the enemy halted in confusion.
Before they could recover, three hundred men from the "King's Own"
4th Foot dashed up on the double, their cartridge boxes rattling on
their hips and their fingers loading shells into their Snider rifles as
they ran.

"Commence firing from both flanks!" bawled an officer.

Rifle fire was added to the rocket bombardment, and the enemy
retreated in disorder, English bullets pursuing them as they fled. One
running man suddenly leaped in the air and then fell on his face,
clawing the ground in agony. Another, about to jump behind a boulder,
was stopped in mid-air when a bullet crashed through his brain. Still
another was hit squarely on the head by a rocket and blown into a
ravine.

Re-formed by their chiefs, the Abyssinians attempted a flanking
movement in an effort to get at the baggage train, but the captain in
charge exclaimed, "By Jove!" and his men drove them back with their
Snider rifles, the most modern breech-loading guns then known. Those
who stayed to fight were wiped out by the bayonets of the Sepoys.

After fighting all day, the army marched back to its camp for the
night. As Stanley rolled himself in his buffalo robe and lay down to
sleep, he heard the jackals and hyenas feasting on the dead and still-
dying on the slopes before Magdala.

The next morning, the casualties were counted. British losses totaled only one officer and thirty-one privates wounded; not a single British soldier had been killed. Stanley accompanied Captain Sweeny of the 4th Foot who was out to count the Abyssinian dead. Seventy-five enemy warriors had managed to live through the night and were carried to the British field hospital; five hundred and sixty corpses were thrown into shallow graves by a burial detail.

Sir Robert sent a messenger to Theodore stating his demands: complete submission, the release of the prisoners, and the surrender of Magdala. Before the messenger could reach the fort, however, he met two of the captives themselves coming down to the British camp with a note from King Theodore. Several messages were exchanged by Theodore and Sir Robert during the course of the day. Finally, late in the afternoon, Theodore, fearful of British firepower after witnessing the destruction of his finest troops, was persuaded to try to appease the British commander by releasing all the prisoners voluntarily. By seven o'clock that evening the captives, together with their servants and their servants' servants, had reached the British camp.

Stanley expected to see an emotional scene as the men and women who had been captive for so long reached the camp of their deliverers. Instead, the released prisoners displayed no emotion at all and the English officers only screwed in their monocles to survey the appearance of the newcomers. It turned out that not quite all of the prisoners were accounted for. In his hurry to leave, one of the missionaries had forgotten his sick wife and had to scurry back to Magdala in the middle of the night to fetch her!

Theodore had hoped that the release of the prisoners would satisfy the British and that now they would return to the coast. But Sir Robert wanted Theodore's complete submission and the surrender of Magdala. So, the next morning, the army again marched out of camp. In orderly columns, to the music of their regimental bands, the men trudged back up the slopes to the Abyssinian stronghold. Behind the infantry came the cavalry, followed by the elephants and the artillery. There were no scouts, and no attempt was made to conceal their movements. When they arrived before the gates of Magdala, the attack was begun with an artillery barrage followed by volleys of musketry. While this was going on, Stanley was shown the naked bodies of more than three hundred prisoners Theodore had massacred and thrown into a ravine two days before. It made a good item.

When the barrage was over and it was time for the British troops to make the final assault, it was learned that scaling ladders, powder charges, and axes to breach and surmount the walls had been left in camp. No one had thought to bring them! Undismayed—or perhaps inured to such lack of foresight—the British soldiers proceeded to tear down the secondary defenses with their hands and rifle butts and to swarm over the walls. Soon men were cheering, British flags were hoisted, and the bands were playing "God Save the Queen." Incredibly, not a single British soldier was killed in this final assault, and only seventeen men were wounded. The dying King Theodore was found by some Irish soldiers; he had shot himself in the mouth with a pistol, a present from Queen Victoria. The soldiers roughly dragged him to a hammock where he died a few moments later.

Now that the battle was over, the looting began. Native beer was soon found and the soldiers drank deep. Theodore's treasure was discovered and noisy quarrels broke out over its distribution. Stanley was shocked to see that foremost in the scramble for the loot were the ex-prisoner missionaries.

Two days later, Magdala was blown up by the engineers and, on the morning of April 18, 1868, the British expeditionary force started back for the coast. Stanley asked permission to send a courier with his news dispatches on ahead of the victorious army, but his request was refused; he was forced to put his stories in the bag with the official report and the dispatches of the English reporters. General Napier had sent word of the victory at Magdala to his government and had received congratulatory messages from the Queen and the Royal Duke of Cambridge. The English public, however, had not yet been informed of the event. Apparently the government was waiting for more details of the campaign before releasing the information.

On June 1, when the army arrived back at Zula, the enthusiastic young Stanley wrote, "And thus the Modern Crusade became numbered with past events, to be remembered of all men, in all lands, among the most wonderfully successful campaigns ever conducted in history."

Leaving Zula by the first troop ship, Stanley arrived in Suez, where he had hoped to send off his stories by telegraph. Instead, he learned that his ship and all its passengers would have to remain in quarantine for five days. Nevertheless, he managed to get a long dispatch smuggled to his friend the telegraph operator, and his story was sent over the wires to London and from there to the New York *Herald*. It was the first news story to get out—and it was a long time before any others could be sent. No sooner had Stanley's story gone over the wires than the cable broke between Alexandria and Malta. The telegraph was out of commission for weeks!

In England, Stanley's stories were greeted with surprise and incredulity. This was a new kind of journalism to the British. Their national vanity was piqued that an American newspaper man should have beaten their own correspondents and even the British government's announcement. There were denunciations of the *Herald,* and Stanley was called an impostor. He and his paper were vindicated three weeks later when the official dispatches were published; Stanley's success was rewarded by his being made a permanent employee of the *Herald* at two thousand dollars a year.

Stanley was jubilant over his first taste of fame, but he was already looking for new arenas in which to display his talents. While waiting for further instructions in Alexandria he wrote in his journal: "I . . . must keep a sharp look-out that my second 'coup' shall be as much of a success as the first. I wonder where I shall be sent to next."

# CHAPTER IV

# *Escape from Bliss*

THE UNLOVED, unwanted bastard had carved out a place for himself in the world. He had been laughed at, rebuffed, and disbelieved, but he had been right and he had succeeded. He had found his own peculiar key to life: through danger and adventure he could find both escape and recognition. But one success was not enough. He looked forward eagerly to additional assignments from Bennett, and they came in rapid succession.

Stanley's next coup was of quite a different nature from what he had anticipated. From Alexandria, Bennett sent him to Crete, where an insurrection was brewing. On August 20, 1868, Stanley was on the island of Syra where a kindly old Greek named Christo Evangelides acted as his guide around the little island's principal town. Seeing the reporter's frank admiration for the young girls they saw, Evangelides suggested that it might be a good idea if Stanley married a Greek girl.

In his journal that night Stanley wrote, "Up to this moment it never had entered my mind that it must be some day my fate to select a wife. Rapidly my mind revolved this question. To marry requires means, larger means than I have. My twelve hundred pounds would soon be spent; and on four hundred pounds a year, and that depending on the will of one man, it would be rash to venture with an extravagant woman. Yet the suggestion was delicious from other points of view. A wife! My wife! How grand the proprietorship of a fair woman appeared! To be loved with heart and soul above all else, forever united in thought and sympathy with a fair and virtuous being, whose very touch gave strength and courage and confidence! . . . how my warm imagination glows at the strange idea!"

Evangelides painted the virtues and beauties of Greek women in the most alluring terms, but although Stanley showed great interest, he doubted that he would ever find such a virtuous beauty as the old Greek pictured. But Evangelides assured the young man that if everything were left to him a suitable wife would be chosen. The very next day, Evangelides hopefully proposed that Stanley marry his own daughter, Calliope! Virtuous, Calliope may have been, but she was no beauty and Stanley thought: "She is not one to thaw my reserve."

That evening, the undiscouraged Evangelides led him to the home of some friends. Here he was introduced to Virginia, a shy young beauty who seemed on first glance to meet all his requirements for a wife. She was sixteen years old, and her features reminded him of the Empress Eugénie. To Stanley's horror, however, Evangelides immediately introduced the subject of marriage in his conversation with Virginia's parents. Their allusions soon became quite personal and Stanley's face began to flush.

Virginia's mother turned to the embarrassed young man and asked, "Are you married?"

"Heaven forbid," he replied quickly.

"Why?" she said, smiling. "Is marriage so dreadful?"

"I am sure I don't know, but I have not thought of the subject."

"Oh, well, I hope you will think of it now; there are many fair women in Greece; and Greek women make the best wives," she counseled.

"I am quite ready to believe you, and if I met a young Greek lady who thought as much of me as I of her, I might be tempted to sacrifice my independence."

"I am sure," said the mother, "if you will look around, you will find a young lady after your heart."

Stanley bowed, but his face burned.

Virginia spoke French fluently but knew very little English. In spite of this, he found himself strongly attracted to the girl, although he denied even to himself that he was actually in love. Shortly after this first interview he left town for a few days, and apparently wrote a letter in which he expressed his desire to marry the fair Virginia. When he returned, there was a self-conscious evening with the family when he was introduced to the girl's two older brothers and a younger sister. They scrutinized him carefully, and even on the little girl's face he read, "I wonder if he will suit me as a brother-in-law."

The next day—it was now September 10—a friend of the family came to Stanley's room to inform him that the marriage had been satisfactorily arranged; he had but to name the day. After receiving assurances that the matter was really settled and that there was no honorable retreat, Stanley said, "As my business admits of no delay, I should like the marriage to take place next Sunday."

"All right," said the man, "next Sunday suits us perfectly." He went out, leaving a quivering Henry Stanley.

The marriage now seemed inevitable. That evening, Stanley visited his fiancée's house again, and was allowed to see Virginia. "In a short time, whatever misgivings I may have had as to the wisdom of my act were banished by the touch of her hand, and the visible trust in her eyes. There was no doubt as to her ultimate responsiveness to the height and depth of love. As yet, naturally, there was no love; but it was budding, and, if allowed to expand, there would be no flaw in the bloom. If I know myself at all, I think that my condition was much the same. All that I knew of her I admired; and, if she were as constant in goodness as she was beautiful, there would be no reason to regret having been so precipitate."

He was aroused from these thoughts by the girl's mother, who evidently had been talking with her neighbors. She brought up the point that Stanley was really a stranger in town and that it might be wise to wait a bit to see if he was what he represented himself to be.

Stanley quickly agreed. Here was a reprieve, if not an actual pardon. Three days later he boarded a ship for Smyrna. He noted in his journal that "Virginia was quite affectionate, and, although outwardly calm, my regrets are keener at parting than I expected. However, what must be, must be."

Two weeks later he wrote to Evangelides and to Virginia's mother telling them not to expect his return to Syra. Stanley was frightened out of his wits by the prospect of marriage and, seeing what he hoped was an honorable escape, he bolted. And so the pretty, young Greek girl was added to the St. Asaph Workhouse, the *Windermere,* the Confederate Army, and the United States Navy—all deserted by Henry Stanley.

For the next two months Stanley, free and heart-whole once more, traveled from city to city and country to country, covering assignments for his paper: Smyrna, Rhodes, Athens, Beirut, and Alexandria were visited in succession. A rebellion was brewing in Spain, and he was sent off to cover it. He had barely completed his first interview, with the rebel general, when he was ordered to London. There he received a surprising commission.

It had been reported that the famous African explorer and missionary, Dr. David Livingstone, was on his way home from East Africa. On the chance that he might be able to intercept the great man and obtain the first interview with him, Stanley was ordered to go to Aden, at the southern end of the Arabian peninsula, and wait for him. Off he went, arriving in Aden on November 21, 1868. For two and a half months he waited for some word of Livingstone; but the wait was in vain. Livingstone was still in the African interior. The talk of his return home had been only rumor. It was not yet time nor was Aden the place for these two men to have their famous meeting.

Waiting was the thing Stanley hated most. Without action he became restless and unhappy. He complained of the heat and the dust; he read Herodotus, Josephus, and handbooks on Egypt, Greece, the Levant, and India; and he worked his account of the Magdala campaign into book form with the intention of publishing it some day (it came out five years later). On New Year's Day, 1869, he resolved to give up smoking, but gave up the attempt after only six days because he found the suppression of his one vice took up too much of his time. He meditated on the nature of happiness: "If to be happy is to be without sorrow, fear, anxiety, doubt, I have been happy; and, if I could find an island in mid-ocean, remote from the presence or reach of man, with a few necessaries sufficient to sustain life, I might be happy yet; for then I could forget what reminds me of unhappiness, and, when death came, I should accept it as a long sleep and death."

But these dismal thoughts vanished when, on February 1, he was ordered back to London. He was in quite a different mood when, on February 20, he wrote:

"At sea, under a divine heaven! There is a period which marks the transition from boy to man, when the boy discards his errors and his awkwardness, and puts on the man's mask, and adopts his ways. The duration of the period depends upon circumstances, and not upon any defined time. With me, it lasted some months; and, though I feel in ideas more manly than when I left the States, I am often reminded that I am still a boy in many things. In impulse I am boy-like, but in reflection a man; and then I condemn the boy-like action and make a new resolve. How many of these resolutions will be required before they are capable of restraining, not only the impulse, but the desire, when every action will be the outcome of deliberation? I am still a boy when I obey my first thought; the man takes that thought and views it from many sides before action. I have not come to that yet; but after many a struggle I hope to succeed. . . .

"It is well for me that I am not so rich as the young man I met at Cairo who has money enough to indulge every caprice. I thank Heaven for it, for if he be half as hot-blooded and impulsive as I am, surely his life will be short; but necessity has ordained that my strength and youth should be directed by others, and in a different sphere; and the more tasks I receive, the happier is my life. I want work, close, absorbing, and congenial work, only so that there will be no time for regrets, and vain desires, and morbid thoughts. In the interval, books come handy. I have picked up Helvetius and Zimmerman, in Alexandria, and, though there is much wisdom in them, they are ill suited to young men with a craze for action."

Although Stanley's quick mind was rapidly absorbing knowledge and he was working desperately to mold his own character, he found difficulty in making himself liked—especially by Englishmen, whom he seemed particularly anxious to impress. Recently in Egypt he had found himself in a railway compartment with two young English gentlemen who were a year or two younger than himself. He had provided himself with water, sandwiches, and oranges, but his shy and silent English companions had not. When the heat and the sand made their life uncomfortable, Stanley offered to share his water and provisions with them. The young Englishmen were grateful, and they were soon on what Stanley felt was a friendly basis. He apparently talked a great deal, explaining to them the historical significance of the scenes they were passing and perhaps describing some of his own experiences in this part of the world.

Arriving at Suez, they all went to the same hotel. As Stanley was known there, he was shown to his room at once. While washing, he heard voices in the adjoining room and, thanks to the thin walls, he overheard the conversation of his English traveling companions. They were talking about him. "Had I been a leper or a pariah, I could not have been more foully and slanderously abused," he said.

Stanley had committed one of the cardinal sins of the educated man by displaying his knowledge too ostentatiously. This experience at Suez was not an isolated one; similar incidents had occurred twice before in recent months. No wonder he dreamed of an island where he could escape from civilized men. But Stanley would not have been content to remain on a lonely island even if he had found one, for there were the devils of ambition at his heels. The setbacks his pride suffered only drove him harder on the road to success. He felt that he must achieve greater distinction before he would be accepted and not ridiculed among gentlemen.

His next assignment was back in Spain where rebellion and counter-rebellion were keeping the country in an uproar. From Madrid he wrote a revealing letter to an acquaintance who had urged him to take a vacation:

"You know my peculiar position, you know who, what, and where I am; you know that I am not master of my own actions, that I am at the beck and call of a chief whose will is imperious law. The slightest inattention to business, the slightest forgetfulness of duty, the slightest laggardness, is punished severely; that is, you are sent about your business. I do not mean to be discharged from my position. I mean by attention to my business, by self-denial, by indefatigable energy, to become, by this very business, my own master, and that of others. Hitherto, so well have I performed my duty, surpassing all my contemporaries, that the greatest confidence is placed in me.

"I have *carte blanche* at the bankers'; I can go to any part of Spain I please, that I think best; I can employ a man in my absence. This I have done in a short space of eighteen months, when others have languished on at their business for fifteen years, and got no higher than the step where they entered upon duty. How have I done this? By intense application to duty, by self-denial, which means I have denied myself all pleasures, so that I might do my duty thoroughly, and not exceed it. Such has been my ambition. I am fulfilling it. Pleasure cannot blind me, it cannot lead me astray from the path I have chalked out. I am so much my own master, that I am master over my own passions. It is also my interest to do my duty well. It is my interest not to throw up my position. My whole life hangs upon it—my future would be almost blank, if I threw up my place. You do not—cannot suppose that I have accepted this position merely for money. I can make plenty of money anywhere—it is that my future promotion to distinction hangs upon it. Even now, if I applied for it, I could get a consulship, but I do not want a consulship—I look further up, beyond a consulship.

"My whole future is risked. Stern duty commands me to stay. It is only by railway celerity that I can live. Away from work, my conscience accuses me of forgetting duty, of wasting time, of forgetting my God. I cannot help that feeling. It makes me feel as though the world were sliding from under my feet. Even if I had a month's holiday

I could not take it; I would be restless, dissatisfied, gloomy, morose. To the devil with a vacation! I don't want it."

Despite the discouragements of his youth, Stanley's confidence in himself and his abilities remained unshaken. His will to succeed, whatever the odds, became a grim determination. Austere self-denial and rigid fidelity to duty—these were the qualities that would raise him above his fellows.

Stanley spent six months in Spain, from March to September, 1869, writing vivid descriptions of the fighting. He wrote about typical participants as well as the leaders in the conflict, and he painted for the readers of the New York *Herald* word pictures of the scenery and the countryside, the battles and the barricades. At one point he spent thirty-six hours on a rooftop watching the rebels throw up a barricade in a street and defend it against the repeated assaults of government troops.

Told that there was hot fighting in Valencia and being unable to get there by land, he took a boat and, after a great deal of difficulty, reached the city. He wandered from street to street looking for a hotel, frequently being stopped by suspicious soldiers with fixed bayonets. At last he found a hotel. To reach it, however, he had to pass through twenty feet of murderous crossfire. "But twenty feet," he later wrote. "Count three and jump! I jumped, took one peep of the barricades in my mid-air flight, and was in the hotel portico, safe, with a chorus of 'bravos' in my rear and a welcome in front!"

Bravery won Stanley men's respect, if his cultural attainments did not. But he never ceased his efforts to educate himself. With his quick mind and retentive memory, languages came easily. He had been in Spain only three months when he knew enough of the language to make a speech before a Spanish audience. Later, he even contributed articles to Spanish newspapers. He had already taught himself French and later, in Africa, he had no trouble learning Swahili, some Arabic, and dozens of African dialects.

The test of both his intelligence and his courage was soon to come. Without previous warning, Stanley was recalled from Spain and ordered to Paris to meet with James Gordon Bennett, Jr., the son and chief assistant of the *Herald's* publisher. There, on October 27, 1869, he received certainly one of the most extraordinary sets of assignments ever given to any newspaper reporter. Arriving in Paris in the middle of the night, he went straight to the Grand Hotel where young Bennett was staying. The two young men were both twenty-eight at this time.

Stanley knocked on the door to Bennett's room and heard a voice call "Come in."

Bennett was in bed, and when he saw his visitor he asked, "Who are you?"

"My name is Stanley."

"Ah yes! Sit down," said Bennett, throwing on a robe. "I have important business on hand for you. Where do you think Livingstone is?"

"I really don't know, sir."

"Do you think he is alive?"

"He may be and he may not be."

"Well, I think he is alive, and that he can be found, and I am going to send you to find him."

"What!" exclaimed Stanley. "Do you really think I can find Dr. Livingstone? Do you mean me to go to Central Africa?"

"Yes, I mean that you shall go and find him wherever you may hear that he is, and to get what news you can of him. And perhaps the old man may be in want; take enough with you to help him should he require it. Of course, you will act according to your own plans, and do what you think best—*but find Livingstone!*"

"Have you considered seriously the great expense you are likely to incur on account of this little journey?"

"What will it cost?" Bennett asked abruptly.

"Burton and Speke's journey to Central Africa cost between three thousand and five thousand pounds and I fear it cannot be done under twenty-five hundred."

"Well, I will tell you what you will do. Draw a thousand pounds now; and when you have gone through that, draw another thousand, and when that is spent draw another, and when you have finished that, draw another thousand, and so on; but, *find Livingstone.*"

Thinking of the future, Stanley said, "I have heard that should your father die you would sell the *Herald* and retire from business."

"Whoever told you that is wrong, for there is not enough money in New York City to buy the New York *Herald.* My father has made it a great paper, but I mean to make it greater. I mean that it shall be a newspaper in the true sense of the word. I mean that it shall publish whatever news will be interesting to the world at no matter what cost."

"After that, I have nothing more to say," said Stanley—and then proceeded to ask another question: "Do you mean me to go straight on to Africa to search for Dr. Livingstone?"

"No! I want you to go to the inauguration of the Suez Canal first, and then proceed up the Nile. I hear Baker is about starting for Upper Egypt. Find out what you can about his expedition, and as you go up describe as well as possible whatever is interesting for tourists; and then write up a guide—a practical one—for Lower Egypt; tell us about whatever is worth seeing and how to see it.

"Then you might as well go to Jerusalem; I hear Captain Warren is making some interesting discoveries there. Then visit Constantinople and find out about that trouble between the Khedive and the Sultan.

"Then—let me see—you might as well visit the Crimea and those old battlegrounds. Then go across the Caucasus to the Caspian Sea: I hear there is a Russian expedition bound for Khiva. From thence you may get through Persia to India; you could write an interesting letter from Persepolis.

"Bagdad will be close on your way to India; suppose you go there and write up something about the Euphrates Valley Railway. Then, when you have come to India, you can go after Livingstone. Probably you will hear by that time that Livingstone is on his way to Zanzibar; but if not, go into the interior and find him. If alive, get what news of his discoveries you can; and if you find he is dead, bring all possible proofs of his being dead. That is all. Good night, and God be with you."

"Good night, sir," Stanley said. "What is in the power of human nature to do I will do; and on such an errand as I go upon, God will be with me."

At eleven o'clock that night Stanley boarded the Marseilles express and set out on a whirlwind tour of the Middle East. From Marseilles he went to Port Said to witness the ceremonies accompanying the opening of the Suez Canal. Then he traveled up the Nile to Philae, where he arrived just in time to prevent a duel between a man named Higginbotham, who had been chief engineer on Sir Samuel Baker's expedition, and a young Frenchman who thought himself insulted when Higginbotham had mistaken him for an Egyptian because he was wearing a fez. To the readers of the *Herald,* he sent back stories of the wonders of Egypt and descriptions of the people. One of the sights he described was the mummy vendors who sold their wares on the streets of Thebes, and who could be heard querying, "Buy a nice foot, sir?"

From Egypt, he hurried on to his other assignments. In January, 1870, he was in Jerusalem, where he was shocked by the commercialization of the holy places and disgusted with the sectarian rivalries he found among the Christian churches. In February he was in Constantinople, where he arranged to meet Edward Joy Morris, the American Minister who had befriended him after the ill-fated expedition with Cook and Noe. It was Stanley's desire to repay Morris the hundred and fifty pounds he had borrowed, but Morris informed him that the matter had long since been settled. Morris and Stanley became friends, and Stanley was almost a daily visitor for dinner. Morris was impressed by the changes that had taken place in Stanley since he had last seen him. "The uncouth young man whom I first knew had grown into a perfect man of the world, possessing the appearance, the manners and the attributes of a perfect gentleman. . . . Instead of thinking he was a young man who had barely seen twenty-six summers [sic] you would imagine that he was thirty-five or forty years of age, so cultured and learned was he in all the ways of life."

In March, after leaving Constantinople, Stanley was walking through the old battlefields of the Crimean War. From there he went through the Caucasus, arriving, in the middle of April, at Baku, on the Caspian Sea, where he was impressed with the civilizing influences the Russians had brought to that area.

At Odessa he saw a carnival where the mad abandonment of both men and women shocked him. He found it hard to resist the "fair gauzy nymphs" who tempted him to relax his stern virtue, but "the shame of it more than any morality" prevented him from taking advantage of the carnival spirit.

Three weeks later he was in Teheran, Persia, describing the palaces of the Shah, the exotic bazaars, and the strange customs of the Persians. Then he went on to Persepolis, seat of the great kings of ancient Persia, where he examined and measured the major ruins, slept under a broken portal and, on an ancient wall, carved a crude diamond shape in which he incised:

STANLEY
NEW YORK HERALD
*1870*

Arabia and India were next on his list, and then he was free to leave for Zanzibar, where he planned to begin his search for Livingstone.

Throughout this time, he had been reading everything he could find about Livingstone and poring over books by other explorers to glean details of African life and African exploration. He had also been acquiring some personnel. In Palestine he picked up a Christian Arab boy named Selim for an interpreter, and on the bark that took him from Bombay to Mauritius he hired the ship's first mate, a Scotsman named William Farquhar. All three arrived in Zanzibar by an American whaling ship on January 6, 1871, nearly fifteen months after Stanley had received his assignment to find Livingstone.

CHAPTER V

# *Finding Livingstone*

OTHER CONTINENTS have shifted and changed—their surfaces have been torn and folded by glaciers and violent upheavals of the earth—but the vast bulk of the foundation of Africa, except for the Great Rift and the extreme north and southwest, is almost a solid block of rocks which have rested virtually undisturbed for two hundred million years. Along its over sixteen thousand miles of coastline there are very few bays offering safe anchorage for ships, and much of the shore is simply sandy beach protected by reefs. Thus, although lying close at hand to Asia and Europe, early explorers found it easier to sail across the broad Atlantic than to penetrate the great continent at their feet. Of course, the narrow strip of land along the northern coast was known, but the vast Sahara to the south was an effective barrier to land exploration. The slender finger of the Nile jutted inland and led to the early cultivation of the land along its banks, but even its source was unknown. By the middle of the nineteenth century— a mere hundred years ago—only isolated sections of the coast were known by Europeans. The enormous bulk of the continent—more than eleven million square miles of land—was unknown; its great mountains, lakes, rivers, and forests were unexplored, its people a mystery. The words "unknown" or "unexplored territory" marched in large letters across its maps, or, as Swift said:

> So geographers, in Afric maps,
> With savage pictures fill their gaps,
> And o'er inhabitable downs
> Place elephants for want of towns.

In addition to the inhospitable terrain, half-caste Arab slavers often jealously guarded what they regarded as their hunting grounds. Slaves

55

and ivory, brought out of the interior by unscrupulous Arab traders, were almost the only products exported by the immensely rich continent. The focal point for the East African slave and ivory trade was the tiny island of Zanzibar, perched off the east coast of Africa just below the equator. Since earliest recorded times Zanzibar had been under Arabian cultural influence; but due to its importance as a trading center, it had attracted Indians and other Asiatics; successive waves of invaders—Turks, Portuguese, Arabs, and Africans—had rolled over the island, leaving their biological backwash; and the slave trade had brought Negroes of every East African tribe to the island who, in time, mixed and intermarried with the Arabs and Asians. But, although small, the population of Zanzibar was (and is today) one of the most heterogeneous in the world. Most of the so-called Arabs had a strong mixture of Negro blood, and, while believers in Islam and wearing Arabic dress, their features and coloring were Negroid. The language of Zanzibar was Swahili, and the spread of this tongue until it became the *lingua franca* of East Africa is an indication of the extent of Zanzibarian influence.

Although the sultans of Zanzibar vaguely laid claim to hundreds of thousands of square miles of the African mainland—covering what is today Kenya, Tanganyika, and southern Somalia—they made no effort to chart their domains, erect boundaries, or even to effectively govern the land. Local Arab settlements on the mainland, although owing allegiance to the Sultan, were, in effect, autonomous. The Sultan was content to collect his tax from each slave and each piece of ivory that was brought out. The African mainland, as regarded by the Zanzibari Arabs, was simply a great sea from which men of enterprise could extract a seemingly unlimited number of slaves and elephant tusks.

Until the middle of the nineteenth century, surprisingly few Europeans followed in the steps of the Arab traders. Isolated European explorers—perhaps wanderers would be a better description—had penetrated some sections of the interior, but they paid little attention to geographical detail and did comparatively little to advance the world's knowledge of Africa. Perhaps the first of the real explorers of central Africa were that strange, brave, and venturesome man Richard Francis Burton (1821-1890), the translator of the *Arabian Nights* and one of the first Christians to enter the holy city of Mecca, and John Hanning Speke (1827-1864). These two men made a brief expedition into Somalia where Burton became the first white man ever to visit the Somali capital of Harrar. Then, in June, 1857, Burton and Speke started from Zanzibar and followed an old Arab caravan route into the interior. A year later, after considerable hardship, they reached the settlement of Ujiji on the shores of Lake Tanganyika. They did not explore this important lake, but contented themselves with simply finding it. Retracing their steps, they returned to the Arab town of Tabora. Burton was seriously sick by this time, so Speke alone made a trip north until he came to Africa's largest lake, which he named Victoria Nyanza (Lake Victoria). Speke was sure that the lake flowed into the Nile, but Burton could never bring himself to believe that his partner had made such an important discovery, and the two men became bitter enemies.

To prove his theory, Speke made another expedition to Africa in 1860, this time accompanied by James A. Grant (1827-1892). They went back to the Victoria Nyanza and traveled around its shores until they reached the populous and well-organized Negro kingdom of Uganda (today, Buganda, the largest province of modern Uganda). It was there they discovered the waters of Victoria spilling over a great falls into a river they believed to be the Nile. Following the river down, they met Samuel White Baker (1821-1893) advancing up the White Nile through the formidable sudd. Baker was disappointed to learn that Speke and Grant had already found the "source of the Nile," but he went on to discover the Albert Nyanza in 1864.

Burton, Speke, Grant, and Baker had all established reputations as African explorers, and they had all made important discoveries. But the explorer who surpassed them all was the mild-manned Scottish Presbyterian missionary: David Livingstone. Born of poor parents at Blantyre, Scotland, near Glasgow, on March 19, 1813, he went to work in a textile mill when he was only ten years old. Developing an early passion for books, he spent a good part of his meager earnings on them. At nineteen, he was promoted to cotton spinner and, at the same time, attended classes in Greek, medicine, and religion at the University of Glasgow with the view of becoming a foreign missionary doctor. He succeeded so well that by the time he was twenty-five he had passed the tests necessary to become a Licentiate of the Faculty of Physicians and Surgeons and was sent as a probationer to a parish in Essex County, England.

Originally, he had hoped to go to China, but as he was about to leave England the Chinese Opium War broke out, and he was sent to South Africa instead. He was twenty-eight when he arrived at Cape Town and, after a seven-hundred-mile journey inland, he reached his first African post: the Presbyterian mission station at Kuruman, Bechuanaland, established twenty-five years earlier by Robert Moffat. For the next five years he led a comparatively settled life. He married Mary Moffat, daughter of the mission's founder, and raised a family of three boys and a girl.

In 1845 he moved with his family to a place called Kolobeng, where he established the most remote mission on the African continent. From here he began a series of exploratory trips still farther into the interior, frequently accompanied by his wife and children. He soon became convinced that his work lay not in opening up new missions but in becoming a pioneering missionary, one who would open up roads where others could more easily follow to establish missions.

For the next twenty years he blazed trails through South Africa, opening to the eyes of the civilized world nearly one third of the continent. By 1849 he had crossed the great Kalahari Desert, and discovered Lake Ngami. Six years later he was exploring on the Zambezi, discovering, on November 17, 1855, one of the world's greatest cataracts, which he named Victoria Falls. Lake Nyassa and the Livingstone Mountains were added to his findings as he went on and on, filling the map of South Africa with rivers, mountains, lakes, and deserts where before they had been marked as unknown territory. Often delayed, often detoured, often turned back, he continued his explorations. His wife died in South Africa and his children were sent back to England to be educated, but he continued his work. Livingstone was a careful observer, and wherever he went he made copious notes on geography, botany, zoology, and a host of other subjects. But he never forgot that he was a missionary; he believed the slave trade to be the greatest deterrent to the progress of civilization in Africa, and, through his books and articles, he aroused considerable feeling in Europe against the entire institution of slavery. The slave trade was the "open sore of the world."

At long last, in 1864, Livingstone returned to England, but he was soon persuaded by the Royal Geographical Society to return once more in order to solve the problems connected with the watershed between Lake Tanganyika and Lake Nyassa. Livingstone, now fifty-two years old, left England on August 14, 1865, crossing over to the mainland from Zanzibar seven months later and starting up the River Rovuma. In December, 1866, some of his men returned to Zanzibar with the news that Livingstone was dead. So convincing was the story that for a long time it was generally believed, and the civilized world mourned his passing. There were some, however, notably Roderick Murchinson, famous geologist and President of the Royal Geographical Society, who were not altogether convinced of the truth of the story. Close questioning of the men who had returned with the tale revealed contradictions and improbabilities. Through the London *Times,* Murchinson made public his doubts and stirred up considerable controversy. To settle the matter, the British government dispatched an expedition to search for Livingstone, but the venture was only partially successful. Although the searchers did not find Livingstone, they did return with what seemed to be ample and satisfactory evidence that the missionary was still alive, and their report was later substantiated when letters from Livingstone dated February, 1867, and July, 1868, were brought out of the interior.

As no further news was received except vague and sometimes fantastic rumors from Zanzibar, most people came again to assume that the great man was dead. But the interest Livingstone had generated, not only in Africa and the slave trade, but in his own personal welfare, led James Gordon Bennett, Jr., to believe that it would be a great news story if the missionary could actually be found—dead or alive— and the world's doubts and anxieties resolved. To accomplish this great task, young Bennett selected Henry Stanley.

When Stanley, on the American whaler *Falcon,* arrived on Zanzibar in January, 1871, there was still no word of Livingstone. Neither was there any word from Bennett. Stanley had only eighty dollars in his pocket with which to equip his expedition, but he was loath to sit around waiting for definite instructions. He immediately set about borrowing enough for his entire expedition. Fortunately, he was assisted in this matter by Captain Francis R. Webb, a former naval officer who was now the United States Consul in Zanzibar.

On the surface, Stanley seemed an odd choice for a man to lead the search for Livingstone. Standing only five feet five inches high and weighing a hundred and sixty-five pounds, he had a broad chest and short legs on which were stuck a pair of large feet. His hands were small and red, and on the little finger of his left hand he wore a signet ring. His hair was black above a round, florid face in which were perched a pair of gray, boyish eyes that were strangely penetrating. He was only twenty-nine years old, and he had never before led or organized an expedition (if we discount the short, ill-fated trip to Turkey); indeed, he had never before been a leader or even an employer of men. Nevertheless, he seems to have been aware of his handicap, for he took every opportunity to learn all that he could about traveling in Africa and dealing with its natives.

One of the many problems facing him was the question of currency. Stanley knew that beads, wire, and cloth would be needed for money, but he did not know the kinds or quantities that would be required. Most tribes would take only certain kinds of beads. In Unyamwezi the natives would take red beads but would refuse all other kinds; black beads were the currency of the inhabitants of Ugogo, but with all other tribes they were useless; egg-shaped beads were valuable in Ujiji and Uguhha, but were unacceptable to the people of any other region. The desired beads—some as tiny as sesame seeds and some as large as marbles—were not of the kind that could be easily or cheaply procured in Europe or America. These were quite special beads that had been used in Africa for centuries; many were very old, hand-drilled Venetian beads that had acquired a patina through age and handling. Fake beads were costly and difficult to manufacture. Besides, the African was not easily fooled when it came to his own money. Stanley searched the bazaars of Zanzibar for the millions of beads that would be needed.

Similar difficulties were presented by the wire and cloth. Since everything Stanley wanted to take with him would have to be carried on the backs of *pagazis* (bearers or carriers), it would be a waste of manpower as well as goods to take more than was absolutely essential.

Native currency was, of course, only one of thousands of items that had to be purchased or made before the expedition left Zanzibar. Once they had crossed over to the mainland, they would be on their own; anything forgotten would have to be done without. Stanley spent eight thousand dollars on native currency alone, and before the expedition was over he spent a total of twenty thousand dollars—a sizable amount for those days. He had some qualms about spending so much of his employer's money (particularly since he had borrowed it), but he decided to abide by the old sailor's maxim: "Obey orders if you break owners!"

As important as the supplies were the men who would go with him. In addition to Farquhar, the mate, and Selim, the Arab boy from Palestine, he also hired an Englishman named John Shaw who, until shortly before, had been third mate aboard the American ship *Nevada*.

In the selection of the Zanzibaris, Stanley located Wanyamwezis, or freed Negroes, who had accompanied other explorers on expeditions into the African interior. He was able to locate six who had done faithful service for Burton, Speke, and Grant, including Mabruki, known as the "bullheaded one," and Bombay, who was made captain of the *askaris,* or soldiers. Bombay was left to select eighteen other men who would also serve in the escort as askaris. He was to receive eighty dollars a year, the other "faithful" forty dollars a year, and the remainder of the men three dollars a month.

In addition to the tents, food, medicine, clothing, arms, ammunition, cloths, wire, and beads, Stanley also purchased twenty donkeys and two boats. The latter he stripped down so that only the timbers and thwarts would be carried. Instead of the boards, he set Shaw to work making double canvases covered with tar that would serve as skins for the boats. All of their equipment and supplies were packed in bales, bags, or boxes, depending on their contents. Each piece of the thousands of yards of sheeting and cloth had to be specially packed. All of the various kinds and qualities of cloth—American sheeting (known as Merikani), cloths of Muscat, Cutch, and India—were cut into lengths of a *doti* (four yards) and were laid in alternate layers on the ground. Each bale contained some of each type of cloth so that the loss of one bale would not unduly deplete the supply of any one kind of material. When the cloths had been piled up until they weighed about sixty-eight pounds, they were wrapped in a doti of cloth and tightly bound with rope. They were then pounded by two men until the bale was one solid roll, three and a half feet long, a foot wide, and a foot deep. The roll was placed in a mat bag, and cradled in three long sticks arranged as a fork. In this form, the bale could be carried on the shoulders of pagazis for hundreds, even thousands, of miles.

Beads, strung and unstrung, were carried in long, narrow, cotton bags. These could not weigh more than sixty-two pounds, as they were considered a little more difficult to carry than bales of cloth. Wire was arranged in coils—generally six to a load—and weighing not more than sixty pounds in all. The coils were carried on five-foot poles, three coils at each end. Other supplies and equipment had to be made up into portable shapes and weights. Not knowing how long he would be gone, Stanley stocked his expedition with what he hoped would be sufficient goods to last him for two years—plus supplies for Livingstone, should he find him alive and in want. When he completed his purchases, he found that he had over six tons of material to be carried into the interior! Most all of it would have to be carried by the pagazis, because in the whole of Central Africa there was hardly a wagon or a cart to be found; and because of the tsetse fly, there were few transport animals either.

On February 6, 1871, just twenty-eight days after his arrival in Zanzibar, Stanley, together with his white officers (whom he found drunk in a native saloon at their departure time), askaris, supplies, donkeys, and two horses, boarded four Arab dhows and crossed the twenty-five miles of water separating the island of Zanzibar from the town of Bagamoyo on the mainland of Africa. His plan was to head for the village of Ujiji on the shores of Lake Tanganyika, seven hundred and forty-two miles due west from the coast. It was in this village that Livingstone had last been heard from, and he hoped to learn something of his whereabouts after he arrived there.

At Bagamoyo, Stanley wanted to procure additional pagazis and start immediately for the interior. But he learned that things were not done so simply in Africa. Pagazis seemed unobtainable, and the Arab who undertook to act as his agent tried to swindle him at every turn. This delay at Bagamoyo was an anxious one, for the rainy season would soon be upon them; streams would be swollen, the flatlands would become bogs, and marching in the mud and rain would be slow and difficult. But delay did not mean rest, as Stanley was careful to inform Bennett: "It was work all day, thinking all night; not an hour could I call my own."

He had decided to move his expedition in small groups as far as Tabora in Unyamyembe because he had been told that large caravans moved slowly, inviting attack. But it was two exasperating weeks before he was able to obtain enough pagazis to send out his first caravan, and nearly two hair-tearing months before he was able to leave himself with the sixth and last contingent. On March 21, 1871, with a sigh of relief that he was on his way at last, Stanley marched out of Bagamoyo with twenty-seven pagazis; Asmani, the *kirangozi*, or guide, a giant of a man who led the way carrying the American flag; Captain Bombay in charge of twelve askaris and seventeen loaded donkeys; Selim, the Arab interpreter; one cook and a boy; and, last of all, Shaw, ex-mate, and now in charge of the rear guard. At the head of the caravan was Stanley, called *Bana Mkuba* (Big Master) by his people. The proud young man described himself as "the vanguard, the reporter, the thinker, the leader of the expedition." His patience and determination had already overcome the first obstacles, and he was on his way to find Livingstone at last!

Completed, the expedition consisted of three white men, twenty-three askaris, a hundred and fifty-seven pagazis, four chiefs, and five additional men with miscellaneous duties, a total of a hundred and ninety-two men. At the beginning there were two horses and twenty-seven donkeys, but, thanks to the tsetse fly, most of these beasts did not last long. The baggage was made up into a hundred and sixteen loads consisting of fifty-two bales of cloth, sixteen bags of beads, seven loads of wire, twenty loads of boat fixtures, three loads of tents, four loads of clothes and personal baggage, two loads of cooking utensils and dishes, one load of medicines, eight loads of bullets, powder, small shot, and cartridges, and three loads of instruments, European provisions, soap, and candles.

To defend his expedition, Stanley had purchased a shotgun, two carbines, four rifles, eight pistols, twenty-four flintlock muskets, two swords, two daggers, a boar spear, two American axes, twenty-four hatchets, a battle ax, and twenty-four long knives. A formidable array of weapons! Thus equipped, Stanley thought himself ready for anything.

Describing his state of mind at this time, he said, "My mission to find Livingstone was very simple, and was a clear and definite aim. All I had to do was to free my mind from all else, and relieve it of every earthly desire but the finding of the man whom I was sent to seek. To think of self, friends, banking-account, life-insurance, or any worldly interest but the one sole purpose of reaching the spot where Livingstone might happen to rest, could only weaken resolution. Intense application to my task assisted me to forget all I had left behind, and all that might lie ahead in the future.

"In some ways, it produced a delightful tranquillity which was foreign to me while in Europe. To be indifferent to the obituaries the papers may publish tomorrow, that never even a thought should glance across my mind of law-courts, jails, tombstones; not to care what may disturb a Parliament, or a Congress, or the state of the Funds, or the nerves excited about earthquakes, floods, wars, and other national evils, is a felicity few educated men in Britain know; and it compensated me in a great measure for the distress from heat, meagerness of diet, malaria, and other ills, to which I became subject soon after entering Africa."

But the troubles of this first expedition soon drove away any tranquillity of mind that he enjoyed. The country he had to traverse was not jungle, but savannah, rough and infertile. The hot and humid climate, with temperatures that reached 128 degrees, made the least

movement difficult; its enervating influences sapped the strength of
the body and eroded the will. The coming of the rainy season added
to his troubles by swelling the rivers and streams and bogging down
men and animals in mud and slime. Each of the many rivers they had
to cross required herculean efforts of mind, body, and spirit.

Insects of all sorts attacked the men and beasts. They were not only
a constant source of annoyance by day and by night, but they carried
diseases from the sick to the healthy, from the dying to the doomed.
Stanley himself was laid low by no less than twenty-three attacks of
fever in the thirteen months the expedition lasted. Many of these attacks were so severe that he was unconscious for long periods.

Dysentery, elephantiasis, smallpox, and a host of tropical diseases
attacked the expedition, rendering many of the men physically helpless and most of them demoralized. William Farquhar was the first
white casualty. His legs swelled from the dreaded elephantiasis, and
he had to be left in a native village. Stanley left him with six months'
supply of beads and cloth, but he died only a few days after the expedition went on.

In spite of all difficulties, Stanley pressed on in his search for Livingstone. He was "possessed by a feeling of power to achieve," and he
refused to be distracted or deflected from his duty. "Find him! Find
him! Even the words are inspiring," he wrote in his diary. There was
certainly little else to inspire him.

Hardly a day passed without some problem to be solved. The difficulties presented by nature could be borne or surmounted, the troubles
created by men were more complex and constituted, perhaps, the
greatest obstacle to the success of the expedition. Stanley learned that
leadership involved problems of discipline, morale, and organization.
The difficulties of communicating in a variety of languages added
more complications. Stanley was just learning Swahili (or, technically,
Kiswahili), the most important of the East African languages. At least
a smattering of native grammar was necessary in order to know where
you were and whom you were dealing with. In the matter of prefixes,
for example: U— commonly indicated a country, Wa— a people, M—
a person, and Ki— a language. Thus, the natives of Ugogo were called
Wagogo, and when one Mgogo spoke to another they talked in Kigogo.
But as in all grammars, there were exceptions: Stanley was headed for
Ujiji, a name normally associated with a country, from its prefix, but,
although at one time it may have been the center of a country, it was
now but a tiny village.

Although he made many mistakes of leadership in the first few months on the march, he learned his lessons with astonishing rapidity. Up to this point, his life had been primarily that of an observer of men and events. He had seen and he had recorded. Now he needed all of his stored-up impressions and experiences to give him the wisdom he required to meet the strange and severe demands made on him.

The men who had contracted to serve Stanley and to carry his loads had never heard of Livingstone, and they were not motivated by any feelings higher than a desire to earn enough money to fill their stomachs and clothe their bodies. When the opportunity presented itself, many of them deserted, stole or lost the goods they were carrying, or, feeling tired, simply went to sleep beside the path. It was a never-ending struggle to keep them together and to keep them moving.

In addition to the problems created by his own men, Stanley ran into difficulties with a multitude of native chiefs. He was following an old Arab caravan route—the way taken by Burton, Speke, and Grant. The tribes they encountered were not hostile, but each chief demanded his *honga*, a tribute for permission to pass through his territory. Naturally, there was no set rate among the savages, and they often asked for immense amounts of cloth, beads, or wire. Each time they encountered a tribe, a halt had to be made while Stanley haggled with the chief or his representative over the amount of honga. When the expedition reached the land of Ugogo, inhabited by numerous tribes and subtribes, each with its petty chief who had to be placated, Stanley began to fear that he would be beggared before he ever found Livingstone. Exasperated and outraged, he sometimes lost his temper, but he learned that once he had lost control of himself he had also lost control of the situation. Threats, rage, and harsh words were of no avail against the chiefs; patience, understanding, shrewdness, and resourcefulness accomplished almost everything.

Demands for honga were not the only source of annoyance. When Stanley's horse died in Kingaru, he ordered it buried deep in the ground about twenty yards from camp. The chief of Kingaru professed to be most disturbed by this incident. He was indignant that a horse should be buried on his land without his permission and demanded two doti (eight yards) of cloth in payment. Keeping his temper, Stanley asked him:

"Are you the great chief of Kingaru?"

"Huh-uh. Yes."

"The great great chief?"

"Huh-uh. Yes."

"How many soldiers have you?"

"Why?"

"How many fighting men have you?"

"None."

"Oh! I thought you might have a thousand men with you, by your going to fine a strong white man, who has plenty of guns and soldiers, two doti for burying a dead horse."

"No, I have no soldiers. I have only a few young men."

"Why do you come and make trouble then?"

"It was not I; it was my brothers who said to me, 'Come here, come here, Kingaru, see what the white man has done! Has he not taken possession of your soil, in that he has put his horse into your ground without your permission? Come, go to him and see by what right.' Therefore, I have come to ask you, who gave you permission to use my soil for a burying ground?"

"I want no man's permission to do what is right. My horse died. Had I left him to fester and stink in your valley, sickness would visit your village, your water would become unwholesome and caravans would not stop here for trade. They would say, 'This is an unlucky spot, let us go away.' But enough said; I understand you to say that you do not want him buried in your ground. The error I have fallen into is easily put right. This minute my soldiers shall dig him out again and cover up the soil as it was before and the horse shall be left where he died."

Stanley called out to Bombay to take some men and dig up the dead horse. The chief saw that he had gone too far and cried, "No, no, master! Let not the white man get angry. The horse is dead, and now lies buried. Let it remain so, since he is already there, and let us be friends again."

On June 23, after an exceptionally rapid march (Stanley traveled almost twice as fast as had Burton and Speke), the expedition arrived at Tabora in the country of Unyanyembe, two hundred and twelve miles from the coast. This town was then the principal Arab settlement in Central Africa, and the first major stage on the route to Ujiji. Here Stanley caught up with his other four caravans, and stopped to rest and reorganize. He was well received by the Arabs in Tabora, who were in the process of holding a council of war when he arrived.

The Arabs were agitated by the actions of the chief of the adjoining region of Uyoweh. This chief, a man named Mirambo, was a former pagazi who had turned robber; he had seized power in Uyoweh, and was now terrorizing the surrounding regions. After making war on several neighboring tribes, Mirambo challenged the power of the Arabs of Unyanyembe. Already he had levied tribute and turned back several caravans, and now he was determined that no others would be permitted to pass from Tabora to Ujiji.

After a lengthy debate, the Arabs decided to make war on Mirambo and to end his lawless reign. Stanley, who was admitted to their councils, volunteered to help, since a successful conclusion would enable him to take the Arab caravan route to Ujiji.

Taking his entire expedition to Mfuto, a short march from Tabora, he left the pagazis with his supplies and, with his fifty askaris, joined forces with the Arab army of over two thousand slaves and soldiers marching on Mirambo. At first, the army was successful; they captured a few villages and took a few prisoners. Then they set out to take Wilyankuru, Mirambo's main stronghold.

Unfortunately, Stanley was put out of action at this point by a serious attack of fever. Lying sick in a captured village, he was aroused from his bed by Selim who told him in a hurried voice that the Arab army had been defeated and the men were fleeing in retreat. Four of Stanley's men had been killed, and all but seven of the remainder were running away. Of the seven askaris who stayed behind, only Selim was really faithful—the rest were simply caught by Stanley before they could escape. Even Shaw was in the process of deserting him when, feverish and weak, he staggered from his hut. Gathering the remnants of his fighting force together, he led them back to Mfuto, reaching there safely shortly after midnight. Stanley was quite touched by the devotion of the Arab boy, Selim, who had risked his own life to warn him of the danger. He asked Selim why he, too, had not run away and left him. "Oh, sir," the boy replied naïvely, "I was afraid you would whip me."

After the defeat of the Arab army at Wilyankuru, all roads to Ujiji seemed blocked. But Stanley was determined to go on, and he decided to strike south, making a wide detour of Mirambo's territory. A new difficulty arose, however, to prevent him from carrying out his plan. All but thirteen of his men were so frightened by Mirambo that they refused to go any farther, saying that they had agreed to go as far as Ujiji only by the Arab caravan route. Although he offered to pay triple the standard rate, he still had difficulty obtaining new pagazis. Shaw, at this point, became completely demoralized and worthless; he disgusted Stanley by being more interested in sleeping with the native women than in reaching Ujiji. There were other troubles, too: Mirambo followed up his victory by attacking Tabora and burning it to the ground; Selim was laid low with fever; and one of the best askaris died of smallpox.

In the midst of all this woe, there appeared one bright spark in the form of a little black slave boy who was given to Stanley by an Arab of Tabora. The boy's name was Ndugu M'hali (My Brother's Wealth), but as Stanley did not like this name, he called some of his men together and asked them to select a better one for the boy. One suggested "Simba" (Lion), another "Ngombe" (Cow), Bombay thought "Bombay Mdogo" (roughly, Bombay, Jr.) would suit the boy, while one wit raised a laugh by suggesting "Mirambo." Finally, Ulimengo, the "maddest and most harebrained" man in the expedition, pronounced "Kalulu" (the Swahili term for the young of the blue-buck antelope), and, as this seemed to fit the slim boy with the bright eyes and quick movements, everyone had to agree that Kalulu was the perfect name. Stanley called for a tin pan of water and, while Selim held him, christened him with the words, "Let his name henceforth be Kalulu, and let no man take it from him." This playful ceremony must have called up for Stanley the memory of the day he received his own name from his foster father. Although Selim acted the part of both parent and godfather, it was Stanley who adopted the boy.

At last, on September 13, after spending three months in Unyanyembe, Stanley was able to muster fifty-four men who were willing to make a dash by a southern route for Ujiji. During the first day's march, however, twenty men deserted. A search party was able to recover only nine of them, and the next day two more deserted. In desperation, Stanley chained several together in order to keep them with him. Now Shaw, who had been begging Stanley to turn back, came down with a fever and protested that he was too sick to continue the march. Stanley let him return to Unyanyembe, where he soon died.

Stanley himself was harassed by severe attacks of fever, but he continued his march through what is today western Tanganyika, a rolling grassland, home of the zebra, the hartebeest, the giraffe, and the lion. Meat was plentiful, and his men, who had been reluctant to come, were now reluctant to leave such a pleasant country. Mutiny was brewing.

On the morning of October 1, after a two-day rest stop, Stanley ordered Asmani, the giant kirangozi, to sound the horn for departure. The men grumbled to themselves, Bombay was surly, and Asmani was heard to say that he was sorry he had come. Nevertheless, the men slowly picked up their loads and marched out. Stanley left the camp last to drive on the stragglers. In about a half-hour he saw his caravan at a dead stop ahead of him. Bundles and boxes were thrown on the ground, and the men were standing in small groups talking excitedly.

Taking his double-barreled shotgun from Selim, Stanley loaded both barrels with buckshot, then, adjusting his revolvers for ready action, he walked calmly toward them. The men grabbed up their guns. On his left he saw the heads of two men crouched behind a giant anthill, the muzzles of their muskets pointing toward the path. Stopping, Stanley raised his gun and aimed at their heads, shouting at them to walk toward him. Reluctantly, they stood up, but one of them, the giant Asmani, slid his finger over the trigger of his musket.

Stanley told him to drop his weapon or he would kill him. Asmani did not obey. Instead, he continued to advance with a smirk on his ugly face and a look of murder in his eyes. His companion sneaked around to Stanley's rear. He was coolly putting powder in the pan of his musket when Stanley suddenly swung his shotgun on him and ordered him to drop it. As the musket fell from his hands, Stanley gave him a vigorous poke in the chest with the muzzle of his gun, knocking him to the ground. Whirling quickly to face Asmani again, he was on the point of pulling the trigger when the bullheaded but faithful Mabruki came up behind the mutineer and swept the gun from his hands. The mutiny was over.

After this incident, Stanley extracted a solemn promise from his men to remain faithful to him until they should find Livingstone. The promise was kept in good faith.

Other troubles plagued the expedition as they marched out of the land of plenty into more desolate territory. Food and water became scarce. On October 29, after marching for twenty hours without food, they had only tea for supper, and Stanley carved on the trunk of a tree: "Starving. H.M.S."

A few days later they met a native caravan coming from the direction of Ujiji. Asking the news, Stanley was startled to hear that a white man had just arrived at Ujiji.

"A white man?" he asked.

"Yes, a white man."

"How was he dressed?"

"Like the Master" (meaning Stanley).

"Is he young or old?"

"He is old. He has white hair on his face, and is sick."

"Where has he come from?"

"From a very far country away beyond Uguhha, called Manyuema."

"Indeed! And is he stopping at Ujiji now?"

"Yes, we saw him about eight days ago."

"Do you think he will stop there until we see him?"

"Don't know."

"Was he ever at Ujiji before?"

"Yes, he went away a long time ago."

It was Livingstone! It could be no other. Wildly excited and mad with impatience, Stanley offered two extra doti of cloth to each man if he would march without a rest halt to Ujiji.

His impatience was heightened by the fear that if Livingstone heard that a white man was coming he would run away. He had been told by Sir John Kirk, the British consul in Zanzibar, that Livingstone was a very difficult man to get along with, that he wanted to be left alone and not to be interfered with. In consequence, Stanley anticipated finding a crusty misanthrope at the end of a long and painful search through Central Africa. When one day away from Ujiji, Stanley had his helmet chalked and a fresh puggree folded around it. His new flannel suit was unpacked and his Wellington boots were waxed so that he would make as good an impression as possible upon the white man with the beard. He wanted to minimize, as far as he was able, the chances of a rebuff from the old gentleman. He remembered that Livingstone was an Englishman, and that his encounters with Englishmen had not always been pleasant.

On Friday, November 3,* 1871, the two hundred and thirty-sixth day from Bagamoyo, Stanley and his men were only a six hours' march from their goal. The skies were clear and it was a beautiful morning as they set out on the last lap of their search. Stanley's heart was pounding with excitement. Would the white man still be there? What if he was not Livingstone after all? Climbing over the crest of a hill, they saw Ujiji and the shimmering blue waters of Lake Tanganyika lying below them. As they started down the slope to the town, Stanley ordered the flags unfurled and the guns loaded. Leading the expedition was the smiling Asmani bearing the American flag. Nearing the

* Stanley thought it was November 10, and this is still the accepted date, but he had become confused in his dates during his attacks of fever at Tabora.

village, they fired a volley to warn the inhabitants of their approach.

Susi and Chumah, Livingstone's faithful servants, met them on the path, and ran back to tell their master that a white man with a flag was coming to see him. Before Stanley reached the edge of the village Susi came running breathlessly back to ask Stanley his name. He had told the Doctor the news, but Livingstone was incredulous; he wanted to know the name of the white man. In his excitement, Susi had forgotten to ask. Now Susi ran back with the name, meaningless to Livingstone, of Henry Morton Stanley.

Stanley described in his journal how the only two white men in all equatorial Africa from the Zambezi to the Nile met: "The head of the expedition had halted, and the kirangozi was out of ranks, holding his flag aloft, and Selim said to me, 'I see the Doctor, sir. Oh, what an old man! He has got a white beard.' And I—what would I not have given for a bit of some friendly wilderness, where, unseen I might vent my joy in some mad freak, such as idiotically biting my hand, turning a somersault, or slashing at trees, in order to allay those exciting feelings that were well-nigh uncontrollable. My heart beats fast, but I must not let my face betray my emotions, lest it should detract from the dignity of a white man appearing under such extraordinary circumstances.

"So I did that which I thought was most dignified, I pushed back the crowds, and, passing from the rear, walked down a living avenue of people, until I came in front of the semi-circle of Arabs, before which stood the 'white man with the beard.' As I advanced slowly toward him I noticed that he was pale, and he looked wearied and wan, that he had grey whiskers and mustache, that he wore a bluish cloth cap with a faded gold band on a red ground round it, and that he had on a red-sleeved waistcoat, and a pair of grey tweed trousers. I would have run to him, only I was a coward in the presence of such a mob—would have embraced him, only, he being an Englishman, I did not know how he would receive me; so I did what moral cowardice and false pride suggested was the best thing—walked deliberately to him, took off my hat and said:

" 'Dr. Livingstone, I presume?'

" 'Yes,' said he, with a kind smile, lifting his cap slightly.

"I replace my hat on my head, and he puts on his cap, and we both grasp hands, and I then say aloud:

" 'I thank God, Doctor, I have been permitted to see you.'

"He answered, 'I feel thankful that I am here to welcome you.' "

The two white men then proceeded to the veranda of Livingstone's house where the old man insisted that Stanley occupy his own seat. Stanley gave Livingstone a packet of letters from home, but the old explorer left them unopened on his knees and asked for news of the outside world.

"No, Doctor," Stanley said, "read your letters first, which I am sure you must be impatient to read." Only a month earlier Livingstone had written in his diary: "I am in agony for news from home." But now that he had news, he told Stanley: "Ah, I have waited years for letters, and I have been taught patience. I can surely afford to wait a few hours longer. No, tell me the general news: how is the world getting along?"

So with letters from his family and his friends lying beside him, he listened to the young reporter telling him of the world's events during the past few years: the Suez Canal was now open; General Grant was President of the United States; the "Pacific Railroad" had been completed; the Spanish revolution had driven Queen Isabella from the throne; Prussia had humbled Denmark and annexed Schleswig-Holstein; France had cowered before the armies of Bismarck and Von Moltke; and the transatlantic cable had been laid. Thus the reporter and the missionary passed their first evening together.

Livingstone hardly seemed like the crusty misanthrope who had been described to him by Kirk, back in Zanzibar. Stanley was impressed by the courtesy, dignity, and patience of the old missionary, but he was on his guard nevertheless and was reluctant to tell whom he represented or why he had come. Strangely enough, Livingstone was too polite to ask.

When Stanley woke up that first morning in Ujiji, he felt like a child awakening on Christmas morning. This was the day he had been waiting for! He had really found Livingstone! As he lay on his bed (a primitive four-poster with a palm-leaf mattress), he felt that he had every reason to be proud of himself. But disquieting thoughts disturbed his pride. What if Livingstone refused to give him a letter to Bennett? What proof would he have then that he had really found him? What would be Livingstone's reaction when he heard that he represented an American newspaper instead of a government or a geographical society? Would he want to give him, a reporter, news of the great discoveries he had been so laboriously gleaning for the past six years? These were things which must be thought out carefully. What should he do now? He decided to think over these problems while taking an early morning stroll along the lake shore. He climbed out of bed as quietly as he could and quickly dressed. The door creaked horribly as he eased it open, but his stealth was unnecessary. Livingstone was already up and sitting on the veranda.

"Hello, Doctor! You up already? I hope you have slept well?"

"Good morning, Mr. Stanley. I am glad to see you. I hope you rested well. I sat up late reading my letters. You have brought me good and bad news. But sit down."

"Now, Doctor," said Stanley, about to take the plunge, "you are probably wondering why I came here?"

"It's true, I have been wondering. I thought at first that you were an emissary of the French government, in place of Lieutenant Le Saint, who died a few miles above Gondokoro. I heard you had plenty of boats, plenty of men and stores, and I really believed you were some French officer, until I saw the American flag; and, to tell you the truth, I was rather glad it was so, because I could not have talked to him in French; and if he did not know English, we had been a pretty pair of white men in Ujiji! I did not like to ask you yesterday, because I thought it was none of my business."

"Well, for your sake I am glad that I am an American, and not a Frenchman, and that we can understand each other perfectly without an interpreter. I see that the Arabs are wondering that you, an Englishman, and I, an American, understand each other. We must take care not to tell them that the English and Americans have fought, and that there are *Alabama* claims left unsettled, and that we have such people as Fenians in America who hate you. But, seriously, Doctor—now don't be frightened when I tell you—I have come after *you!*"

"After me!"

"Yes."

"How?"

"Well, you have heard of the New York *Herald?*"

"Oh, who hasn't heard of that despicable newspaper?"

"Without his father's knowledge or consent, Mr. James Gordon Bennett, son of Mr. James Gordon Bennett, the proprietor of the *Herald,* commissioned me to find you, to get what news of your discoveries you would like to give, and to assist you, if I can, with means."

"Young Mr. Bennett told you to come after me, to find me out, and help me? It is no wonder, then, you praised Mr. Bennett so much last night!"

"I know him, I am proud to say, to be just what I say he is. He is an ardent, generous, and true man."

"Well, indeed! I am very much obliged to him; and it makes me feel proud to think that you Americans think so much of me. You have just come in the proper time, for I was beginning to think that I should have to beg from the Arabs. Even they are in want of cloth, and there are but few beads in Ujiji. That fellow Sherif has robbed me of all. I wish I could embody my thanks to Mr. Bennett in suitable words; but if I fail to do so, do not, I beg of you, believe me the less grateful."

"And now, Doctor, having disposed of this little affair, Ferajji will bring breakfast, if you have no objection."

In finding Livingstone, luck for once was on Stanley's side. Had he arrived in Ujiji a few weeks earlier or a few weeks later, he might never have found the wandering missionary who had arrived there only thirteen days before.

Livingstone had discovered a broad, swift river, flowing north, no one knew where, in the country of the Manyuema in the middle of Africa. The natives called the river the Lualaba, but Livingstone believed it was actually the main stream of the Nile, and he had followed it through seven degrees of latitude (from 11° south to a little north of 4° south). He had wished to follow it to its mouth, or until he was certain that it was the Nile, but he had gotten as far as the village of Nyangwe when he was forced to turn back by a lack of canoes and the unwillingness of his followers to continue with him. Also, Arab slavers had cheated and robbed him of his supplies, and he was desperate when he arrived, sick and nearly destitute, at Ujiji.

In his journal, Livingstone described Stanley's arrival: "But when my spirits were at their lowest ebb the good Samaritan was close at hand, for one morning Susi came running, at the top of his speed, and gasped out, 'An Englishman! I see him!' and off he darted to meet him. The American flag at the head of a caravan told of the nationality of the stranger. Bales of goods, baths of tin, huge kettles, cooking pots, tents, etc., made me think, 'This must be a luxurious traveller, and not one at his wit's end like me.' It was Henry Moreland [sic] Stanley, the travelling correspondent of the New York *Herald,* sent by James Gordon Bennett, junior, at an expense of more than four thousand pounds, to obtain accurate information about Dr. Livingstone if living, and if dead, to bring home my bones. . . . I am not of a demonstrative turn—as cold, indeed, as we islanders are usually reputed to be—but this disinterested kindness of Mr. Bennett, so nobly carried into effect by Mr. Stanley, was simply overwhelming. I really do feel extremely grateful, and at the same time I am a little ashamed at not being more worthy of the generosity. Mr. Stanley has done his part with untiring energy; good judgement, in the teeth of very serious obstacles."

Although Livingstone was amazed and flattered by the concern the civilized world felt for him as evidenced by the New York *Herald* Expedition, Stanley, cautious and respectful, still half expected to be repulsed by the old explorer. But the friendship which began so formally was to grow and deepen in the next four months, during which they were in daily, intimate contact with each other. Stanley was surprised and captivated by this man of high morals. The bitter misanthrope turned out to be "a sweet opposite."

Ostensibly, Stanley was a reporter sent a long way to find a famous man feared lost. Having found him, he was to interview the man, secure evidence of his success, and return to write the story for his newspaper. In reality, the situation was more complex. For the long, difficult search for Livingstone had also been a search for himself. In the thousand-mile trek from Zanzibar to Ujiji, he had met with many formidable obstacles and had overcome them all; in the process he had formed even higher concepts of his own character than he had previously thought possible. Always before, he had solved his problems by running away from them. This time, using sheer grit and will power, he had faced his difficulties boldly and had pressed forward determinedly. It had paid off. Henry Stanley would never again run away from anything.

Writing of Livingstone later in life, Stanley said, "He preached no sermon, by word of mouth, while I was in company with him; but each day of my companionship with him witnessed a sermon acted. The divine instructions, given of old on the Sacred Mount, were closely followed, day by day, whether he rested in the jungle-camp, or bided in the trader's town, or savage hamlet. Lowly of spirit, meek in speech, merciful of heart, pure in mind, and peaceful in act . . . had my soul been of brass and my heart of spelter, the powers of my head had surely compelled me to recognize, with due honor, the Spirit of Goodness which manifested itself in him. . . . But my every-day study of him, during health or sickness, deepened my reverence and increased my esteem. He was, in short, consistently noble, upright, pious, and manly, in all the days of my companionship with him."

Livingstone's patience and forbearance impressed Stanley the most.

He would listen in wonder as Livingstone gave only a mild rebuke to a servant whom he found lazy or downright dishonest—Stanley would have beaten the man. This difference between the two men was not lost on Stanley's servants, one of whom was heard to remark to one of Livingstone's men, "Your master is a good man—a very good man. He does not beat you, for he has a kind heart, but ours—oh! he is sharp, hot as fire!"

A veritable saint, Livingstone may have been, but he had his moments of moodiness when he wanted to be left to himself, and, although the arrival of Stanley gave him fresh strength of body and mind, he was an old man who had lived much alone, and sometimes he found the company of the eager young reporter something of a strain. Once, when he was sitting gazing into nothingness and drawn into his own thoughts, Stanley could not resist asking him what he was thinking about:

"A penny for your thoughts, Doctor," he said.

"They are not worth it, my young friend, and let me suggest that, if I had any, possibly, I should wish to keep them."

Stanley deserved the rebuke, for he occasionally became somewhat presumptuous in their conversations together. Once he even ventured a criticism of the methods used by missionaries to bring Christianity to the African.

"How would you go about it?" Livingstone asked him.

"I would certainly have more than one or two missionaries. I would have a thousand, scattered not all over the continent, but among some great tribe or cluster of tribes, organized systematically, one or two for each village, so that though the outskirts of the tribe or area might be disturbed somewhat by the evil example of those outside, all within the area might be safely and uninterruptedly progressing. Then, with the pupils who would be turned out from each village, there would be new forces to start elsewhere outside the area."

It never occurred to Stanley that it might not be tactful to tell the most famous missionary alive how missions should be organized. But the very fact that he was thinking along these lines indicates the influence Livingstone exerted over the reporter. Their relationship was soon close to that which had existed between Stanley and his foster father. Indeed, in a letter to his friend Horace Waller in England, Livingstone wrote of Stanley, "He behaved as a son to a father."

Together, Livingstone and Stanley undertook an expedition by boat around the northern end of Lake Tanganyika, discovering that the

Rusizi River flowed into Lake Tanganyika instead of out of it as had been believed. On this excursion, which lasted from November 15 to December 11, 1871, Stanley allowed Livingstone to be the leader and bowed to his wishes in everything throughout the trip, although the men, equipment, and native currency were all Stanley's.

A sidelight of this trip was the naming, by Livingstone, of a small group of tiny islands in Lake Tanganyika as "New York Herald Islets" in honor of the paper that had sent Stanley. Unfortunately, the name did not stick and today they are generally called—when they are mentioned at all—by their native name: Kavuneh.

By the end of December, Stanley decided that he must leave Ujiji. He wanted to bring the ailing old missionary out with him, but he was unable to persuade him to come. Livingstone was determined to complete his explorations before quitting Africa. He told Stanley he wanted to prove that the Lualaba was the Nile, but it may have been that he who had spent so many years of his life in Africa wanted to die there. His wife was dead, one of his sons had been killed in America fighting in the Union Army, and his other children were now all grown.

Livingstone accompanied Stanley as far as Unyanyembe to pick up the supplies that had been left there. Stanley promised to return with all speed to Zanzibar, purchase a few more supplies, and engage some faithful men who would be sent to join Livingstone in Unyanyembe. The war with Mirambo was still in progress and local pagazis were unobtainable.

Before parting, Livingstone entrusted Stanley with a box filled with letters, diaries, and other papers to be carried to the outside world. Included were letters to his family; to Lord Granville, the British Prime Minister; to his old friend Sir Roderick Murchison (who died before the letter could reach him); and to James Gordon Bennett, Jr., thanking him for sending Stanley with supplies to relieve him. On March 14, 1872, the two men, who were so different and who had met and become fast friends under such extraordinary circumstances, sadly parted. They were never to meet again. Stanley was the last white man ever to see Livingstone alive.

Writing to Agnes Livingstone two years later, Stanley wrote of her father: "I loved him as a son, and would have done for him anything worthy of the most filial. The image of him will never be obliterated from my memory, it is so green with me when I think of the parting with him, that I almost fancy sometimes that it is palpable. . . ."

The trip back to the coast was easier than the trip inland had been. Most of the goods had been turned over to Livingstone, and the pagazis had no reason to desert while on their way home. There was one incident, however, that gave Stanley an anxious moment.

The expedition had been marching in the rain for days through half-flooded fields in which they frequently sank in mud up to their knees. They encountered numerous rivers and streams, swollen and overflowing. On April 13 they came to a branch river that was narrow, but too deep for fording. Finding a large tree growing on the bank, they cut it down so that it fell across the stream. Over this felled tree the men, bestriding it, cautiously moved their bales and boxes. One young pagazi, who was carrying the box containing Livingstone's letters and journals, decided that this method was too slow. Stanley had already crossed to the other side when he saw him wading into the river with "the most precious box of all on his head"! The success of Stanley's mission depended upon the safe return of those papers. How would he be regarded if after finding Livingstone and being entrusted with his valuable papers, he lost them on the way home? Stanley whipped out his revolver. Aiming at the pagazi's head, he shouted, "Look out! Drop that box and I'll shoot you!"

The other pagazis stopped their work to watch their poor comrade, threatened by pistol and flood. The man himself seemed more afraid of the pistol—or perhaps it was the determined look in the eyes of his master. Slowly he eased his way forward in the water. Suddenly he stepped in a hole! Pagazi and box almost disappeared from sight. Stanley was in agony. Fortunately, the pagazi was able to keep the box out of the water and to recover himself. After a few desperate efforts, he managed to get both himself and the box safely on shore. Stanley breathed a sigh of relief, and transferred the box to a more cautious and sure-footed man.

On May 6, only fifty-four days after leaving Tabora, they reached Bagamoyo. There Stanley was met by Lieutenant William Henn of the Royal Navy, who was in charge of the Livingstone Search and Relief Expedition tardily sent out by the Royal Geographical Society. With him was W. Oswell Livingstone, twenty years old and youngest of the missionary's sons. With the arrival of Stanley, Lieutenant Henn resigned as the expedition's leader. There was talk of taking the supplies to Livingstone anyway, but this idea was soon abandoned and the expedition was dissolved.

Crossing the channel to Zanzibar the next day, Stanley discharged

his own men and paid them each a bonus. He then re-engaged twenty
of the best of them and, collecting thirty-four more good men, he sent
them all off with some additional supplies to become the followers of
Dr. Livingstone.

In all, Stanley had traveled 2250 miles in 411 days. Fifteen hundred miles were through country never before seen by any white man.
The expedition had taken the lives of eighteen pagazis and askaris as
well as Shaw and Farquhar. Stanley himself had lost seventy-six
pounds in his bouts with malaria and dysentery, and his black hair
showed streaks of gray. But the reporter-turned-explorer was too ex-
hilarated to count the cost—he had found Livingstone!

On May 29, 1872, Stanley left Zanzibar for Europe to face fame
and disillusionment.

# CHAPTER VI

# *A Taste of Fame and Fortune*

STANLEY'S SOCIAL WORLD, despite his wide travels among men of all nations and many types of characters, was a narrow one. Always among men, he was never a part of any group. He knew the surface characteristics of many men but he knew no man well and, conversely, no man knew Stanley. He had built up a careful shell around himself and painted it with colors that he hoped would make him accepted by the men among whom he moved.

His first inkling of what awaited him on his return occurred at Bagamoyo when a Lieutenant Llewellyn Dawson, an officer of the Royal Geographical Society's Livingstone Relief Expedition that had been too late in starting, told him that England would not be pleased with his success because he was an American. But Stanley was completely unprepared for the reception that greeted him in Europe. Although Stanley expected to be praised for his accomplishment, he did not anticipate the extent of the tremendous interest, and the idolization and vilification that would soon be his.

Arriving in Marseilles, on August 2, 1872, he went straight to Paris, where he became the hero of the hour. The Paris correspondent of the *Herald* cabled: "He is sought for, honored, feted, talked about in a way that will turn his head if he has a head capable of being turned. He is interrupted by newspaper reporters, importuned by correspondents of the pictorials for sketches and scenes from his travels, and generally lionized to an extent that has astonished him beyond measure."

Bennett, always jealous of news he regarded as exclusively his, thought his correspondent was giving away too much of the story. He sent Stanley a terse cable: "Stop talking."

Although the Paris Geographical Society hastily met and stuffily pronounced him an impostor, most French newspapers hailed Stanley in the most extravagant language. The finding of Livingstone was compared in greatness to Hannibal's march on Rome, Napoleon's passage of the Alps, and Sherman's march to the sea. Stanley's name was on everyone's lips, and all were eager to learn more about him. A Paris paper, *Le Soir*, uninhibited by a lack of facts, announced the arrival of Lord Stanley, son of the great Lord Derby, who, at the instigation of the New York *Herald*, had nobly undertaken to find Dr. Livingstone, the great traveler.

In England, the news of Stanley's exploit created the greatest excitement. "I have seldom, if ever, known anything create so widespread and intense an interest throughout the country," wrote J. B. Braithwaite, a prominent Quaker, in a letter to Livingstone. But it was an excitement of controversy, not of triumph. Several newspapers, led by the *Standard* and the *Spectator*, were voicing suspicions that reflected the feelings of many Britons, piqued that their own David Livingstone had been rescued by an American journalist who had succeeded where the Royal Geographical Society and the British government had failed. The *Standard* called for an investigation of Stanley's story. The paper "could not resist some suspicions and misgivings"; it found "something inexplicable and mysterious" in the tale.

Major General Sir Henry Creswicke Rawlinson, President of the Royal Geographical Society, set the tone for the nation's wishful thinking in a letter to the *Times*. Stanley did not discover Livingstone, he said, but rather it was Livingstone who had found Stanley. This slanderous but quotable quip was to be heard long after Rawlinson had changed his mind and the Geographical Society had passed a vote of thanks to Stanley.

A mixed welcome was given Stanley when he arrived in London on August 2. He received a letter of thanks from Agnes Livingstone, the missionary's daughter, and he was the guest of Lord Granville and the Duchess of Argyle. But insinuations and doubts continued to be expressed in some newspapers. The strongest proofs of the truth of Stanley's story were the letters and papers Livingstone had sent back with him, but when some of the letters were published they were immediately attacked. Some claimed that they were forgeries; they laughed at Stanley for being a ridiculous and clumsy pretender. It was even said that he had not been to Africa at all.

The climax of this critical barrage came at a meeting of the Geographical Section of the British Association for the Advancement of Science in Brighton on August 15. Three thousand people, including all of the great geographers, many prominent scientists, and the ex-Emperor and Empress of France, had assembled to hear speeches on Africa. Stanley was asked to give a talk and, as this was his first public appearance in England, he was the central figure of the occasion. He had prepared a brief paper dealing only with his exploration with Livingstone of the north end of Lake Tanganyika. Unexpectedly, he was called on to give an account of his entire expedition. He found himself placed on trial. The *Daily Telegraph* described him as speaking with composure and self-possession, but in his journal he wrote that his stage fright was so extreme that he could only begin after three attempts.

The learned members of the association cringed at Stanley's unscientific approach. He began his talk by saying, "I consider myself in the light of a troubadour, to relate to you the tale of an old man who is tramping onward to discover the sources of the Nile."

When he had finished, there was a general discussion. Several tactless comments were made. Francis Galton, a cousin of Charles Darwin, who was president of the association, remarked that they were gathered not to listen to "sensational stories" but to *"serious facts"!* Colonel James Grant, the African explorer, gave a speech in which he criticized portions of Livingstone's letter to Bennett; he then went on to label Livingstone's belief that the Lualaba River was actually the Nile an "extravagant idea." Other speakers echoed these sentiments. Stanley arose to state his belief that Livingstone's theory was correct. He called on his audience at least to respect the idea because it had been advanced by a man who knew more about Africa than any other living man. He concluded with a fervent eulogy of Livingstone and a biting condemnation of the "armchair geographer," awakening from his nap to dogmatize about the Nile while Livingstone was devoting his life to the long, hard search in Central Africa for the true facts.

That evening, Stanley was invited to a dinner at the Royal Pavilion given by the Brighton and Sussex Medical Society in honor of the distinguished men attending the conference. It turned out to be a most unhappy affair. As one newspaper reported it: "The harmony of the evening was disturbed by a very unfortunate occurrence. The 'Health of the Visitors' was coupled with the name of Mr. Stanley, and that gentleman, when he came to speak of his meeting with Dr. Livingstone, believed that he heard some expression of incredulity among the audience. With great vehemence he declaimed against being so received or treated, and withdrew from the room in great indignation."

The president of the society tried to explain the incident in a letter to the editor of the London *Mail*: "Mr. Stanley, who had but recently returned into the room (having left with the Mayor, after the third toast had been given, to be present at the theatre), commenced his reply in a grotesque and humorous strain, expressing his surprise that he should be called upon to return thanks, when there were visitors present whose eloquence would rival that of Demosthenes, Pericles, or even their own Daniel Webster. He said, likewise, in a jocose manner, that Dr. Livingstone had administered pills, potions, and plaisters to the natives.

"These remarks were made with considerable gesticulation, which, if not intended, was certainly calculated to excite and encourage laughter, and some such feeling may have naturally been expressed by one or more of the gentlemen present, but I firmly believe with no intention of casting a sneer or offering any disrespect to Mr. Stanley. Mr. Stanley then hastily left the room, saying that he did not come here to be ridiculed or laughed at.

"This conduct of Mr. Stanley's naturally caused the greatest surprise and vexation among the whole company, and his departure was so sudden that it was impossible for me as chairman to exercise that tact which some of the papers censured me for not showing.

"This, sir, is the 'plain, unvarnished tale.'"

On August 20, in a letter published in the *Daily Telegraph*, addressed to the *Saturday Review*, and through it to all his jeering enemies, Stanley lashed out: "If the *Saturday Review* wishes to know what I resent, let it be understood that I resent all manner of impertinence, brutal horse-laughs at the mention of Livingstone's name, or his sufferings . . . all statements that I am not what I claim to be—an American; all gratuitous remarks such as 'sensationalism,' as directed at me by that suave gentleman, Mr. Francis Galton . . . ; and all such nonsense as the *Spectator* has seen fit to attribute to my pen."

The shell Stanley had built around himself was not thick enough to protect his hypersensitive nature. His sudden fame, the unexpected and unjustified attacks upon his character, and the criticism of his idol, Livingstone—combined with his discomfiture in polite society and his ineptness as a public speaker—made him a thoroughly disappointed and miserable man. The whole experience was an embittering one for him. Much later in life he wrote in his notebook: "All the actions of my life, and I may say all my thoughts, since 1872, have been strongly coloured by the storm of abuse and the wholly unjustifiable reports circulated about me then."

And in another place in his notebook he wrote: "It was owing to repeated attacks of the Public and Press that I lost the elastic hope of my youth, the hope, and belief, that toil, generosity, devotion to duty, righteous doing, would receive recognition at the hands of my fellow creatures who had been more happily born, more fortunately endowed, more honoured by circumstances and fate than I. It required much control of natural waywardness to reform the shattered aspirations. For it seemed as though the years of patient watchfulness, the long periods of frugality, the painstaking self-teaching in lessons of manliness, had ended disastrously in failure."

Stanley needed more than fame and distinction. As Dorothy Tennant, who later became his wife, wrote of him after his death: "He had in his nature much of the woman, the *ewigweibliche;* he craved fame far less than love and confidence." But he would not admit this, even to himself.

Not everyone doubted Stanley's story. In fact, most people regarded him as a true hero. There were only a few newspapers that attempted to discredit him, while others, such as the *Times,* the *Daily News,* the *Daily Telegraph,* and *Punch,* were among his champions. When Livingstone's family confirmed beyond question the authenticity of the letters and papers he had brought back, the charges of forgery which had been leveled at him were squelched and his triumph over his accusers was complete. But Stanley was not a very forgiving person, and the memory of the injustices done him remained with him forever, tormenting and embittering him.

Most of the animosity shown toward him came from men in professional and intellectual circles, and, in a way, he should have expected it. Stanley was a sensation, and sober geographical societies looked with suspicion on the sensational amateur. And there were other, more personal, reasons why he should have expected his cool reception from the learned men of England. In his letters from Africa, he had not always been circumspect in his criticism of men known and respected for their work in Africa. He had severely censured Sir John Kirk, British Consul in Zanzibar and a former companion of Livingstone on his Zambezi expedition, for negligence in sending supplies for Livingstone into the interior and for giving him a false impression of Livingstone's character. Kirk was well known, and he had many influential friends in England who doubtless did not take kindly to these charges made by a young upstart American newspaper reporter. The famous explorers Burton, Speke, and Sir Samuel Baker were slightingly referred to in his letters, and even the president of the Royal Geographical Society was sneered at and his pronouncements mocked. When Stanley wrote these letters, he had regarded himself only as an enterprising American reporter who could with impunity take the liberty of smearing English heroes. He did not realize that he was about to join their ranks, and that many of these men would later become his friends.

Perhaps another reason for the English reception of Stanley was the coolness in the relations between the governments of Great Britain and the United States at this time. Many Americans were still incensed over English sympathies for the Confederacy during the Civil War, and even Stanley's own paper, the *Herald,* was editorializing that as there was an "irrepressible conflict" between the two countries it had better be settled at once by war! Yet, only two days after the Brighton episode Lord Granville, the Minister for Foreign Affairs, presented Stanley with a gold snuffbox set with more than five dozen diamonds, a present from Queen Victoria. Inside the lid was inscribed:

*Presented by*
HER MAJESTY, QUEEN VICTORIA
*to*
HENRY M. STANLEY, ESQ.
*in recognition of the prudence and zeal
displayed by him
in opening communication with*
DOCTOR LIVINGSTONE,
*and thus relieving the general anxiety
felt in regard to the fate of
that distinguished traveller.*

*London, August 17, 1872.*

On October 6 Stanley traveled to the home of the Duke of Sutherland in Scotland to be presented to the Queen. The audience lasted only ten minutes, but the regal Victoria made an indelible impression on him. He was surprised to find that she was even shorter than he was, but he was most impressed by her gracious dignity and royal manner. On the other hand, the impression he made on the Queen was quite different. She saw him only as "a determined, ugly little man—with a strong American twang."

In London, on October 21, he was somewhat belatedly honored by the Royal Geographical Society. At a banquet in his honor, he was presented with the Victoria Medal, highest award of the society. Also, Sir Henry Rawlinson offered a complete public apology for his conduct.

Following the banquet, Stanley left again for Scotland. But the cheers of the Scots, the medals and gold snuffboxes, could not erase from his mind the Brighton episode. On October 23, at a banquet given in his honor by the city officials of Glasgow, he told his audience how he had been treated by the English at Brighton: "I spoke what was in my heart, and related to them his [Livingstone's] sufferings, and I hoped that narrative to them would make such an impression upon them that they would sympathize with the old traveler, and believe the story I told them. I then sat down, fancying I had made an impression; but, Englishmen, the sequence [sic] was really pathetic; how it harasses my feelings every time I think of it!

"One gentleman got up and said, 'Ah, Dr. Livingstone says he has seen cannibals there, and men eating pigs there. Impossible. Dr. Livingstone is wandering; he has been much farther west than he thought.' That gentleman sits down, and another gentleman rises, and every time I find I have another antagonist. So I take my notes. Dr. Bunkum says, 'I feel convinced that Dr. Livingstone has not discovered the sources of the Nile.' That gentleman sits down, and Cad, Jr., says, 'Well, Dr. Livingstone will by and by begin to say what I have said. I do not believe in his arbitrary way of settling the sources of the Nile, because I do not understand it.'

"So Cad, Jr., bows to the audience, and then takes his seat, and then I am asked to rise and reply. I have got my notes, and remark that one gentleman had said because Dr. Livingstone saw no gorillas on the Lualaba he must have been much farther west than he really thought, because I never saw any gorillas in Uganda. The gentleman forgets that between that point and Dr. Livingstone's points there were eight degrees of longitude. The gentleman might have said, 'I have seen St. Paul's Cathedral,' and another gentleman in France might have said, 'You are mistaken, sir; there is no St. Paul's Cathedral in France, therefore there can be none in England.' What was the end of it all? The gentlemen got up and with great suavity, an elongated smile, and with sweet sympathy said, 'We are very much obliged to Mr. Stanley; but we do not want sensational stories. We want facts.'

Well, I might have risen and like the Irishman, said, 'Shure, begorra, all I have said are facts.' "

Stanley's humor was too bitter to be successful and too subjective for satire.

In Hamilton, Scotland, where Livingstone's father had lived for many years, Stanley was given another medal and was made an honorary citizen. Edinburgh and Leith also gave him warm and hospitable welcomes. Between receptions, banquets, and ceremonies, he somehow managed to complete his book, *How I Found Livingstone in Central Africa*. (It was published by Sampson Low, Marston and Company in November of 1872, only three months after his arrival in Europe.) Edward Marston, one of the partners in the publishing house, told Stanley that the book "received an ovation seldom, perhaps never before accorded a book of travel."

His fame caused him to receive a flood of letters from strangers filled with questions and requests. Relatives and acquaintances from his early years became suddenly affectionate, and also acquisitive.

As soon as his book was in the presses, Stanley sailed on the steamship *Cuba* for America, arriving in New York on November 20. He was greeted at the dock by a huge red banner with the words, "Welcome home Henry Stanley." A special delegation from the Herald Club, made up of employees of the *Herald,* was waiting with a carriage to take him to the offices of the paper that had sent him to find Livingstone. In the *Herald* library, almost the entire staff was on hand to welcome and congratulate him. But there was one important person who was not there. James Gordon Bennett, Jr., the man who had sent Stanley to Africa, remained in his den, calmly writing a letter. Thomas Connery, the editor of the *Herald* and President of the Herald Club, finally took Stanley in to Bennett. The interview lasted only ten minutes. Bennett had hoped to boost the circulation of his paper by sending Stanley after Livingstone; he had not planned to share his paper's glory with his "hired hand." His reporter's fame provoked first displeasure and then a jealousy that grew into hatred as Stanley returned from other expeditions after even greater exploits. Men who worked closely with Bennett have related how he would explode when Stanley came into the news. "Who was Stanley before I found him?" Bennett would rage, "Who thought of hunting for Livingstone? Who paid the bills?"

Bennett's hatred lasted as long as Stanley lived, but if the explorer was aware of it, he never revealed it. In subsequent expeditions he was to discover and name a mountain and a river after his employer. Bennett was shrewd enough to conceal his animosity, and never allowed it to prevent him from capitalizing on Stanley's abilities and achievements.

In the United States, Stanley again made the rounds of receptions and banquets. The most brilliant of these affairs was a reception given him at the Lotus Club in New York two days after his arrival. It was attended by distinguished men from all professions, and as soon as Stanley entered the club he was greeted with loud cheers and applause. Again he told the story of how he had found Livingstone, and, bitterly, of the reception given him by the English at Brighton.

On November 24, Dr. Livingstone's elder brother, John, came to New York from his home in Listowell, Ontario, to thank Stanley personally for what he had done for his brother.

Of all the eulogies given Stanley, orally and in print, perhaps no one put his exploit into perspective better than Mark Twain when he once introduced the explorer in Boston: "When I contrast what I have achieved in my measurably brief life with what he has achieved in his possibly briefer one, the effect is to sweep utterly away the ten-story edifice of my own self-appreciation and to leave nothing behind but the cellar. When you compare these achievements of his with the achievements of really great men who exist in history, the comparison, I believe, is in his favor.

"I am not here to disparage Columbus. No, I won't do that; but when you come to regard the achievements of these two men, Columbus and Stanley, from the standpoint of the difficulties they encountered, the advantage is with Stanley and against Columbus. Now, Columbus started out to discover America. Well, he didn't need to do anything at all but sit in the cabin of his ship and hold his grip and sail straight on, and America would discover itself. Here it was, barring his passage the whole length and breadth of the South American continent, and he couldn't get by it. He'd got to discover it. But Stanley started out to find Doctor Livingstone, who was scattered abroad, as you might say, over the length and breadth of a vast slab of Africa as big as the United States."

But America had its doubters, too. Many had to agree with one newspaper that confessed, "There is but one *Herald* and Stanley is its profit"; for the *Herald* was an aggressive, swashbuckling paper, and it had many enemies. Chief among them was the New York *Sun*, then rising rapidly into prominence under the leadership of Charles A. Dana.

The managers of the *Sun* felt that if they could discredit Stanley they would be striking a solid blow at the rival *Herald*. Other papers followed the *Sun's* lead.

"There is a growing suspicion that the alleged discovery of Livingstone, the African explorer, by Stanley of the New York *Herald,* is a monstrous sell, only equaled by the great moon hoax of several years ago," one newspaper said.

Another reported that, "The number of those who regard the *Herald* Livingstone story as a huge humbug are increasing. It is thought that Dr. Livingstone could never have written such letters as those published in the *Herald* over his signature. Think of a scientific man, say Agassiz, giving to the world such stuff as this, as part of the fruits of years of toil."

But while other papers only guessed and cast doubts and suspicions, the *Sun* set about proving that the public was being deceived by Stanley and the *Herald*. They struck where Stanley was most vulnerable. His exploit had stirred the imagination and curiosity of the public; people wanted to know all about the man who had accomplished such a feat. Particularly, everyone wanted to know where he had come from. Who was he? What were his origins? Unfortunately, these were the very questions Stanley wanted most to evade. He feared the disclosure of his illegitimate birth. Then, too, there was probably a legal question involving his nationality. He proudly proclaimed himself an American citizen, but, technically, he had entered this country illegally when he jumped ship in New Orleans, and he had never become naturalized. His desertions from the Confederate Army and the Union Navy, if known, would also reflect little credit on him.

The first solid bit of evidence dug up by the *Sun* was a series of accusations brought forth by Lewis H. Noe, the boy who had deserted the navy with Stanley and accompanied the ill-fated Stanley-Cook expedition to Turkey. On August 24, 30, and 31 (while Stanley was still in England), the *Sun* printed Noe's charges: a mixture of truth and half-truth. According to Noe, Stanley was a deserter from the United States Navy, he had attempted to murder an old Turk, he had cruelly whipped Noe on his bare back and forced him to steal food, he had issued a worthless check in Constantinople, he was not an American but a Welshman, and his name was simply an alias he had assumed after he came to America.

Bennett sent these clippings from the *Sun* to Stanley, asking him to reply to them. Most of the charges of course were true, but in Stanley's present position they were embarrassing. He attempted to side-step the whole affair with an air of injured innocence. In a letter to Bennett dated September 13, 1872, he wrote: "To enter upon a detailed refutation of the various charges and accusations falsely levelled at me by this eccentric youth would be undignified and unworthy of me; it would but serve to bring the contemptible newspaper and its unmanly correspondent into greater prominence than they deserve. I content myself with simply asserting that the statements of this man Noe, insofar as they concern me, consist of a series of the most atrocious falsehoods that the most imaginative villain could have devised to the detriment of any one man's reputation.

"They are oft-recurring questions to me, 'Wherein have I incurred any man's hostility? Why should people attack my private character? How have I injured any person so much as to induce him to vilify me in this manner?' It is with the utmost confidence that I can reply that, intentionally, I have never injured any living man."

Stanley's reluctance to disclose the place and circumstances of his birth created a world-wide side issue in the newspapers of the day. A Welsh paper, the Carnarvon *Herald*, was on the right track: "Who do our readers imagine this enterprising 'Stanley' is? We are glad to be able to state on the best authority, that he is a young Welshman, who was born thirty-two years ago in the town of Denbigh. His mother is alive and well at the present time and keeps the public house known as the 'Cross Foxes,' St. Asaph. Stanley is not the real name of the eminent explorer, but John Thomas."

Subsequently, this version was corrected by the paper, which said, "Mr. Stanley's proper name is John Rowlands, and his mother at the present time keeps a public house called the 'Castle Arms,' close to St. Hilary's church, Denbigh, and not a house at St. Asaph, as above stated. His grandfather on the paternal side was the late Mr. John Rowlands, farmer, of Segroid, near Denbigh, and on the maternal side the late Mr. Moses Parry, butcher, Denbigh."

But the truth that the Welsh paper had uncovered was pushed aside by the stories put out by the larger journals. The New York *Herald* disposed of the Welsh claim in a cavalier manner: "There is evidently a mistake here. John Thomas is not known to *Herald* fame. The person described . . . has possible existence in the regions of Bohemia; but, though we have a faint recollection of having heard the aristocratic name before, the great Ap Thomas is unknown to us. Mr. Stanley is neither an Ap Jones nor an Ap Thomas; he is simply a native American. Missouri, and not Wales, is his birthplace. So the Denbigh lady must look for her long-lost Thomas in another direction."

Canada, Ohio, Boston, and many other cities, states, and countries tried to claim the famous man. A Scottish paper said his real name was Garret Baldwin, while an Irish paper countered by claiming his name was Baldwin Garry. A French paper maintained that the name Stanley was a corruption of Stanislaus, and that Stanley was no less than one of the descendants of the last King of Poland, who had settled in France.

So great was the interest Stanley had created that even before he arrived in the United States he had made arrangements with a promoter named Rullmann in New York to give a series of sixty lectures throughout the country for thirty thousand dollars, or five hundred dollars each. He also agreed to give forty more lectures at the same price if Rullmann wanted them. The first lecture took place on December 3 at Steinway Hall in New York. The auditorium was decorated with the American flag Stanley had unfurled at Ujiji, spears, swords, rusty guns, and other souvenirs of his African trip. For added interest, John Livingstone and Kalulu, whom Stanley had brought back with him, appeared on the platform.

Stanley had not yet learned the art of public speaking, and his talk was a jumble of stories about Livingstone and his search for him, mingled with a bitter defense of himself against the accusations of the *Sun.* Even the *Herald* was cautious in its praise of this first lecture: "The hall was full and though its human contents were, perhaps, a little too well bred to be very eagerly enthusiastic, they lent throughout an attention which was neither extinguished by the necessary dryness of much of the material spread before them, nor sated by the bright glimpses occasionally offered them of what life really is among the untutored savages of the great unknown continent."

His second lecture was panned—even by the *Herald,* which said: "Mr. Stanley's elocution is bad, though it improves as he gets into his discourse, and might be made acceptable if his manner of treating his subjects was such as to insure a partial forgetfulness of his faults of oratory. Unfortunately this was not the case—lecture goers care little to be told of Livingstone as a missionary or Livingstone as a traveller— and consequently this part of his lecture last night was intolerably dull. Mr. Stanley has utterly mistaken the necessities of the platform. His map of Central Africa is not used, and the specimens of cloths which he brings on the stage are quite as useless, for he does not know how to make his hearers interested in them by making them illustrative of his subject. He overlooks the personal and the peculiar, and treats only of the geographical and commonplace. All this is unnecessary, and it would be cruel to Mr. Stanley not to say so. If he has half the courage before an average civilized audience that he showed in the wilds of Africa he can at once overcome his deficiencies. To do this he, of course, must forego his manuscript, and forgetting the singsong and doleful monotone in which his voice is too often pitched, simply talk to his auditors of what he saw, heard and suffered while doing his duty so nobly to the *Herald,* to humanity and to science."

The critic who wrote this stinging article was George Seilhamer, one of Bennett's chief sycophants. Sensing Bennett's true feelings, he knew that his jibes at Stanley would actually please his chief. Later he confessed to Joseph I. C. Clark, the night editor, that "I simply made the truth sound raw and when Bennett sent for me the next day to reproach me severely, as he did, I could see that he was really gratified." Stanley's lecture tour ended abruptly with his third lecture.

His book, *How I Found Livingstone in Central Africa,* received better treatment than his lectures. Although there were many slighting references to his lack of literary style, the book was a tremendous success. The entire first edition was sold within a week, and it was to go through many more editions in both England and the United States. Probably most people would agree with Florence Nightingale, who wrote to Monsieur Mohl: "It is, without exception, the very worst book on the very best subject, I ever saw in all my life." To her, the entire affair seemed much like the story of Humpty Dumpty, "when all our government, all our Societies, all our Subscriptions, and all the Queen's men could not set Livingstone up again!"

Unlike the failure of his lectures, the criticisms of his book did not greatly disturb Stanley. In a letter to Marston, his publisher, he said, "I have received several of the notices in the English press, and I am glad to see they take it so kindly; they are not half so severe as I would have been on *it,* though some have stooped to downright falsehoods, but the majority of them have been very gracious indeed. I suppose I must prepare myself for attacks from certain weeklies, but I can bear them without flinching."

Second only to Stanley as an object of interest and curiosity was Kalulu, the little African boy he had brought back with him. Stanley, who as a boy and as a young man had felt the need for a father, now tried to be one, and Kalulu became the first of his adopted sons. He was about eleven years old when he arrived in Europe, and he was described as being robust, with bright eyes and an intelligent face. Kalulu was watched, interviewed, and reported on almost as much as Stanley himself. Everything he saw and did was described in the newspapers. In France when he put on his first suit of European clothes the event was fully covered by the press. Someone had given him a red velvet purse with gilt embroidery which he was anxious to display, but, being unaccustomed to pockets, he had to have help in getting it out.

The boy knew a little English, but most of his interviews were conducted with Stanley acting as an interpreter. Like a proud father, he was eager to have Kalulu perform for the newsmen. Stanley would hold up a picture of Livingstone and the boy would call out, "Lifinston!"; when asked to sing, he would break into a Swahili song; Stanley would tell the boy to pray like a Moslem, and Kalulu would get on his knees and imitate the motions he had seen the Zanzibaris perform so often, complete with the fly swatting and mosquito slapping that usually accompanied the prayer in insect-ridden Africa.

In December, 1872, there were no less than three separate theaters in New York offering entertainment based on Stanley and his expedition. One was a series of burlesque lectures given by theatrical manager Don Bryant. A second was a farce called *King Carrot* which Stanley saw and enjoyed very much. One scene showed a room full of decrepit old men representing the Royal Geographical Society who promptly fainted en masse when Stanley walked into the room. The third was a lavish musical comedy produced by Josh Hart and featuring the vaudeville team of Harrigan and Hart. Neil Warner, a well-known actor, played Stanley. There were nine scenes in all, including fights between the Arabs and Mirambo, conversions to Christianity by Harrigan and Hart, and a "coconut shuffle" by the Congo Dancers. The play was called *Africa,* and on December 8 the entire front page of the *Herald* was bought to advertise the spectacle. Stanley saw this play, too. In the last scene Livingstone, almost dead, attempts to pawn his watch to an Arab for a slice of pineapple when a great commotion is heard off stage. In a few minutes, Stanley and his expedition march on and stride back and forth. At last Stanley pushes aside a huge cactus, sees Livingstone, tips his hat, and says, "Dr. Livingstone, I presume?" Everyone roared—everyone except Stanley. He could not understand it. What should he have said? Perhaps he should have said nothing and simply handed Livingstone his card. The laughter of the audience tore at his heart.

By April, 1873, the shows about him had folded and the fickle public had become interested in other matters, so Stanley returned to England with Kalulu. He asked Edward Marston to put the African boy in a good school, and Marston sent him to the Reverend J. Conder at Wadsworth, the same school his own son, Arthur, attended. In a letter to the publisher from Pamplona dated June 11, 1873, Stanley wrote: "I enclose a letter for your son, Arthur. I fear from the hearty, friendly way in which your son speaks of Kalulu, that he will get too spoilt. I am exceedingly obliged to you for your kindness, and shall ever remember it."

In a paternal spirit, Stanley attempted to write a novel for boys. It was called *My Kalulu,* and, although it was based upon stories he had heard from Kalulu, the guide Asmani, the Tabora Arabs, and other people he had met and talked with during his search for Livingstone, it was an extremely dull book. In the preface, Stanley promised his readers that if the book were successful he would write others in the same vein. But when the novel was published in 1874, it was not a success, and he wisely refrained from ever writing another.

On May 2, 1873, Stanley once again reported to Bennett in Paris. Here in this city where Bennett had first summoned his reporter from Spain and told him to find Livingstone, he now sent the same man back to Spain to cover the Carlist War. Although they were not to hear of it for some months, Livingstone had died only the day before in the heart of Africa. The war in Spain gave him an opportunity to escape from the world of lectures, banquets, receptions, honors, criticisms, and attacks. Although he worked hard covering the fighting, he found it a welcome relief.

Fortunately for his restless nature, England embarked on another military expedition to Africa. The warlike and savage Ashantees on the Gold Coast had been harassing the Fantees, a tribe under the protection of the British. At intervals for the past half-century there had been friction between the British and the Ashantees. In 1823 a British force of six hundred men under Sir Charles McCarthy had been defeated and massacred by the Ashantees, and it was said that their chieftain, Kofi Karikari, or "King Coffee" as he was called in England, still had Sir Charles' skull, bound with gold bands, which he used as a drinking cup. In 1863-1864 the English, again defeated by the Ashantees, were forced to retreat to the coast in disorder. Then, in 1873, a new army, under Major General Sir Garnet J. Wolseley,

K.C.B., was organized to deal with them. It was to cover this expedition for the New York *Herald* that Stanley returned to Africa.

When he arrived at Cape Coast Castle on the Gold Coast he found that the campaign had not yet begun. Although General Wolseley with a staff of officers and a few soldiers had landed and established a headquarters, the main body of troops had not arrived. The basic plan of the campaign was simple. As in Abyssinia, the English intended to land an army on the coast, set up a supply base, and then march inland. This time their destination was Coomassie (Kumasi), the Ashantee capital. Not much thought seems to have been given as to what would be done when the army reached there, but it was generally agreed that a British army on the scene would put things to rights and teach a lesson to the audacious savages who had dared to challenge the might of the British Empire.

Stanley was eager to follow the army to Coomassie, but as the staff was still waiting for the troops, there was nothing for him to do but wait. Sir Garnet proved singularly uncommunicative about his plans, and Stanley was almost at a loss for anything to write about. The absence of news and the inactivity forced upon him put the restless and impatient Stanley in a terrible state of mind. He took out his ill will on everything and everyone who came to mind. He sent back long reports to his paper criticizing the selection of Cape Coast Castle as a starting point, the English policies that led to the war, the handling of the supplies, and the character of the local natives. As usual, he was filled with ideas and suggestions as to what should have been done, how the present situation could be improved, and what must be done to insure the future success of the campaign.

He even developed his own medical theories. Malaria, he felt, was caused by a deficiency of ozone in the air. "It has been proved," he said, "that if a man spent twelve hours in a hot bed of malaria, and lived the next twelve hours where the ozone is pretty well developed, the quantity of ozone inhaled into the lungs would be sufficient to neutralize the malaria taken into the system. When a person cannot move so quickly into an ozonic atmosphere, twenty grains of quinine should be taken, which is said to contain the same quantity."

While highly critical of Sir Garnet and the British preparations for the war, he was outright contemptuous of the Fantees, against whom the war was ostensibly being launched. "Two hundred and five years has this town been in the possession of the British, and yet out of its population of twenty-thousand souls I doubt whether there are a thousand of them who understand English. The people are as barbarous, untutored, and superstitious as though they had never seen an Englishman's face. They are as wild in appearance, as naked in body, as filthy in their habits as any tribe of savages I have ever seen. Their fetish idols, and medicine and Mumbo Jumbo rites, are visible in the streets of Cape Coast. The bizarre fantastics in which women caper about nude, and ancient hags disagreeably remind you of the bonyness of the human body in old age, and little consciousless children prank and hop, involved inextricably between the pedal extremities of their grandmothers, form a picture utterly unsuited, I should say, at least, for any portion of the British colonies."

After a month of waiting at Cape Coast Castle, Stanley set out to locate Captain J. H. Glover, who was organizing a force of irregulars to attack the right flank of the Ashantees. Taking a steam launch, the *Dauntless,* which, with his usual foresight, he had brought with him, he traveled down the coast to the mouth of the Volta and then up the river to Captain Glover's camp. Stanley found much to admire in this officer: "Glover compels men to love him. There is something specially attractive in him; all who come in contact with him thaw before his general kindliness of manner. There is no affectation about him; he is a plain, hearty, genuine man."

Glover was also a man of action who saw to everything himself and made things run smoothly. In addition, unlike General Wolseley, he was willing to talk about what he had done and what he planned to do.

While Stanley and the English reporters covering the war sat in idleness, Sir Garnet and his people busied themselves with a number of minor skirmishes with the Ashantees, and in organizing the stores and supplies that poured into the base. As in Abyssinia, the engineers went ahead to prepare camps and build roads for the advancing army.

At last, in mid-December, the troops arrived. The army consisted of the Rifle Brigade, the Royal Welsh Fusiliers, the 42nd Highlanders (the Black Watch), a battalion of marines and sailors, a battery of artillery, a company of Royal Engineers, two battalions of West Indian troops, a battalion of Houssa artillery, and two battalions of native allies. It was not as colorful an array as had been assembled in Abyssinia, particularly since the Highlanders had left their kilts behind, but it was a formidable assemblage of the might of the British Empire and everyone was confident they could easily do the job.

On January 6, 1874, the army set out for Coomassie. It was a tedious march, and for the most part uneventful. For a while it even looked as though King Coffee would sue for peace, and there would be no war at all. The soldiers cursed because they would have come so far for nothing; the officers feared they would have no chance to distinguish themselves; Stanley and the other correspondents were anxious lest they would be unable to file stories of battles and victories; and all were concerned that England would be unable to take adequate revenge for past wrongs.

A number of letters were exchanged between Sir Garnet and the Ashantee king, and messengers and envoys were kept busy going to and fro between the leaders of the two forces. Stanley wrote, "That he (King Coffee) will fear treachery on the part of the white men, some deep scheme of revenge, some bloody massacre, some wholesale spoliation, is the only hope left to the English that they will not be permitted to enter Coomassie bloodlessly or without some opportunity of inflicting a punishment on the savages, that it may become a tradition with them of what may be expected should they venture to attack any territory under the protection of white men again."

These fears proved groundless, for while King Coffee never ceased to profess his desire for peace, he took no definite steps to establish it, so on January 15 the British army started across the Prah River and entered Ashantee country. It was a grisly march. Each village they encountered had placed its human sacrifice in the middle of the path. The sacrifice was sometimes a young man and sometimes a woman. The severed head was turned to meet the advancing army while the body was evenly laid out with the feet toward Coomassie.

On the twenty-second they peacefully entered Fomannah, capital of the Ashantee province of Adansi. The degree of the Ashantee's culture surprised them. They found ornately carved woodwork and evidence of a high degree of skill in the use of tools. In one house Stanley discovered a thirty-year-old copy of the London *Times*.

On January 29 the action they had been waiting for began with the capture of a village called Borborassi. Three men were killed and seven were wounded in this encounter. Ashantee losses were estimated to be about fifty. The enemy was extremely brave, but he could not compete with the modern armaments of the English. Two days later, when the battle of Amoaful was fought and won, the campaign's success was practically assured. On February 4 the British army achieved another victory at the village of Ordahsu just outside Coomassie and entered the Ashantee capital that night.

All the troops were quartered on one street in Coomassie, and no attempt was made to secure the town. The Ashantees roamed the streets, carrying off their goods, arms, and ammunition, so that by morning the town was stripped of all the valuables that would have brought prize money into the pockets of the victorious soldiers. This failure to make the most of a victory was interpreted as a sign of British weakness by King Coffee, who had escaped. Stanley was incensed, but as a reporter, he was unable to give an order or even make a suggestion. His frustration as a mere witness almost burst the limits of his self-control.

The fighting in this war had not seemed exciting to Stanley. When he awoke to his first morning in Coomassie, he set about at once to see what he could find of a sensational nature in the city itself. He located what he described as "the Golgotha of Coomassie," a sacred grove where King Coffee and his predecessors had executed their prisoners and slaves and had made human sacrifices. Braving the terrible stench of decomposing corpses, Stanley saw thirty or forty decapitated bodies in the last stages of corruption. Skulls were piled in heaps and scattered over a wide area, and Stanley roughly calculated that over a hundred and twenty thousand people must have been slain in this grove since the founding of the Ashantee Kingdom.

The following day Coomassie was set afire, and the British army left for the coast. Their hasty retreat was due to a shortage of food and the fear that they would not be able to reach the coast before the rainy season began. Five days after they left, Captain Glover's force entered the now deserted ruins of Coomassie, but the war was over. By the end of February the army had reached the coast and had set sail for home.

Nothing in Stanley's account of the expedition indicates that he took any personal share in the fighting. But in Lord Wolseley's memoirs, written many years after the event, describing the battle of Amoaful, he said: "Not twenty yards off were several newspaper correspondents. One was Mr. Winwood Reid, a very cool and daring man, who had gone forward with the fighting line. Of the others, one soon attracted my attention by his remarkable coolness. It was Sir Henry Stanley,* the famous traveler. A thoroughly good man, no noise, no danger ruffled his nerve, and he looked as cool and self-possessed as if he had been at target practice. Time after time, as I turned in his direction, I saw him go down to a kneeling position to steady his rifle, as he plied the most daring of the enemy with a never-failing aim. It is

---

* Stanley, of course, was not "Sir Henry" at the time.

nearly thirty years ago, and I can still see before me the close-shut lips, and determined expression of his manly face, which, when he looked in my direction, told plainly I had near me an Englishman in plain clothes, whom no danger could appall. Had I felt inclined to run away, the cool, unflinching manliness of that face would have given me fresh courage. I had been previously somewhat prejudiced against him, but all such feelings were slain and buried at Amoaful. Ever since, I have been proud to reckon him among the bravest of my brave comrades; and I hope he may not feel offended if I add him amongst my best friends also."

Stanley was on his way home from the Ashantee war when he learned of the death of David Livingstone. The missionary had died at a place called Ilala, near Lake Bangweulu, on May 1, 1873. His faithful followers had brought his body out of Africa, and it was now on its way back to England. This news had a profound effect upon Stanley. In his notebook he wrote:

"Dear Livingstone! another sacrifice to Africa! His mission, however, must not be allowed to cease; others must go forward and fill the gap. 'Close up boys! close up! Death must find us everywhere.'

"May I be selected to succeed him in opening up Africa to the light of Christianity! My methods, however, will not be Livingstone's. Each man has his own way. His, I think, had its defects, though the old man, personally, has been almost Christ-like for goodness, patience, and self-sacrifice. The selfish and wooden-headed world requires mastering, as well as loving charity; for man is a composite of the spiritual and earthly. May Livingstone's God be with me, as He was with Livingstone in all his loneliness. May God direct me as He wills. I can only vow to be obedient, and not to slacken."

In his mind, Stanley ticked off what remained to be done in Central Africa: Livingstone had died trying to solve the mystery of the Lualaba River; John Hanning Speke died before he could prove that the Victoria Nyanza was one lake, rather than a cluster of lakes as had been maintained by Richard Burton; Lake Tanganyika was known, but it had never been circumnavigated; Sir Samuel Baker had sailed along the northeastern shores of Lake Albert, but the extent of that lake was not known.

For a man with a vast store of restless energy and a consuming ambition, Africa presented a challenge and a wide field in which to work; for an idealist without a cause, Africa offered the highest: the development of civilization and Christianity; for a leader of men without followers and a master builder without materials, Africa extended millions of men and resources beyond compare; for a man with a limitless curiosity and an overpowering desire to satisfy it, Africa, in all of its beauty and horror, lay waiting to be seen if he had the courage and the indomitable will to go there. Stanley was the man, and Africa was his destiny. If he could unravel some of the geographical mysteries that the greatest African explorers had been unable to solve, the world would be forced to acknowledge his feats, and to recognize him for what he was rather than what he had been or how he came to be born.

He formed great plans, but he did not at once reveal them. Back in England, he hastily put together his newspaper stories of the Ashantee campaign, added his account of the Abyssinian war, and published both together under the title of *Coomassie and Magdala.*

On April 15, 1874, the English mail steamer *Malwa* arrived in Southampton bearing the body of David Livingstone. A crowd of fifty thousand was on hand to see the body taken off the ship and put on a train for London. Three days later, the great explorer was buried in Westminster Abbey with a funeral that one spectator described as "the grandest ever witnessed during the present generation." Stanley was one of the pallbearers, occupying the foremost position on the right.

A few days after the funeral, Stanley walked over to 135 Fleet Street, the offices of the *Daily Telegraph.* To Edward Levy-Lawson, the proprietor of the paper, he pointed out how much of Africa was still unknown. He then laid out a plan for an African expedition, to be led by himself and sponsored by the paper, that would attempt to penetrate the Dark Continent and explore its mysteries.

"But do you think you can settle all these interesting geographical problems?" Lawson asked him.

"Nay, Mr. Lawson, that is not a fair question. I mean to say I can do my level best, that nothing on my part shall be lacking to make a systematic exploration which shall embrace all the regions containing these secrets; but Africa includes so many dangers from man, beast, and climate, that it would be the height of immeasurable conceit to say I shall be successful. My promise that 1 will endeavour to be even with my word must be accepted by you as sufficient."

"Well, well! I will cable over to Bennett of the New York *Herald,* and ask if he is willing to join in this expedition of yours."

The cable was sent. In New York that same day, Bennett, sitting at his desk, tore open the telegram and read it. Reaching for a blank cable form, he wrote, "Yes. Bennett."

# CHAPTER VII

## Return to Africa

ANNOUNCEMENTS in the London *Daily Telegraph* and the New York *Herald* told their readers that the two newspapers had united to send an expedition to Central Africa under the leadership of Henry M. Stanley. The purpose of the enterprise, as outlined by the *Daily Telegraph*, was "to complete the work left unfinished by the lamentable death of Dr. Livingstone; to solve, if possible, the remaining problems of the geography of Central Africa; and to investigate and report upon the haunts of the slave traders. . . ."

No sooner was the announcement made than Stanley was besieged by applicants eager to accompany the expedition. Over twelve hundred letters were received from all kinds of people, qualified and unqualified, who clamored to go with him: army officers, sailors, cooks, mechanics, waiters, spiritual mediums, and "magnetizers." But he turned down all of these and chose as his white companions two young brothers named Francis and Edward Pocock who were reputed to be honest, trustworthy, and familiar with small boats. He also hired a young hotel clerk named Frederick Barker whose only qualification seems to have been his intense desire to go to Africa.

Many sent presents of items they thought would be useful to him: canteens, watches, pistols, water bottles, cigars, packages of medicine, Bibles and religious tracts of all sorts, dogs, poems, gold rings, and tiny silk banners. Most of these were left in England, but Stanley did take two mastiffs that were presented to him, and he purchased three other dogs besides.

Stanley was now a veteran of one African expedition of his own and he had accompanied two others. Carefully and methodically he estimated his wants and bought his supplies. Besides the usual equipment, he also ordered the construction of three small boats. One of these, which he called a barge, he designed himself. It was forty feet long, six feet wide, and thirty inches deep, of Spanish cedar three eighths of an inch thick. When finished, it was divided into five sections, each eight feet long, so that it could be carried by pagazis. This boat, christened the *Lady Alice*, was to see good service.

On August 15, 1874, Stanley, with Kalulu, Frederick Barker, and the Pocock brothers, set sail from England for Zanzibar. Almost immediately after their arrival Stanley set out for a brief exploration of the delta of the Rufiji River. Returning to Zanzibar, he began to make his purchases of beads, wire, cloth, and other items necessary to complete his expedition. He also searched for men who would act as chiefs, boatmen, askaris, and pagazis. All who had faithfully followed him on the Livingstone Search Expedition, or had served with Livingstone, were immediately hired. Among these was Manwa Sera, who not only had served with Speke and Grant and had been in charge of the second caravan of the Livingstone expedition, but also had been chief of the party sent back by Stanley from Zanzibar to accompany Livingstone. Manwa Sera was given a jet necklace and a heavy seal ring, and was appointed head chief of the Anglo-American Expedition. Other veterans given positions as chiefs included the sage Safeni, the bullheaded Mabruki, and the faithful Zaidi.

In hiring new men, Stanley did his best to sort out the cripples, the misfits, and the rogues. In this, he was not entirely successful. One man, named Msenna, turned out to be the most notorious ruffian in Zanzibar. When the merchants of the island learned that he was to accompany the expedition, they breathed sighs of relief at the prospect of being free from his villainies for a season. Begging to be taken, Msenna had assumed such a "contrite penitent look" and had wept so copiously that Stanley hired him. Unfortunately, many of the men—white and black— were taken along for no other reason than that they appealed to Stanley's innate sentimentality.

Three hundred and fifty-six men were finally selected, and Stanley made a sort of marriage contract with them—a general policy to guide them throughout the expedition. They swore to carry his loads and to go with him wherever he might direct, to stand by him in time of trouble, and to serve him faithfully. Stanley, on his part, swore to treat them kindly, minister to them when they became sick, judge them fairly in their differences, and to be a "father and mother" to them.

On November 12, 1874, Arab dhows were loaded with the animals and supplies and, although only two hundred and twenty-four men reported, these, with the white men and the wives of the chiefs, cast off from Zanzibar and headed for the mainland. Three hours after landing at Bagamoyo the town was in a ferment. A mob of furious men with bloody faces and wild eyes, together with women in rumpled and torn dresses, presented themselves to Stanley.

"What's the matter," he demanded.

"Matter!" echoed one man. "Matter enough. The town is in an uproar. Your men are stealing, murdering, robbing goods from the stores, breaking plates, killing our chickens, assaulting everybody, drawing knives on our women after abusing them and threatening to burn the town and exterminate everybody. Matter indeed! Matter enough! What do you mean by bringing this savage rabble from Zanzibar?"

It was several exasperating hours before Stanley could quiet this mass of irate natives and Arabs by locating the guilty parties and locking them up in native huts. It was not a happy beginning.

Stanley had intended to pause in Bagamoyo long enough to recruit additional pagazis, but, because of the uproar caused by his men, he wisely decided to start for the interior after only four days. Boxes and bundles had been packed with great care, and the pagazis who carried them were selected according to their strength and age. Strong men were given sixty- to seventy-pound bales of cloth, short men were given the bead sacks weighing fifty to fifty-five pounds, men from eighteen to twenty years old carried forty-pound boxes of ammunition and stores, older men were given the boxes containing the photographic equipment and the scientific instruments, while one man, recommended for his steady and cautious tread, was given the twenty-five-pound box containing the three chronometers packed in cotton. The twelve kirangozis, or guides, carried the coils of wire and were armed with Snider rifles. Many of them were to become part of the boat's crew and ranked second only to the chiefs. In a special category were the men selected to carry the sections of the boat. These were individuals noted for their great strength who were also practiced bearers. To each section of the boat, four men were assigned who relieved each other in pairs. They were given more pay than even the chiefs—Manwa Sera excepted—and in addition they received double rations and were granted the privilege of bringing their wives along.

Stanley's first project was the circumnavigation of the Victoria Nyanza, but the march from the coast to the lake was a difficult one.

There were some unusual problems. Unbeknown to their leader, Stanley's men had carried off several women from Bagamoyo. Soldiers were sent out to bring them back, and there was a near-mutiny when Stanley made his men give the women up. The two prize mastiffs given Stanley in England soon died from the heat, and there was the old problem of desertions.

At first the expedition followed the same slave and ivory caravan route toward Tabora that Stanley had taken in his search for Livingstone, but late in December they struck northward into unexplored territory. They were soon in serious trouble. The land through which they were passing was beautiful open country, but famine in the land made it inhospitable for such a large caravan. To make matters worse, their local guides deserted and the new ones they obtained promptly got them lost.

The year 1875 did not begin auspiciously for the expedition; the month of January saw a series of terrible hardships and catastrophes. One day, five men in the rear of the column straggled too far back and took a wrong path. When Manwa Sera and a search party went to look for them, they found three men dead from the heat, lack of food, and exhaustion. The remaining two were never seen again.

Shortage of food was their principal problem. The inhabitants of the country were unfriendly and suspicious, and the expedition was forced to pay ten times the value for such food as the sullen natives were willing to sell. By January 9 they were close to starvation. Although enough oatmeal was found in the medical stores to give each man two cups of thin gruel and two lion cubs were caught and made into a stew, they barely kept alive.

Sickness plagued them, too. By January 15 there were thirty men on the sick list, including Edward Pocock. Stanley diagnosed Edward's illness as typhus, and he knew that he could not last. The young man died on January 17. Although they had been on the march for only two months, twenty people had died and eighty-nine had deserted—a loss of one third of the expedition!

Until now, the natives, while not friendly, had refrained from attacking the caravan. But four days after the death of Edward Pocock, the weak and stumbling expedition reached a place called Vinyata in the country of Ituru where all of their friendly overtures were met with hostile demonstrations. Not a banana or a root would the Ituru natives sell, and they hovered on the expedition's flanks and rear to watch for stragglers. One man who had fallen behind was found with over thirty spear wounds in his body. On January 23, Soudi, a young Zanzibari, staggered into camp with two spear wounds and his temple laid open by a whirling knobstick. Breathless and sobbing, he told how he and his brother had been attacked while looking for food and how his brother had been killed.

Later that same day, Stanley's men suffered their first direct attack from the Ituru natives. After an hour of vicious fighting, the savages were driven off, but the expedition gained only a brief respite. Early the next morning the enemy returned, this time reinforced by hundreds of natives from adjoining districts. Stanley quickly organized his askaris, and several pagazis who volunteered to become temporary soldiers, into seven well-armed detachments of ten men each. With each of them Stanley sent along a messenger who acted as a "getaway man." One detachment was left in camp to defend the pagazis and the loads, two were kept as a reserve force, and the remaining four were sent out in different directions to drive back the enemy.

The first detachment was thrown into disorder and, except for the messenger, was completely wiped out. Manwa Sera was dispatched with the reserve force, and he arrived just in time to save eight men from the second detachment. The third group lost six men, but kept moving forward. The fourth detachment, under the wise and prudent Safeni, was able to overcome and set fire to several villages.

The soldiers returned to the camp about four o'clock in the afternoon, bringing with them several oxen, goats, and baskets of grain. They had driven off their enemies and secured some badly needed food, but the expedition's losses from this day's fighting were twenty-one askaris and one messenger killed and three men wounded.

The next day, several forays were made on the camp, but they were beaten off by a few volleys from the expedition's rifles and muskets. More pagazis volunteered as askaris, and Stanley sent out another force. This time, his men kept together, and they were successful in driving the enemy from their strongholds and burning their villages.

The way was clear for them to move forward once more. With desertions, sickness, and casualties from the fighting, their losses had been so heavy that now there were not enough healthy people to carry all the supplies. Some of the goods had to be burned, and the riding asses and even the chiefs were called on to carry loads. Besides the three Europeans, the expedition now consisted of two hundred and six men, twenty-five women, and six boys.

Continuing the march at a faster pace, they left Ituru behind them.

On February 9 they reached the village of Mombiti, where the natives were friendly and they were able to purchase food. They were able also to engage additional pagazis who agreed to carry their goods as far as Victoria Nyanza. Without further difficulties then, they arrived at the small village of Kagehyi (at or near present-day Mwanza) on the shores of Lake Victoria on the twenty-seventh of February. Here Stanley made friends with the natives, and established a semipermanent camp where he could leave the bulk of his expedition while he took the *Lady Alice* on an exploratory trip around the lake. When all of the preparations had been made, he called for volunteers to man the boat. No one stepped forward. He asked several men individually if they would not go with him. Each professed that he knew nothing about boats and that he was a coward on the water. Stanley had gained the respect of his men, but he had not yet acquired their complete confidence and devotion.

At last Manwa Sera spoke up, "Master, have done with these questions. Command your party. All our people are your children, and they will not disobey you. While you ask them as a friend, no one will offer his services. Command them, and they will all go."

Following this good advice, Stanley selected a crew of ten good men, and appointed the prudent Safeni as the coxswain. Leaving detailed instructions with Frank Pocock and Fred Barker on what they should do and how they should act during his absence, he set sail on the Victoria Nyanza on March 8, 1875. Victoria is the largest lake in Africa and, except for Lake Superior, the largest fresh-water lake in the world, covering twenty-six thousand square miles. There had been considerable controversy in Europe over its size and importance. So now Stanley prepared to take careful notes and measurements as he sailed along its two thousand miles of shore line, recording every cove, river, and island he found.

At first, he had little trouble with the natives. Although he had a number of narrow escapes, he was forced to fight only once during his first month on the lake. Battles were frequently prevented by Stanley's calm and peaceful attitude, a lesson he had learned from Livingstone. He often remained seated and smiling in the boat while spears were poised only a few feet from him and the savages, sometimes drunk, were screaming their intention to kill him.

Early in April, they drew near the kingdom of Uganda, then the best-organized Negro state on the continent. Stanley was most interested in meeting Mtesa, the *kabaka* or king, of Uganda, of whom

Speke had written. When still several days from the court of the
African monarch, he was met by emissaries of Mtesa, and, under their
protection, he and his men were guided to Usavara, then the capital of
Uganda.

As the *Lady Alice,* escorted by war canoes, approached land, Stanley
saw several thousand people arranging themselves into two dense lines
perpendicular to the shore. As they drew closer, he saw at the far end
of the rows, standing by gaily colored flags, several men in beautiful
robes of red, black, and white. He landed to the din of hundreds of
muskets being fired into the air, drums pounding furiously, and men,
women, and children roaring great shouts of welcome. Stanley strode
through the cheering lines of people to where the brilliantly dressed
chiefs stood waiting for him. There he bowed politely and was courte-
ously received by the dignitaries sent to meet him. The head of this
delegation was none other than the *katekiro,* or prime minister, of the
country.

Stanley was at once taken by the reception committee to a circle of
grass-thatched huts surrounding a larger house, which he learned was
to be his quarters. Inside the large hut, the katekiro and a few of his
chiefs sat down with him and began a long series of questions in
Swahili about his health, the purpose of his visit, Zanzibar, Europe
and its people, the seas, the heavens, angels and devils, priests, doctors,
craftsmen, and dozens of other subjects. When at last they had completed their questioning, they wrung his hand and seemed to congratulate him as though he had just completed an important examination—
as indeed he had. Some of the chiefs left immediately to tell the kabaka
about the white man and his wisdom, and soon servants arrived from
Mtesa, bringing fourteen oxen, sixteen goats and sheep, over thirty
fowls, milk, yams, Indian corn, rice, eggs, and wine.

A few hours later, Stanley was summoned to meet the kabaka himself, whom he found to be a tall, clean-faced, large-eyed, nervous-
looking man dressed in a tarboosh, black robe, and a white shirt belted
with gold. Stanley was quite taken with Mtesa, and immediately con-
jured up great plans for the African monarch.

"Mtesa has impressed me as being an intelligent and distinguished
prince, who, if aided in time by virtuous philanthropists, will do more
for Central Africa than fifty years of Gospel teaching, unaided by such
authority, can do. I think I see in him the light that shall lighten the
darkness of this benighted region; a prince well worthy the most hearty
sympathies that Europe can give him. In this man I see the possible

fruition of Livingstone's hopes, for with his aid the civilization of Equatorial Africa becomes feasible," he recorded in his diary that evening.

Mtesa was at this time a Moslem, having been converted to Islam some years before by an Arab named Muley bin Salim. Stanley got the notion that he should convert the kabaka to Christianity. "I shall destroy his belief in Islam, and teach the doctrines of Jesus of Nazareth," he wrote in his diary after his fifth interview with him.

He took on the self-appointed task with his usual vigor and intelligence. Avoiding doctrinal matters, he told the kabaka the story of Christ and tales from the Old Testament; he explained the ethics of the Ten Commandments and the golden rule. So well did he preach and reason that all other business was postponed, and the court became a regular seminary. At the end of twelve days he had made such an impression that Mtesa decided to observe the Christian Sabbath as well as the Moslem Sabbath and ordered the Ten Commandments to be written on a board where he could see and study them every day.

About this time, a Frenchman, Colonel Linant de Bellefonds, arrived at the court of Uganda. He had been sent by General Charles Gordon, Governor General of the Sudan, to establish official communications between the Sudan and Uganda. De Bellefonds did not stay long, but Stanley was glad to see him—or, more particularly, to be seen by him. In a letter to his friend and publisher, Edward Marston, dated September 27, 1875, Stanley wrote: "They will not doubt my meeting Bellefonds, will they? I mean the British and American people. On Lake Albert I hope to meet other whites, so that there may be many witnesses of my being in Africa."

In the same letter, Stanley wondered about the success of a competitor, Verney Lovett Cameron (1844-1894), a British naval officer who was on his way to becoming the first European to cross Africa: "Has Cameron emerged from Africa yet? If so, what success has he had? If I come through, his journey will be a mere tour compared with mine; though if he arrives in England safe he will deserve all the applause he can get. I am, however, not labouring for applause, I am labouring to establish a confidence in me in the minds of right-minded people, which my vicious foes robbed me of."

Stanley entrusted De Bellefonds with this letter as well as one to the *Daily Telegraph* which contained an appeal for a large number of missionaries to be sent to Uganda. On his return to the Sudan, De Bellefonds was murdered. When his body was found, Stanley's letters were discovered concealed in his boots. Eventually, the letters found their way to England where the *Telegraph* published them in November, 1875. They created an immediate effect (five thousand pounds were contributed that very day). With the funds collected, missionaries were sent out, and Christianity began to flourish in the remote African kingdom.

Stanley, having laid the groundwork for such great political and religious changes, now wished to push on and continue his geographical explorations. He announced his intention, however, to return to Uganda with his complete expedition in about a month. Reinforced by canoes and men lent by Mtesa, Stanley set out to explore the western shores of the Victoria Nyanza.

One evening, about two weeks after leaving the kabaka's court, the party pulled their canoes on a beach for the night. The natives they encountered seemed friendly at first, but at midnight they were awakened by loud drumming, which continued throughout the night. At dawn, Stanley saw between two hundred and three hundred natives, all in war costume and armed with spears, bows and arrows, shields, and long-handled cleavers, standing silently not thirty paces from him. Recognizing an elderly man as one who had given him a cup of native wine the previous evening, he advanced toward him.

"What means this, my friend?" he asked. "Is anything wrong?"

"What do you mean by drawing your canoes on our beach?" the man demanded.

"We drew them up lest the surf should batter them to pieces during the night. The winds are rough sometimes, and waves rise high. Our canoes are our homes, and we are far from our friends who are waiting for us. Were our canoes injured or broken, how should we return to our friends?"

"Do you know this is our country?"

"Yes, but are we doing wrong? Is the beach so soft that it can be hurt by our canoes? Have we cut down your bananas or entered your houses? Have we molested any of your people? Do you not see our fires by which we slept exposed to the cold night?"

"Well, you must leave this place at once. We do not want you here. Go!"

"That is easily done, and had you told us last night that our presence was not welcome to you, we should have camped on yonder island."

"What did you come here for?"

"We came to rest for the night, and to buy food, and is that a crime? Do you not travel in your canoes? Supposing people received you as you received us this morning, what would you say? Would you not say they were bad? Ah, my friend, I did not expect that you who were so good yesterday would turn out thus! But never mind; we will go away quickly and quietly, and the Kabaka Mtesa shall hear of this, and judge between us."

At the mention of Mtesa's name, the man became less imperious. "If you wish food, I will send some bananas to yonder island, but you must go away from here, lest the people, who wish to fight you, should break out."

Stanley and his men embarked in their boats and rowed to the off-shore island. About ten o'clock the natives sent them ten bunches of green bananas.

While his men were occupied with the bananas, Stanley seized the opportunity to take a solitary walk on the little island. "With all the ardour of a boy, I began my solitary exploration," he wrote. "That impulse to jump, to bound, to spring upward and cling to branches overhead, which is the characteristic of a strong green age, I gave free rein to. Unfettered for a time from all conventionalisms, and absolved from that sobriety and steadiness which my position as a leader of half-wild men compelled me to assume in their presence, all my natural elasticity of body came back to me. I dived under the obstructing bough or sprang over the prostrate trunk, squeezed into almost impossible places, crawled and writhed like a serpent through the tangled undergrowth. . . ."

He was brought back to the realities of his world by the discovery of six half-decomposed bodies, only partially covered with dried grass and rocks. One of the skulls had been cleaved with a hatchet, and it was obvious that they had all been murdered only a few days earlier.

Stanley rushed back to his party, and, loading his men into their boats, quickly left this inhospitable area.

Shortly after this Mtesa's escort of canoes deserted Stanley, and he was left with the *Lady Alice* and his own crew to continue on his way.

A few days later, the expedition had one of its most hair-raising encounters on the Victoria Nyanza. Having spent the night before shivering, supperless, and sleepless, crouching in a pouring rain, the men sailed for Bumbireh Island where they hoped to find friendly natives with whom they could barter for food. The island was about eleven miles long and two miles wide and contained about fifty small villages, each with an average of twenty huts. Herds of cattle grazed on the slopes, and here and there patches of ground had been cultivated. Extensive banana groves marked the sites of most of the villages. In all, Stanley felt that there was "a kindly and prosperous aspect about the island."

As they sailed along the shore looking for a suitable place to land, they caught sight of a few figures running along the banks. To their dismay, they heard them sound the familiar and melodious war cry used by most Central African tribes, "Hehu–a hehu–u-u-u!" It was loud, long-drawn, and ringing; its notes sounding both alarm and defiance.

By the time they had found a cove and turned the *Lady Alice* in toward shore, a great crowd of shouting, gesticulating natives had gathered on the bank. About fifty yards from shore, Stanley told his men to stop rowing while he appraised the situation. Safeni, the coxswain, spoke up then and said, "It is almost always the case, master, with savages. They cry out, and threaten and look big, but you will see that all that noise will cease as soon as they hear us speak. Besides, if we leave here without food, where shall we obtain it?"

This last argument seemed unanswerable, so they rowed slowly in. Safeni and another man stood up to talk with the natives. Putting on their most pleasing smiles, they explained by gestures and words that they were hungry, that they came in peace, and that they wanted to make friends. The words and gestures seemed to have a good effect, for in a few minutes spears were lowered, bows were unstrung, and stones were dropped. The natives consulted among themselves for a few moments and then several of them came into the water toward the boat, smiling and talking pleasantly. Suddenly, however, they laid hold of the gunwale and seized the painter. With a rush, they carried the *Lady Alice* up the bank, dragging the boat and its astonished crew for twenty yards over the rocky beach.

"Then ensued a scene of rampant wildness and hideous ferocity beyond description," Stanley later recalled. "The boat was surrounded by a forest of spears, over fifty bows were bent nearly double, with leveled arrows, over two hundred stalwart demons contended as to who should deliver the first blow. When this outbreak first took place, I had sprung up to kill or be killed, a revolver in each hand; but as I rose to my feet, the utter hopelessness of our situation was revealed to me."

Some of the boat's crew were beaten, Safeni was given a push that sent him sprawling, and one native even tugged at Stanley's hair, apparently under the impression that it was a wig. The best course was to appear unconcerned and calm, Stanley decided. His men tried to follow his example. At first, these tactics seemed to be successful; the riot and noise subsided somewhat. Then, about fifty more excited natives arrived on the scene and rekindled the smoldering fury.

One elderly man, whom Stanley later discovered to be Shekka, the king of Bumbireh, appeared to be restraining the people from proceeding too far. Stanley tried to talk to him, showing him beads, cloth, and wire. This was a mistake, for at the sight of these riches the savages' greed and selfishness were awakened. Nevertheless, Shekka called together some of his chief men and retired several yards away to have a *shauri,* a council or discussion. Next to wine, women, and war, there was nothing the savage African delighted in more than an opportunity to hold a shauri. Half of the crowd followed the king to listen. Presently a messenger from Shekka came to the boat and beckoned to Safeni.

Stanley said, "Safeni, use your wit."

"Please God, master," Safeni replied.

The rest of the natives around the boat followed Safeni as he walked to the shauri. Stanley watched him. "I saw him pose himself. A born diplomatist was Safeni. His hands moved up and down, outward and inward; a cordial frankness sat naturally on his face; his gestures were graceful; the man was an orator, pleading for mercy and justice."

When Safeni returned, his face was radiant. "It is all right, master, there is no fear. They say we must stop here until tomorrow."

"Will they sell us food?" Stanley asked.

"Oh, yes, as soon as they finish their shauri."

But while Safeni was giving his report, six men rushed up to the boat, seized the oars, and made off with them. This action was gleefully applauded by the other natives, who now believed the white man and his crew were helpless and could not possibly escape. It was nearly noon, and most of the savages retired to their villages for lunch. Some women came to stare at them, laughing among themselves. Stanley and the Zanzibaris tried to be friendly and gave them some beads. In return, the women calmly assured them that they would certainly be killed unless they succeeded in making blood brotherhood with Shekka.

About three o'clock in the afternoon, they heard the loud, deep booming of war drums. Soon a long line of natives, their faces smeared with black and white pigments, sprang up along the crest of the hill

Stanley at 17.

Stanley in 1882.

*(Photograph by Messrs. Thomson, New Bond St., London)*

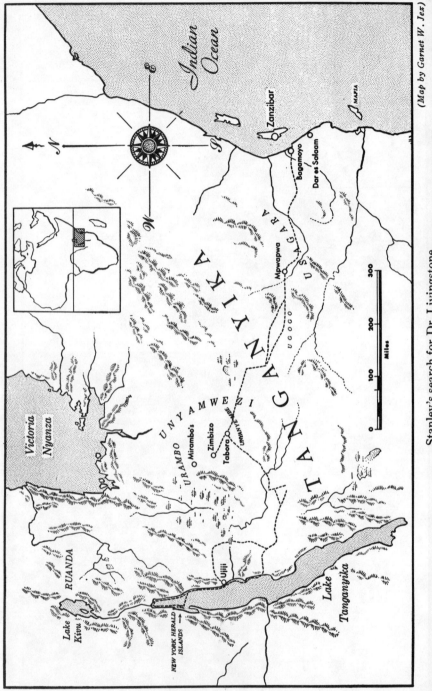

Stanley's search for Dr. Livingstone.

(*Map by Garnet W. Jex*)

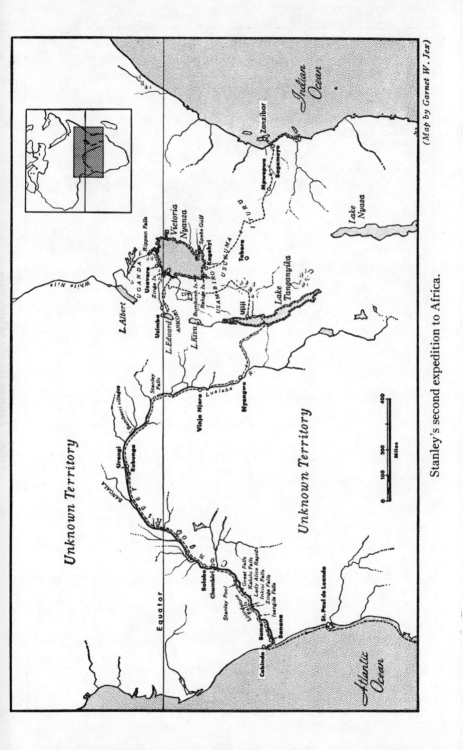

(Map by Garnet W. Jex)

Stanley's second expedition to Africa.

Tippu-Tib, the world's greatest slaver.     Emin Pasha, governor of Equatria.

*Opposite page*: Officers of the Rear Guard, Emin Pasha Expedition:

      *Top left*: John Rose Troup

      *Top right*: James Jameson

      *Center*: Major Edmund Barttelot

      *Bottom left*: Herbert Ward

      *Bottom right*: William Bonny

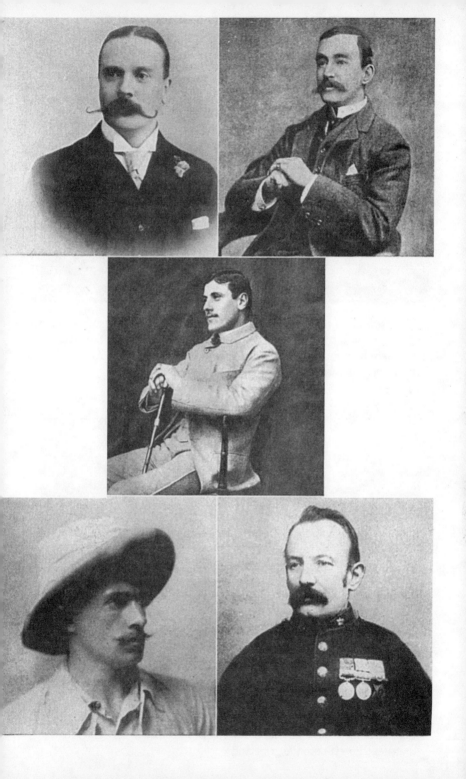

Stanley with officers of the Advance Guard of the Emin Pasha Expedition. *From left to right:* Surgeon Thomas H. Parke, Captain Robert Nelson, Stanley, Lieutenant William G. Stairs, and Arthur J. Mounteney-Jephson.

*(Illustration from* In Darkest Africa*)*

The Advance Guard of the Emin Pasha Expedition emerging from the Great Forest onto the grasslands.

Dorothy Tennant Stanley.

nley in 1890 after the Emin
ha Expedition.

*(Photograph by Mrs. Frederic Myers)*

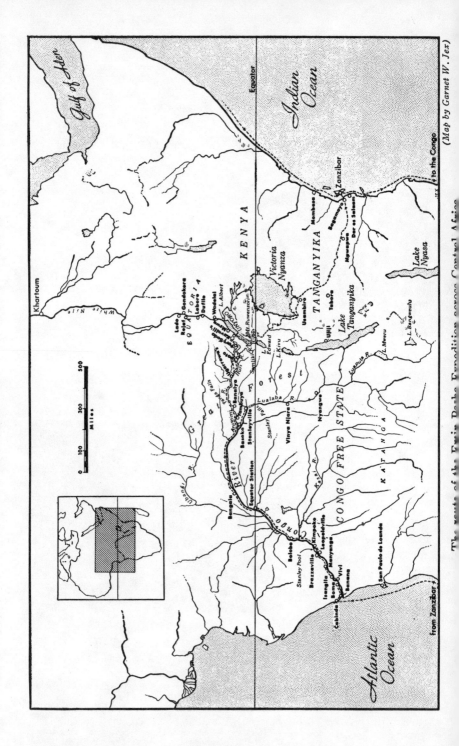

The route of the Emin Pasha Expedition across Central Africa

(Map by Garnet W. Jex)

overlooking the beach. There was no mistaking their hostile intentions. Waving their weapons and shouting shrilly, they were kindling themselves into a fighting fervor. Safeni, who up to this moment had firmly maintained that the savages would make friends with them, was astounded. In the understatement of the trip he said, "Truly, master, this is trouble."

Suddenly, one tall young warrior came running down the hill and pounced on a Kiganda drum. It was only a curio Stanley had picked up; he let him have it. Retreating with his prize, the warrior called out, "If you are men, prepare to fight!"

"Good," Stanley said, "the sentence is given, suspense is over. Boys, if I try to save you, will you give me absolute submission, unwavering obedience?—no arguing or reasoning, but prompt, unhesitating compliance?"

"Yes, we will; we swear!"

"Do you think you can push this boat into the water?"

"Yes."

"Just as she is, with all her goods in her, before those men can reach us?"

"Yes, certainly."

"Stand by, then. Range yourselves on both sides of the boat, carelessly. Each of you find out exactly where you shall lay hold. I'll load my guns. Safeni, take these cloths on your arm, walk up toward the men on the hill; open out the cloths one by one, you know, as though you were admiring the pattern. But keep your ears open. When I call out to you, throw the cloths away and fly to us, or your death will lie on your own head! Do you understand?"

"Perfectly, master."

"Then go."

Meantime, Stanley loaded his pistols, his elephant rifle, his double-barreled shotgun, his Winchester repeater, and two or three Sniders belonging to the men.

"Lay hold firmly; break the boat rather than stop; it's life or death," Stanley told his men.

Safeni was about fifty yards off. The natives' eyes were fastened on him, wondering why he came. Taking one of his cloths, Safeni leisurely began his pantomime.

"Now, boys, ready?" Stanley whispered.

"Ready! please God, master!" they replied.

"Push!" he commanded, "push, Saramba, Kirango! Push, you villain, Baraka!"

"Ahee, master! Push it is."

The Zanzibaris bent their heads and backs and strained their arms. The boat moved. They drove her stern first, her keel plowing the gravel and crunching through the stony beach. Safeni had gained only a few precious seconds before the quick-eyed natives saw the moving boat. With wild cries, they swept down the hill.

The boat was nearing the lake now, and Stanley called, "Safeni! Safeni! Safeni!"

Safeni threw down his cloths and ran, the natives close behind him. The boat glided swiftly into the water, carrying the crew far out with her—so frantic was the impetus with which she was launched. "Swim away with her! Don't stop!" Stanley shouted.

A tall warrior came bounding over the ground like a springbok after Safeni, his spear poised for the cast. As the balanced spear was about to fly, Stanley fired his Winchester repeater. The bullet perforated the warrior, and flew through a second man. At the edge of the lake, Safeni hesitated for a moment.

"Jump, Safeni!" Stanley called.

As the natives closed in on him, drawing their bows, Safeni dived. Stanley's rifle steadily dropped his nearest pursuers. In a few moments, the native warriors were crowding the shore and deftly working their bows. Arrows began to fall in the boat, piercing the thwarts and quivering in the mast. Stanley exchanged his rifle for his shotgun and sent two devastating charges of duck-shot into the massed flesh of his enemies. In a few moments more they were a hundred yards away from shore, and the arrows were falling harmlessly in the water behind them. Stanley lifted one of the Zanzibaris into the boat and ordered him to lend a hand to the others while he reloaded his guns. They waited for the swimming Sefani and drew him safely on board.

A point of land about a hundred yards long jutted out on the east side of the cove. To escape into the lake, the boat would have to pass by it. Some of the natives saw this and made a rush for the point, but Stanley's guns commanded the exposed position, and he forced them to retreat.

As soon as the dripping crew were all on board, they snatched up their rifles; but Stanley ordered them to leave their weapons alone and instead to tear up the bottom boards of the boat and use them as paddles. Stanley now saw a new danger threatening them. Two hippopotamuses, their great mouths open, were advancing toward them. He thought how ironical it would be if, after narrowly escaping the savages on shore, they should be crushed in the water. One of the hippos was within ten yards of the boat before Stanley neatly punctured his skull between the eyes, with a three-ounce ball. The second hippo received similar treatment.

The baffled and furious natives, seeing their prey escape, dashed to man two canoes that were drawn up on the beach at the northwest corner of the cove. Stanley dropped two warriors, but the others succeeded in launching the canoes. Meanwhile, two other canoes were seen coming down the eastern coast of the island. Realizing that they would be unable to escape, Stanley stopped his boat and waited. Taking careful aim at the swiftly advancing enemy, he killed five men with four shots. Still they came on.

Loading his elephant rifle with explosive bullets, he waited until the foremost canoe was about eighty yards from him. Then, taking deliberate aim at a spot on the canoe "between wind and water," he fired. The shell struck home, tearing a large fragment from the brittle wood. The canoe sank. The next canoe met the same fate. The others turned back. As they slowly paddled the *Lady Alice* into the lake, Stanley heard a voice behind them cry out, "Go and die in the Nyanza!"

It seemed an even chance that they might. They were in an open boat without oars, around them was hostile country, and they had been without food for forty-nine hours. They hoisted their sail, but two hours later it fell dead calm. Using the thin, weak bottom boards, they were barely able to make three quarters of a mile per hour as they paddled throughout the night. The next morning a gale drove them off their course, but they doggedly continued their paddling. Nightfall found them only seven miles from an island, but to their dismay another storm drove them away from it. Rain and spray filled the boat and great waves tossed them about. It was all they could do to keep the *Lady Alice* bailed out.

About midnight the gale subsided and the moon came up, casting a weird light on the heaving face of the lake. Up and down they rocked in their small boat. The strange moonlight revealed to Stanley the dark forms of his wretched, disheartened Zanzibaris crouching in front of him. At long last dawn came, and he saw an island about twelve miles to the south. Rousing his exhausted men, he urged them to again take up the boards and paddle on.

It was two o'clock in the afternoon before they landed on the un-inhabited island. Crawling out of the boat, the men threw themselves onto the warm sands to rest. But they had to find food—and soon. It had been seventy-six hours since they had eaten last. Stanley sent two men in one direction and two more in another, while the others were ordered to make a fire. Stanley took his shotgun and went to look for birds. Within half an hour he was back in camp with two large, fat ducks. The foraging Zanzibaris came back with two bunches of bananas and some luscious berries resembling cherries. Stanley broke out some coffee given him by De Bellefonds and they prepared for a feast—bananas, ducks, berries, and coffee! After a good meal, a pipe of tobacco! Stanley described the event as "one of the most delicious evenings I ever remember to have passed." He named this bountiful bit of land "Refuge Island."

Three days later, they arrived back at Kagehyi, their circumnaviga-tion of the Victoria Nyanza completed. They were welcomed to their home base with loud shouts of joy from the Zanzibaris and the smiling faces of Kalulu and Frank Pocock. But when Stanley asked after Frederick Barker, he was told that the hotel clerk who wanted to see Africa had come down with a fever and had died twelve days earlier. Also dead was Mabruki, the bullheaded. He had been a veteran of many an expedition, having faithfully served Burton, Speke, Grant, Livingstone, and Stanley himself on his first expedition. Mabruki and five other men had died of dysentery.

Stanley needed rest and food; on weighing himself, he discovered that he had lost sixty-three pounds since leaving Zanzibar. But before he could begin to improve his condition, three attacks of fever reduced his weight to a mere hundred and eight pounds.

In spite of his weakened state, Stanley set to work trying to obtain sufficient canoes to take his entire expedition to Uganda by water. He succeeded, finally, in securing enough from a friendly tribe in an ad-joining region. Remembering Bumbireh, he purchased and took with him six tons of grain, millet, maize, and sesame and five hundred pounds of rice.

On June 20 he and all of his people set out. Stanley hoped to be able to reach a small group of islands before nightfall, but strong head winds and the inexperience of most of his men with canoes slowed them, and darkness found them still on the water. As there was no moon and the boats could not see each other, Stanley stood up from time to time and waved a candle as a beacon, at the same time calling out threats of punishment to those who strayed out of line.

The expedition proceeded for about three hours in this fashion and was nearing its destination when Stanley heard shrill cries for "the boat." Hurrying to the spot where the cries originated, he was able to distinguish round, dark objects floating in the water. They were the heads of men from a foundered canoe. Stanley took all of the frightened people on board the *Lady Alice* and retrieved four bales of cloth, but a box of ammunition and four hundred pounds of grain had sunk.

They moved forward, but they had gone hardly a mile when once more there were frenzied, piercing cries from out of the night. "The boat, oh, the boat!" Steering for the spot, Stanley again saw by the light of a taper made from pages of a book he had been reading that afternoon, the heads of struggling men and women and floating bales of cloth beside an overturned canoe. Four more bags of grain and five guns had sunk, but fortunately no lives were lost. Stanley and his crew hauled all of the people into the badly overloaded *Lady Alice*. If a breeze came up they would have to lighten the load or the boat would sink.

Through the darkness, Stanley shouted to his people that if any more canoes started to founder they should dump the grain and beads overboard, but hang on to the canoe until he could save them. The order was no sooner out than he heard more cries: "Master, the canoe is sinking! Quick, come here! Oh, master, we cannot swim!" Going to their assistance, he heard other cries: "The boat! Oh hurry—the boat, the boat!" Then cries from another: "Come to us, master, or we die! Bring the boat, my master!" One by one, the rotten canoes were sinking and his people were becoming panicky.

In response to their pleading, Stanley called out sternly, "You who would save yourselves, follow me to the islets as fast as you can. And you who are crying out, cling to your canoes until we return."

So saying, he turned his boat forward and urged his men to row hard. The moon came up, and they caught sight of the island just ahead of them. Stanley shouted encouragement to his crew, as behind him he heard the piteous cries of "Master! oh master! bring your boat—the boat!"

The island rose larger and clearer into view as they pushed the overloaded *Lady Alice* as fast as she would go. Landing, they shot out the goods and hurried off the passengers, then raced back to the foundering canoes. On the way they passed two canoes speeding like arrows for the island. Stanley called out to them to unload quickly and return for the others. "It is what we intend to do, Inshallah!" the coxswain Uledi called.

Reaching the spot where the canoes were sinking, Stanley set to work picking up the people in the water and such goods as he could recover. He was soon joined by Uledi and his younger brother, Shumari. Thanks to their help, he was able to save all of his people, but he lost five canoes, a case of ammunition, twelve hundred pounds of grain and—worst loss of all—five guns.

The shortage of canoes now forced Stanley to move his expedition forward in relays. He would paddle his canoes to a suitable spot for a camp and then send the boats back to bring up the remainder of the expedition. They limped on in this fashion until they arrived at an island only eight miles from Bumbireh, where he and the crew of the *Lady Alice* had had such a narrow escape. Here he learned through friendly natives that Shekka, the Bumbireh chief, was planning to prevent them from returning to Uganda. But Stanley was able to make an ally of a nearby tribe. This tribe handily captured Shekka, together with two of his head men, and turned them over to him as hostages. Reinforcements also came. A party of Waganda and Wazongora arrived, led by a chief named Sabadu, who had been sent out by Mtesa to search for them.

The natives of Bumbireh now made peaceful overtures, even promising to sell food to the expedition. To test this promise, Sabadu and some of his Waganda rowed over to purchase bananas. As treacherous as ever, the Bumbireh natives attacked the party, killing a chief and wounding eight other men. Shortly after this incident, Stanley learned through spies that the savages planned to invade his little island and attack his camp.

These people could be cured of their ferocity and treachery only by force, he decided. Gathering his askaris and the fighting men of Sabadu, he set out on a punitive expedition to Bumbireh. As they approached the island, he saw the natives gathered on the shore. Rowing within a hundred yards of them, he drew his boats into a line and anchored. Once more he offered to make peace, but his offer was scornfully rejected. He ordered his men to fire a broadside into the densely packed savages on the shore. The volley scattered them, but they tried to strike back with their bows and arrows. All of the arrows fell short, however.

Stanley brought his boats to within fifty yards of shore, and told his men to fire at will. Fleeing from the rifle and musket fire, the savages retreated from the river banks and hid among the grass and stones. Stanley then made a feint, as though he were going to land. At this, the savages rushed toward them by the hundreds, but Stanley, pulling his boats up short, again poured a volley into their ranks. This mass slaughter proved too much for them, and they turned and fled over the hills. His work of chastisement was complete, Stanley felt. The Waganda wanted to land and continue the fight, but he refused to allow this, threatening to fire on the first man who landed.

The way to Uganda and the court of Mtesa was now clear, and he reached there in the middle of August. He intended to enlist the kabaka's help in his projected expedition to Lake Albert, but he found Mtesa preparing for a war against the Wavuma, a rebellious tribe that had been subject to him.

Since Mtesa was unable at this time to spare enough men to escort Stanley through the hostile regions that lay between Uganda and the lake, he was forced either to wait until the war was over or go on to Lake Tanganyika without visiting Lake Albert. But as Mtesa assured him that the war would be a short one, he decided to accompany the African monarch's army and see how they fought. He also hoped to utilize the enforced delay by continuing his religious instructions to Mtesa.

But the war lasted over two months, and in the end it was Stanley who devised the means for ending it. Mtesa had gathered a force that, with camp followers and retainers, Stanley estimated to be a quarter of a million people. With this mighty array he set out to subdue the Wavuma.

The rebels lived on a large island in the Victoria Nyanza, and although Mtesa possessed a considerable fleet of canoes, he was unable to effect a landing or to gain a decisive victory. At last Stanley received permission to carry out a scheme which he had contrived for inducing the Wavuma to submit. Taking three large canoes, he had them lashed side by side. On this foundation he constructed a large wooden tower adorned with banners. A herald was sent to the Wavuma to tell them that a terrible thing, filled with all the potent charms of Uganda, was to be sent against them and, if they did not submit, their entire island would be annihilated. The craft was then loaded with men and sent in perfect silence toward the enemy island. Approaching within fifty yards of the shore, it halted, and a solemn voice from within the tower cried out, "Speak! What will you do? Will you make peace with Mtesa, or shall we blow up the island? Be quick and answer."

The Wavuma were not long in making up their minds; they submitted to an unconditional surrender. The war was over.

Besides ending the war with the Wavuma, Stanley had also gained a personal triumph with Mtesa. By the end of the campaign the kabaka and his court were completely converted to Christianity.

But Stanley was anxious to get on with his work. When Mtesa returned to his capital, Stanley reminded him of his promise to supply him with an escort for the exploration of the lake known as Muta Nzige, which Stanley believed was Lake Albert. Mtesa kept his promise, giving him an army of over two thousand Waganda warriors. On New Year's Day, 1876, the exploring army set out for the lake. They did come close to what is now known as Lake Edward, but the Waganda warriors proved so untrustworthy and cowardly and the natives of the region around the lake were so numerous and hostile that they were forced to retreat to the Victoria Nyanza.

Here Stanley parted with his Waganda escort, who returned to Uganda—taking one hundred and eighty pounds of Stanley's beads with them. The expedition now turned south until, on March 27, they arrived at Ujiji, where Stanley had found Livingstone nearly five years before. Leaving Frank Pocock and the bulk of the expedition here, Stanley set sail in the *Lady Alice* for a trip around Lake Tanganyika. He completed the circumnavigation of the lake in fifty-one days, proving that it was the longest fresh-water lake in the world. Although the voyagers encountered several bad storms, they had little difficulty with the natives and all returned to Ujiji safe and healthy.

Stanley had now been in Africa for two years, and he had accomplished two of his geographical objectives: the exploration of both the Victoria Nyanza and Lake Tanganyika. These lakes, which had hitherto been indicated on maps of Africa with blue blobs, could now be fairly accurately drawn and placed with certainty.

One last project remained for him if he was to complete the work of Livingstone, and this was the greatest and most formidable task of all. He had yet to learn if the Lualaba River, whose course Livingstone had traced for thirteen hundred miles, was the Nile, the Niger, or the Congo. Livingstone had believed that it was the Nile, and had sacrificed his life in trying to prove it. He had also known that it might well be the Congo, but he had resisted the idea. In his journal he once wrote: "I am oppressed with the apprehension that after all it may turn out that I have been following the Congo; and who would risk being put into a cannibal pot and converted into a black man for it?"

Stanley now prepared to take his expedition to the town of Nyangwe, where Livingstone had turned back, and start this last great project from there. He was plagued, however, by the same problem that had so hampered Livingstone: desertions. When his men learned where they were going, many of them took the opportunity to slip away before they left Ujiji. Stanley was finally forced to take some of his less trustworthy men under armed guard. Once started, the trip to Nyangwe was without serious incident and the expedition arrived there on October 27, 1876.

# CHAPTER VIII

# *Down the Long River*

NYANGWE, almost in the exact center of the continent, was the westernmost locality inhabited by the Arab traders from Zanzibar. Standing on the east bank of the broad, mysterious Lualaba River, it was to the Arabs what the horizon was to early sailors. Beyond the river, superstition taught and experience had proved that it was unsafe to travel. To the north the Lualaba was cannibal country for as far as any man knew. To enter this region was suicide. So convincing were the horror-filled tales of those who had ventured even a few miles up this river, that such intrepid explorers as Livingstone and Lovett Cameron had turned back.

There was a fascination about this north-flowing river. The section of it that was known was so broad and swift that geographers, cartographers, and explorers were convinced that somewhere it must empty into the sea, but its course, its tributaries, and its destination were unknown. Was it a part of the Congo, the Niger, or the Nile?

Livingstone had been strongly attracted by the Lualaba and its riddle, but he had been unable to go beyond Nyangwe.

Lieutenant Cameron, with an expedition boasting forty-five Snider rifles, felt his force not strong enough to fight the savages that lined the river banks. He had not dared to go beyond Nyangwe. Certainly it would not have been a disgrace if Stanley, too, had turned back here. He had already accomplished much, and he could have circled south, taken his expedition through more easily explorable country, and ended up at Zanzibar. In fact, there was every reason for not attempting the exploration of the river. His men were demoralized by the very thought of such an undertaking, his force was believed too small to repel the attacks of the fierce river tribes, and he did not have, nor was he able to purchase, a single canoe to supplement the *Lady Alice.*

Lack of canoes presented Stanley with perhaps his biggest problem. Native canoes were made from a single large log, laboriously hollowed out and shaped by hand. It took many days of work for skilled hands and primitive tools to make one of them. To the African living by lakes or rivers, the dugouts were invaluable, and, once made, the owners were reluctant to part with them. The idea of attempting to explore a river without the aid of boats might seem foolhardy, but Stanley was determined to conquer the Lualaba. He had his own reasons. First of all, he wanted to follow the river because this was what Livingstone had wanted to do, and Stanley wanted to complete his work. But there was a more personal reason as well. At Brighton, he had been laughed at for defending Livingstone's contention that the Lualaba was the Nile. Now he wanted to prove to the world that he and Livingstone had been right, to have the last laugh on the "armchair geographers." When the expedition was over and the Lualaba proved to be the Congo, Stanley refused to admit that he had believed the river to be the Nile, but in a letter to Marston written September 23, 1874 —two days after his arrival in Zanzibar—he wrote: "Continue sending my letters to Zanzibar until the end of May, 1875, then cease until you hear from me again, which will probably be *via the Nile.*"

Stanley had kept his plans to himself, not even discussing them with Frank Pocock, his last remaining white companion. Now, however, he discussed the pros and cons of their future with young Pocock. Should they tackle the river or should they circle south through Katanga? Frank, unaware that his chief had long ago made up his mind, suggested that they toss a coin to decide their fate. Stanley agreed, handing Frank a rupee. The best two out of three was to decide the matter. Heads for the north and the Lualaba; tails for the south. The coin landed tails up, not once or twice, but six straight times. Disregarding the rupee, they drew straws—short straws for the south and long straws for the Lualaba. Again fate gave them their warning; they drew only short straws. Setting aside both rupee and straws, Stanley said, "It's no use, Frank. We'll face our destiny, despite the rupee and the straws. With your help, I'll follow the river."

The decision sealed the fate of Frank Pocock. He was never to reach the sea.

Stanley knew that to explore the Lualaba he would have to supplement his expedition with a force strong enough to give him some chance of succeeding. To obtain this force, he had to deal with Hamid bin Mohammed, commonly called Tippu-Tib, a man who was rapidly becoming the greatest slave trader the world has ever known. This man possessed the only organized force, and was thus the greatest power, in the area.

Tippu-Tib was born on Zanzibar of a well-to-do Arab family about 1832. His grandmother on his father's side was a Negro, and Tippu-Tib retained her Negroid features. The son of an ivory and slave trader, it was only natural that he should become one himself. He started while a very young man—he was probably still in his teens—and his audacity, combined with extraordinary luck, made his first expeditions extremely profitable. Instead of following in the tracks of the other Arab traders, he struck out into new country and developed new techniques. For the most part, the Zanzibar Arabs had contented themselves with "legitimate" trading; that is, they would exchange beads, wire, cloth, and other goods brought from the coast for the ivory and slaves of the inland tribes. This was the method Tippu-Tib intended to use when he entered the country west of Lake Tanganyika, but circumstances led him to the discovery of a more profitable system.

Coming to a large village where the inhabitants appeared to be friendly, Tippu-Tib and his men accepted their invitation to enter the town. Fortunately for them, they took the precaution of concealing their muskets under their robes. Once inside, the savages, thinking them defenseless, fell on them with their spears and arrows. But when Tippu-Tib and his men started shooting them down with their muskets, the natives, unfamiliar with firearms, fled in terror. Inside the huts, Tippu-Tib found a fortune in ivory. Rounding up the disorganized natives, he shackled them with chains and forced them to carry their own ivory back to Zanzibar where both prisoners and ivory were sold. This low-overhead method of obtaining slaves and ivory in exchange for a few musket balls and gunpowder soon became Tippu-Tib's standard operating procedure. He had learned that "in Africa the gun is king."

On subsequent expeditions, Tippu-Tib would enter a new country, make friends with one tribe and then, as every tribe was always feuding with its neighbors, offer to help with the wars. Supported by one tribe he would subdue the surrounding tribes and take his share of the slaves and ivory. Then he would turn about and destroy the tribe he had been "helping." It seemed a wonderful system for a slaver!

Although these early successes made him rich, Tippu-Tib, like many a successful businessman, plowed his profits back into the business—in this case, guns and ammunition. A few years before meeting Stanley, the wily Arab had made his greatest coup of all—but this time without firing a shot. According to his own account—and there is no one to dispute the story—Tippu-Tib came to rule over, or at least to gain control of, a large district known as Manyuema through an almost incredibly simple trick. He had heard of a country on the Lualaba River known as Uterera, where, it was said, there was a fabulous amount of ivory. From a renegade native Mterera, Tippu-Tib managed to learn a great many intimate details about the tribe, including the interesting story of the daughter of the chief who long ago had been carried off by a neighboring tribe and had not been heard of since. When Tippu-Tib reached Uterera, he was able to astound the Waterera by his knowledge of local customs, tribal secrets, and the genealogy of their chiefs. He told them that he was the son of the chief's captured daughter, and thus the grandson of the present chief, Kasongo, now living in a village of the same name. If Tippu-Tib is to be believed, Kasongo, an old man, immediately resigned as chief and turned the country over to his "grandson." Tippu-Tib lost little time in rounding up the available ivory: 200 tusks weighing 374½ *frasilas* (a frasila is about 35 pounds). Later he milked the country for a good deal more, using the men, many of whom were cannibals, as his henchmen when he raided the surrounding tribes for more slaves and ivory.

At their first meeting at Nyangwe, Stanley saw immediately that he was dealing with no ordinary Arab. In the heart of primitive Africa Tippu-Tib dressed like a wealthy Arab on the streets of Zanzibar: his clothes were spotlessly white, a new fez was on his head, and his dagger was splendid with filigree. Stanley described him as a "tall, black-bearded man, of Negroid complexion, in the prime of life, straight and quick in his movements, a picture of energy and strength. He had a fine intelligent face, with a nervous twitching of the eyes, and gleaming white and perfectly formed teeth." But apart from his appearance, his manner and his intellect marked him as the most remarkable non-European Stanley had met in Africa.

Tippu-Tib had power and wealth in a land where little else was respected. He was shrewd and he was unscrupulous, but he was also brave. In the pursuit of ivory and slaves he was completely ruthless and cruel; in the course of his business he and his slave raiders killed thousands of men, women, and children and sold additional thousands into slavery. Yet, one of his daughters-in-law, still living today in

Zanzibar, recently spoke of him as "the kindest man who ever lived."

This strange man had an unusual trait for one of his character and occupation: he liked white men. He had helped Livingstone and he had helped Cameron; now he was anxious to help Stanley—within reason. But Stanley's request for an escort down the Lualaba did not seem reasonable to Tippu-Tib. When even the prospect of ivory and slaves could not tempt him to venture into the unknown land to the north, why should he risk his skin for the sake of a white man who said he only wanted to see where the river went? The Arab did not understand white men who ignored ivory and slaves to follow rivers and look at mountains, but white men fascinated him; he wanted to help. Stanley was the most persistent white man Tippu-Tib had ever met, and his determination to make this trip intrigued him. At last, after a good deal of discussion, he agreed to accompany Stanley for sixty marches down the river for the sum of five thousand dollars.

The presence of Tippu-Tib and more than seven hundred of his followers gave assurance and confidence to Stanley's people, who otherwise would have mutinied rather than go a single mile down the dreaded river. On November 5, 1876, Stanley marched out of Nyangwe at the head of an array of nearly a thousand men, women, and children. On their backs were provisions and stores of all sorts, and the *Lady Alice* carried in sections.

On the first day the country was open and the marching was easy, but on the second day they entered the gloomy forest of Mitamba. Here they had to hack their way through thick, matted jungle that made each step painful. In their first week of marching they covered only forty miles. And, although they did not know it, scarcely one mile was in the direction of their ultimate destination—the Atlantic Ocean to the west. Stanley excepted, the entire expedition was discouraged. Even Tippu-Tib was appalled by the savage nature of the country and resolution oozed out of him. He begged to be released from his contract. It took two hours of cajoling before Stanley was able to persuade him to continue for at least twenty marches more.

The terrain became even more difficult. The jungle was now so thick that it shut out not only every ray of the sun, but also every moving particle of air; each breath became a gasp as they wormed their way forward.

At first, Stanley had carried the *Lady Alice* overland with him because he did not want to be separated from the main body of his expedition. But the boat was difficult to carry through the pathless jungle and on the nineteenth of November he launched it on the Lualaba. Uledi, the young Zanzibari who had distinguished himself when the canoes were sinking on the Victoria Nyanza, was appointed coxswain. The expedition was now divided into two unequal parts: Stanley with the crew of the *Lady Alice* went on the river, while Tippu-Tib and the bulk of the expedition continued to travel on land.

In the beginning they saw no signs of the natives who had such a reputation for ferocity. Village after village was passed, but they were all deserted—the inhabitants had fled at the first sight of such a large caravan. The empty villages, however, spoke eloquently of the depraved nature of their occupants. Rows of skulls lined the streets, and well-gnawed human bones littered the huts and yards. In fleeing, the natives had left all of their belongings behind them, but Stanley ordered that nothing be touched, hoping that word of his forbearance would be communicated to the tribes ahead and that they would come to realize that his mission was a peaceful one.

Rowing down the river, they occasionally caught sight of a black man peering at them from the bushes. Frequently they heard peculiar war cries coming from the jungle—cries that sounded like "Ooh-hu-hu." On November 23, Stanley and the boat crew reached the point where the Ruiki River empties into the Congo. As the Ruiki was about a hundred yards wide, Stanley knew that the land party would have to be ferried across when it reached this point. Landing, he built a strong camp near the mouth of the tributary and waited for the land party to join them. Night fell, but there was still no sign of Tippu-Tib.

The next day Stanley left a few men to guard their *boma* while he took the remainder and rowed up the Ruiki, thinking he might find his land party camped farther upstream. Returning in the afternoon without having found the rest of the expedition, he heard shots mingled with cries of "Ooh-hu-hu" as he approached his camp. He ordered his men to row at full speed. Rounding a bend, he saw the mouth of the Ruiki blocked by war canoes filled with savages. They were attacking his camp with spears and arrows, while its few defenders were replying with musket and rifle fire.

With loud shouts, Stanley and the crew of the *Lady Alice* bore down upon the attackers, firing as they came. Seeing the white man, the savages turned their canoes about and fled, still chanting their harmonious and strange war cry of "Ooh-hu-hu." The result of the expedition's first fight on the Congo was one dead native lying face downward in the mud of the river bank.

The following day Tippu-Tib and the land party came up, and the expedition continued to struggle forward. Other battles followed in the days ahead, but now the greatest danger was from disease. Smallpox broke out among them, and from the eighth to the eighteenth of December they lowered twelve corpses into the Congo. The dead were not buried on land for fear the cannibals would dig up the bodies and eat them.

Fortunately, they came upon six broken, old, and abandoned canoes (one of them Stanley estimated to be a hundred years old). They were repaired and used to transport the sick and wounded. The water-borne part of the expedition now became a badly matched combination: reconnaissance unit and floating hospital. It was not just a matter of coasting down a calm and placid river; often the water became treacherous. A few days after they acquired the canoes, one of them overturned in a stretch of rapids. Although no lives were lost, four of the precious Snider rifles sank in the Congo.

In spite of difficulties on river and on land, sickness, and the hostility of the natives, the expedition pushed on, the monotony of their efforts relieved only by the frequent accidents, native attacks, and the splashes of weighted corpses sinking in the Congo. It was demoralizing, it was exhausting, and to all but Stanley their toils seemed pointless and impossible. Again and again Tippu-Tib urged him to turn back before it was too late, but Stanley remained obdurate.

On December 18 the expedition entered a region called Vinya-Njara. Steering his little flotilla close to shore, Stanley was searching the dense green jungle for a suitable campsite when he heard a sudden scream of pain. Turning around, he saw a guard in one of the hospital canoes falling, an arrow fixed in his chest. Now all the rowers, strengthened by fear, pulled hard on their oars, and the canoes moved quickly downstream out of danger. Locating a small clearing, the men landed. They immediately began the construction of a brushwood barricade while scouts were sent out to delay the approach of the enemy. In an hour they had completed their defenses, and the scouts were recalled.

It was only a few minutes before the savages were upon them. Beaten off, they came back again and again, launching their spears with great force into the camp. At times they came so close in their wild charges that the muzzles of the expedition's muskets were almost pressing against their chests. Only forty men were well enough to man the barricades; the sick and wounded crouched fearfully in the boats. The yells of the attackers, the booming of their war horns, the crack of the rifles and muskets of the expedition, mingled with the screams of the women and children, created an unnerving din. All were badly frightened; some tried to run away, but they were kept at their posts by the clubbed muskets of Uledi and Frank Pocock. For two hours they fought desperately for their lives. Then, just at dusk, the savages called a retreat.

They did not go far, however, and the sounds of their ivory war horns could be heard echoing through the jungle and over the river. Arrows, their tips soaked in poison, continued to drop into the camp and stick quivering in the earth. Under such circumstances, sleep seemed out of the question; yet, many were so exhausted from the physical and emotional strain of rowing and fighting that they dozed. To keep his men alert it was necessary for Stanley to detail Frank and two of the chiefs to fill pots of cold water from the river and to circulate among the Zanzibaris, dousing the head of any man who tried to sleep.

Toward midnight, Stanley detected a dark form stealthily creeping on all fours toward their little stockade. Silently crawling over to Uledi, he told him to take two men and attempt to capture the savage. Stanley watched while Uledi wriggled through an opening in the fence and cautiously circled toward the unsuspecting native. Suddenly, Uledi pounced on the dark form and called out for assistance. The other two Zanzibaris sprang to his aid, but quick rustling in the foliage warned that the savage's friends were coming to his relief. The expedition's rifles and muskets fired a fusillade into the bushes while Uledi and his men brought in their prisoner. Arrows fell in showers now as the natives attempted to retaliate. After a brisk but short exchange, there was again quiet except for the occasional whizz of an arrow.

Dawn found the defenders still staring at the dark jungle from behind their barricade. The greatest sufferers were the sick, who had been forced to spend this night of terror in the open canoes; three of them died of smallpox during the night. It was obvious that they could not stay in their present position indefinitely. They all needed food and the sick and wounded needed rest and attention. Even if they were able to by-pass these people, Tippu-Tib with the land party would certainly be ambushed.

After a breakfast of roasted bananas cooked in the shelter of the river bank, Stanley set out in the *Lady Alice* for a reconnaissance. Only a quarter of a mile down the river from his camp he found a large town, consisting of a series of villages in a uniform line along the river bank.

Unquestionably, these were the homes of the natives who were attacking him. He decided to capture the nearest village.

Returning to camp, he quickly loaded his people into the boats and
pushed off. On the river they ran a gantlet of arrows, but no one was
hit. They rowed swiftly, and soon they were opposite the first village.
Landing, Stanley led his fighting force up the steep banks and into the
town—it was deserted. The village consisted of a single street, three
hundred yards long, with huts pressed one against the other so that
the backs of the huts formed a solid wall on two sides. By cutting down
trees to block up each end, the expedition made the village easily
defensible.

The sick (there were now seventy-two of them, over half of whom
had smallpox) were taken out of the canoes and hustled into the village
where they were allotted quarters in the huts. Stanley quickly posted
his men at tactical locations throughout the town and sent three or
four sharpshooters up the tall trees along the river where they could
shoot down on any of the enemy who might try to hide in the tall
grass around the village. No sooner had they finished these precautions
than the natives launched a wild, determined attack. The battle lasted
until noon, when Stanley took twenty-five men and made a sally. He
succeeded in clearing the skirts of the village, and they were free from
attack for the rest of the day. During this encounter, Uledi caught
another prisoner.

Stanley now set about strengthening his fortifications and clearing
his field of fire. First, he sent out scouts, fanning them in a crescent
around the end of the village. Then the rest of his men set to work
cutting down the weeds and tall grass in a hundred-yard-wide semi-
circle; the same thing was then done for the opposite end of the village.
This would give them a clear field and effectually prevent any native
from approaching unseen. After a scant lunch of bananas, Stanley
directed the construction of marksmen's nests, fifteen feet high and
capable of holding ten men, at each end of the street. By the end of
the day, they had made a snug fort out of the village.

That night, all was calm—except for the patter of arrows on the
roofs of the huts. The next morning, however, the enemy suddenly
came running out of the jungle into the clearing. But the fortifications
surprised them, and they quickly retreated into the foliage. Although
invisible, the savages could be heard blowing their war horns and
shouting excitedly.

About noon, a large flotilla of canoes was seen coming up the river along the opposite shore. Stanley estimated that there were between five and eight hundred men packed in the dugouts. Paddling about a half-mile upstream, the enemy turned, formed line, and came down the river with a rush toward the village, shouting and blowing their war horns. At the same moment, a mass of arrows flew into the village from the jungle. It was a well-planned, concerted land and river attack. Finding that the men in the marksmen's nests could handle the situation on the land side, Stanley took twenty men and ran down to defend the river banks.

Crouching in the bushes along the water line waiting for the enemy, Stanley looked over the taut, ready expressions on the faces of his Zanzibaris. They were seasoning rapidly, he thought with satisfaction. Every man knew now that he must fight or resign himself to be thrown, a headless corpse, into the river. They had been living a precarious existence, but their continued success in overcoming the obstacles they had encountered had given them confidence in their own superiority. Their ingenuity, courage, and stamina had not diminished in the face of death or in the continuing presence of fear.

The savages were soon upon them, and in spite of the superiority of their guns, Stanley and his men might well have been overcome through the sheer weight of the numbers ranged against them had not Tippu-Tib and the advance column of the land division made their appearance. The natives in the jungle signaled to those in the canoes; the arrows ceased to fall and the savages on the water, screaming their rage, retreated behind an island in the middle of the river.

Tippu-Tib and his people had frightened off the natives more by their numbers than by their vigor, for they were in a wretched state. Living on poor food—and little of that for the past three days—they were exhausted from their efforts to cut their way through the dense, matted jungle where they had frequently lost their way. They would have to rest before they could go on, and the only place to stop was in Stanley's fortified village. This meant a continuation of the war with the natives of Vinya-Njara. The expedition's casualties already totaled four men killed and thirteen wounded in the fighting with this determined tribe. They were too numerous to defeat by force, and they had courage in abundance. If they were to be defeated it would have to be through some stratagem—and Stanley had a plan.

The natives on the river had last been seen going behind the island in the middle of the stream. They had probably camped there for the night, intending to renew their attacks tomorrow. If he could slip behind the island under the cover of night and steal their canoes, he would score a major victory. They would, he reasoned, consider the loss of their precious dugouts a more serious defeat than the loss of any battle, regardless of their casualties. To those who lived on the banks of the Congo, good stout canoes were more valuable than human life. Besides, he could use the canoes himself.

He outlined his plan to Frank Pocock and a select detail of men. They made their preparations, and that night about ten o'clock, Stanley with the crew of the *Lady Alice* and Frank with crews for four of the small canoes stole out on the river with muffled oars. Fortunately for their enterprise, it was a rainy, gusty night and quite dark. Cautiously, they approached the island. Pocock took up his position at the lower end, spreading his canoes across the mouth of the channel between the island and the opposite bank. Stanley in the *Lady Alice* crept silently along the far shore of the river until he was opposite the upper end of the island. Then he whispered his orders to Uledi, who steered the boat across to within a few yards of the island. Resting on their oars, they drifted down the dark stream, carefully watching the shore.

This was a bold venture, for if they were detected now they would stand little chance of escaping. Trapped in the narrow channel, their silhouettes could be seen by the natives on shore while the men in the boat would not be able to see them. Should the natives find them and take to their canoes, they could quickly cut off the *Lady Alice* and overwhelm her tiny crew. A single guard, a solitary native made wakeful and restless by the rain and looking out over the river, would doom them all. But the dark island showed no signs of any human being; there were only the usual jungle noises mingled with the sounds of the wind and the rain in the vegetation.

Suddenly, Stanley saw a light—a camp fire! He signaled to his men to row cautiously toward it. As they drew near, he saw the dark shapes of eight long canoes. He eased the *Lady Alice* right up under the high banks, and he and Uledi slipped out. Crouching on the shore and hidden by the shadows of the trees, only a few feet separated them from the natives, dozing by their fires, their weapons handy. Carefully, they crept along the slippery shore line. The canoes were secured to the banks by rattan ropes fastened to stakes driven into the clay banks. At first, they tried to pull out the stakes, but they were buried too deeply. Using their knives, they were forced to saw through the tough rattan. As soon as the ropes were cut they seized the canoes and pushed them far out into the channel. The two men watched for a moment to see them caught by the swift current, to be carried down to where Frank and his crew were waiting to catch them. Then Stanley and Uledi climbed back on board the *Lady Alice*.

Again the oars silently pulled at the water and they glided along the shore, watching for more canoes. In a few minutes they spotted another camp fire, and again Stanley and Uledi slipped ashore. There were only four canoes here, but their rattan ropes were cut and they were pushed into the river. Still farther down the channel they came upon the largest camp of all with twenty-six canoes tied up along the river bank. Numerous fires were burning in the enemy camp and, as they slid along under the high banks, they could hear the murmur of voices and the coughing of the naked natives as they shivered by their fires. One by one, the canoes were cut loose and set adrift, each with its paddles and bailing scoops. It was a tremendous haul.

When the *Lady Alice* reached the lower end of the island, Stanley found Frank and his men struggling to control the thirty-eight canoes, some of them fifty feet long, that had been sent down to them. They were fighting a losing battle against the current that was carrying them downstream. Stanley relieved them of twelve of the canoes and strung them behind the *Lady Alice*. With the aid of the sail to help the rowers, they were able to tow their captured prizes back to their fortified village and turn them over to the men in camp. Racing back, he found that Frank was barely holding his own against the current. When Stanley relieved him of another batch of canoes, they were able to keep together and bring the rest of them back to their village. By five o'clock in the morning they were all safely in camp, tired but exuberant over the success of their mission.

Shortly after sunrise, cries of rage could be heard from the savages who had been deprived of their most cherished possessions. Where the slaughter from the expedition's rifles and muskets had failed to discourage the natives of Vinya-Njara, the loss of their canoes effectively extinguished all their desire for further combat. They readily accepted Stanley's offer to hold a shauri, and two hours later peace terms were arranged. Stanley returned fifteen of their canoes, and paid them what he considered a fair price for the ones he kept. He also released the prisoners Uledi had captured.

Although they were safe for the time being, the swelling sick list, the high death rate from smallpox, the constant attacks of the natives, and the daily struggles to move through the dense jungle had completely exhausted the strength and drained the will of Tippu-Tib and his followers; the Arab told Stanley that he would go no farther. Seeing that he was determined and that nothing he could say would change his mind, Stanley decided to let him go, although he was still bound by his agreement to make eight marches more. Actually, now that he had the twenty-three Vinya-Njara canoes, Stanley no longer felt that he needed Tippu-Tib. He had enough boats to put all of his people on the water, and Tippu-Tib, when he left, could take back with him the numerous sick and wounded.

Stanley's principal concern was the psychological effect Tippu-Tib's impending departure would make on his own people. To encourage his men to go on with him, he made them an impassioned speech:

"Into whichever sea this great river empties, there shall we follow it. You have seen that I have saved you a score of times when everything looked black and dismal for us. That care of you to which you owe your safety hitherto, I shall maintain until I see you safe and sound in your own homes and under your own palm trees. All I ask of you is perfect trust in whatever I say. On your lives depends my own; if I risk yours, I risk mine. As a father looks after his children, I will look after you. It is true that we are not as strong as when the Wanyaturu attacked us, or when we marched through Unyoro to Muta Nzige, but we are of the same band of men, and we are still of the same spirit. Many of our party have already died, but death is the end of all; and if they died earlier than we, it was the will of God, and who shall rebel against His will? It may be we shall meet a hundred wild tribes yet who, for the sake of eating us, will rush to meet and fight us. We have no wish to molest them. We have moneys with us, and are, therefore, not poor. If they fight us, we must accept it as an evil, like disease, which we cannot help. We shall continue to do our utmost to make friends, and the river is wide and deep. If we fight, we fight for our lives. It may be that we shall be distressed by famine and want. It may be that we shall meet with many more cataracts, or find ourselves before a great lake, whose wild waves we cannot cross with these canoes; but we are not children, we have heads and arms and are we not always under the eye of God, who will do with us as He sees fit? Therefore, my children, make up your minds as I have made up mine, that as we are now in the very middle of this continent, and it would be just as bad to return as to go on, that we shall continue our journey, that we shall toil on and on, by this great river and no other, to the salt sea!"

In such a way, Ulysses must have spoken to his Greeks in the middle of their homeward voyage. When Stanley had finished, the Zanzibaris cheered. Manwa Sera jumped up and added his sentiments to those of his chief. The brave and faithful Uledi stood up too and, speaking for the crew of the *Lady Alice,* said that even if the others would not go with them they would take Stanley and Pocock down the river. Stanley thanked them all and declared a three-day holiday with feasting, dancing, and canoe races. This was Christmas Day, 1876.

During this holiday, Stanley and the Zanzibaris gave names to all of their captured canoes. Stanley gave such names as *Livingstone, Herald,* and *Telegraph* while the Zanzibaris chose *Mtesa, Shark,* and *Mirambo.* The greatest event, however, was a foot race run by Tippu-Tib and Frank Pocock. The Arab took the race seriously, even practicing beforehand. The course was three hundred yards, from one end of the village to the other. Tippu-Tib, although older, won easily, beating the young Englishman by a good fifteen yards, and winning the silver goblet and cup Stanley had offered to the winner.

On December 27, Stanley separated his people from Tippu-Tib's and moved them to a new camp on an island. When they arrived, Stanley was pleased to find that not a single person had attempted to desert. No stronger proof of Stanley's influence over his followers could be given than their willingness to follow him still farther down this inhospitable river. They dreaded the dangers and hardships that awaited them, yet they went on. The day they left Tippu-Tib at Vinya-Njara and started their journey alone, nearly every man was sobbing as he rowed.

Stanley tried to encourage them: "Sons of Zanzibar, lift up your heads and be men. What is there to fear? Here we are all together, like one family with hearts united, all strong with the purpose to reach our home. See this river, it is the road to Zanzibar! When saw you a road so wide? Strike your paddles deep, and cry 'Bismillah,' and let us go forward."

But the Zanzibaris responded with wan smiles; he could not erase their gloom. They would follow him, but they could not be happy. They knew that they had a great deal to fear, and that the road to Zanzibar their leader pointed out to them was a long road indeed. Without knowing where they were going or why, they dipped their oars, bent their backs, and rowed.

Down the river they went, day after day, the sounds of drums and war horns in their ears. Almost daily now they were attacked by swarms of savages. They poured out of their villages and filled their canoes with eager young warriors, their bodies painted and grotesquely adorned with feathers and the skins of wild animals. "Meat! Meat!" they screamed as they massed for the attack. To the cannibals, Stanley's expedition must have seemed like a herd of ownerless cattle straying among them. Stanley was dismayed by the instant hatred he and his men seemed to inspire. These people did not know him; they did not want to know him. He was only a stranger, and they proposed to eat him.

Stanley was fascinated by these men who seemed the living embodiment of the spirit of hatred: "There was a fat-bodied wretch in a canoe, whom I allowed to crawl within spear-throw of me; who, while he swayed the spear with a vigour far from assuring to one who stood within reach of it, leered with such a clever hideousness of feature that I felt, if only within arm's length of him, I could have bestowed upon him a hearty thump on the back, and cried out applaudingly, 'Bravo, old boy! You do it capitally!'

"Yet not being able to reach him, I was rapidly being fascinated by him. The rapid movements of the swaying spear, the steady wide-mouthed grin, the big square teeth, the head poised on one side with the confident pose of a practiced spear-thrower, the short brow and square face, hair short and thick. Shall I ever forget him? It appeared to me as if the spear partook of the same cruel inexorable look as the grinning savage. Finally, I saw him draw his right arm back, and his body incline backwards, with still that same grin on his face, and I felt myself begin to count, one, two, three, four—and *whizz!* The spear flew over my back, and hissed as it pierced the water. The spell was broken." Stanley shot him.

The expedition's firearms (consisting of forty-eight rifles and muskets) always got the better of the spear-throwing natives, although there were frequent casualties. To protect the rowers, Stanley ordered his men to collect and save all of the captured or abandoned shields after every battle. These were used to bulwark the canoes, making them look like the galleys of the ancient Vikings. By this time, there was no longer a distinction between pagazi and askari—almost every man was both a rower and a soldier. Those without guns armed themselves with captured spears, which they threw back at the next hostile tribe they encountered.

One day, about two o'clock in the afternoon, they were attacked from both sides of the river simultaneously. The natives had apparently been expecting them, for they were in full war paint, half of their bodies being painted white and the other half red with broad black stripes. They paddled to the attack in the largest canoes Stanley had ever seen; one of them, with a bas-relief crocodile carved on its side, was over eighty-five feet long. This great canoe made the mistake of singling out the *Lady Alice* for its victim. Stanley bade his men to hold their fire until the canoe was only about fifty feet away, then he gave the order that sent a murderous volley into the gaudily painted crew. Unable to turn their large craft soon enough, the survivors jumped overboard and swam for shore, leaving the giant canoe in the hands of the expedition. This prize was promptly named the *Crocodile* by the delighted Zanzibaris.

Although they had lost their largest canoe and had been beaten off, the savages were far from finished. Retreating downriver, they alarmed the other tribes on both sides. The river narrowed here, and the expedition rowed between banks filled with savages, pounding their drums, screaming their wild cries, and blowing their ivory horns. Suddenly, above the din created by the natives, they heard the ominous roar of a cataract just ahead of them. The choice before them now was a bitter one: would they prefer to be drowned in a cataract or have their throats slit by cannibals?

From the roar, the cataract sounded like certain death; but they had overcome native warriors before. Stanley quickly decided to fight. Dropping anchor within fighting distance of the right bank, they began to fire. After fifteen minutes of combat, Stanley saw that it would be impossible to land here. Retreating into the middle of the river, they rowed upstream a little way and then divided their forces for an attack on the left bank. Manwa Sera took four canoes and slid downstream while Stanley led the rest of the expedition in a skirmish with the natives on the shore. When all attention was directed toward Stanley and the bulk of the expedition, Manwa Sera and his men made a landing downriver and started a land attack on the enemy's flank. As soon as Stanley heard the shots on shore, he dashed in for a landing under a shower of arrows and spears. The strategy was successful, and they established a beachhead, although they had to fight from tree to tree until sunset.

The expedition worked until ten o'clock that night building a boma or stockade of brushwood. Then, without food or fires, they lay down to sleep. They were up at four o'clock in the morning preparing for the hard and dangerous day that lay ahead of them. The battle got under way about ten o'clock and continued without pause until three in the afternoon. The savages were beaten off, leaving the expedition with casualties of two killed and ten wounded.

The next day, Stanley set out to reconnoiter the cataract. Although he could not know it, this was the first of a series. There were seven of them stretching along fifty miles of the river; it was to take them nearly a month to get past them. (The seven cataracts are today called Stanley Falls.) The portage around the first cataract took seventy-two hours of hard labor and constant fighting, and it set the pattern for the others. Exhausted from the strain of pulling and pushing the heavy canoes and fighting off the hostile natives, the expedition at last launched its boats on the river again—only to find another cataract just two miles ahead.

Meanwhile, war horns and drums on both sides of the river and on the islands told them that they were completely surrounded by hostile tribes. It was almost dark now and they could not escape. Reasoning that the islanders would be less numerous than the mainland tribes, Stanley rushed his canoes toward a large island in the middle of the river about five hundred feet above the beginning of the waterfall. Driving their canoes straight for the bank, they quickly landed and threw up a slight brushwood fence to protect their camp, while the islanders fled to their howling friends on the left bank of the river.

In a small village near their boma they found an old woman of about sixty-five who, because of a large ulcer on her foot, had been unable to escape. She was carried into camp and treated kindly. Stanley tried to talk to her, but he could make out very little of what she said. He did learn that the island was called Cheandoah and belonged to the Baswa tribe and that the tribe on the left bank were the Bakumu.

The next day, Stanley explored the island and tried to determine the best way to get his expedition around the falls and through the savages. He concluded there was no easy way out, and they would have to fight their way through the combined Baswa and Bakumu. Early the following morning, the expedition embarked, made their way up the river about a mile, and then attempted to land. The enemy awaited them. After a stubborn fight the savages were driven from the banks and the expedition landed. Leaving Frank with four muskets and sixty axes, Stanley led thirty-six men in a determined attack on the Baswa and Bakumu, and drove them backward into the Bakumu villages. The natives had piled up heaps of brushwood and cut down trees to protect their villages, but Stanley outflanked them and forced an entrance.

The huts were fired and the Bakumu and Baswa were dispersed. The battle was over; they returned to their camp, where Frank had succeeded in building a strong stockade.

The expedition was now divided into two parts: one group to work at night and the other during the day. A picked body of men with axes and guns blazed a trail three miles long through the jungle along the river bank and around the waterfall. Dried palm branches and bundles of cane smeared with gum frankincense were brought from the village and tied to trees along the path to light up the jungle for the night workers. Bomas were established at intervals, and as soon as the path was made and a new camp constructed, the canoes, baggage, women, children, sick, and wounded were carried to the new site. The Bakumu and Baswa continued to harass them, but after seventy-eight hours of exhausting, nerve-tearing work, the portage was made, and they once more launched their canoes on the river.

Below the second cataract there was a two-mile stretch of rapids leading to the third cataract. In spite of the danger, Stanley decided to float the heavy canoes through the rapids; the baggage and most of the expedition were taken overland. The crew of the *Lady Alice,* being the best boatmen, began the dangerous task of working the canoes down the river in the swift current. Six canoes were safely taken downstream to the camp near the edge of the falls. The seventh canoe, manned by Zaidi and two other men, wobbled dangerously in the rushing water, then upset. Zaidi clung to the canoe, but the other two men swam toward an island, where they were saved by Uledi and Manwa Sera in the eighth canoe. Zaidi swept on downstream with the overturned canoe.

Just at the brink of the falls, in the middle of the stream, the canoe struck a narrow, pointed rock and split. Half of it was swept over the falls and dashed to pieces; the other half wedged itself against the rock. It was to this half that Zaidi clung. Lifting himself onto the rock, he perched there, wet and forlorn, shivering in the rain, while those on shore who had witnessed the catastrophe hurriedly summoned Stanley. Quickly, Stanley took in the situation and sent his men scurrying into the jungle to collect rattans for a cable. When this was completed, the rope was tied to a small canoe and cautiously lowered downstream. But before it could reach the unfortunate Zaidi, the rope suddenly snapped and the canoe darted past him. Over the falls it went, became engulfed in the waves, split, and was pounded to splinters in a matter of seconds.

Although Zaidi was only fifty feet from the shore, the roar of the cataract drowned out all the words of encouragement and advice shouted at him. He sat silent and unmoving, anxiously watching the futile efforts of those on shore to save him. They tried to toss him poles tied to creepers, but they could not reach him. It seemed that Zaidi's doom, although protracted, was certain.

But Stanley devised another plan. Taking a second canoe, he had his men make three ropes, each ninety yards long, out of one-inch rattans twisted together and strengthened by all of the tent ropes. One cable was fastened to the bow, another to the stern, and the third to the side of the canoe. These were to be held by men on the shore. A shorter cable, thirty yards long, was tied to the stern for Zaidi to grab. Two men were needed to man the canoe, so Uledi and Marzouk, one of the boat's crew, volunteered. Starting from upstream, the boat was lowered toward Zaidi. But just as it came within reach the strong current carried the canoe to one side of the rock close to the edge of the cataract. It had to be hauled back by the men on shore.

Five times the attempt was made without success. The sixth time, the canoe came within ten yards of Zaidi, and Uledi threw him the short rope attached to the stern. The rope struck him on the arm and he grabbed it. Lowering himself into the water, he was instantly carried over the falls—but he clung tenaciously to the rope. Those on shore hauled away with all their strength, and in a moment Zaidi's head emerged above the boiling water. Just as it appeared that he might be saved, the bow and side cables attached to the canoe snapped. The canoe whipped around, and then the stern cable broke! Like an arrow, the free canoe raced toward the edge of the cataract.

Fortunately, there was a tiny islet in the river here, and the canoe was swept around the far side of it. Zaidi, still holding on to the rope, acted as a kedge anchor, swinging the canoe against the rocky islet. Uledi and Marzouk leaped out and in a few moments pulled up the dripping Zaidi, still holding the rope. Although all three men were safe for the time being, it seemed only a reprieve. Stanley did not dare risk any more men in canoes, and night was fast approaching.

Stanley now attempted to get a small rope to the three men stranded on the rock. He tied a stone to a long piece of whipcord and the best throwers in the expedition tried to throw it to the stranded men. After nineteen failures, Uledi finally caught the rock and pulled in the whipcord. The tent rope, which had parted before, was tied to the whipcord, and then a stout rattan creeper was fastened to the rope. But it was getting quite dark, and all operations had to cease until morning. The men on the rock spent a sleepless and wretched night waiting for the dawn. Cold, hungry, and afraid to move, they did not even have the solace of conversation. The roar of the churning water pouring over the cataract and crashing on the rocks below deafened them to all but the sound of the watery force which, at the slip of a foot, would sweep them over the falls and crush them on the rocks.

When the sun came up, the efforts of those on shore to save the stranded men were renewed. Thirty men with guns were sent to protect thirty others who searched for rattans in the jungle. By nine o'clock in the morning they had enough material to make a stout line from the shore to the rocky islet and to furnish light cables for each man to tie around his waist. Uledi was the first to try the dangerous experiment. Tying a rope around his waist—the other end was held by ten men on the shore—he took hold of the rattan rope bridge. Hand over hand, the waves dashing against his face and tearing at his body, he worked his way toward shore. By jerking his body upward occasionally, he managed to keep from being suffocated by the waves. A dozen willing hands were waiting to haul him on shore.

Zaidi came next. He had already given ample proof of both his courage and his tenacious grip. He arrived safely. Last of all was Marzouk, the youngest of the three. He struggled fiercely, but when halfway across he nearly lost his hold; he stopped, suspended in the wild, tearing water. Afraid that in his despair he would lose his grip altogether, Stanley shouted harshly, "Pull away, you fool! Be a man!" The boy continued his desperate struggles until at last he reached the arms of his cheering friends.

The Zanzibaris now set to work making a three-mile path wide enough to enable them to carry the canoes around the falls. Although they were not molested by the natives during this portage, millions of tiny red ants tormented them. They covered each leaf and blade of grass; soon, the bodies of every member of the expedition were blistered by their bites, and Stanley felt as though his scalp had been scarified by a steel comb.

No sooner had the expedition launched their boats than the cannibals were upon them again. But Stanley was able to lure the warriors away from their villages and hold them at bay until Manwa Sera with a detachment made a flanking attack on the village, rounding up the women, children, and a herd of goats. Seeing their families and livestock in the hands of the strangers, the savages sat stunned in their canoes, overwhelmed by the disaster that had overtaken them. They fully expected to see these innocents slaughtered before their eyes. When the amazing white man made peaceful overtures, the native chief readily agreed to make friends with Stanley. In less than an hour, the incisions had been made in the right arms of Stanley and the chief; the medicine man had pronounced the magic words as they held one cut against the other and the two became blood brothers.

Once peace had been established and the captives returned, this tribe proved quite helpful to the expedition, supplying information regarding the river and loading the expedition's canoes with bananas. They also permitted Stanley to inspect their villages where he found the typical artifacts of a Congo Iron-Age culture: baskets, fishnets, and bundles of wooden spears with iron points. Human skulls ornamented the village streets, and human ribs, thighbones, and vertebrae lay scattered about the huts.

The next day, January 19, 1877, the expedition resumed its voyage. They met only deserted villages, and when night approached they were able to locate a pleasant spot on the river bank to make their camp. When they awoke at sunrise, they discovered with dismay that they were surrounded on the land side by a huge net. Stanley knew that behind the net lurked spearmen; they were being trapped like big-game animals! Pitting his intelligence against the cunning of the savages, he dispatched Manwa Sera with a detachment of thirty men a half-mile up the river with instructions to land and come up on the man-hunting sportsmen from behind. After waiting an hour for Manwa Sera to get into position, Stanley ordered a loud blast on a horn as a signal for the concerted attack to begin.

Four Zanzibaris with shields, covered by ten men with rifles and thirty men with spears, advanced to cut the net. Several spears came hurtling at them from the bushes, but no one was hit. As soon as they had passed through the net, Stanley and his men fired a fusillade into the undergrowth and then charged. Shadowy forms were seen retreating. Suddenly, there were sharp screams of pain from the foremost Zanzibaris. They hopped from one foot to the other, blood streaming from their feet. "Keep away from the path!" they yelled.

The path bristled with sharp-pointed cane splinters that cut the bare feet of the Zanzibaris to the bone. Nevertheless, the attack went on, and the retreating savages were driven into the arms of Manwa Sera and his men in their rear. Stanley's pincer movement was successful, and eight prisoners were taken. They were Wane-Mpungu, cannibals with filed teeth and two rows of ugly tattoo marks on their foreheads.

Under questioning, the captives confessed that they lay in wait for man-meat. They also told how, in addition to the strangers they were able to capture, they ate their own old men and women. Stanley took these prisoners with him to point out the remaining cataracts, which the Wane-Mpungu said they would encounter a few miles down the river. Their captive guides warned them to avoid the treacherous water on the left side of the river as they approached the falls; so, following their advice, the expedition made camp on the right bank. Here Stanley released his prisoners and returned their weapons to them.

While still preparing camp, they were again attacked. When, after an hour of hot combat, the natives retreated, Stanley and his men followed up their advantage and were able to capture two wounded natives. Stanley dressed their wounds and treated them kindly, and they rewarded him by talking volubly. Unfortunately, very little of what they said could be understood. Some geographical information was obtained, however, and Stanley was able to compile a list of over two hundred words of their language which he hoped would be useful to him in dealing with the next tribe. As usual, the captives were released unharmed after they had given all the information they could.

Four days later, the expedition was attacked in such numbers that had they not been prepared they would have been easily overwhelmed. Fortunately, they had thrown up a protecting screen of brushwood which served as camouflage and as some protection from the arrows and spears. Again and again the savages rushed their boma. The notes of their war horns, the furious beating of their drums, and their screaming rage and hatred filled the jungle. Not until sunset did the attacking hordes retreat. There were no alarms during the night, but the next morning the Zanzibaris steeled themselves for the dangerous routine of fighting man and jungle to get their boats around the falls.

To their astonishment, they were left to make their way around the cataracts in peace. Going out with a small force to reconnoiter, Stanley found large villages, which must have housed several thousand inhabitants, completely deserted! Not a single native was to be found. Silence, except for the dull rumble of the cataract, reigned over the forest.

With the sixth falls behind them they came to the seventh and last a few miles down the river. At this point, the Congo was a mile in breadth and the water roaring over the precipice made the earth tremble for miles around. Fortunately, they were not molested in their portage, and at last, on January 28, it was done; the boats were once more on smooth-flowing water. Everyone was in high spirits, feeling that with the cataracts and their ferocious guardians behind them the worst was over.

# CHAPTER IX

# Cannibals and Cataracts

THE WORST WAS FAR from over. However hard they tried, the conflicts with the natives could not be avoided. "As day after day passed, we found the natives increasing rather than abating in wild rancour and unreasonable hate of strangers. At every curve and bend they 'telephoned' along the river their warning signals; the forests on either bank flung hither and thither the strange echoes; their huge war drums sounded the muster for resistance. Reed arrows, tipped with poison, were shot at us from the jungle as we glided by."

The terrible strain of fighting for their lives every day began to have its effect on every member of the expedition. The incessant, long-lasting enmity shown by every tribe they encountered made them feel like baited animals. Everything in the shape of a man raised his spear and screamed his rage at them as soon as they appeared.

While he was concerned by the fate of his men and the success of his expedition, Stanley never revealed any personal fear. Although he wrote of the terrors they faced and the horror of the terrible incidents of their journey, he apparently set down only the feelings he thought would be expected of him under such circumstances. He was blessed with a psyche that was incapable of absolute terror. He never knew the shock of sickening fear that paralyzes mind and body. Stanley thrilled to danger but he always remained clear-headed, capable of taking whatever action was needed. As he passed through battle after battle unscathed, he developed a feeling that divine eyes were watching out for his welfare; that he was destined for a special mission in life; that he would not die until his work was finished.

Stanley was always genuinely more concerned for the welfare and safety of his men than for himself. What precautions he took for his own safety were with the thought in mind that his Zanzibaris would be helpless without his guidance and leadership. For it was he who devised the plans that outwitted the cunning natives, and it was he who would have to map the strategy that would enable them to overcome the human and natural obstacles that lay ahead. His proven ability to lead made his people dependent upon him. By this time, most of them were truly devoted to him, and over and over again he speaks of his "faithfuls." Knowing nothing of his aims or their importance, they followed him because they had blind, almost unreasonable faith in him. Their devotion meant much to this unloved man.

Even as they died, his followers bore him no ill will for leading them to this barbarous and unfriendly river. On being told that Amina, the wife of one of his chiefs, was dying in the attempt to give birth to a child, Stanley drew the *Lady Alice* alongside the canoe where she lay. She was conscious, but very weak. "Ah, master!" she said, "I shall never see the sea again. Your child Amina is dying. I have so wished to see the cocoanuts and mangoes; but no—Amina is dying—dying in a pagan land. She will never see Zanzibar. The master has been good to his children, and Amina remembers it. It is a bad world, master, and you have lost your way in it. Good-by, master; do not forget poor little Amina."

Stanley has been called ruthless, but he was no harder on his people than he was on himself, and he really did regard these simple, brave, faithful people as his children. The bright-eyed Kalulu, the brave Uledi, the intelligent Manwa Sera, the stolid Zaidi, the diplomatic Safeni— he loved them all. For their part, if they did not love him, they at least respected him and developed a great affection for him. For Stanley, this was a more satisfying relationship than any he had experienced in the civilized world. The hatred of the natives they encountered drew all of them closer together.

In the long series of battles and skirmishes they had fought, each encounter tended to be much like the others. There were the same screaming and howling, the same drums and war horns, and the same wild and furious fighting. Although so far they had always emerged victorious, they had sustained casualties, and victory was often won by a close margin. On February 1, 1877, they had one of their most desperate encounters. Early that morning they had beaten off an attack and were rowing languidly down the river, knowing that the faster they rowed the sooner they would encounter more hostile tribes.

About one o'clock in the afternoon they were bothered by natives in dozens of small canoes who, although they did not make a direct, mass attack, made threatening gestures and occasionally attempted to throw a spear. Along the river banks there was much shouting and beating of drums. An hour later they came to the mouth of the Aruwimi River, one of the Congo's largest affluents. Looking up this river, Stanley saw an awe-inspiring sight: a flotilla of gigantic canoes which eclipsed in both size and numbers anything that they had yet seen!

Stanley tried to escape. Forming his boats in a line, he ordered his men to row hard down the river. Stanley in the *Lady Alice* acted as a rear guard. But as it soon became apparent that they could not out-run the huge, many-paddled war canoes, Stanley decided to stand and fight. He shouted to his men to drop their anchors. Four of his canoes pretended to not hear the order, and continued their furious paddling until the *Lady Alice* overtook them and chased them back. He formed his boats in a battle line consisting of eleven double canoes anchored ten yards apart with the *Lady Alice* taking up a position fifty yards above them. The noncombatants—men, women, and children—raised the shields around each pair of canoes.

His defenses in order, Stanley sized up the fast-approaching enemy: "There are fifty-four of them! A monster canoe leads the way, with two rows of upstanding paddles, forty men on a side, their bodies bending in unison as with a swelling barbarous chorus they drive her down toward us. In the bow, standing on what appears to be a plat-form, are ten prime young warriors, their heads gay with feathers of the parrot crimson and grey: at the stern, eight men, with long paddles, whose tops are decorated with ivory balls, guide the monster vessel; and dancing up and down from stem to stern are ten men, who appear to be chiefs. All the paddles are headed with ivory balls, every head bears a feathered crown, every arm shows gleaming white ivory arm-lets. From the bow of the canoe streams a thick fringe of the long white fibre of the Hyphene palm. The crashing sound of large drums, a hundred blasts from ivory horns, and a thrilling chant from two thousand human throats, do not intend to soothe our nerves or to in-crease our confidence."

The monster canoe aimed straight for the *Lady Alice*, its many paddles beating the water into foam and its sharp prow raising jets of water on either side. Stanley called out a stream of advice and en-couragement to his men: "Be firm as iron. Wait until you see the first spear, and then take good aim. Don't fire all at once. Keep aiming until you are sure of your man. Don't think of running away, for only your guns can save you."

He just had time for one look around him. Frank was on the right flank with a choice crew and a good bulwark of black shields. Manwa Sera occupied the left flank, and the sides of his canoe bristled with guns. The men seemed tolerably steady, Stanley thought.

Then the monster canoe was upon them. It seemed at first as though she intended to ram the *Lady Alice,* but suddenly it swerved, discharging a broadside of arrows. Stanley and his Zanzibaris replied with their rifles and muskets. For several minutes the air was full of spears and bullets, and the din of the shouting savages and the reports of the guns went echoing back and forth between the jungles on either side of the river. Then the enemy retreated about two hundred yards upstream to re-form for another attack.

Seeing that they were disorganized for the moment and seemingly shaken by the failure of their initial charge, Stanley decided to attack. "Our blood is up now. It is a murderous world, and we feel for the first time that we hate the filthy, vulturous ghouls who inhabit it."

Lifting anchors, the expedition sped upriver after the natives who, seeing the disciplined flotilla bearing down on them, turned their canoes about and fled. Hot in pursuit, Stanley followed them along the right bank of the river. Rounding a point he saw them tumbling into their villages. Close upon them, the Zanzibaris made straight for the banks, landed, and chased their enemies through their villages and into the jungle.

The battle won, Stanley sounded the recall. While gathering his people together for re-embarkation, a Zanzibari came up to report that he had found a *meskiti,* or temple, where there was ivory "as abundant as fuel." Following the man, Stanley found himself under a large circular roof supported by thirty-three tusks of ivory erected over an idol that stood four feet high, painted bright red with camwood dye, with black eyes, hair, and a beard. He gave permission for his men to loot the meskiti, a decision that later caused him to be censured by the Aborigines Protection Society and by some of the press in England.

Besides the tusks, one hundred other pieces of ivory were collected. Splendid carvings, weapons, tools, and utensils all indicated that this tribe (Basoko) was more clever, intelligent, and artistic than any other people they had encountered so far in their descent of the Congo. There were long ivory war horns; beautifully carved paddles ten feet long, some of them with iron points; ceremonial spears, six feet long; great long knives in bright iron-mounted sheaths on belts of red buffalo and antelope; barbed spears of all sizes; and ingeniously carved stools, flutes, staffs, and masks of wood. But there were also numerous skulls mounted on poles, and around them were scorched human ribs and, near a fire, Stanley saw a gnawed piece of a thin human forearm.

By five o'clock in the afternoon they were back in their boats, rowing once more down the great river. They had now traveled three hundred and forty geographical miles north since leaving Nyangwe. The fight near the mouth of the Aruwimi was their twenty-eighth; seventy-nine people had died on the expedition so far—thirty-three of them in battle—and there were not thirty men in the entire expedition who had not been wounded. They were still in the middle of the continent and their exploration of the Congo was not even half completed. So far they had traveled mostly north, but the river was veering westward more and more, leading Stanley to the conclusion that they would eventually end up at the Atlantic Ocean. He still did not know whether it was the Congo or the Niger, but regardless of its original name, he decided that the river should be renamed the Livingstone—a name that did not stick.

Whether this river, which sapped their energy, took their lives, and strained their courage, was the Congo, the Nile, or the Niger meant little to the Zanzibaris. In any case, they had a long, long way to go—and the journey would be hard. No one knew this better than Stanley, yet he also knew that he would never turn back.

Throughout all of the trials and difficulties that beset him, Stanley, the reporter, kept his notebook up to date. One of his entries reads: "Livingstone called floating down the Lualaba a foolhardy feat. So it has proved, indeed, and I pen these lines with half a feeling that they will never be read by any man; still, as we persist in floating down according to our destiny, I persist in writing, leaving events to an all-gracious providence."

As they continued to row down the dark river, they found that the fury of man abated somewhat—but nature continued to be malevolent. Sudden storms threatened the boats with destruction, and a shortage of food threatened them with starvation. Fortunately, at this juncture they arrived in the region of Rubunga. Here they were well received by elaborately tattooed natives who were willing to trade food for wire and beads and the expedition gained a much needed respite.

Although the inhabitants of Rubunga had never seen a white man before, they had in their possession four antique Portuguese muskets.

The Zanzibaris were jubilant, regarding the guns as an encouraging sign that they were approaching civilization at last. Stanley was not so pleased. What if they encountered hostile tribes armed with these weapons? Their captured shields had served to ward off arrows, darts, and spears, but they would hardly protect them from musket balls fired at close range. The expedition's twenty muskets and twenty rifles would be no match for any sizable force well equipped with guns—even ancient Portuguese muskets.

The Rubunga natives guided them down the river to the next tribe, a people called Urangi. Again there was friendly trading, and Stanley began to hope that the character of the river people was changing for the better. As they left the Urangi village and were rowing down the river, they noticed a large number of Urangi approaching them in canoes. At first, they paid little attention to them. Then, the sound of a shot echoed across the water, and a puff of smoke was seen drifting away from a Urangi canoe. A Zanzibari fell to the bottom of his boat —killed by a ball from a Portuguese musket! But the treacherous Urangi did not possess many guns, and they were not particularly daring. Although they were soon beaten off, their attack underscored the new danger.

A few days later, on February 14, Stanley's worst fears were almost realized. During the morning they had rowed between islands that blocked their view of the river banks. When they came to the end of one long island, they suddenly found themselves in full view of a settlement on the right bank. At first Stanley hoped they would be able to creep past the village without being detected, but soon they heard sharp, quick taps on a small drum. In a few moments the first drum was answered by a second and then a third, until the news of their presence was being drummed for miles down the river. It was only a few moments later that the great war drums were thundering the call to arms.

In spite of the danger threatening them, Stanley calmly landed on a small island, and, as it was noon, shot the sun, observing that they were now at north latitude 1° 7' 0". This task completed, they embarked again, and started carefully down the river, the *Lady Alice* in the lead, Frank's canoe on the right flank, and Manwa Sera's on the left. It was not long before they saw the canoes of the natives advancing toward them. They were Bangala, the most militant natives on the Congo. Later, this tribe would furnish most of the men for the army and police force of the Congo Free State, but now they were bent on destroying the first white men to enter their country. The warriors were the most brilliantly decorated of any they had yet seen. Burnished copper and brass flashed among them, and, from a distance, they appeared to be wearing white caps like university mortarboards; their war cry, too, smacked of a college yell as they rent the air with, "Yaha-ha, Ya Bangala! Ya Bangala! Yaha-ha-ha!" But this was not a football game. These young men were out to kill—and they were armed with muskets!

In spite of their obviously hostile intent, Stanley was determined to make peace with them if it was at all possible. As the *Lady Alice* edged toward them, he stood up in the prow, holding a long piece of red cloth in one hand and a coil of brass wire in the other. *"Senneneh!"* Stanley called, "Peace!" The Zanzibaris rested on their oars, and sat still but watchful as they drew near the wild Bangala. Again Stanley called out to them "Senneneh!" But they did not answer. Three or four Bangala canoes approached Frank, threatening him with their weapons. Frank sprang up, aiming his rifle, but Stanley immediately ordered him to sit down. Again Stanley called out to the Bangala, offering to give some brass wire to the nearest man. The Bangala liked to trade, he had been told, but they liked to fight better. Suddenly, a volley from the canoes that had threatened Frank poured into the *Lady Alice,* wounding three men. Other Bangala fired into Frank's canoe, wounding two more. There could be no peace now; shields were raised and the guns of the expedition were quickly played upon the natives.

The battle began in earnest, each village sending out its quota of warriors. The Bangala were numerous, they were daring, and they were well equipped with muskets. The Anglo-American Expedition would have ended here except for one fortunate circumstance: the Bangala did not have proper ammunition for their weapons. Instead of musket balls, they loaded their guns with jagged pieces of iron and copper ore. The effect was similar to that of shotguns: while murderous at close range, the muskets did not have the penetrating power they would have had if they had been properly loaded. Consequently, although the shields of the expedition were scarred and dented in this encounter, they were not penetrated.

In this fight, as in all of the other combats on the Congo, Stanley rode in the prow of the *Lady Alice,* and the short, stout white man in knickers and a high-crowned cap was a more frequent target than any other man on the expedition. Yet he came through every battle unscathed. He attributed part of his good fortune to the color of his skin. Speaking of an incident during the fight with the Bangala, when no less than nine muskets were pointed at him simultaneously, he said, "Had I been a black man I should long before been slain, but even in the midst of a battle curiosity stronger than hate or bloodthirstiness arrested the sinewy arm which drew the bow, and delayed the flying spear. And now, while their thin flint hammers were at full cock, and the fingers pressing the triggers of the deadly muskets, the savages became absorbed in contemplating the silent and still form of a kind of being which to them must have appeared as strange as any unreal being the traditions of their father had attempted to describe. 'White!'

"Of course the slightest movement on my part would have been instantly followed by my death. Though it was unpleasant to sit and feel oneself to be a target of so many guns, yet it was the wisest plan."

The battle continued throughout the afternoon. By three o'clock Stanley counted sixty-three war canoes opposing him, each with an average of five muskets—over three hundred guns against forty! Time after time they charged the canoes of the expedition. In their persistence and bravery they reminded Stanley of the Ashantees. They were skillful, too. One young chief, distinguished by a headdress and cape of white goatskin with his arms, legs, and neck covered by wreaths of thick brass wire, was extremely adroit in maneuvering his canoe. He would charge straight toward the *Lady Alice*, swerve his boat sharply to fire a broadside, and then cut back instantly so as to present only a thin line of upright figures to the sights of the expedition's guns. He set an example for his fellow tribesmen who tried to emulate his actions. Finally Manwa Sera managed to wound him in the thigh with a Snider bullet, and he retired to the shore. With his departure the firing became desultory, and about five-thirty in the afternoon the Bangala gave up the contest.

This was their thirty-first fight. A few weeks later, on March 9, they had their thirty-second and last fight with the savages of the Congo. Few professional soldiers have fought as many battles in a lifetime as had Stanley and his Zanzibaris during these past four months. Although in the forefront of every battle, not an arrow, spear, dart, or discharge of musket touched Stanley. It is little wonder that he felt himself under divine protection!

Three days later they reached a lakelike expansion of the river that Frank named Stanley Pool. They had made good progress after passing Stanley Falls, in spite of the natives; Stanley calculated that they had now traveled 1235 miles since leaving Nyangwe. Hostile natives made their existence on the river perilous, but cataracts and rapids were the greatest deterrents to their progress. The expedition's experiences at Stanley Falls were terrible, but there had been only seven cataracts; now, directly ahead of them, just past Stanley Pool, stretched another series containing no less than thirty-two cataracts, and the struggle to get around them was to prove a desperate one. Stanley named them Livingstone Falls.

Accidents now became a daily occurrence as the men toiled with the boats and supplies over slippery rocks. One man dislocated a shoulder; another suffered a severe concussion; Stanley fell thirty feet into a chasm, but miraculously escaped with only a few bruises. Many canoes were lost, too. In order to work them as close to the falls as possible before they would have to be taken out and laboriously hauled overland, the boats were maneuvered along the shore line by men on the banks. But the current was often so swift that it swept the canoes from the grasp of the Zanzibaris trying to hold them in check.

By the afternoon of March 28, the expedition had just completed the portage around the second cataract when a scouting party reported that a mile below there was a good campsite, a broad strip of sand lining a bay near the third cataract. Stanley decided that they should try to reach it before sunset. Embarking in the *Lady Alice*, he instructed the canoes to follow him, warning them to keep close to the bank and avoid the strong current in midstream.

Just before reaching the inlet, the boats had to round a narrow point of land jutting out into the river. Here the current was swiftest, but once around the point they could enter the cove without difficulty and land at a point not six hundred yards from the brink of the cataract. The *Lady Alice* and the first three canoes following her negotiated the point and arrived safely. Just as Stanley was beginning to congratulate himself on a good day's work, he saw the fourth canoe, the *Crocodile*, with its helpless crew swept away from the point and carried to the middle of the river. On board was Kalulu, the boy Stanley regarded almost as his son. Gliding swiftly, it headed straight for the falls. Nothing could stop it. Stanley and the men with him could only watch in agony as the boat plunged over the cataract. It whirled around three or four times, then dived into the depths to return, stern upward and empty, in a few moments. Kalulu and seven men were drowned.

Before they could recover from the shock of this catastrophe, another canoe, a small one carrying two men, was seen in midstream heading for the falls. Over it went, but somehow managed to stay upright and afloat. The men struggled hard to save it and to edge close to the far shore. At last they succeeded, and both jumped to safety. "As we observed them clamber over the rocks to approach a point opposite us, regarding us in silence across the river, our pity and love gushed strong toward them, but we could utter nothing of it. The roar of the falls completely mocked and overpowered the human voice," Stanley recorded.

Following the first disaster, Stanley had dispatched two men up the river to reiterate his warning about the current in the middle of the river. Before his messengers could reach the remainder of the expedition, a third boat, a small one manned only by young Soudi, the boy who had barely escaped being murdered in Ituru two years before, darted past. As he went by, the boy called out, "I am lost, master!"

"We watched him for a few moments, and then saw him drop," Stanley wrote. "Out of the shadow of the fall he presently emerged, dropping from terrace to terrace, precipitated down, then whirled around, caught by great heavy waves, which whisked him to right and left, and struck madly at him, and yet his canoe did not sink, but he and it were swept behind the lower end of the island, and then darkness fell upon the day of horror."

Stanley named this cataract Kalulu Falls. Here eight men had drowned, two were separated from them by a raging torrent and three canoes were lost. It was indeed a dark day! Soudi was not drowned, however. Clinging to the canoe, he was carried downstream, and for over an hour after dark he rode the mad waves. At last he floated near a rock and scampered ashore. Holding on to his canoe, he pulled it safely on the rock with him. No sooner had he done this than he was seized from behind, tightly bound, and taken by two natives to their village.

The next day, tribesmen from miles around came to the village to see the fine slave that had been captured. Fortunately, one of the visitors had seen Soudi before in the company of Stanley. This man charged that Soudi's captors had stolen the boy from the white man, and he painted a frightening picture of Stanley and his stick that belched smoke. He so terrified the men who had made the capture that they took Soudi back to his canoe, begging him not to tell his master of the affair. As Soudi was sitting by his boat wondering what he should do, the other two men who had survived the descent over the falls came upon him. The three of them decided they would try to rejoin the expedition by paddling Soudi's canoe across the river. The current was swift, but they were successful in making the opposite bank, although they were carried a mile downstream. Once landed on the right bank, they lost no time in making their way back to Stanley and their friends.

Accidents continued to occur. One canoe, containing fifty ivory tusks and a sack of beads, was upset and its cargo lost; four men had narrow escapes from drowning and were saved only by the bravery of Uledi; Stanley himself tumbled into a small basin and was almost drowned. Cataracts and rapids were so numerous that they developed a standard routine for their portages. Frank Pocock would lead most of the expedition overland to some cove or recess on the other side of the waterfall or stretch of rapids. There he would put the older men, women, and children to work constructing a camp while the working force, consisting of the younger men, would return to assist Stanley in maneuvering the boats along the banks of the river or in hauling them overland along the route Stanley had marked out.

When Stanley attempted to keep his boats in the water through a stretch of rapids, hawsers of rattan would be made and tied to the boats. These would be held by men walking along the bank. Once, however, the *Lady Alice*, with Stanley, Uledi, and the entire crew on board, was swept from the hands of those on shore. Away shot the boat to the center of the churning river. Oars were useless. The mighty Congo was compressed into a narrow torrent, rushing swiftly between high cliffs.

Describing his feelings, Stanley said, "Never did the rocks assume such hardness, such solemn grimness and bigness, never were they invested with such terrors and such grandeur of height, as while we were the cruel sport and prey of the brown-black waves, which whirled us around like a spinning top, swung us aside, almost engulfed us in the rapidly subsiding troughs, and then hurled us upon the white rageful crests of others."

In a matter of minutes they were tossed two miles down the river and were being carried past their advance campsite. Frank Pocock saw them go by and cried out in despair. Down the torrent they went, trying as best they could with helm and oars to steer the boat. Suddenly they heard a heavy rumbling noise, and the river around them heaved upward. The *Lady Alice* was impelled to the top of a watery mound. Stanley shouted to his men to pull hard on their oars. A few hard, frantic strokes took them to the lower side of the mound before it subsided to begin its fatal circling. They had narrowly escaped a huge whirlpool. They had no time to consider their deliverance, however, for a moment later they were whisked over a small waterfall. Although they were spun around several times, they somehow managed to stay afloat. Presently they discovered that they were able to manipulate their oars, and finally they worked their boat to shore. Stanley christened this stretch of water the Lady Alice Rapids.

From March 16 to April 21, a period of thirty-seven days, the expedition had traveled only thirty-four miles. Their progress was to become even slower. On April 22 they reached a huge cataract called Inkisi. The natives said this was the last waterfall, and Stanley hoped they were right. But to get around Inkisi Falls, it was necessary to pass over a small mountain rising precipitously a thousand feet.

When Stanley announced that they would carry the canoes over the mountain, the natives, and even Stanley's own men, were incredulous. Some of the expedition's large canoes were made of heavy teak and weighed over three tons. It seemed an impossible undertaking, but, negotiating with the local tribe, Stanley secured the assistance of six hundred natives for the price of forty cloths. After starting the men on their task, he then led the bulk of the expedition with all their goods to a site on the river below the falls. Here they established a camp, made friends with the natives, and set to work making new canoes to replace some of those lost in the rapids and falls.

It took two weeks for the natives and Zanzibaris to carry the canoes over the mountain, and Stanley decided that the men who had worked so hard deserved a few days' rest. It was during this period that the theft of a considerable number of beads was discovered. This was serious, for the fate of the expedition depended upon this currency. Stanley's supplies of negotiable goods was already low, and they had even gone without meat when it was available in order to conserve the precious beads. Stanley demanded to know the name of the thief, vowing that whoever he was, he would be severely punished. Then he was told that the thief was none other than Uledi, the bravest, most capable, and devoted of all his followers.

At first Uledi denied his guilt, but Stanley ordered all the coxswain's belongings brought before him. Inspection revealed enough beads to buy two days' rations for the entire expedition. Calling an assembly of all his people, Stanley asked the oldest and wisest of the chiefs what should be done with the thief. They replied that if it had been any other man, they would vote for death by drowning in the river. Since it was Uledi, they voted that he should be let off with a sound flogging. Stanley then turned to the crew of the *Lady Alice*, the men who had worked closest to Uledi since the expedition had started its voyage down the Congo. They begged that if Uledi must be whipped the blows should not be severe.

Uledi's brother, Shumari, and his cousin, Saywa, were next asked what should be done with their thieving kinsman. Each of them pleaded that half of Uledi's lashes be given to him. Saywa kneeled and embraced Stanley's legs saying, "The master is wise. All things that happen he writes in a book. Each day there is something written. We black men know nothing, neither. have we any memory. What we saw yesterday is today forgotten. Yet the master forgets nothing. Perhaps if the master will look into his books he may see something in it about Uledi. How Uledi behaved on Lake Tanganyika; how he rescued Zaidi from the cataract; how he has saved many men whose names I cannot remember from the river; how he worked harder on the canoes than any three men; how he has been the first to listen to your voice always; how he has been the father of the boatboys, and many other things. . . ."

Stanley at last felt justified in tempering justice with mercy—and following the dictates of his heart. "Very well," he said, "Uledi, by the voice of the people, is condemned, but Shumari and Saywa have promised to take the punishment on themselves; Uledi is set free and Shumari and Saywa are pardoned."

During these few days of rest another unusual incident occurred. Stanley was sitting in front of his tent when he heard shrill war cries. Looking up, he saw a long line of warriors, armed with muskets, advancing on the camp. They were the local natives who until now had been quite friendly to the expedition and Stanley could not imagine what had aroused them.

Instead of preparing for a fight, Stanley took Safeni, the wise chief who had been his coxswain on the Victoria Nyanza, and went out to meet them. He asked them why they came in such an unfriendly fashion. What complaint did they have against him? They replied that they had seen the white man writing in a book. This, they said, was very bad. It meant their goats would die, their country would waste away, and their women would become sterile. They demanded that he destroy his book.

By this time, Stanley had filled his notebook with enough material to make two large volumes. In it were valuable geographic notes, sketches of localities, and observations on the tribes and their languages. He could not sacrifice the fruit of all his labors and trials. Nevertheless, he told the warriors to wait and he would bring them the offending book.

Leaving Safeni as a pledge, Stanley went back to his tent. There he rummaged through his box of books until he found his large, worn, and well-thumbed edition of Shakespeare. It was about the same size as his notebook, and it had a similar cover. He took this to the waiting natives. Showing them the book, he asked what they wanted done with it.

"It is a fetish. You must burn it," they told him.

Stanley took the book and walked over to the nearest fire. Sadly, he tossed his Shakespeare into the flames and piled brush fuel over it. The natives sighed in relief, and departed satisfied.

Before long three new canoes had been made, and the men were rested. Although Stanley now lacked the active assistance of Frank Pocock, he felt it was time to renew their journey.

Frank had long ago worn through all of his shoes, and for some time he had been wearing makeshift sandals. These proved inadequate protection, and ulcers had developed on the soles of his feet. The sores were so painful that he was no longer able to walk, but had to be carried from campsite to campsite. For a young man as energetic as Frank, this lack of mobility was irksome. Nevertheless, he managed to make himself useful by mending clothes and repairing bags, and, in spite of his pain and comparative inactivity, he remained cheerful. Often he was able to raise Stanley's spirits by his lively songs and general good humor.

Frank Pocock, who started the expedition as little more than Stanley's servant, had long since become a companion and friend to whom Stanley could talk. He entrusted Frank with many of the supervisory responsibilities, and among the Zanzibaris he was known as the "little master."

On the morning of June 3, after a seven-day rest halt, the expedition was preparing to move on. Two miles down the river was Massassa Falls; just beyond Massassa was Zinga Falls. Stanley decided to go overland to the Zinga Falls area to make friends with the natives and to select a new campsite. He left instructions for Uledi to take a stout canoe and make a reconnaissance of Massassa Falls, warning him to be careful and not to take any chances with the treacherous river.

Stanley proceeded to Zinga and had a successful shauri with the natives, one of whom boasted that he had seen the ocean. After completing his negotiations, Stanley climbed onto a high rock overlooking the entire falls area to check on the progress of his men. Searching the river with his field glasses, he spotted a long, dark object tumbling about in the fierce waves above Zinga Falls. It was a capsized canoe with several men clinging to it!

Stanley called out to some of the men with him to take cane ropes and run to a point that he saw the canoe must pass before being swept over the falls. Kacheche, Wadi, Rehani, and ten other men ran toward the river. Meanwhile, Stanley watched helplessly as the men struggled to right the canoe. He saw them lift themselves onto the keel and attempt to work the overturned boat toward shore. Finally, as they drew near the land, he saw them abandon the canoe and swim ashore while the canoe shot over the great Zinga cataract.

In a few minutes, Kacheche, breathless and horror-struck, gave him the bad news: only eight out of the eleven men in the canoe were saved. "Three are lost!" he gasped, "and—one of them is the little master!"

"The little master, Kacheche?" Stanley stared at him, unwilling to believe what he had just heard. "Not the little master?"

"Yes, he is lost, master!" Kacheche replied.

Turning to the dripping Uledi who came to make his report, Stanley asked what Frank had been doing in the canoe in the first place. Sadly, Uledi told his story. Just as he was about to leave on his reconnaissance, Frank had crawled on all fours to the river bank and told Uledi that he must take him too. Uledi tried to argue with him, but Frank demanded that he be put in the canoe. Manwa Sera came up and tried to dissuade him too, but Frank, with a sick man's impatience, brushed their arguments aside and compelled the crew to lift him in. The current was swift, but the canoe was well manned and they kept control of their vessel. As they neared the booming cataract, Uledi steered toward the shore, guiding the boat into a little cove just above the cataract. Jumping out on the bank, he climbed over the rocks until he had a clear view of the waterfall. In a few minutes he returned to the canoe.

"Little master, it is impossible to shoot the falls. No canoe or boat can do it and live," Uledi announced.

In England, Frank had been a bargeman and he did know a great deal about the water and about boats. Besides, he was an excellent swimmer, and had frequently stated that he did not believe anyone who was a good swimmer could be drowned in the Congo. He told Uledi: "I can't believe this fall is as bad as you say it is. The noise isn't like that of the fall we just passed, and I feel sure that if I went to look at it myself I'd soon find a way."

"Well, if you doubt me, send Mpwapwa and Shumari and Marzouk to see, and if they say there is a way I will try it if you command me."

Frank sent two men to examine the falls, but they returned in a few moments, averring that the falls were impassable by water. Frank laughed. "I knew what you would say. The Wangwana are always cowardly in the water. You are always magnifying little ripples into great waves. If I had only four white men with me I would show you whether we could pass it or not."

These were brave men who had proven their valor many times; and had Frank been able to walk, and to see the falls for himself, he would never have doubted these men whom he himself respected so much.

"Little master," said Uledi gravely, "neither white men nor black men can go down this river alive, and I do not think it right that you should say we are afraid. As for me, I think you ought to know better. See! I hold out both hands, and all my fingers will not count the number of lives I have saved on this river. How can you say, master, I show fear?"

"Well, if you don't, the others do," Frank retorted.

"Neither they nor I am afraid. We believe the river to be impassable in a canoe. I have only to beckon to my men, and they will follow me to death—and it is death to go down this cataract. We are now ready to hear you command us to go, and we want your promise that if anything happens, and our master asks, 'Why did you do it?' that you will bear the blame."

"No, I won't order you. I'll have nothing to do with it. You're the chief in this canoe. If you'd like to go—go, and I'll say that you are men, and not afraid of the water. If not, stay, and I'll know it's because you are afraid. It appears to me easy enough, and I can advise you. I don't see what could happen."

Thus challenged, Uledi turned to his crew and said, "Our little master is saying that we are afraid of death. I know there is death in the cataract, but come, let us show him that black men fear death as little as white men. What do you say?"

"A man can die but once."

"Who can contend with his fate?"

"Our fate is in the hands of Allah!"

"Enough," Uledi said, "take your seats."

"Now you're men!" Frank cried.

Uledi shouted, "Bismillah, let go the rocks and shove off!"

"Bismillah!" echoed the crew.

In a few seconds they were in midstream. They tried to get to the other side of the river where Frank thought he had seen smooth-flowing water, but it soon became apparent that they would not be able to make it. The current was carrying them broadside over the cataract. Quickly, Uledi turned the prow forward in a desperate effort to shoot the falls—but it was too late!

Over the falls they plunged. Flying water leaped into the canoe. The currents spun them around as though they were on a pivot, and then sent them whirling down to the yawning whirlpools. A huge, spinning abyss waited for them; it caught the canoe and violently sucked it under. When the maelstrom closed, a great body of water belched upward; the canoe was shot dripping into the bright sunlight. It hung there for an instant with several half-drowned men clinging to it, and then moved away from the whirlpool area. Uledi quickly collected his faculties and counted the men still hanging to the canoe. There were eight of them, but the "little master" was not among them. Then, close by, the water again heaved upward, and out of the water appeared the head of Frank. The Zanzibaris heard a loud moan from him. Leaving the comparative safety of the canoe, Uledi struck out toward him, but before he could reach him they were both sucked down for a second time. Uledi came up, exhausted and faint, but Frank Pocock was gone forever.

When Uledi had finished his story, Stanley said to him, "Ah, Uledi, had you but saved him, I should have made you a rich man."

Sadly and wearily Uledi replied, "Our fate is in the hands of God, master."

Eight days later, a native fisherman, attracted by something strange floating in the water, paddled toward it; he was horrified to find the upturned face of a dead white man.

The death of his young companion who had been with him constantly for nearly three years was a bitter blow to Stanley. First Kalulu, now Frank. So deep was his grief that for the first time in his life he thought of suicide.

The loss of the "little master" had a depressing effect on the rest of the expedition, too. At first, the Zanzibaris were stupefied; then they lapsed into an apathetic sullenness and a complete lack of feeling for themselves and for their comrades. The slightest illness caused them to lean against a rock or to crouch by the camp fire in an attitude of despair. They became unnaturally silent, and would not open their lips even to ask for medicine. When questioned about their ailments, they hardly bothered to reply. It seemed that overfamiliarity with diseases, severe accidents, and violent and painful deaths had finally obliterated the fear of their own death. They became convinced that they would all die, and that if they died now instead of tomorrow they would have one less day of pain and hardship to endure.

Two days after Frank's death there was a mutiny. There was no violence; the men said simply that rather than follow Stanley any farther down the hated river they would remain where they were and work for the local natives. Stanley spoke to them, concluding: "While you stay with me, I follow this river until I come to a point where it is known. If you don't stay with me, I still will cling to the river, and will die in it." With this he turned and walked away. A tent boy came to tell him that thirty-one men had packed their belongings and left. Stanley sent Manwa Sera and Kacheche to follow and plead with them. They overtook the malcontents about five miles from camp, but they were unable to persuade them to change their minds.

The next day Stanley sent Manwa Sera and Kacheche around to the surrounding villages to ask the help of the chiefs in preventing the deserters from passing through their territories. The chiefs co-operated so well that it was not long before the jungle for miles around was resounding to the beats of war drums. Two of the men came back, reporting that already the mutineers regretted their departure. The following day Manwa Sera and Kacheche again went out to find the deserters, and this time they brought them all back.

Stanley continued to have trouble with his tired, hungry, and dis-pirited men. One man caught stealing cassava was held captive by the natives until Stanley agreed to ransom him with 150 dollars' worth of cloth. When the offense was repeated, he was forced to warn his peo-ple that anyone else found stealing would be left behind to spend the rest of his life as a slave. This threat was issued not only as a deter-rent to further robbery, but also because their supplies had dwindled dangerously low; the expedition could not afford to pay out huge quantities of goods as ransom without risking future starvation.

Slowly and painfully they worked their way around two more falls, but at the cost of another man's life and the loss of one of their new canoes. The Zanzibaris regarded these disasters with fatalistic indifference; they were only further signs of the impending doom that would soon engulf them all. In a month they had traveled only three miles. Ahead of them were at least three more cataracts.

They struggled on, but the natives around them became more and more sullen and resentful of their presence. They began to demand absurdly high sums for their food, and the ribs of the hungry Zanzibaris began to protrude through their shrinking skins. Another man caught stealing cassava had to be left behind as a slave because the price demanded for his release was more than four times the value of all their remaining goods. To encourage his people, Stanley told them that they were now only a few miles from the ocean. The announcement produced the desired effect; the Zanzibaris were as jubilant as their hunger and misery would allow them to be. One man seemed to be actually frenzied by the news. It was the sage and normally reserved Safeni—the man who had been coxswain of the *Lady Alice* during the circumnavigation of the Victoria Nyanza. Safeni ran to Stanley shouting, "Ah, master! El hamd ul Illah! We have reached the sea! We are home! We are home! We shall no more be tormented by empty stomachs and accursed savages! I am about to run all the way to the sea to tell your brothers you are coming!"

With this, Safeni set his parrot on his shoulder and darted off into the jungle. It was a few minutes before Stanley could realize that the wise and sensible man was now a lunatic. Men were sent off to find him and bring him back, but they returned alone. The sage Safeni was never seen again.

Lack of food had reduced them all to hideous, bony frames. Sickness flourished in the expedition, and men who had survived cannibals and cataracts were felled by disease. Food could have been obtained by force, but Stanley held to his principles: he would not use his weapons unless attacked.

On July 30, six of his men were wounded and three more were captured while trying to steal food from the natives. The unfortunate captives had to be left behind; Stanley could not ransom them. The next day the expedition reached Isangila Falls, only a few days' march from the sea. Quadruple ration money was issued, and Stanley even distributed his personal belongings among his people so that they could buy food. Even so, they were able to purchase very little.

Since it was now absolutely certain that the river they had been following for so long was indeed the Congo and as there were more rapids and falls ahead, Stanley decided that they could now abandon it and travel the rest of the way by land. The gallant *Lady Alice,* which had carried Stanley for nearly five thousand miles, was lifted onto a pile of rocks above the Isangila cataract and left to rot.

By August 2, they were only a few miles from Embomma (Boma), where they would find white men and food. The natives they encountered now were familiar with white men—and white men's products. They refused to sell their food for beads, wire, or cheap cloth and laughed when these things were offered to them. They demanded rum! Enervated by hunger, Stanley did not see how they would be able to drag themselves the last few miles. There were only a hundred and sixteen people left with the expedition now, and forty of them were on the sick list, with more falling ill every day.

Two days later they reached the small village of Nsanda. Here Stanley spent four hours arguing and pleading with the arrogant village chief to persuade him to provide a guide so that he could send a letter to the Europeans at Embomma. At last the chief reluctantly agreed, and Stanley sat down to compose a letter. He sketched their desperate plight and outlined their requirements. "The supplies must arrive within two days," he wrote, "or I may have a fearful time of it among the dying." The letter was addressed, "To any gentleman who speaks English at Embomma." He signed it, "H. M. Stanley, Commanding Anglo-American Expedition for the Exploration of Africa." Then followed a postscript: "You may not know me by name: I therefore add, I am the person that discovered Livingstone in 1871.—H. M. S."

Similar messages were written in Spanish and French, and all three letters were given to Uledi who, with three other men, started out for Embomma on August 4. Meanwhile, the expedition resumed its slow, weary march through this land where the white man was known and had made rum the local currency.

Two days later they met the returning Uledi. With him were pagazis bearing food, tobacco, cloth, rum, and a letter of welcome from the Europeans at Embomma. Stanley's people were jubilant. They had reached the end of their long journey. There would be no more fighting with hostile natives, no more treacherous rapids, no more cataracts to block their progress. The back-breaking toil and the dangers were over, and they had good food with which to stuff their starving bellies.

On the morning of August 9, 1877, nine hundred and ninety-nine days after their departure from Zanzibar, they met civilization in the form of four white men who had come out to welcome them. Arriving in Embomma at midday, Stanley was given a royal reception and treated to all of the delicacies this remote outpost of civilization could provide.

On the eleventh, a steamer took them to the coastal town of Cabinda, and eight days later another ship carried them to Luanda in Angola, where they had another wait for a ship to Capetown. On board the ships and during their delays at Cabinda and Luanda, Stanley's followers were left with nothing to do for the first time in years. The letdown was tremendous for them. They surrendered themselves to the benumbing influences of listlessness, and developed a fatal indifference to life. Four people died at Luanda and three more on the remainder of the trip back. One poor woman, wife of the unfortunate Safeni, breathed her last on the day after arriving in Zanzibar.

At Capetown, while Stanley was being feted and honored, his ship was anchored in the bay. For the first three days after landing, blustering gales prevented him from returning to the ship. When he was finally able to go on board again, he found his people unusually depressed. When he asked the reason one of them replied:

"You will return to Ulyah [Europe], of course, now."

"Why?"

"Oh, do we not see that you have met your friends, and all of these days we have felt that you will shortly leave us."

"Who told you so?" Stanley asked, smiling at the suppressed bitterness visible in their faces.

"Our hearts; and they are very heavy."

"And would it please you if I accompanied you to Zanzibar?"

"Why should you ask, master? Are you not our father?"

"Well, it takes a long time to teach you to rely upon the promise of your father. I have told you over and over again that nothing shall cause me to break my promise to you that I would take you home. You have been true to me, and I shall be true to you. If we can get no ship to take us, I will walk the entire distance with you until I can show you to your friends at Zanzibar."

"Now we are grateful, master."

From this day on, there were no more sad faces among the Zanzibaris. The devotion displayed by his people made a very deep impression on Stanley, and who can say what part this father-child relationship had in drawing this fatherless man back again and again to the Dark Continent?

A British man-of-war took the explorers on the final lap from the Cape of Good Hope to Zanzibar. Of the three hundred and fifty-nine people who had left Bagamoyo with Stanley three years before, only eighty-two returned to Zanzibar with him. Added to those who came back, however, were six children who were born on the expedition—one of them the child of the unfortunate Safeni and his wife. Of the thirty-six women who started out on the expedition, only twelve returned, plus one woman from the Victoria Nyanza region who had married a Zanzibari chief. One hundred and seventy-three, including fifty-nine of Tippu-Tib's people, had died on the march. Of these, fifty-eight were killed in battles with the natives, forty-five were felled by small-pox, nine starved to death, and fourteen were drowned. Ulcers, typhoid fever, overdoses of opium, crocodiles, and other causes accounted for the rest.

The price of Stanley's victory was high. What had he accomplished? Neither before nor since has any single African expedition accomplished so much. To realize the importance of his work, it is necessary to look at a map of Central Africa before Stanley's expedition. In spite of the explorations of Livingstone, Burton, Grant, Baker, and Schweinfurth, the maps of Central Africa were largely blank spaces. The existence of the Victoria Nyanza, Lake Tanganyika, and the Congo River were known, but their outlines, exact locations, and connections were conjectural. In addition to surveying these great lakes and the world's second longest river, Stanley discovered new lakes and marked a streak of "known territory" across twenty-five degrees of longitude on Africa's map.

Even more important than the geographical discoveries were the political and commercial implications of his explorations. The great powers of the world were suddenly made aware of the potentials of the great continent. At this time less than one fifth of Africa was claimed by European nations; only seventeen years later there were scarcely a hundred square yards left unclaimed. This neglected giant of a land became an object of intense interest to millions of people throughout the world. The end of Stanley's expedition marked the beginning of the history of modern Central Africa, and Stanley was to have an important part to play in its political and cultural development.

Stanley was only thirty-seven when he completed his expedition, but his adventures had prematurely aged him. His hair, black when he started, was almost gray, and he looked ten years older than he was.

By December 13, 1877, Stanley had paid off his followers, the relatives of the deceased, and all of his creditors, and was ready to depart from Zanzibar. All of his people came down to see him off. When he was about to step into the small boat that would take him out to his steamer, they shoved the boat out into the water and then lifted him up and carried him on their heads through the surf to the boat.

Even after he was on board the steamer, several of them manned a lighter and rowed out to say good-by to their leader once more—Uledi, Zaidi, Manwa Sera, and the rest of the chiefs were there. They assured Stanley that, if he wished, they would go with him to see him home to his own country; all of them swore they would not leave Zanzibar again until they heard he had reached his home safely. Stanley said of them: "For me they are heroes, these poor ignorant children of Africa, for, from the first deadly struggle in savage Ituru to the last staggering rush into Embomma, they had rallied to my voice like veterans, and in the hour of need they had never failed me."

## CHAPTER X

# *Founding an Empire*

O F ALL THE GREAT African explorers, Stanley alone followed up his explorations by developing the vast untamed area he had revealed. Stanley had the nineteenth-century faith in the virtues of civilization and material progress. He believed mankind would be bettered if only he could "pour the civilization of Europe into the barbarian of Africa." Trade would surely bring culture and religion in its wake. In his mind isolation was the great curse of Central Africa; if European businessmen and missionaries would open up the great continent to the civilized influences of the modern world, the African Negro would emerge from barbarism, and there would be an end to tribal wars, superstition, slave hunting, and cannibalism.

Stanley felt also that the opening of the African interior to trade would be advantageous to the European, for, besides ivory, there were rare woods, ores, palm oil, valuable nuts, and other natural resources that would well repay the effort of going several thousand miles to get them. The 1,425,000 square miles of the Congo basin comprised a tract of land comparable in both extent and resources to the Mississippi or the Amazon. The Congo River, fully three thousand miles long and pouring twelve million cubic feet of water every second into the Atlantic, was a tremendous source of power. It was the natural channel by which civilization could be infused into Central Africa if the formidable obstacles, both physical and human, could be overcome.

The mouth of the Congo was discovered by a Portuguese seaman named Diogo Cam around 1482, and he named the river Rio de Padrao. Later it came to be called the Zaire on Portuguese maps. The river would doubtless have given up its secrets long before Stanley's time if its navigation were not blocked by nearly two hundred miles of cataracts and rapids, these being surrounded by rugged hills near the river's mouth. In 1816 the British government dispatched a scientific expedition under the command of Captain James Kingston Tuckey to explore the Congo River. The expedition was able to penetrate only a hundred and seventy-two miles inland before it was turned back by the cataracts and by a high death rate. Of the fifty-six Europeans on the expedition, eighteen died, including Captain Tuckey, although they spent less than three months on the river. Their fate effectively discouraged all further exploration until Stanley's descent of the river in 1876-1877.

Stanley's plan for the development of the Congo was to cut around the cataracts and rapids, first by a wagon road and later with a railroad. Then steamers could be launched on the river and a chain of stations, which would serve as trading centers and military garrisons, could be built up the river into the heartland.

Stanley could not wait to get back to England before revealing his great plan. His letters to the *Telegraph* hinted at the vast and inviting political and commercial possibilities the Congo offered to Great Britain. But, initially, Stanley had no desire to accomplish these ambitious plans himself.

Arriving in Europe in January, 1878, he was met at Marseilles by two representatives of Leopold II, King of the Belgians, who tried to persuade him to return to Africa at once under the auspices of an organization known as the *Association Internationale Africaine*, headed by Leopold himself. Stanley refused this offer. His body was emaciated and his constitution was nearly wrecked; he needed and wanted rest.

But before he could take time out for recuperation, he had one more task to fulfill: his publishers were anxious for a book describing his journey across Africa. Just four months after his return he submitted the manuscript for *Through the Dark Continent*, a book that in published form covered more than a thousand pages in two volumes. Now, at last, he was free from all work, cares, and responsibility for the first time in his life.

He sampled all of the famous European resorts: Trouville, Deauville, Dieppe, and Switzerland. The more he tried to rest, the more he fidgeted. He wanted to "lounge," but he had never learned how. He was tormented by "morbid feelings." Freedom from work he found "insipid and joyless." Lack of responsibility he found unbearable. When, in August, 1878, one of Leopold's representatives again asked to meet with him in Paris to discuss the Congo, Stanley readily agreed, but nothing tangible came of this meeting.

In September he went to England, where he was given a hero's welcome. Indeed, the whole world hastened to do him honor for his achievement. King Umberto of Italy sent him his portrait with a complimentary inscription, the Khedive of Egypt sent him a medal, all of the leading geographical societies gave him gold medals, the Prince of Wales paid him tribute, and many chambers of commerce, European governments, and learned societies honored him. In the United States, a unanimous vote of thanks was passed by both the Senate and the House of Representatives. For most people there were no longer any doubts concerning the success or the abilities of the most famous African explorer alive; in final homage, wax museums hastened to make up tableaux of Stanley surrounded by wild beasts and cannibals.

But there were also a few bits of criticism. A member of Parliament denounced him for his retaliation upon the natives of Bumbireh, the Aborigines Protection Society deplored the looting of the ivory meskiti, and there were a few ugly whispers that it was strange none of the white men who went into Africa with Stanley ever came out. As Stanley lectured throughout the country on the commercial advantages to be gained by the development of the Congo area, both the British government and the English merchants turned a deaf ear to him. His latest achievements in Africa had won him world-wide fame, but his ideas on the development of the Congo basin were called quixotic. Civilizing the natives was a job for missionaries and he was denounced by the pious as a mere adventurer who put commerce before religion.

When, in November, 1878, Stanley was asked to come to Brussels for a personal interview with Leopold, he accepted. He found that the Belgian king had already assembled a number of prominent people from England, Germany, France, Belgium, and Holland who were interested in the development of West Africa. A committee—the *Comité d'Étude du Haut Congo*—was formed with Leopold as its president for the purpose of studying the possibility of doing further work in the Congo area.

Two months later, Stanley was on his way back to Africa. He had accepted the offer of the committee to put what were essentially his own ideas into practice. While stores and equipment were being assembled in Europe, he hurried off to Zanzibar to recruit some of his "faithfuls" for this new venture. While in the neighborhood of the island, he found time to complete a number of other tasks. Technically, the *Comité d'Étude du Haut Congo*, for whom Stanley worked, was at this time separate from the African International Association. Nevertheless, both organizations had Leopold as their president and guiding spirit and their aims were similar. When the leader of the first African International Association expedition, which had been sent out from East Africa, ran into difficulties in Unyanyembe, Stanley sent off a long letter giving the expedition's leader detailed instructions on what he should do and how he should do it. He also organized and sent out a second African International Association expedition into East Africa. In addition, he made some exploratory excursions up the Wami and Rufiji rivers and took trips to Dar es Salaam and the island of Mafia.

In the later part of May, 1879, Stanley and sixty-eight Zanzibaris, three fourths of whom had served with him on his last expedition, set sail from Zanzibar for the mouth of the Congo by way of the Red Sea and the Mediterranean. The following entry is from Stanley's journal: "August 15, 1879. Arrived off the mouth of the Congo. Two years have passed since I was here before, after my descent of the great river, in 1877. Now, having been the first to explore it, I am to be the first who shall prove its utility to the world. I now debark my seventy Zanzibaris and Somalis for the purpose of beginning to civilize the Congo basin."

What a magnificent presumption! One man with less than a hundred followers, three fourths of whom could neither read nor write, presumed to bring civilization to several millions of the most savage people on earth living in one of the world's most remote and inhospitable regions with a debilitating, furnace-like climate and filled with wild beasts, dense jungles, treacherous rivers, and insects carrying exotic and fatal diseases! Add to these realities the fact that Stanley had comparatively meager funds (initially, sixty thousand dollars), and was not backed by any recognized government. It was a glorious dream, but like most dreams, it seemed to bear little relation to the realities of life.

During the five and a half years he was engaged in the project he was subjected to a continual stream of exasperating and frustrating experiences. Man and nature seemingly conspired to bring him to defeat or to drive him to utter distraction. But of the two, man was his greatest cross—particularly the white Europeans.

Stanley, who could be the most tactful of men when dealing with Arabs or African natives, somehow seemed to feel that this quality was unnecessary—or should be unnecessary—when dealing with Europeans. Certainly a part of the difficulties that were to come were due to this failing, but he did have a great deal to contend with in his relationships with his white officers, a conglomeration of Americans, Danes, Englishmen, Belgians, and Frenchmen. Some were little more than technicians who had never worked with natives before; many were gentlemen who had never worked with their hands and were shocked to find that they were expected to do so. From the very beginning of the expedition, they complained, became affronted, and haggled over their contracts. Almost all of them clamored for expense money of all kinds; they wanted free tobacco, clothes, wine, board, and decent lodging. One said that he would not stay in the Congo unless these items were given to him. Another said that if he was expected to drive a steam launch unassisted he must have higher pay, and that if he was to be sent into the interior his pay should be increased still more.

Quarrels also broke out among them over their proper rank. An engineer of a steamer protested because he was not accorded the same rank as the expedition's general accountant. Men in charge of the larger boats complained because they were forced to eat at the same table with men who commanded smaller boats. Many of them threatened to write letters of complaint to the *Comité d'Étude du Haut Congo* or to the newspapers. In spite of difficulties with his men and mechanical difficulties with the four boats they had brought with them, Stanley took his force up the Congo as far as they could navigate and there planted his first station, Vivi (later moved and called Mataddi). After negotiating treaties with the natives for the use of the land, the real work began. First of all, a road had to be built from Vivi to Isangila, around the first set of rapids and cataracts. The road had to be more than a mere path over the rocks and through the trees; it had to stand up under heavy loads in both rainy and dry seasons. Consequently, Stanley planned to build his road of crushed rock, covered over with a thin layer of clay wherever possible. While the natives and Zanzibaris looked on, he picked up a sledge hammer and patiently taught them how to crush big rocks into little ones. This simple feat earned him his African name: Bula Matari (Breaker of Rocks). By this name he became known throughout the Congo from Stanley Falls to the sea.

The building of the fifty-two-mile road from Vivi to Isangila took nearly a year—from March 18, 1880, to February 21, 1881—and Stanley estimated that in marching and countermarching over the road he walked 2352 miles. The road cost the lives of six Europeans and twenty-two natives and Zanzibaris; in addition, thirteen whites had to be invalided home. There was little glamour in this task. It was hard, back-breaking toil for whites and blacks alike. They worked ten hours a day, six days a week, in rocks and stubborn scrub in a hot and enervating atmosphere. Their diet consisted of beans, goat meat, and sodden bananas.

The Zanzibaris proved good workmen, and Stanley was even able to induce some of the local natives to work regularly for wages—a novelty to them. But the slowness of their progress led to uneasiness back in Belgium, and the *Comité d'Étude du Haut Congo* could not resist sending suggestions for speeding up the work. Stanley, however, had no patience to spare for their anxieties, and in the summer of 1880 he wrote these comments to Colonel M. Strauch, chairman of the committee:

"You have instructed me to convey a steamer and a boat to Manyanga station, and another boat to Stanley Pool, and build three stations—one at Vivi, one at Manyanga, and one at some convenient point on the shores of Stanley Pool; for which task I obtained sixty-eight Zanzibaris, and as many west-coast natives as I could induce to enter into our service; the number of the latter, despite my best efforts, is today exactly sixty-six. On this morning's sick list, which is only an average number, I have sixteen invalids, who, with boys and cooks, make a non-working number of twenty-four, leaving me with an effective working force of 110 men, who are to convey fifty-four tons into the interior, and have yet to make a road 125 miles long before Stanley Pool is reached.

"I beg to inform you that if the whole talent and genius of Belgium were here to assist my progress with their advice, they could not increase my working force, but they might add to my burdens and sick list. I am quite satisfied with my people; they perform all that can be reasonably expected of them. To expect they should do more would be criminal ingratitude in me.

"These and similar facts have been repeated to you since February of this year. The truths they describe should by this time be clearly obvious, so that I am somewhat ashamed to iterate and repeat them.

"Our part in the committee's project is easily demonstrable. We will continue to perform it effectively and zealously, but by the enclosed balance sheet of work done you may be able to calculate how fast our advance must be forward, so long as we have only these few men. Whatever number you add to our force of *working* men you may easily calculate our increased rate of progress. Whatever orders or suggestions you give or make will be instantly obeyed. Double our power, and we will double our speed; treble the working power, and our speed will be three times quicker. With sufficient men we could be at Stanley

Pool within one month. If you send us no more men, then we will go on as we can, steadily and faithfully."

Stanley did go on, but he encountered unexpected political complications. On November 7, 1880, Lutete Kuna, a native of Nsanda who was working for Stanley, came rushing into camp with a piece of paper on which was written in pencil, "Le Comte Savorgnan de Brazza." As this name meant nothing to Stanley, he questioned Lutete. The Negro told him how he had unexpectedly encountered a tall white man in a neighboring village. "Francess, he tells me he is—who kept firing at the trees with a gun that shoots many times. Now, Bula Matari, tell me why do white men shoot at trees? Is it to kill the bad spirit?"

"Perhaps," Stanley said, "but what more?"

"Oh, after he found out I belonged to your company, he gave me that piece of paper and told me to carry it to you."

An hour later, Count de Brazza entered Stanley's camp with fifteen men, principally Gabonese sailors, all armed with Winchester repeating rifles. De Brazza was a wealthy and enterprising Frenchman, ten years younger than Stanley, who, hearing of his work, had, with the aid of the French government and, strangely enough, the International African Association, rushed across West Africa from Libreville on the coast of Gabon to a point on the Congo River far above Stanley. He had worked his way down the north bank of the river, concluding treaties with the native tribes that placed them under French protection.

It was some time, however, before Stanley discovered exactly what De Brazza had done. Although somewhat puzzled by his presence, Stanley helped him on his way down the river. During his two-day stay in the camp, Count de Brazza inspected the road and, looking at the rocky mass of Ngoma which they had yet to pass, remarked, "It will take you six months to pass that mountain with those wagons. Your force is too weak altogether for such work as you are engaged in. You should have at least five hundred men."

Stanley certainly agreed that he needed more men; but since he did not have them, he struggled on with what he had, completing the road three months later. Now began the laborious task of hauling the boats and supplies over the road to Isangila, building another station, launching the boats, and transporting the supplies eighty miles upstream to Manyanga, where a third station was to be built. At Isangila, incidentally, Stanley discovered that the gallant *Lady Alice* of his previous expedition had been broken up by the natives for her tacks and nails.

By May 1, 1881, the station at Manyanga, a hundred and forty miles above Vivi, was completed. Four days later, Stanley, after twelve full months of uninterrupted good health, came down with a violent attack of fever. At first he was more exasperated than alarmed by the attack—it kept him from his work. But the next day, in spite of heavy doses of medicine, the fever increased. On May 9, now suffering from nausea, he had his tent moved to the top of a hill about two hundred and eighty feet above the river. By May 11, the fever was worse. Twenty grains of quinine dissolved in hydrobromic acid did not seem to help, so the next day Stanley increased the dosage to thirty grains. For the next six days he was unconscious most of the time, being aware only of the fact that he was being cared for by Mabruki and Dualla, his servants. One of his officers, Lieutenant Braconnier, came daily to suggest some new remedy to him, but Stanley held tenaciously to the belief that he could be cured only by taking larger and larger doses of quinine. On the fourteenth day of his fever he was so weak that he could not sit up or even lift his arms. Limp and nerveless, he was raised up by Mabruki and Dualla to take fifty grains of quinine.

Two days later, on May 20, it seemed to him that his sickness had reached a climax. He had a strong presentiment that he was going to die. His work was unfinished—but he was dying. He had to give some last words of encouragement to his people. Mabruki was sent to call all of the Europeans and Zanzibaris to his bedside, while Dualla prepared a mixture of *sixty* grains of quinine and some hydrobromic acid in an ounce of Madeira wine. Downing this kill-or-cure solution, Stanley sent Dualla to hasten up his people before it was too late for them to hear his final words. He heard the rush of feet outside his tent. Lifted up, he could see that the walls of the tent had been raised and that his faithful Zanzibaris were sitting in a circle around him. His white officers stood at the foot of his bed. He struggled hard to keep control of his senses as the powerful drugs he had taken coursed through his emaciated body and dulled his fevered brain.

Albert Christopherson, a young Danish sailor who was a favorite of Stanley's and who seems to have been much like Frank Pocock, stood beside him and took his hand as with all his strength he strove to utter the words that his lips and tongue could not form. At last he was able to speak one clear and intelligible sentence. So relieved was he at this success that he cried out, "I am saved!"

Then he lost consciousness for twenty-four hours. He awoke weak, but hungry; his weight was down to a hundred pounds, but he felt that he was at last on the road to recovery. By the end of May he felt

well enough to sit in a chair outside his tent and to be carried about
the camp. Then, on July 4, when he received the good news that a large
body of recruits had arrived from Zanzibar, his recovery seemed
complete.

Although still weak, he resumed his work with undiminished passion.
Oddly enough, Stanley had little trouble with hostile natives; the same
people who had attacked him in 1877 were now eager to make friends
with him. He attributed this change to the slowness of his progress.
As he saw it, this allowed ample time for the reputation of Bula Matari
to travel up the river. His name became so respected that his officers
were frequently saved from the necessity of fighting with warlike
natives by calling out that they were the "sons of Bula Matari."
Eventually, his African name came to be synonymous with his government, and it was so used long after he left the Congo. Even today,
natives in the Belgian Congo who are working on government projects
will sometimes say that they are "working for Bula Matari."

As step by step he extended his chain of stations up the Congo,
Stanley negotiated with the chiefs of the tribes along the river's southern banks, purchasing from them not only their lands but essentially
the sovereignty of their people as well. Few objected to this procedure,
but some of the chiefs who had been paid for their lands and rights
became greedy for more of the white man's goods. One of the most
troublesome was a powerful chief called Ngalyema. Pretending that he
had not been paid at all, he sent message after message to Stanley—
first demanding, then threatening. As the messages failed to elicit the
riches he sought, he decided to pay a personal visit. Through the jungle
grapevine, Stanley heard of Ngalyema's coming and prepared to receive
him.

When Ngalyema strode into Bula Matari's camp—accompanied by
his warriors dressed in battle paint and bearing freshly sharpened
spears—he found Stanley alone and calmly reading a book in front of
his tent. As he approached, Stanley jumped to his feet and greeted
him warmly, calling him "brother" to remind him that they had
mingled their blood and had sworn to be blood brothers in a common
African ceremony. Ngalyema was taken off guard by this exhibition of
friendship, but he coolly restated his extortionate demands. As he
talked, his eye was taken by a large gong prominently displayed beside
the tent. He demanded to know what it was, but Stanley warned him
not to touch it as the gong was a powerful fetish. Ngalyema imperi-
ously ordered that it be struck. Stanley begged the chief not to force

him to strike it as the sound of the gong would cause armed men to spring out of the ground and drop from the trees.

Ngalyema's curiosity got the better of him; the temptation was too great; he insisted that it be struck at once. Still protesting, Stanley finally hit the gong a thwack that rocked the jungle with its echoes. At once the foliage sprouted armed men. They sprang up from the grass and dropped from the branches of every tree. Screaming and waving their muskets, they ran straight for Ngalyema's warriors. Forgetting their war paint and dropping their spears, these stalwarts fled, leaving their chief clutching at Stanley's coat and begging for deliverance. Stanley slapped the gong once more, and his Zanzibaris fell into orderly ranks and stood obediently at attention.

Although Ngalyema learned his lesson that day, its moral did not long remain with him. Stanley was forced to deal with him time and time again, and it was many months before the savage learned that he could neither frighten nor deceive Bula Matari.

Stanley regarded the Africans as children who must be taught many lessons. He saw himself as their teacher, and he knew that he must be patient. In his dealings with the natives he always seemed to have an inexhaustible fund of patience; with his European officers, he had very little. When a native broke a promise—as Ngalyema did time after time—he was never surprised or even very irritated, but set about patiently to woo him back into friendship and to teach him that he must live up to his promises.

Stanley did not believe that such tolerance was necessary in dealing with his Europeans. To him, this undertaking was a crusade. He felt that the Europeans should share his vision, but to them it was simply an agonizing and purposeless job. Their lack of foresight and querulousness exasperated Stanley. His rigid demands and lack of understanding infuriated them.

The men did have cause for complaint. They were expected to work until they dropped—and drop they did. One man out of every nine died from a fatal accident or from disease, and nearly half of the remainder quit before the expiration of their three-year contracts. The Congo became known as the "white man's grave."

On the other hand, Stanley was not being unreasonable. He did not feel that equatorial Africa was dangerous to men of common sense, and he was appalled by what he regarded as the stupidity and unsuitability of the Europeans sent to him. In a report to Colonel Strauch he mentioned one officer "whose conduct has revealed to me an amount of selfishness that has been a novelty to me from its intensity and peculiarity." The Belgian committee received a constant stream of letters from Stanley begging for more competent officers. For the most part, they sent him gentlemen instead of leaders, dandies instead of workers.

Stanley did not feel himself to blame for the failure of his officers: "Being of an open temper and frank disposition, and always willing to hear what my officers or men had to say, though as a leader of men I could not hob-nob with my officers, they ought to have found no difficulty in understanding me. The black man certainly was never at a loss to do so."

Stanley had no real friends and many enemies among his officers. Even Albert Christopherson, his favorite, left him when his contract expired. While the Zanzibaris and the Congo natives would suffer abuse and quickly forget it, the white men harbored smoldering resentments after they had been caught up short by their quick-tempered leader. He gained a reputation as a hard man. In answer to this he said, "One is not likely to be hard with persons who perform their duties; but it is difficult to be mild, or amiable, with people who are absolutely incapable, and who will not listen to admonition without bristling with resentment."

Perhaps the differences in outlook and temperament between Stanley and his European subordinates can best be illustrated by the case of Lieutenant Braconnier, already mentioned. To Stanley, young Braconnier seemed simply incompetent, unsuited by education or temperament for the task of empire building in Central Africa. At one time, he charged, Braconnier, who should have known better, had stood by and allowed an inexperienced young Austrian officer with six Zanzibaris to enter a small overloaded boat on the treacherous Congo. Fifteen minutes later the boat had sunk, and all seven men were drowned. On another occasion, during the building of the wagon road from Vivi to Isangila, when Stanley was laid up by a fever, Braconnier was asked to supervise the work of getting a boiler wagon down a steep hill. Ten minutes after undertaking this task, boiler, wagon, and Braconnier were *hors de combat*.

But the worst charge leveled against the Belgian officer was the neglect of his station. Braconnier was once appointed to take charge of one of the most important stations on the Congo, Leopoldville, today a modern city and the capital of the Belgian Congo. When Stanley saw the station four months after Braconnier took charge, it was in ruins and the surrounding natives had been turned from friends into enemies by the station commander. Stanley put up with this sort of incompetence for nearly three years before sending the lieutenant back to Europe.

Braconnier, in turn, developed that mixture of dislike and respect that was typical of the officers serving under Stanley. He once gave the following analysis of his former chief: "He is a man of sudden resolutions and irresolutions. Ten minutes before he starts he hardly knows himself whether or where he is going. No one can admire Stanley's qualities more than I. He is a man of iron—easily discouraged, indeed, but quick to regain courage; full of dogged will, which is his strength, and a splendid leader. In his dealings with the natives, whatever lies people may say of him, he is invariably kind, merciful, and politic. He can palaver with them. He respects their religions, their customs, their traditions. There is not an atom of truth in the iniquitous accusations of cruelty brought against him and the officers in general. But he has one fault, he is not so unselfish as he might be. He is far too inconsiderate of his European fellow-workers, and more esteemed than liked. He treats his white companions as though he were a little king— lives apart, never 'chums' with them, and at certain moments would think it justifiable to sacrifice any one of them to his own safety. I never asked him for 'reasons.' Sometimes he would say to me, 'Braconnier, strike your tents, we start in ten minutes.' Had I been foolish enough to say, 'Where are we going?' he would have answered, 'Mind your own business, not mine.' I have watched him smoking under his tent, knowing all the time his officers had no tobacco, and it would never occur to him to offer them a pipe. You must live with him a long time to understand him. However long you might know him I doubt that you would ever become his friend."

Aware of the expense of sending out Europeans, Stanley was always reluctant to discharge the officers who had been sent to him—even though he considered most of them to be utter fools. The *Comité d'Étude du Haut Congo*, established by Leopold to set policy and to act as a base for supplies, was also responsible for sending out the Europeans who were to be Stanley's officers. But the committee had a difficult time. Some men would come out to the Congo, spend a few weeks, then send in their resignations and go home. One man arrived at Banana Point, at the very mouth of the Congo, and immediately turned around and went home without even having the courage to see Vivi.

Stanley had a high, solitary concept of leadership and he paid for his aloofness with loneliness. He wrote, "I have had no friend on any expedition, no one who could possibly be my companion, on an equal footing, except while with Livingstone."

But there was always his duty, his work. For him it was a shining vision that absorbed him completely. "Though altogether solitary, I was never less conscious of solitude," he wrote, "though as liable to be prostrated by fever as the youngest, I was never more indifferent to its sharpest attacks, or less concerned for its results. My only comfort was my work. To it I turned as a friend. It occupied my days, and I dwelt fondly on it at night. I rose in the morning, welcoming the dawn, only because it assisted me to my labour; and only those who regard it from a similar temperament could I consider as my friends. Though this may be poorly expressed, nevertheless, those who can comprehend what I mean will understand the main grounds."

Stanley could not understand, and had little use for, those who held their duty more lightly than he did. While engaged in the building of Leopoldville, he received word that the chief of Vivi station had suddenly quit and gone home. Although bound by a formal contract, he had not even bothered to send Stanley a letter of resignation! How could he found a nation with such stuff as this?

Fortunately, this particular information was accompanied by news of the arrival of a hundred additional Zanzibaris. Nothing could have pleased him more. He had developed, through experience, a tremendous partiality for the Zanzibari. To Colonel Strauch he wrote, "The only people on whom my words take due effect and create a prolonged impression are the foreign coloured employees"—that is, the Zanzibaris. They were brave, they were malleable, and some were very loyal. Many of those now with him, like the brave Uledi, had been with him in the rough days of his second expedition across Africa. Some, who had survived many other perils with Stanley, died on this project. Soudi, the young man who had been wounded in Ituru in 1875 and who had had such a narrow escape when he went over Kalulu Falls in 1877, was finally killed in the Congo by a water buffalo in 1881.

But as fond as he was of the Zanzibaris, Stanley had to admit that many of them were incredibly stupid. One man had used a musket for three years and still could not remember whether the powder or the ball should be loaded into the muzzle first. Sometimes their stupidities were ludicrous. Rushing down the Congo in a canoe one day, Stanley caught sight of a good place for a camp and steered toward the shore. He called to the man in the bow to seize the tough grass growing on the bank so as to stop the boat. "Hold hard, Kirango!" Stanley called. "Please God, master," the man cried as he leaped from the canoe and grabbed the grass while the boat swept on down the river.

With all of his difficulties with his men and officers, one wonders how anything was accomplished. Yet progress was made. When Leopold-ville was finished in the early part of 1882, Stanley looked on it with satisfaction and special pride. It consisted of an impregnable block-house, a village with broad streets, gardens with bananas and veg-etables, and well-stocked storehouses. There was even a smooth promenade where Stanley envisioned Europeans strolling on Sunday afternoons to look at the river, cataract, mountain, and forests. In his journal for February 5, 1882, he noted: "I perceive from my last accounts from down-river that we are progressing exceedingly well, despite drawbacks caused by faithless Europeans."

What he had accomplished so far had required an iron will and a stern attention to duty. He had no interest in sport—not even hunting. He stalked game only when it was needed for food. He did not play cards or any other game, and he read only to learn. He was a grave and serious man, certainly, but he was not completely devoid of humor —in his own ironic way. When a delegation of clerks came to him to protest a lack of what they considered proper provisions, Stanley listened to them attentively, and then said gravely, "Let us pray."

When a man named Ingham established a missionary station not far from Manyanga, Stanley paid him a visit. Attracted by a bright little native boy there, he patted the boy on the head and said:

"I should not be surprised, Ingham, if this little fellow becomes a bishop."

"I don't know," said Ingham, "he is sometimes very disagreeable."

"A sure sign he will be a bishop," replied Stanley.

His work left little time for pure exploration, but in the spring of 1882 Stanley did make one exploratory trip up the Kwa River. Using one of the steamboats, he took Albert Christopherson, Uledi, and some of his other Zanzibaris and set out on a trip that seemed more like recreation than actual work for the explorer. They discovered an im-portant lake, however, which Stanley christened Lake Leopold.

Returning from this excursion, Stanley came down with another violent attack of fever accompanied by "gastric attacks in the stomach." This illness lasted a full month, and it left him exceedingly weak. Tak-ing advantage of the presence of a well-known African explorer, a German named Dr. Peschuel-Loeche, Stanley decided that he could leave the work in his hands while he returned to Europe to convalesce. Leaving Vivi station the middle of July, he arrived in Lisbon on September 21, 1882.

In October, he was setting forth to present to the committee of the *Association Internationale du Congo,* which had taken over the functions of the old *Comité d'Étude du Haut Congo,* a complete report on what he had accomplished. He had done all that had been expected of him and more. Five stations had been built, reaching four hundred and forty miles inland; a steamer and a sailboat had been launched on the Upper Congo (above Stanley Pool); a small steamer and a lighter maintained communication between Isangila and Manyanga; and a wagon road had been built between Vivi and Isangila. Stanley then outlined to the committee all that still needed to be done. They agreed with him and promised to do all that he suggested provided that he return to the Congo and complete the work himself. Because of his poor health, Stanley was reluctant to return immediately. He wanted to have his teeth fixed in Brussels and to rest in southern Spain in the hope that the climate would cure his respiratory ailments. But with the promise that a suitable assistant would be sent who could take care of the stations on the Lower Congo while he was occupied in extending the chain of stations and making treaties with the natives on the Upper Congo, he consented to return to Africa after only six weeks in Europe.

Stanley wanted a man to assist him who would be solid and reliable; a man of sufficient reputation and depth of judgment to inspire respect in his subordinates. He wanted a man who would not only work himself, but would see to it that others worked. Still complaining about the Europeans who had been sent to him, he said: "These people had already given me more trouble than all the African tribes put together. They had inspired such disgust in me that I would rather be condemned to be a-bootblack all my life than to be a dry-nurse to beings who had no higher claim to manhood than that externally they might be pretty pictures of men."

The committee promised him faithfully that within the next few months they would find a man who would meet Stanley's requirements, and send him to the Congo. So, on November 23, 1882, he sailed from Cadiz, arriving at the mouth of the Congo River on December 14.

He was heartsick and wrathful when he found that much of his work had gone to ruin in his absence. In his trip up the Congo he found one neglected station after another. At Vivi he learned that the steamers had been taken possession of by a party that had attached itself to the expedition, originally for the purpose of providing transport on the Lower Congo, but which, by some strange process, dominated the expedition by withholding all the steamers and boats and landing goods where it pleased them, usually a mile below the landing place. When he arrived at Leopoldville, his greatest pride, Stanley found the storerooms empty, the gardens overgrown with weeds, the houses for the native workers crumbling, the boats uncared for, and the whole place in a state of near-siege through the alienation of the natives.

Peace, order, progress, and work followed shortly after his arrival, but he could not be everywhere at once. Here is a partial report of only one day's news and activities:

"March 24th. Dispatched Lieutenant Orban with thirty-one men to Vivi, to hurry up by forced marches a caravan with brass rods. . . .

"Received news to-day that a Mons. Callewart had been killed and decapitated at Kimpoko, the station near head of Stanley Pool on the south bank. . . .

"This evening I received by courier letters from down river. Second chief at Vivi declaims against asking him to manage the duties of chief, second chief, and shopkeeper, and declares he will not—suffer who may. His letter is remarkable for impoliteness, and is replete with gross accusations against a number of people.

"The officer in charge of the transport of a whaleboat from Vivi to Isangila, having fifty-eight men with him, writes that he cannot, and will not, carry the boat with such a limited number.

"The chief of Manyanga writes that the chief in charge of Vivi is acting an 'infamous comedy,' that his letters demanding supplies are unanswered.

"He also writes that Mons. Luksic, an Austrian marine officer, has committed suicide by shooting himself through the head."

Stanley worked his way through these crises and set out by steamboat up the Congo. His job for the next year and a half was to make treaties with the natives of the tribes along the river banks and to establish more stations. Over four hundred treaties were made, and the foundations of the *État Indépendent du Congo* (Congo Free State) were firmly established.

Just when Stanley despaired of ever finding men who would be able to build and maintain stations as he thought they should be built and maintained, he was heartened to find that one station he had built right on the equator—and thus named Equator station—had blossomed into a model little settlement under the direction of two young

Belgian army officers: Lieutenant Vangele and Lieutenant Coquilhat. They had built themselves a house of clay and fitted it with window frames and doors; they had made themselves chairs, tables, and stools and had even put curtains up at the windows; clay barracks had been constructed for the men; drainage had been adequately provided for; thriving gardens had been planted, barns built for fowl and goats. For the first time, Stanley saw the realization of his dreams. This station, seven hundred and sixty miles from the coast, was to continue to prosper. Today it is the modern city of Coquilhatville.

The trip up the river awakened many memories. He was pleased that he was able to make blood brotherhood with most of the savage tribes he had fought six years before. Even the wild and warlike Bangala made friends with Bula Matari, although there was a tense moment in the negotiations when they discovered that he was the same man who had passed through their country before and defeated them on the river.

In the minds of the natives, there was an aura of wonder about Stanley's first trip down the river. The curiosity he had excited then was heightened by his return in that wonder of wonders, a steamboat. The bales of cloth, the quantities of brass rods, and the usual trinkets and beads that were first given as presents and later offered in trade, opened up the Congo to commercial intercourse with the white man. It was Stanley's hope that this wonder, this curiosity, would be changed to friendliness, respect, an eagerness to trade, and eventually a desire to emulate civilized ways. By his diplomacy, his patience, and his understanding of the primitive Negro mind and psychology, he laid a foundation for this dream. That it failed to materialize as he had imagined was due to no fault of his.

The inhabitants of the Congo had a long way to go before they could even approach a civilized state. The tattooed and naked savages lived in what seemed like barbarous depravity. Their Stone- and Iron-Age world was almost without morals by our standards. These primitive people lived little better than animals in a world which their imagination filled with witchcraft, superstition, and terror.

Lieutenant Vangele of the Equator station was once asked by the local natives of the Bakuti tribe to sell some of the men who were working for him. They assumed that the loyal and obedient Zanzibaris were his slaves. The young lieutenant turned down the request, but he was curious and soon learned why they were wanted. An old chief had died, and the Bakutis planned to make a human sacrifice. Lieutenant

Vangele was a witness to what happened to the fourteen native slaves they were finally able to obtain.

All of the slaves were bound with their hands tied behind them. One at a time, they were taken to a sapling that was bent nearly double. The slave was made to kneel and the end of the sapling was tied to his head and then released so that his neck was drawn taut. The executioner now advanced with a broadsword, and, like a golfer about to make a drive, he twice put the blade on the man's neck where he wanted to cut and then drew his weapon back. The third time he struck, cutting the head from the body. The head was thrown high in the air by the released sapling and bounded along the ground several yards away. When all the slaves had been dispatched in this manner, the heads were boiled until the skin came off and the skulls were placed on poles around the old chief's grave. The headless bodies were thrown into the Congo, and the blood-saturated soil was scooped up and buried with the chief.

Herbert Ward, another of Stanley's officers, recorded seeing a similar ceremony. Just before one of the slaves was to be decapitated, however, a relative of the dead chief came up to the doomed slave and gave him a message to relay to the spirit of the departed. He concluded his message with ". . . and tell him when you meet, that his biggest war canoe, which I inherit, is *rotten*."

Slavery was a common evil throughout the African continent. Tribe raided tribe, but it was the Arabs and certain Europeans who put the business on a wholesale basis. Whole villages were destroyed, and sometimes entire areas covering many hundreds of square miles were completely depopulated by the slave raiders. Chained, yoked, and starved, the poor savages were often forced to march thousands of miles to the coast to be sold at slave auctions if they survived. It was a multimillion-dollar infamous industry.

Although not apparent at first, the founding of the Congo State was one of the first major blows to the slave business. Perhaps the founding of this African nation, although less spectacular than his other exploits, was Stanley's greatest accomplishment. But even Stanley could not do everything that had to be done. While he was on the Upper Congo there would be disturbing events on the Lower Congo; while he was straightening out affairs in the Lower Congo, trouble would develop in the Upper Congo. The able assistant, promised by the Belgian committee, had not arrived.

For a while, Stanley had high hopes that the famous English general,

Charles Gordon—"Chinese Gordon"—would come out to help him. At one point, Gordon had agreed to come and had even written to Stanley saying that he was looking forward to working for him. Of this episode Stanley wrote: "There was a man at that time in retreat, near Mount Carmel. If he but emerge from his seclusion, he had all the elements in him of the man that was needed: indefatigable industry; that magnetism which commands affection, obedience, and perfect trust; that power of reconciling men, no matter of what colour, to their duties; that cheerful promise that in him lay security and peace; that loving solicitude which betokens the kindly chief. That man was General Gordon. For six months I waited for his coming; finally, letters came announcing his departure for the Soudan; and soon after, arrived Lieutenant-Colonel Francis de Winton, of the Royal Artillery, in his place."

Whatever his other qualities, De Winton was not a Gordon, and Stanley was disappointed. By 1884, when De Winton arrived in the Congo, Stanley's work was almost finished—and so was Stanley. He had been in the Congo for more than five years. He had built a line of garrisoned stations for fourteen hundred miles up the Congo, acquired sovereignty of the land from the natives, and made friends with them, established an elaborate political and commercial organization, built roads and even a small stretch of railroad, launched two steamers on the Upper Congo and three on the Lower Congo, brought peace and order to a land of anarchy, and opened up a rich and fertile country to trade and civilization. Already some traders and missionaries had ventured up the river and established trading posts and missions. On April 10, 1884, the United States Senate authorized President Arthur to recognize the African International Association as the governing power on the Congo. Although this action was criticized in the American press and condemned by several European governments, recognition by other countries followed.

Stanley turned his command over to De Winton and left the Congo for Europe, leaving Vivi on June 6 and arriving at Plymouth on July 29. Four days later he crossed the Channel to give his report to Leopold at Ostend. The physical and political developments achieved in the Congo had begun to interest the world. Africa, the sleeping giant, was at last awakening.

As Africa opened up more and more, the countries of Europe took an increasing interest in African colonies. On February 26, 1885, that shrewd German statesman Bismarck called a conference in Berlin. It opened on November 15 and was attended by representatives of Germany, Belgium, Austria-Hungary, Denmark, Spain, the United States, France, Great Britain, Italy, the Netherlands, Portugal, Russia, Sweden, and Turkey. Like boys slicing up a choice melon, the diplomats of Europe carved out great chunks of land and marked them as their own. Strangely enough, at this conference Stanley participated as a technical adviser to the United States, one of the few countries that did not want to taste the melon.*

It was in the paper that resulted from this meeting, "The General Act of the Berlin Conference," that the term "spheres of influence" was used for the first time. This document laid down the ground rules for the exploitation of the world's second largest continent. A few months later, all pretense of giving the Congo an international character was abandoned and the Congo Free State was established under the sovereignty of King Leopold II. Here was a most curious kind of country. While Leopold remained King of the Belgians, the Congo state belonged to him personally, not to Belgium. In fact, the Belgian Chamber declared that the relationship between Belgium and the Congo Free State would be "exclusively personal." Seventy-nine times larger than Belgium, it was the largest private domain in history.

This queer nation, the personal property of a king who never saw it, lasted for twenty-four years. It fell through a failure to carry out the humanitarian principles that Leopold had never ceased to profess and that Stanley had tried so hard to establish. Stanley's ideals were betrayed by the men who followed him. The abominable treatment of the natives by Leopold's officers after the departure of Stanley created a world-wide scandal. Popular feeling in the United States and Britain ran high, and a storm of abuse fell upon the European king of the Congo. There was an uproar in the American and British press, and Theodore Roosevelt, Vachel Lindsay, and Winston Churchill were among those who denounced Leopold and his Congo representatives.

In 1910, the reluctant Belgian government, with Leopold's consent, annexed the territory, and it ceased to be an independent power. As a colony of Belgium, under the name of the Belgian Congo, it exists today as one of the most stable of all African colonies and as the largest producer of an element of which both Leopold and Stanley were ignorant: uranium.

*Just six months before the conference began, Stanley made a trip to the United States. In the Superior Court of New York County he was naturalized a citizen on May 15, 1885.

# CHAPTER XI

## *Another Mission*

TERRIBLE AS STANLEY's sufferings had been on previous expeditions to Africa, they were to be completely overshadowed by his last venture. In terms of size, difficulty, danger—everything except the importance of its objective—this final expedition was his greatest. It demanded the most of his ability, his character, and his stamina. The events creating the cause of the expedition were already taking place in the Sudan. The stage was set, many of the principal characters were in their places, and the opening words of the prologue were now being spoken. The drama was beginning, but the leading actor was as yet unaware of the role he was to play.

Stanley required no preparation for his part; he needed only rest, and for the next two years he came as close to relaxing as his restless nature permitted. He wrote a two-volume book on his work in the Congo (published simultaneously in eight languages); he took part in the Berlin Conference on Africa; he lectured and traveled in Europe and the United States; he attended numerous dinners and received more medals, honorary memberships in learned societies, scrolls, testimonials, honorary degrees from universities, and the freedom of many cities.

During this period he apparently became more familiar with polite society and felt more at ease in the drawing rooms of London. He had achieved the distinction he had sought and was content enough to make peace with the English and the scientific societies. The great disillusionment and despair no longer overwhelmed him. His London lodgings were modest ones on Bond Street, where he lived with his servant and his latest adopted African boy, Baruti. As a man who had been received by Queen Victoria and was an intimate of the King of the Belgians, not to mention the Sultan of Zanzibar, he found himself a respected member of the highest society. His lectures and his books had brought him enough wealth to enable him to be independent. He was a famous, respected, and comfortably well-off man. But malicious stories, many of them circulated by men whom he had discharged in the Congo, continued to circulate and unduly to plague his sensitive nature. He still flinched at criticism.

Stanley's interest in Africa remained unabated. When Sir William MacKinnon, head of the British India Steamship Navigation Company, formed a syndicate for the exploitation of the Congo, Stanley served as his technical adviser and entered into negotiations with a representative of his former employer, King Leopold. Sir Thomas Barclay, who acted as Leopold's representative, gives an interesting picture of Stanley at this period: "H. M. Stanley was not a diplomatist. Uncompromising determination was stamped on his features. His angular form and hands were of a piece with his truculent manner. I often shared his very simple midday meal. Then, as always, we conversed à la Stanley, which meant that his words were final. He was unsympathetic yet fascinating, intensely in earnest and ruthless in his idea of duty, yet when off his guard almost sentimentally tender."

Sir Thomas also recorded an amusing account of Baruti. This boy was a member of the cannibalistic Basoko tribe, and he was more savage and untamed than the unfortunate Kalulu had been. Baruti had been captured by an Arab slaver when a child, but later came into the kindly hands of Lieutenant-Colonel Sir Francis de Winton who brought him to England to impress him with "the superiority of civilized customs." Care of the boy was then taken over by Stanley.

Barclay's story illustrates Stanley's character as much as the boy's: "He [Stanley] had a little African boy . . . who was very unhappy in European clothes within the narrow compass of Stanley's flat in Bond Street. One day I came in somewhat earlier than I was wont to do and Stanley was still out. Suddenly the door of the sitting room was thrown open and the little naked savage dashed in, flew madly round the table, springing over the sofa, flying out again, round the flat in the wildest African style, whooping, laughing and gesticulating madly. Stanley's man told me that as soon as Stanley went out, the 'little chap' flung off his clothes and became a savage till Stanley's footsteps were again heard on the staircase. He hadn't the heart to stop him, and stood 'cavey' for him. If Mr. Stanley knew, he was afraid of what might happen."

Several years later when Barclay asked about the boy, Stanley told him, "Poor little chap! He was very unhappy. He needed exercise, and I used to go out on purpose to let him have a run round the place."

But other stories, less innocent, were told of Baruti. One evening in London, when Stanley was gone, Baruti tried to persuade the housekeeper to give him some choice bit from the pantry. On being told that he could not have it, the boy seized the housekeeper's baby and dashed to the top of the stairs. At the top landing, he held the baby over the balusters, threatening to drop him unless he got his way. Stanley had a long way to go before teaching Baruti civilized virtues.

The events that were to lead Stanley back to the Congo were rapidly taking place in the northeast quarter of Africa. The Sudan, roughly a million square miles of land south of Egypt, was a wild and barbarous country, the home of savages and the haunt of Arab slave traders. Egypt had coveted the land since 1820 and, with the help of the British, she succeeded at last in establishing some sort of occupation, if not control, over this vast area. Egypt was a strange, schizophrenic conqueror. The Khedive of Egypt nominally owed allegiance to the Sultan of Turkey, but for some years prior to 1881 the country's affairs were jointly controlled by France and England. In that year an Egyptian officer, Ahmed Arabi, seized control of the government and ousted the British and French. Britain decided to take strong action and invited France to join with her in overthrowing Arabi. The French declined the invitation, and finally Great Britain took matters into her own hands. In July of 1882, British war ships bombarded the forts at Alexandria. A short time later a British force commanded by Sir Garnet Wolseley, the conqueror of Coomassie, landed at Ismailia and engaged the Egyptian forces under Arabi. On September 13, Sir Garnet's troops gained a decisive victory over Arabi at Tell-el-Kebir. The Khedive was returned, and the British assumed sole and almost complete control over Egyptian affairs.

Meanwhile, in the Sudan, there had arisen a man named Mohammed Ahmed who proclaimed himself the Mahdi, or Messiah, of Islam. While the British and Egyptians were concerned with disorders in Egypt, the Mahdi had grown powerful, raised an army, and now wielded an ever increasing influence over the wild Sudanese tribes. Unfortunately, the man who might have prevented this uprising was now in Europe. Charles "Chinese" Gordon, the "Christian soldier" who was the military hero of England and occupied a place in the hearts of the English somewhat akin to the devotion inspired by General Douglas MacArthur in the United States during World War II, had been governor general of the Sudan from 1872 to 1880 and had effectively brought a degree of order to that chaotic land. In each province he had installed capable European administrators: an Italian, Romolo Gessi, was the governor of the province of Bahr-el Gazal (he was later succeeded by an Englishman, Frank Lupton, an ex-sea captain); Darfur was governed by a young Austrian, Rudolf Slatin; and Equatoria, the southernmost province, was in charge of a Prussian doctor who called himself Mohammed Emin. Gordon and his provincial governors were, for the most part, capable and energetic, but the Egyptian civil servants, officers, and other officials were not. When Gordon left the Sudan in 1880, all of his work began to crumble.

Although allegedly religious in origin, Mahdism owed much of its popularity to the general hatred of the corrupt government in the hands of the Egyptian administrators, who could not be kept honest by the handful of European beys and pashas. At first the Egyptian and English governments did not take the Mahdist uprising seriously. When, finally, they found time to send some troops to capture the Mahdi, he was already too strong. The troops sent against him promptly deserted and joined the ranks of his militant followers. A second force was repelled. With each defeat of the Egyptians, the Mahdist movement gained in prestige and in adherents. By January, 1883, the Mahdi's forces had captured El Obeid, and in November the fanatical dervishes annihilated an army of over ten thousand troops commanded by William Hicks Pasha. In December, Slatin Bey was forced to surrender Darfur, and in February, 1884, Osman Digna, one of the Mahdi's best generals, crushed a force of four thousand Egyptians near Suakin. In April, Bahr-el Gazal fell, and Lupton Bey was sent to the Mahdi in chains to join Slatin as one of the Mahdi's slaves.

Such was the state of affairs when Gordon once more attempted to assume control at Khartoum. He was to have left England on February 6, 1884, for the Congo to help Stanley in the founding of the Congo Free State, but when he was called on to save the situation in the Sudan, he sent King Leopold his resignation and on January 18, 1884, he sailed for Egypt. There was a great deal of confusion as to exactly what Gordon's orders were. Certainly his understanding of them was not the same as that of the English government which had sent him. Most of the English public—and probably Gordon himself—felt that although he brought no troops with him he would be able to quell the revolt and restore order in the Sudan. Her Majesty's government was under the impression—or later pretended to be under the impression—that Gordon's mission was only to evacuate the European and Egyptian officials and their families from the region.

Arriving in Khartoum in February, 1884, Gordon found the situation already out of hand, and by March 12 he was trapped there. For months he held out against the Mahdist hordes surrounding him. He sent back frantic messages filled with plans for his own relief, but as all the plans involved sending soldiers, the British government, for political and economic reasons, was reluctant to adopt any of them. Gladstone and his cabinet felt that as Gordon was unable to make an evacuation of the Sudan he should return. In reply to messages from Cairo asking why he did not leave Khartoum, Gordon replied bitterly that he did not leave because the Arabs had shut him in and would not let him out.

At last the government, prodded by strong public opinion that their hero should not be abandoned, sent out a relief expedition under General Wolseley. It arrived exactly two days too late. On January 25, 1885, Khartoum had fallen and its thousands of inhabitants had been massacred. Gordon's severed head was proudly displayed to the Mahdi. The Sudan was now abandoned, and all intercourse with the civilized world was cut off for thirteen years.

When the words "Too late!" reached England in February, 1885, the entire country was shocked and indignant. England's soldier-saint was martyred—and all because the government's aid had been too late. Britons everywhere felt shamed and dishonored. It was a national disgrace, and the words "Too late!" symbolized the loss of Gordon and the whole debacle in the Sudan. Mr. Gladstone's government was never so unpopular. Queen Victoria was so upset that she sent her Prime Minister the following telegram: "These news from Khartoum are frightful, and to think that all this might have been prevented and many precious lives saved by earlier action is too frightful."

Then one day the public became aware that not quite all was lost in the Sudan. There was one lone governor, "the last of Gordon's lieutenants," still valiantly holding out against all odds. This man was Emin Bey, governor of the province of Equatoria. The *Times* printed a letter he had managed to send out to Charles H. Allen, Secretary of the Anti-Slavery Society, dated December 31, 1885, which said: "Ever since the month of May, 1883, we have been cut off from all communication with the world. Forgotten, and abandoned by the Government, we have been compelled to make a virtue of necessity. Since the occupation of the Bahr-Gazal we have been vigorously attacked, and I do not know how to describe to you the admirable devotion of my black troops throughout the long war, which for them at least, has no advantage. Deprived of the most necessary things, for a long time without any pay, my men fought valiantly, and when at last hunger weakened them, when, after nineteen days of incredible privation and suffering, their strength was exhausted, and when the last torn leather of the last boot had been eaten, then they cut their way through the midst of their enemies and succeeded in saving themselves. All this hardship was undergone without the least *arrière-pensée*, without even the hope of any appreciable reward, prompted only by their duty and the desire of showing a proper valour before their enemies."

In a letter to his friend Dr. R. W. Felkin, written on the same date, Emin said: "The Government in Khartoum did not behave well to us. Before they evacuated Fashoda, they ought to have remembered that Government officials were living here who had performed their duty, and had not deserved to be left to their fate without more ado. Even if it were the intention of the Government to deliver us over to our fate, the least they could have done was to have released us from our duties; we should then have known that we were considered to have become valueless."

And in a letter to a missionary written a month later, Emin wrote: "If no danger overtakes us, and our ammunition holds out for some time longer, I mean to follow your advice and remain here until help comes to us from some quarter. . . . My people have become impatient through long delay, and are anxiously looking for help at last. It would also be most desirable that some commissioner come here from Europe, either direct by the Masai route, or from Karagwe via Kabba-Regga's country, in order that my people may actually see there is some interest taken in them. I would defray with ivory all expenses of such a commission."

Through letters such as these and the reports of Dr. Wilhelm Junker, an African explorer who had been with Emin and had succeeded in making his way out, a picture was painted of an ideal governor who had been able to maintain the loyalty of his troops and was holding back the Mahdist hordes pressing down on him from the north. There was some confusion as to Emin's intentions and desires. Sometimes he spoke of evacuating all of his people, and at other times he indicated that he needed only ammunition to hold on to his province. What seemed clear was that this gallant man clinging to his post was badly in need of relief. English newspapers and magazines fanned the flames of public sentiment. Everyone who had known Emin, either personally or through his letters and articles to scientific journals, wrote about his high personal character, his scientific accomplishments, and his wisdom and ability as a governor. In France, Germany, Italy, and Belgium there were similar expressions of concern.

Who was this European with a Turkish name who now found himself in such a predicament in the heart of equatorial Africa? Born in Prussia of Jewish parents in 1840, his real name was Edouard Schnitzer. He grew up a shy, frail boy with a great love of natural history. He studied medicine in Berlin, and became a surgeon in 1864. Almost immediately he set off for Turkey where he obtained employment as a tutor for the children of Ismail Hakki Pasha. When the pasha moved his family to Albania, where he was governor of a province, Emin went along. While Ismail was busy trying to cope with an Albanian revolution, his young German tutor made love to his wife.

When Hakki Pasha conveniently died, Schnitzer took over not only his wife but his children and servants as well. After wandering about Europe for a time, the ex-tutor took Madame Hakki Pasha and the eleven children and servants to the home of his family in Neisse. There he left them and disappeared.

In 1875 he turned up in Alexandria, Egypt. After earning a little money by doctoring among the poor, he made his way south to Khartoum. Europeans were few in the Sudan and there were none, certainly, who had the accomplishments of this man, who now called himself Mohammed Emin. He could play Chopin and Mendelssohn on the pianoforte, he was skillful at chess, and he was familiar with many languages, including Arabic, Turkish, English, Albanian, French, Italian, Latin, and Greek, both ancient and modern. He became widely known for his skill as a doctor, and for his kindliness and his excessive generosity, which led him to give away his money as fast as he acquired it.

He was soon hired as a medical officer on Gordon's staff. Other Europeans died off, Emin remained. He gave to Gordon Pasha that puppy-dog devotion that the English general always seemed to like in his subordinates, and it was not long before he was made governor of the province of Equatoria with the rank of bey.

In appearance, Emin resembled a German professor at a Shriners' convention. His studious expression was enhanced rather than concealed by thick spectacles and heavy black beard, and he habitually wore a red fez perched squarely on top of his head. Although he had been seen praying in mosques and wore a fez, he proclaimed himself a Christian. He had continued his boyhood interest in natural history. Amid the strange flora and fauna of his equatorial province, he daily found new forms of animal and mineral matter which he recorded in his almost miscroscopic handwriting in his notebooks. To the journals of the leading scientific societies of Europe he sent extremely detailed accounts of his thorough observations and experiments. Many museums, particularly the British Museum, were enriched by his carefully prepared collections of insects and bird skins.

Madame Hakki was so far forgotten that Emin took an Abyssinian woman as his mistress and had a child by her. For a while, life was very pleasant for him in his province. Then the Khartoum government fell, and he found himself in a very precarious position. So far the Mahdi had made no serious attempt to conquer the province, but there seemed little doubt that it was only a question of time before Equatoria would feel the full fury of the Mahdist dervishes. With a limited supply of ammunition and all effective communication with the outside world cut off, Emin could not hope to last long.

His appeals and the efforts of his friends to save him fell on deaf ears at first. The English government maintained that as Emin was not an Englishman they were not responsible for him; besides, they did not wish to become politically involved. The German government felt that as Emin was in the service of England and Egypt, it was not their affair. The Egyptian government expressed itself as being incapable of sending relief.

But the people of England were not to be put off. The rescue of Emin was the least they could do for the last of Gordon's officers. They did not know or care about the more sordid facts of Emin's life. They were determined that he should be relieved. Even before a relief committee had been formed or money raised, there was discussion in the press as to the best method of effecting the rescue. Three main routes, all starting from the east coast of Africa were proposed and their merits publicly debated.

In October, 1886, Sir William MacKinnon and Mr. J. F. Hutton, ex-President of the Manchester Chamber of Commerce, spoke to Stanley about the possibility of a relief expedition and asked his advice. Stanley outlined the three possible routes that had been discussed and then proposed a fourth route:

"The whole question resolves itself into that of money. With money enough every route is possible; but as I understand it, you propose to subscribe a moderate amount, and therefore there is only one route which is safely open for the money, and that is the Congo. This river has the disadvantage of not having enough transport vessels in its upper portion. I would propose then to supplement the Upper Congo flotilla with fifteen whaleboats, which will take an expedition to within two hundred miles, at least, of the Albert Nyanza. A heavy labour will be carrying the whaleboats from the Lower Congo to the Upper Congo, but we can easily manage it by sending agents at once there to prepare carriers. There is one thing, however, that must be done—which is to obtain the sanction of King Leopold.

"But it may be we are rather premature in discussing the matter at all. You know I am aware of many projects mooted, and much 'talk' has been expended on each and this may end in smoke—collect your funds, and then call upon me if you want me. If you do not require me after this exposition of my views, let Thomson take his expedition through the Masai Land, and put me down for £500 subscription for it."

In the middle of November Stanley left for America to begin a lecture tour. Before leaving, he sent another letter to Sir William Mac-Kinnon in which he offered his services as leader of the expedition without pay while reminding him that this offer, if accepted, would involve the sacrifice on his part of an income of ten thousand pounds. He also urged that the Congo route be chosen for the expedition and cited his own qualifications: "You must remember that for fourteen years I have been in Africa; that I know personally the region to be traversed within 350 miles of Emin Bey's position at Wadelai; that the three expeditions I have led into Africa have been perfectly success-ful each time; that my recommendation to King Leopold was based upon the celerity of my movements and the economy attending the equipment of the previous expeditions."

Stanley arrived in the United States and began his lecture tour. He had been in the country only two weeks and his tour had extended as far as St. Johnsbury, Vermont, when, on December 11, he received a telegram: "Your plan and offer accepted. Authorities approve. Funds provided. Business urgent. Come promptly. Reply. MacKinnon."

Stanley left immediately, and on Christmas Eve, 1886, he landed in England. Here he learned that MacKinnon and the relief committee had changed their minds and decided on an eastern route. To this proposal Stanley wrote, "Very good, it is perfectly immaterial to me. Let us decide on the East Coast route, via Msalala, Karagwe, Ankori, and Unyoro. If you hear of some hard fighting, I look to you that you will defend the absent. If I could drop this ammunition in Emin's camp from a balloon I certainly would do so, and avoid coming into contact with those warlike natives, but it is decided that the best means of defence must be put into Emin's hands, and you have entrusted me with the escort of it. So be it."

On December 31, Stanley was formally informed of his appointment and began his preparations. The sum of £21,500 had been raised. The Egyptian government had subscribed £10,000 and the rest had been raised primarily by MacKinnon and his relatives and friends. Stanley at once began to order his supplies. From his agent in Zanzibar he ordered 27,262 yards of two dozen different kinds of cloth, specifying the amounts and kinds of each and the length of each piece. He also ordered thirty-six hundred pounds of beads and a ton of brass, copper, and iron wire. He directed that six tons of rice be purchased and carried by two hundred Wanyamwezi porters two hundred miles inland from the coast as a stockpile of provisions. He instructed his agent to recruit six hundred Zanzibari pagazis and to purchase forty pack donkeys and ten riding asses with saddles.

From an English firm he ordered the construction of a steel boat, 28 feet long, 6 feet wide, and 2½ feet deep, divided into twelve sections each weighing seventy-five pounds. As the rifles and ammunition for Emin were to be supplied by the Egyptian government, 510 Remington rifles, two tons of gunpowder, 350,000 percussion caps, and 100,000 rounds of Remington ammunition were sent from Egypt to Zanzibar. In addition, a Birmingham firm donated 35,000 special Remington cartridges. A London firm packed up fifty Winchester repeaters with 50,000 Winchester cartridges, and Hiram Maxim, inventor of the Maxim machine gun, donated one of his ingenious weapons.

Stanley bought and shipped to Zanzibar a hundred shovels, a hundred hoes, a hundred axes, and a hundred bill-hooks. A chemical firm donated nine beautiful chests filled with medicine and surgical equipment. Another company made special tents dipped in sulphate of copper, while a catering firm packed up forty carrier loads of choice provisions for the Europeans. It was to be a great expedition.

As soon as word of the relief expedition was announced to the public, Stanley was besieged with letters of application from men anxious to accompany him. The first man selected was a twenty-five-year-old lieutenant from the Royal Engineers, William Grant Stairs. He had applied by letter and the "concise style and directness of the application" impressed Stanley. He was sent for, and after a brief interview he was hired on condition that he could obtain leave of absence from the army. Lord Wolseley granted the request for leave and Stairs started to work.

The next man to be accepted was William Bonny. He had tried to go on other expeditions, but his letters of application had always been rejected. This time he applied in person, his chest covered with medals. He looked what he was: a noncommissioned officer of the British Army. He had served with the Army Medical Corps in Zululand, the Transvaal, and the Sudan. He was hired as medical assistant after he purchased his discharge from the army. Bonny was forty-three years old. Next to Stanley, he was the oldest white man on the expedition.

John Rose Troup, who had just returned to England after three years' service with the Congo Free State, applied to go. Stanley had known him on the Congo and thought highly of him. He was about thirty-two years old, spoke Swahili, and was a hard and methodical worker. Troup was engaged.

The fourth volunteer was Major Edmund Musgrave Barttelot of the 7th Fusiliers. Although only twenty-seven years old, he had already seen a good deal of service and had distinguished himself in the Sudan and in Afghanistan. He was introduced to Stanley by an acquaintance and was recommended by Lord Wolseley; after a brief interview, he was selected.

Captain Robert Henry Nelson, thirty-six, of Methuen's Horse, was the next officer signed. He had seen service in South Africa, distinguishing himself in the Zulu campaigns. Stanley said of him, "There was merit in his very face."

So far, all the officers selected were men experienced in living in foreign and dangerous surroundings, but the next applicant chosen was of quite a different stamp. He was thirty-year-old Arthur J. Mounteney-Jephson, a distant relative of Gordon, whom some members of the committee felt was "too high class." His chief recommendations were that he was most anxious to go, even without pay, and that the Countess de Noailles, his cousin, offered to donate a thousand pounds to the relief fund if he was accepted. This last argument proved irresistible, and he was allowed to sign the articles of enlistment in spite of his inexperience.

Dr. Rolf Leslie, who had served with Stanley in the Congo Free State, was originally to have accompanied the expedition as medical officer, but he got into a disagreement with the committee over the wording of his contract and backed out at the last minute.

Just as the list of officers was about to be closed, James S. Jameson, thirty-one, applied. He was a naturalist who had traveled a great deal in Borneo, India, Ceylon, the United States, and South Africa, collecting trophies and zoological specimens and sketching fauna and flora. He did not appear to be very strong, and the committee hesitated to engage him. But Jameson, who was independently wealthy, offered to subscribe a thousand pounds for the privilege of going, so he too was engaged.

Each of these men signed an agreement: "I ———— agree to accompany the Emin Pasha Relief Expedition, and to place myself under the command of Mr. H. M. Stanley, the leader of the Expedition, and to accept any post or position in that Expedition to which he may appoint me. I further agree to serve him loyally and devotedly, to obey all his orders and to follow him by whatsoever route he may choose, and to use my utmost endeavours to bring the Expedition to a successful issue. Should I leave the Expedition without his orders, I agree to forfeit passage money, and to become liable to refund all moneys advanced to me for passage to Zanzibar and outfit.

"Mr. H. M. Stanley also agrees to give £40 for outfit, and to pay my passage to Zanzibar, and return passage to England, provided I continue during the whole period of the Expedition. I undertake not to publish anything connected with the Expedition, or to send any account to the newspapers for six months after the issue of the official publication of the Expedition by the leader or his representative.

"In addition to the outfit, Mr. Stanley will supply the following:— tent, bed, Winchester rifle, one revolver, ammunition for the same, canteen, a due share of the European provisions taken for the party— besides such provisions as the country can supply."

Only four of the seven officers who had so far enlisted were to stay with the expedition to the bitter end, and two of them were to leave their bones in Africa. When they signed their contracts, all of them had romantic concepts regarding the nature of their mission. None knew of the trials and horrors they were to face.

Stanley's quarters on Bond Street rapidly took on the appearance of a place of business. It was the headquarters of the expedition, and Stanley, Sir Francis de Winton, and later Stairs and Troup, worked furiously to expedite the business aspects of the venture.

When the arrangements were all but completed, political considerations and the offer of assistance from King Leopold caused the committee to alter its plans again and to adopt the Congo route Stanley had originally proposed. It was decided now to continue the assemblage of supplies and men at Zanzibar and then to ship the expedition around the Cape to the mouth of the Congo. Stanley drew up a new list of the advantages offered by the Congo route:

1. Certainty of reaching Emin.
2. Transport up the Congo by State steamers to a point 320 geographical miles from Lake Albert.
3. Allaying suspicions of Germans that underlying our acts were political motives.
4. Allaying alleged fears of French government that our Expedition would endanger the lives of French missionaries.
5. If French missionaries were endangered, then English missionaries would certainly share their fate.
6. Greater immunity from the desertions of the Zanzibaris who are fickle in the neighborhood of Arab settlements.

Stanley's great concern now was that his expedition would have insufficient transport on the Upper Congo. There was not time to build the whaleboats and send them to Stanley Pool; so, with the exception of the steel boat, they would have to rely upon the already available ships. On January 14, 1887, Stanley crossed the Channel and had a talk with Leopold. The king offered him the use of all of the Congo Free State steamers, but told him he would have to apply directly to the missionaries who owned the other ships on the river. In reply to his request for the use of one of these steamers, the *Peace*, Stanley was told to "repent and believe the Gospel . . . and live hereafter in happiness, light, and joy"—and no, he could not use the boat.

On January 18 Stanley went to Sandringham and explained the expedition to the Prince of Wales. The following evening, Sir William MacKinnon gave a farewell banquet for him, and the next day the S.S. *Navarino* sailed with Stairs, Nelson, Jephson, and supplies for the expedition. Bonny was to have sailed on this ship, too, but he did not quite make it. "Mr. William Bonny started from my rooms with black boy Baruti to Fenchurch Station at 8 A.M.," Stanley wrote in his notebook. "Arriving there he leaves Baruti after a while and proceeds to Tower of London! He says that returning to station at 2 P.M. he found boat had gone. He then went to Gray, Dawes & C., shipping agents, and is discouraged to find that the matter cannot be mended. Baruti found deserted in Fenchurch Station, very hungry and cold. Col. J. A. Grant finds him and brings him to me."

Poor Bonny. He had gotten off to a bad start. Had he known his employer better, he might have returned to the Tower of London and hidden there until Bula Matari left England.

The next day Bonny and Baruti were sent to Plymouth to catch a boat bound for India, they were instructed to get off the boat at Suez and wait for Stanley's arrival. The same day, January 21, less than a month after being named leader of the expedition, Stanley left London on his way to Alexandria, Egypt.

With him was another white man. His name was William Hoffman, and he was Stanley's servant. Not much is known of this man except that he was a cockney and that he accompanied Stanley on the expedition, staying with it to the end. He suffered all the discomforts and hardships with the others, but in the two-volume book of over a thousand pages that Stanley wrote describing his experiences on this expedition the name of William Hoffman does not once appear.

Taking the overland route, Stanley arrived in Alexandria on January 27, 1887. Here he was met by Surgeon Thomas Heazle Parke, thirty, of the Army Medical Corps, who asked to be taken on the expedition. He had heard about the undertaking from his friend Major Barttelot who had stopped off in Egypt to collect some Sudanese soldiers before going to Aden to obtain Somalis. Barttelot had been enthusiastic about the idea of crossing unknown regions to reach Emin Bey; he urged Parke to apply for the position of medical officer. Stationed in Egypt and wrapped up in his own affairs there, Parke had never heard of Emin. When he asked his friend who he was, Barttelot replied that he was "some chap who wants to get out of Africa and can't."

The idea of going with Stanley appealed to the young doctor, an adventurous spirit who had already been through several exciting experiences. He had been awarded the Queen's Medal and the Khedive's Star for his services in the campaign of 1882 against Arabi; he had been senior medical officer of a cholera camp outside Cairo in 1883; and he had accompanied the unsuccessful expedition for the relief of Gordon in 1884-1885. But his chief preoccupation at the moment was in connection with his duties as master of the fox hounds for the Alexandrian Hunt, a position he felt to be "an important charge."

Stanley described Parke as "an extremely handsome young gentleman—diffident somewhat—but very prepossessing." In spite of this good first impression and the fact that he needed a medical officer, Stanley did not at first hire the young Irish doctor, but told him, "If you care to follow me to Cairo, I will talk further with you. I have not time to argue with you here."

Parke's version of this first meeting differs somewhat, but Parke did follow Stanley to Cairo and was engaged without pay as the expedition's medical officer.

In Cairo, Stanley found that there were additional complications to his mission. The Khedive, Nubar Pasha, the prime minister, and—even more important—Sir Evelyn Baring, later 1st Earl Cromer, Great Britain's chief Egyptian representative and virtual ruler of the country, objected to the Congo route. Their doubts were fostered by Dr. Wilhelm Junker and Professor Georg August Schweinfurth, two eminent African explorers then in Egypt. But Stanley was able to persuade Sir Evelyn of the soundness of his plan and Nubar Pasha and the Khedive deferred to the judgment of the Englishman.

On February 2, Stanley had breakfast with Khedive Tewfik and was given a firman, in Arabic and English, to be given to Emin. The firman praised Emin's defense of his province and raised him to the rank of pasha. It also gave him liberty to return to Cairo or to remain where he was, as he saw fit. If he remained, however, he could not expect to receive further aid from the Egyptian government.

On the following day Stanley left Cairo, picked up Surgeon Parke, and headed for Suez, where they were joined by Jameson, Bonny, and Baruti. Parke just had time to play in a cricket match before they all proceeded to Aden, where they met Major Barttelot with his Sudanese soldiers and Somali boys. After changing ships here, they set out on the last lap of their trip to Zanzibar. All of the officers had first-class passage except Bonny, who was given second-class accommodations. On the way they passed a ship carrying Dr. Oscar Lenz, leader of one of the two unsuccessful expeditions that had previously tried to reach Emin from the east coast.

On February 22, they arrived at Zanzibar, where Stanley's agent had managed things so well that they were almost ready to embark the supplies and men. But before this could be done, Stanley had a secret mission to accomplish by which he hoped to further the cause of the expedition and to do a favor for King Leopold. Tippu-Tib was in Zanzibar, and Stanley had business with him. The Arab was a much greater man now than he was when he had escorted Stanley on the first lap of his trip down the Lualaba. He had invested his money in guns and gunpowder and was now virtual ruler of a vast area from Lake Tanganyika to Stanley Falls. He had become the biggest slave and ivory trader in all Africa.

Stanley proposed to Tippu-Tib that he supply men to assist the expedition by carrying some of the loads to Emin Pasha and then help to bring back the large store of ivory which Emin was said to possess. Tippu-Tib could be paid in ivory, and, in addition, Stanley would convey him and his personal retinue from Zanzibar to Stanley Falls. Stanley had one other ace to play. There had been trouble between Tippu-Tib's men and the forces of the Congo Free State at Stanley Falls. The Arabs and their subjugated natives, the Manyuema, had attacked the Free State station there and had wiped out the garrison. So far, the State had not attempted to retake the station, but the land was still claimed by King Leopold. Stanley's novel proposal was that Tippu-Tib be made the *wali*, or governor, of the Stanley Falls area in the name of the Congo Free State. He was to fly the Free State flag and to pay allegiance to the Free State government. For this he would receive a salary of thirty pounds a month. This arrangement would prevent further clashes between the Europeans and the Arabs, and it would be some measure of assurance that Stanley's expedition would not be attacked by the slavers.

Tippu-Tib accepted this offer. When the news of the agreement reached Europe, it created a sensation. Europeans could not understand why it was necessary to deal with such a notorious slave trader. Gordon, that most Christian soldier and destroyer of slavers, had once created a similar sensation when, in order to relieve tension in the Sudan, he had released a politically powerful slaver imprisoned in Cairo and reinstated him in the Sudan. Stanley and Gordon, for all of their dreams, were practical men. Stanley knew that the Free State would not be able to reconquer the Stanley Falls region for some time and that when it did there would be bloodshed. His agreement would bring at least a temporary peace and would assure him that there would not be a war raging in his rear while he made his final dash for Emin Pasha.

While on Zanzibar, Stanley also put through one other little project that English diplomats had been trying to accomplish for eight years. Germany had grabbed off as her own a large section of East Africa, now Tanganyika Territory. Much of this land should have been given to Britain in the opinion of many Englishmen. Now Stanley obtained from Seyyid Barghash, the Sultan of Zanzibar, a concession for trade and exploitation of what is today Kenya. His friend William MacKinnon, who had formed the Imperial British East African Company, could exploit the concession for Britain's benefit.

Stanley may not have known how to negotiate with Europeans, but with Africans of whatever race or nationality he had few peers as a diplomat. It took him exactly two days to accomplish these important negotiations.

On February 24, 1887, the expedition embarked. The group that sailed from Zanzibar was a heterogeneous one:

| | |
|---|---:|
| Whites | 9 |
| Zanzibari men | 600 |
| Zanzibari boys | 23 |
| Sudanese | 62 |
| Somalis | 13 |
| Tippu-Tib & Co. | 97 |
| TOTAL | 804 |

Included in Tippu-Tib's group, incidentally, were thirty-five of his wives.

Many of the Zanzibaris were men who had accompanied Stanley on previous expeditions or had worked for him during the founding of the Congo Free State. Frederick Holmwood, British Acting Consul General in Zanzibar, in a letter to the Marquis of Salisbury, wrote: "Mr. Stanley personally attended at the muster of the Zanzibar porters which took place before embarkation: a considerable number of these had served under him on former occasions, and his immediate recognition of them, accompanied in every instance with the recollection of their names, and generally of some little incident in connection with their former service, evidently afforded especial gratification; indeed, this trait, or gift, which he eminently possesses, together with a practical knowledge of the Swahili language, would alone account for his undoubted popularity and great influence among his native followers."

When all the men and goods had been loaded on board, the expedition sailed for the Congo via Cape Town. The ship was only two hours out of port when trouble began. Conditions on board were crowded and uncomfortable, and friction immediately developed between the Sudanese soldiers and the Zanzibaris. A battle was well under way before Stanley discovered it. Looking down the hatch, he saw a bloody free-for-all in progress. Using planks, firewood, and spears, the huge Sudanese were trying desperately to hold their own against the more numerous Zanzibaris. All were yelling and screaming in the crowded hold. Stanley's commands could not be heard in the uproar so, calling for his officers, he waded in with a stick, concentrating on the noisiest ones. Nelson, Bonny, and Jephson followed his example, and it was not long before order was restored and the Sudanese could be removed to another part of the ship. Surgeon Parke set the broken bones and sewed up the gashes.

The trip to Cape Town was without further serious incident, and Stanley had an opportunity to size up his officers. He jotted down his impressions of some of them. Of Major Barttelot he said, "Barttelot is a little too eager, and will have to be restrained. There is abundance of work in him, and this quality would be most lovely if it were always according to orders. The most valuable man to me would be he who had Barttelot's spirit and 'go' in him, and who could come and ask if such and such a work ought to be done." Stanley did not discover the major's tragic, fatal flaw: he hated every man whose color was black.

Mounteney-Jephson, whom Stanley had at first considered "too effeminate," he found to be "actually fierce when roused, and his face becomes dangerously set and fixed."

Nelson he described as "a fine fellow, and without the ghost of a hobby." Stairs was "a splendid fellow, painstaking, ready, thoughtful, and industrious, and is an invaluable addition to our staff." Jameson he thought "sociable and good." Of the British Army noncommissioned officer he said, "Bonny is the soldier. He is not initiative. He seems to have been under a martinet's drill."

While he was making these observations, some of his officers were also forming their opinions of him and the expedition. Parke found him "very reticent." Jameson wrote in his diary, "Mr. Stanley, when he throws off his reserve, is one of the most agreeable of men and full of information." But Jameson was crushed when he learned that each officer would be allowed only three pagazis for his personal baggage. This meant that each officer would be limited to 180 pounds and Jameson, who hoped to acquire some interesting specimens of animal and insect life, was forced to discard some of his collecting equipment and to throw away some of his personal belongings. But there was some compensation: "He [Stanley] gave us all the most lovely little medicine-chests today."

On board the ship Stanley issued his first "general orders" to his officers. Militaristically, he divided all of the men into companies. Major Barttelot was put in charge of the Sudanese and each of the other officers was given a company of Zanzibaris—except Bonny, who was placed in charge of the asses and goats. Stanley set up a duty roster of his officers, and they took turns serving as officer of the day. Other instructions in the general orders included the following:

"Each officer is personally responsible for the good behaviour of his company, and for the good condition of arms and accoutrements after distribution.

"Officers will inspect frequently, when on shore, cartridge pouches of their men to see that the cartridges are not lost, or sold to natives or Arabs *en route*. For an intentional loss of one cartridge a fine of one dollar will be imposed; two cartridges, two dollars, and a corporal punishment of five strokes with a rod.

"For trivial offences a slight corporal punishment only can be inflicted, and this as seldom as possible. Officers will exercise a proper discretion in this matter, and endeavour to avoid irritating their men by being too exacting, or unnecessarily fussy: it has been usual with me to be greatly forebearing, allowing three pardons for one punishment."

On March 9, they reached Cape Town, where they were joined by an English engineer named Walker who was to superintend the working of the steamboats on the Congo.

March 18 found the expedition at Banana, on the mouth of the Congo River. There, stuck on a sand bar, they saw the largest of the steamers that was to have taken them up the river as far as Mataddi. The Europeans at Banana did not hesitate to impart other tidbits of news: there was a famine in the lands adjacent to the river; the villages on the way to Stanley Pool were deserted; native pagazis were almost unobtainable; and there was virtually no river transport on the Upper Congo!

The officers were dismayed by these reports, but Stanley was unconcerned. Difficulties such as these were to be expected. Besides, he had no time to worry about them. All obstacles must be overcome—and quickly. There was the haunting fear that his expedition, like the one sent for the relief of Gordon, would be too late. He must hurry. Junker had said, "Emin will be lost unless immediate aid be given him." Emin Pasha himself had written that unless relief were sent soon "we shall perish." Stanley had no intention of letting this happen if he could possibly prevent it. By the evening of the day of their arrival at Banana, he had arranged for the transport of his men and supplies to Mataddi, a hundred and eight miles from the Atlantic near the now abandoned Vivi. This was to be the first lap of their almost frantic trip up the river. On the Lower Congo the expedition soon became known as the "Relief Hurricane."

Landing at Mataddi, they began the march around the cataracts over the road Stanley had spent a year of his life building. There were not enough Zanzibaris to carry all of the loads, but Stanley had sent John Rose Troup direct from London to the Congo to arrange for native transport. It had not been an easy task, but Troup had succeeded. When friction developed, as it immediately did, between the Zanzibaris and the native pagazis going to and fro along the road, Stanley gave orders to supply the natives with pieces of paper on which there was writing—it did not matter what the paper said as neither the Congolese nor the Zanzibaris could read. Then when a native was molested by a Zanzibari, the native would wave the paper in his face and call out, "Bula Matari!"

On the road, Stanley met Herbert Ward, a strikingly handsome and talented young man; an amateur sculptor of considerable ability who had wandered in New Zealand and Borneo before coming to Africa. For several years now he had been working for the Congo Free State. Stanley knew him, and considered him a very promising young man. When he encountered the relief expedition, Ward was on his way down the Congo, having obtained a six months' leave to visit his father in California. On meeting Stanley, however, he changed his plans and offered his services to the expedition. Stanley accepted him.

The Sudanese soldiers proved very troublesome, keeping up a running feud with the Zanzibaris. Stanley ran across one soldier strangling a Zanzibari because the pagazi had accidentally touched his shoulder with his box. The Sudanese carried no loads, only their rifles and personal equipment, but they could not keep pace with the Zanzibaris and were difficult to keep moving. Major Barttelot was sent on ahead with these trouble makers, but he could not push them fast enough, and the main column was continually bumping into them. They were issued provisions to last them for several days, but they ate them up at once and then threatened to mutiny if they were not issued more.

Food for such a large number of men created a tremendous problem. Due to the quick change in plans regarding the route, there had not been time to stockpile provisions along the line of march up the Congo. Besides, there was famine in the country, and food was scarce even for the normal residents. The Zanzibaris tried to steal food from the natives, and this resulted in many clashes. One Zanzibari chief was killed by a native when he attempted to enter a hut, and Stanley was continually hearing complaints about the conduct of his men.

One day as he was sitting on a camp stool in front of his tent Stanley was approached by a native chief who swaggered up, plunged his spear into the ground at his feet, and began a long harangue protesting against the expedition camping so close to his village. While the chief shouted and gesticulated, Stanley did not move a muscle, but sat looking him in the eye. The chief tried in vain to ignore the steady gaze of the penetrating blue eyes, but it was impossible. He faltered, broke down, and stopped. Pulling his spear out of the ground he walked away, ignominiously trailing his spear in the dust behind him. Herbert Ward, who saw this incident, noticed a peculiar smile on Stanley's face as the incident closed.

Another chief came to complain of the raids made by the Zanzibaris on his plantain fields. Again Stanley listened in silence. Then, calling for his bugler to sound assembly, he mustered his men. He took the chief down the long lines of men, pausing occasionally to ask, "Was this the man who robbed you? Or this? Is this the man that caused unhappiness in your homes?"

The confused chief at last shook his head sadly and confessed, "These men all look alike. I do not know which are the robbers."

Speaking in a benevolent tone, Stanley placed his hand on the chief's shoulder and told him, "The next time your peace is disturbed, O chief, place a mark upon the man—*mark* him! Then when we collect our men and when we look all along the line, we shall be able at once to distinguish the culprit!"

On April 10, the heat was excessive, even for the Congo. Stanley, who normally did not notice such minor discomforts, complained of its severity. Many of his officers wore pajamas stuffed in boots and a pith helmet, a common costume on the Congo. Stanley, however, made no concession to the heat and wore his usual braided coat, knickerbockers, and, instead of the conventional topee, what he called a Congo hat, which resembled an army officer's cap with a much higher crown, down the back of which he often suspended a piece of cloth such as was formerly worn by French Foreign Legionnaires.

Stanley's temper was apparently as hot as he was on this particular day, for Surgeon Parke wrote in his diary: "I was again 'pulled up' about the loss of rifles. Mr. Stanley told me that I had lost nineteen rifles, so that by going on at the same ratio I will have lost all the rifles of the expedition long before we reach our destination. This is not a very inspiriting reflection."

Every day saw its losses of men and supplies. Although the Zanzibaris who deserted could not hope ever to return to Zanzibar, many of them apparently felt it was better to forego this prospect than to continue with the expedition. Many had died, and nearly a hundred were too sick to carry loads. Seriously ill men were left with every missionary and at every Free State station they encountered.

On April 21, 1887, the expedition arrived at Leopoldville, where Stanley was paid a visit by his old friend, Ngalyema—who had been so fascinated by the gong. Stanley found him tedious. Everyone seemed to be getting on his nerves.

They were now three hundred and forty-five miles from the Atlantic. Before them stretched a thousand miles of river before they should reach Yambuya on the Aruwimi River, where they would be forced to resume their land journey to Lake Albert. The difficulties Stanley encountered in collecting enough boats to transport his expedition up river put him into a vile temper.

By this time the white officers had realized that the relief of Emin Pasha was not to be a pleasure trip. Some adjusted to the situation and some did not, but all were determined to see the thing through to the finish regardless of the consequences. One of the most disillusioned officers was James Jameson, the naturalist. From Stanley Pool he wrote to his wife:

"The birds and the insects are lovely, but with the work one has to do it is impossible to get anything. All my lovely dreams have been very roughly knocked on the head. I will give you a specimen of a day's work on the march. Barttelot and I started one day as rear guard a little after 6 A.M., and did not reach camp until after 6 P.M., with not a quarter-hour's rest all day. Nothing but beating niggers with a stick, and lifting loads on to their heads, and day after day the same disgusting work. It must take a great deal of glory to make up for it all."

In the same letter, he also related an unpleasant episode concerning his chief:

"We have all had one or two disagreeable moments with Mr. Stanley, but I think they are over for the present. I cannot help admiring him immensely for his great strength of will and power of overcoming difficulties; but there are some points in his character which I cannot admire. . . . Stairs' donkey broke his leg, and he had to shoot it. I saw the broken leg myself. When he reported the matter, Mr. Stanley in-

formed him that he had been told that the leg was not broken, and
that he shot it in a rage; and when asked who had told him, said,
'Tippu-Tib's people.' Stairs then gave him a real good piece of his mind
on the subject. It is impossible for any one calling himself a gentleman
and an officer, to stand this sort of thing. The fact is, this is the first
time Stanley has ever had gentlemen to deal with on an expedition
of this sort."

It was true that Stanley had little experience in working with English gentlemen as his subordinates. He was to find them quite different
from the white men who had been with him on previous expeditions.
It soon became obvious to all of the officers that their leader was partial
to the Zanzibaris and distrusted the white men. Stanley had not forgotten his experiences with Europeans while founding the Free State.
The worst row of all occurred on the Upper Congo. Strangely enough,
the two officers involved, Stairs and Jephson, were already well thought
of and were to become Stanley's favorites.

The incident took place on the morning of May 20 when a number
of Zanzibaris came to Stanley complaining that Jephson and Stairs
had taken food away from them. The Zanzibaris claimed they had
purchased the food from natives. Stanley summoned the two officers
and demanded an explanation. Stairs hotly told him that the men had
stolen the food. Jephson told the same story. In defending themselves,
the officers used language Stanley felt was insubordinate. Flying into
a rage, he stamped up and down, calling Jephson a "God damned son
of a sea cook" and a "God damned impudent puppy." He added, "You
damned ass, you're tired of me, of the expedition, and of my men. Go
into the bush, get, I've done with you. And you, too, Lieutenant Stairs,
you and I will part today. You're tired of me, sir, I can see. Get!
Away into the bush."

When Jephson tried to protest his innocence, Stanley told him, "If
you want to fight, God damn you, I'll give you a belly full."

There was no fight, however, and the officers did not get into the
bush. Instead, there were apologies all around and the expedition
continued its weary way toward Yambuya.

For the most part, the journey from Leopoldville to Yambuya was
the easiest part of the trip. There were frequent stops to cut wood for
the furnaces of the steamboats; there were delays when the boats
grounded on sand bars; the *Stanley* had a gash cut in her bottom by a
snag and almost sank; the *Peace* lost her tiller the first day and later

turned sulky and would only work up thirty pounds of steam; but in spite of these difficulties, the expedition pressed on.

Herbert Ward and William Bonny were left with one hundred and twenty-nine of the weakest men at Bolobo to fatten them up; Troup was left with five hundred loads at Leopoldville; and Major Barttelot was dispatched with an escort in the *Henry Reed* to take Tippu-Tib and his people to Stanley Falls. The remainder of the expedition reached the mouth of the Aruwimi River on June 12.

They were soon opposite the villages of the Basoko, Baruti's tribe. This was a tribe that had rejected all friendly overtures from Stanley in the past. They were very wild and addicted to cannibalism. The boy who had been instructed in London ways eyed the place of his birth with great interest. Encouraged by Stanley, Baruti hailed his tribesmen in their own language. At first the Basoko were suspicious and would not even approach the steamer. Baruti persisted in calling to them until, at last, some canoes approached within easy hearing. Baruti asked for someone by name, and the men on the water relayed the name to those on shore. Finally a man was seen entering a canoe and rowing out toward the steamer. It was Baruti's elder brother whom he had not seen for six years. Baruti asked him how he was and if he did not remember his young brother, but the man only stared at him in silence. Baruti mentioned the names of his parents. The man suddenly showed great interest and drew his canoe nearer.

"If you are my brother, tell me some incident, that I may know you."

"You have a scar on your arm—there on the right. Don't you remember the crocodile?"

The native whooped for joy and, forgetting his fear of strangers, boarded the steamer to give Baruti a hug. The other Basokos followed suit, and there was a mad reunion scene on the deck of the steamboat.

That evening, Baruti was given his choice of returning to his native tribe or remaining with the expedition. Baruti thought he would stay with Stanley, for he might be eaten by his fellow tribesmen or perhaps be carried off again by Arabs. A few days later, however, he got up in the middle of the night and stole a rifle, a brace of pistols, a silver watch, a pedometer, and some other items of Stanley's and decamped in a canoe, probably back to his own tribe. Stanley never heard from him again. It was no great loss. Troup called him a "little imp" and Surgeon Parke, who rarely spoke ill of anyone, referred to him as "an atrocious ruffian."

On June 15, 1887, the expedition arrived opposite the village of

Yambuya, located on the left bank of the Aruwimi, ninety-six miles above the confluence of the Congo and Aruwimi rivers.

Further progress on the steamers was impossible due to the rough water just above Yambuya, but they were now only three hundred and fifty miles, in a straight line, from the point where they hoped to find Emin Pasha. The actual marching distance, however, proved to be nearly twice as far.

# CHAPTER XII

# *The Forest of Darkness*

A LTHOUGH IN TERMS of time the expedition had barely begun, already there were prophets in Europe who were predicting the failure of the Emin Pasha Relief Expedition. In June, 1887, the month Stanley reached Yambuya, several European newspapers were already proclaiming the expedition's doom. Reports read that it had been decimated by famine and the line of march was strewn with the bodies of the dead.

It was certainly true that the expedition had suffered from the serious shortage of food on the Congo—so far fifty-seven men had died and many more were ill and undernourished—but the expedition was far from finished. Stanley now proposed to establish a camp at Yambuya, leaving a rear guard with about two thirds of the loads and one third of the men, while he pressed on with the best and strongest men to reach Emin Pasha and to deliver a portion of the ammunition which, it was believed, was Emin's most vital and pressing requirement. In his imagination, Stanley pictured the beleaguered pasha, hemmed in by howling dervishes, looking vainly for the ammunition that would enable him to hold his province.

The advance guard was to consist of 389 picked men—including Stanley, four officers, and Stanley's cockney servant—armed with 357 rifles. Officers' baggage was further reduced to two loads (120 pounds). The rear guard, counting the men left at Bolobo and Leopold-ville who would later join those left at Yambuya, would consist of 260 men with 139 rifles. The rear guard was placed under the command of Major Barttelot with Jameson as second in command. All of the officers selected to remain at Yambuya were bitterly disappointed when they learned they were to be left behind. Nevertheless, they accepted their fate with good grace and determined to make the best of it.

On June 23, 1887, Stanley took advantage of the departure of the *Peace* and the *Henry Reed* to send a letter to MacKinnon. He concluded by saying that with the departure of the steamers "our last chance of communication with Europe for a few months will be gone." No further authentic news was to be heard from him in Europe until December 21, 1888, eighteen months later.

Before leaving, Stanley wrote fairly detailed instructions for Major Barttelot and gave a copy to Jameson:

Sir,

As the senior of those officers accompanying me on the Emin Pasha Relief Expedition, the command of this important post devolves on you. It is also for the interest of the Expedition that you accept this command, from the fact that your Soudanese company, being only soldiers, and more capable of garrison duty than the Zanzibaris, will be better utilized than on the road.

The steamer *Stanley* left Yambuya on the 22nd of this month for Stanley Pool. If she meets with no mischance she ought to be at Leopoldville on the 2nd of July. In two days more she will be loaded with about 500 loads of our goods, which were left in charge of Mr. J. R. Troup. This gentleman will embark, and on the 4th of July I assume that the *Stanley* will commence her ascent of the river, and arrive at Bolobo on the 9th. Fuel being ready, the 125 men in charge of Messrs. Ward and Bonny, now at Bolobo, will embark, and the steamer will continue her journey. She will be at Bangala on the 19th of July, and arrive here on the 31st of July. . . .

It is the non-arrival of these goods and men which compels me to appoint you as commander of this post. But as I shall shortly expect the arrival of a strong reinforcement of men, greatly exceeding the advance force which must, at all hazards, push on to the rescue of Emin Pasha, I hope you will not be detained longer than a few days after the departure of the *Stanley* on her final return to Stanley Pool in August.

Meantime, pending the arrival of our men and goods, it behooves you to be very alert and wary in the command of this stockaded camp. . . .

The interests now intrusted to you are of vital importance to this expedition. The men you will eventually have under you consist of more than an entire third of the expedition. The goods that will be brought up are the currency needed for transit through the regions beyond the lakes; there will be a vast store of ammunition and provisions, which are of equal importance to us. The loss of these men and goods would be certain ruin to us, and the Advance Force itself would need to solicit relief in its turn. Therefore, weighing this matter well, I hope you will spare no pains to maintain order and discipline in your camp, and make your defences complete, and keep them in such a condition, that however brave an enemy may be he can make no impression on them. . . . Remember, it is not the natives alone who may wish to assail you, but the Arabs and their followers may, through some cause or other, quarrel with you and assail your camp.

Our course from here will be due east, or by magnetic compass, east by south as near as possible. Certain marches that we may make may not exactly lead in the direction aimed at. Nevertheless, it is the southwest corner of Lake Albert, near or at Kavalli, that is our destination. When we arrive there we shall form a strong camp in the neighbourhood, launch our boat, and steer for Kibiro, in Unyoro, to hear from Signor Casati, if he is there, of the condition of Emin Pasha. If the latter is alive, and in the neighbourhood of the lake, we shall communicate with him, and our after conduct must be guided by what we shall learn of the intentions of Emin Pasha. We may assume that we shall not be longer than a fortnight with him before deciding on our return toward the camp along the same road traversed by us.

We will endeavour, by blazing trees and cutting saplings along our road, to leave sufficient traces of the route taken by us. We shall always take, by preference, tracks leading eastward. At all crossings where paths intersect, we shall hoe up and make a hole a few inches deep across all paths not used by us, besides blazing trees when possible.

It may happen, should Tippu-Tib have sent the full number of adults promised by him to me, vis. 600 men (able to carry loads), and the *Stanley* has arrived safely with the 125 men left by me at Bolobo, that you will feel yourself sufficiently competent to march the column, with all the goods brought by the *Stanley*, and those left by me at Yambuya, along the road pursued by me. In that event, which would be very desirable, you will follow closely our route, and before many days we should most assuredly meet. No doubt you will find our bomas intact and standing, and you should endeavour to make your marches so that you could utilize these as you marched. Better guides than those bomas of our route could not be made. If you do not meet them in the course of two days' march, you may rest assured that you are not on our route.

It may happen, also, that though Tippu-Tib has sent some men, he has not sent enough to carry the goods with your own force. In that case you will, of course, use your discretion as to what goods you can dispense with to enable you to march. For this purpose you should study your list attentively.

1st.  Ammunition, especially fixed, is most important.
2nd.  Beads, brass wire, cowries and cloth, rank next.
3rd.  Private luggage.
4th.  Powder and caps.
5th.  European provisions.
6th.  Brass rods as used on the Congo.
7th.  Provisions (rice, beans, peas, millet, biscuits).

Therefore, you must consider, after rope, sacking, tools, such as shovels (never discard an axe or bill-hook), how many sacks of provisions you can distribute among your men to enable you to march —whether half your brass rods in the boxes could not go also, and there stop. If you still cannot march, then it would be better to make two marches of six miles twice over, if you prefer marching to staying for our arrival, than throw too many things away. . . .

Your present garrison shall consist of eighty rifles, and from forty to fifty supernumeraries. The *Stanley* is to bring you within a few weeks fifty more rifles and seventy-five supernumeraries, under Messrs. Troup, Ward and Bonny.

I associate Mr. J. S. Jameson with you at present. Messrs. Troup, Ward and Bonny, will submit to your authority. In the ordinary duties of the defence, and the conduct of the camp or of the march, there is only one chief, which is yourself; but, should any vital step be proposed to be taken, I beg you will take the voice of Mr. Jameson also. And when Messrs. Troup and Ward are here, pray admit them to your confidence, and let them speak freely their opinions.

I think I have written very clearly upon everything that strikes me as necessary. Your treatment of the natives, I suggest, should depend entirely on their conduct to you. . . . Lose no opportunity of obtaining all kinds of information respecting the natives, the position of the various villages in your neighbourhood, &c., &c.

I have the honour to be, your obedient servant,

Henry M. Stanley
*Commanding Expedition.*

After reading this letter over carefully, Barttelot came back to talk with Stanley regarding Tippu-Tib, and he asked why Stanley dealt with such a man.

"I have nothing to do with Tippu-Tib but from necessity, for your sake as well as mine," Stanley told the major. "He claims this as his territory. We are in it as his friends. Supposing we had not made an agreement with him, how long should we be left to prepare for the march to the Albert, or how long would you be permitted to remain here, before you had to answer the question why you were on his territory? Could I possibly leave you here, with my knowledge of what they are capable of—alone? With eighty rifles against probably three thousand, perhaps five thousand guns? Why, Major, I am surprised that you, who have seen Stanley Falls and some hundreds of the Arabs, should ask the question? . . . You know that he [Tippu-Tib] meditated war against the Congo State, and that I had to pass on a relief mission through a portion of his territory. Why how can you—grown to the rank of Major—ask such questions, or doubt the why and wherefore of acts which are as clear as daylight? . . .

"Look at these penciled calculations on this paper—nay, you can keep it if you please. They represent what you can do with your own men, and what you can do assuming that Tippu-Tib really keeps to the letter of his contract. Now I have grounded my instructions principally on your impetuous answer to me at Bolobo. 'By Jove! I will not stay a day at Yambuya after I get my column together!' "

Stanley then went on to cite how the rear column could march, and gave additional reasons for keeping on the good side of Tippu-Tib, concluding with a note of warning regarding the Major's handling of his men:

"Let these reasons sink into your mind, Major, my dear fellow. Yet withal, your column may be ruined if you are not very careful. Be tender and patient with your people, for they are as skittish as young colts. Still, it was with these people, or men like them, that I crossed Africa—followed the course of the Congo to the sea, and formed the Congo State."

"Well, now, say do you think Tippu-Tib will keep his contract, and bring six hundred people?" Barttelot asked.

"You ought to know that as well as I myself," Stanley replied. "What did he say to you before you left him?"

"He said he would be here in nine days, as he told you at Bangala, *Inshallah!*" Barttelot said, mimicking the Arabs who always qualified their statements by adding, "If Allah wills it."

Stanley knew the Arabs of Central Africa very well, and he knew how little credence should be given to their promises. He told Barttelot, "If Tippu-Tib is here in nine days, it will be the biggest wonder I have met."

"Why?"

"Because to provide six hundred carriers is a large order. He will not be here in fifteen days or even twenty days. We must be reasonable with the man. He is not a European—taught to be rigidly faithful to his promise. . . . No, wait for him until the *Stanley* comes, and if he has not appeared by that time he will not come at all."

"But it will be a severe job for us if he does not appear at all, to carry five hundred or six hundred loads with two hundred carriers, to and fro, backwards and forwards, day after day!"

"Undoubtedly, my dear Major, it is not a light task by any means. But which would you prefer; stay here, waiting for us to return from the Albert, or to proceed little by little—gaining something each day —and be absorbed in your work?"

"Oh, my God! I think staying here for months would be a deuced sight the worse."

Major Barttelot now brought up another, more personal, question: was Stanley prejudiced against him or had he heard anything about him that was detrimental to his character? Stanley dismissed these ideas and told him, "Now, Major, my dear fellow, don't be silly. I know you feel sore because you are not to go with us in the advance. You think you will lose some *kudos*. Not a bit of it. Ever since King David, those who remain with the stuff, and those who go to the war, receive the same honors. Besides, I don't like the word 'kudos.' The kudos impulse is like the pop of a ginger-beer bottle, good for a V. C. or an Albert medal, but it effervesces in a month of Africa. It is a damp squib, Major."

Stanley concluded the conversation by reciting two lines from Tennyson's "Ode on the Death of the Duke of Wellington":

> Not once or twice in our fair island story
> Has the path of duty been the way to glory.*

Stanley was now ready to leave. Before him stood a primeval rain forest of unknown depth which had never been penetrated by a white man. When Stanley with his advance force plunged into it, he had no conception of its immensity. He believed he could be through it, make contact with Emin, and return by November; it was now June.

---

* Tennyson's lines:

> Not once or twice in our rough island story
> The path of duty was the way to glory.

In spite of his phenomenal memory and the fact that he repeated the couplet on every appropriate occasion, Stanley misquoted these lines. Perhaps he simply could not resist attempting to improve upon everything, even Tennyson.

The jungle before them was more like a wall of vegetation than a forest. For Stanley it was a "region of horrors." He dreaded the prospect of penetrating its dank loathsomeness. "My imagination began to eat at my will. But when all the virtue in me rose in hot indignation against such pusillanimity, I left the pleasant day and entered as into a tomb. I found it difficult to accustom myself to its gloom and its pallid solitude. I could find no comfort for the inner man, or solace for the spirit. A man can look into the face of the Sun and call him Father; the moon can be compared to a mistress, the stars to the souls of the departed, and the Sky to our Heavenly home: but when man is sunk in the depths of a cold tomb, how can he sing or feel glad?"

It was on June 28, 1887, that the advance column left Yambuya and entered the forest of darkness. Today we know that this vast forest covers an area of some twenty-five thousand square miles. Into a great part of it the sun never shines. Trees often tower a hundred and fifty to two hundred feet high, and the undergrowth rises fifteen feet above the ground. Inside this almost solid mass of vegetation it is always damp, with water dripping from each leaf and petal. The ground is covered with centuries of dead leaves, decayed wood, and rotting vegetation. Every kind of tropical flora grows here, often taking exotic forms. Climbing vines ranging from thin threads of green to giant creepers over half a foot in diameter twist around each trunk and form webby barriers between the trees. Mosses, fungi, and lichens of all kinds abound here, and ferns sometimes have leaves twelve feet long.

All of this steaming green mass teems with insect life. There are grubs, ticks, ants of many varieties, malaria-carrying mosquitoes, and the dreaded tsetse fly. Each step taken by a human dislodges scores of insects or parasites that cling and bite.

Giant snakes creep through the thickets, hang from the vines, and coil around low-hanging boughs of trees. Strange animals live here, like the rare okapi, the black Ituri ratel, the elephant shrew, and the red dwarf buffalo.

The human habitants of this region were then—and are still—among the most isolated and primitive savages known, living out their lives in terror, pain, and dark superstition. Dying, they leave behind no monument, no progress, no history, no hope. Pygmies, the ugly and diminutive Negrillos, here live out their secluded, furtive lives.

Stanley, the great namer of places, could think of no name for this jungle. He called it simply "the great forest." Strangely enough, it still

has no distinctive name, but is variously known as the Great Congo
Forest, the Ituri Forest, the Aruwimi Forest, or the Stanley Forest.

On the expedition's first day of hacking its way through this jungle,
the savage inhabitants made their appearance. Working their slow
way forward, the leading men suddenly came upon a broad, cleared
road, twenty feet wide, at the end of which stood a village. In front
of their huts stood massed ranks of natives with drawn bows. Scan-
ning the road, Stanley noticed half-concealed skewers just visible under
bits of leaves. He quickly formed two lines of twelve men each. The
first line was detailed to pluck the skewers from the road while the
second line covered them with their rifles. Advancing in this fashion,
they steadily drove the natives back through their village and into the
jungle. The now deserted village was occupied by the Zanzibaris, and
the advance column of the expedition settled down to spend its first
night in the great forest.

The savages pelted the camp with arrows and spears throughout the
night, and one Zanzibari wakened to find that two spears had landed
on each side of him, so close that they pierced his sleeping mat and
blanket, almost pinning him to the ground.

In the morning a narrow path was found winding through a manioc
field, and they followed it. Several times they encountered obstructions
in the form of huge fallen trees. They came upon several villages. The
paths to all of them were studded with poisoned skewers.

Each day had its incidents and sometimes even the nights were
disturbed. One night, about three hours before dawn, the camp was
awakened by two voices near by.

The first called out, "Hey, strangers, where are you going?"

The second, acting as an echo, repeated, "Where are you going?"

"This country has no welcome for you."

"No welcome for you."

"All men will be against you."

"Against you."

"And you will be surely slain."

"Surely slain."

"Ah-ah-ah-ah-ah-aah."

"Ah-ah-aah."

"Ooh-ooh-ooh-ooh-ooooh."

"Ooh-ooh-ooooh."

Several of the Zanzibaris laughed at this crude attempt to frighten
them, and the speaker and his parasite fled.

The expedition enjoyed considerable good fortune for the next three weeks. Although barely able to make five miles a day, they did not lose a single man. On July 4, calm water was seen on the river and the *Advance* was launched. As the steel boat weighed the equivalent of forty-four loads and would carry fifty loads plus ten sick men, the column was relieved of much toil. Among the sick was Lieutenant Stairs, who had been carried in a stretcher since leaving Yambuya. The first day on the water they accidentally frightened some natives who abandoned their canoes and fled. The expedition appropriated eleven of the canoes in order to carry more loads and more sick men. They now advanced in the same manner as had Stanley's expedition when he started down the Lualaba River, one party traveling by land and the other managing the boats. This time, however, the route was upstream instead of down.

On July 20, two men, known as Charlie No. 1 and Musa bin Juma, deserted. They eventually reached Yambuya where they told the already disheartened Major Barttelot tall tales of disasters to the expedition.

On July 24, when the land party was being led by Jephson, they made an "astonishing march" of seven and one-half miles in one day. Stanley had now developed a great admiration for this young officer. He said of him, "He was in many things an exact duplicate of myself in my younger days, before years and hundreds of fevers had cooled my burning blood. He is exactly my own height, build and weight and temperament. He is sanguine, confident, and loves hard work."

Stanley himself was no longer the same man who had discovered Livingstone and followed the Congo to the sea. He had a great deal more experience now, but he was older. At forty-seven, the novelty of African travel was long since gone. He worried more and was less able to restrain his impatience and his irritability. His body had been wracked by too many fevers and deprived of too many nourishing meals. He had lost some of his energy, but he had lost none of his spirit. His indomitable will to succeed was, if anything, stronger than ever.

But back in Europe he was already reported dead. In July, a west-coast missionary sent back a story that Stanley had been killed in an engagement with natives over food. Newspapers in all parts of the world reported this. On August 17, the French consul in Zanzibar passed on a rumor that Stanley, after being betrayed by Tippu-Tib, had been murdered on the banks of the Aruwimi River. The French paper *Figaro* even gave the date of this supposed occurrence as June 28. No African expedition had ever drawn forth such a profusion of speculations. The whole world was interested. It was said that a traveler in Greenland had been asked by an Eskimo, "What news of Stanley?"

Stanley had little time to be concerned about events or rumors in Europe; he was completely occupied by the multitude of tasks at hand. On August 13, he was investigating a murder which had taken place the day before. A Zanzibari had been killed by a rifle bullet just outside the camp. While court was being held, Stanley sent a scouting party to the other side of the river to look for food. The investigation had not been long under way when firing was heard in the direction of the river. Stairs, only recently recovered from his illness, took a party of fifty men and headed in the direction of the shots. Stanley went on with his questioning of witnesses. But the firing continued and seemed to increase in intensity. At last Stanley broke up the court and ran with his remaining officers and men toward the river. There he found the first rescue mission engaged in a hot battle with natives hidden in the jungle on the far shore. Lieutenant Stairs, his shirt torn open, was stretched out on the ground, blood streaming from an arrow wound in his left breast.

Leaving Stairs with Surgeon Parke, Stanley hurried to the firing line. He learned that the scouting party in the boat had been attacked while trying to cross the river and had been forced to retreat. He saw that his men were firing wildly into the vegetation, but he could see nothing of the enemy, although their arrows were falling all around him and nine of his men were wounded. Looking carefully, he saw a dark shadow creeping along the ground. He fired at it, and immediately heard a curious, weird wail. Two minutes later the arrows stopped falling.

Stairs' wound was about an inch below the heart. The arrowhead had penetrated an inch and a half into his chest and had broken off. Parke was unable to extract the arrowhead, but, fearing that the arrow had been poisoned, he sucked the wound vigorously. This action probably saved Stairs' life, for all of the other men wounded in this engagement died horrible lingering deaths.

On August 15, the land party, with Jephson, Parke, and Nelson, lost its way, leaving Stanley stranded with the wounded and sick of the river party. Most of the healthy men were sent out to search for the lost column. Remaining with Stanley were "twenty-nine men suffering from pleurisy, dysentery, incurable debility, and eight suffering from wounds." Stairs was in terrible agony from his arrow wound; a Zanzibari who had been wounded in the windpipe was half strangled; and a man who had lost his mind and was described as a "dying idiot" completed the horrors of the little camp by the river. To add to their misery, a violent storm struck them, soaking them through. Surgeon Parke, who should have been on hand to tend to the sick and wounded, was, through no fault of his own, lost with the rest of the land party. Stanley wrote, "I hate to see pain, and take no delight in sick men's groans. I feel pleasure in ministering to their needs only when conscious I can cure."

All of the men were demoralized, and even Stanley was sunk in despondency. Later he wrote, "A few days more of this disheartening work, attending on the sick, looking at the agonies of men dying from lockjaw, listening to their muffled screams, observing general distress and despondency, from hunger, and the sad anxiety caused by the unaccountable absence of their brothers and comrades, with the loss of three hundred men impending over me must have exercised a malign influence over myself. I am conscious of the insidious advance of despair toward me. Our food has been bananas or plantains, boiled or fried, our other provisions being reserved for perhaps an extreme occasion which may present itself in the near future. The dearest passion of my life has been, I think, to succeed in my undertakings; but the last few days have begun to fill me with a doubt of success in the present one."

After six long days the lost column returned, and Stanley counted his people. Of the 388 men who had left Yambuya with him, there now remained 372 of whom fifty-seven were sick or wounded.

The morning of August 31 began as other mornings had. The sun, after struggling through dense clouds of mist, finally appeared about nine o'clock as a pale, indistinct circle of lusterless light filtered through the dense green foliage. Stanley was to describe it as an "evil date." They had now covered half the distance between Yambuya and the lake and the eerie dawn found them already working their way forward through the jungle. Stanley was supervising the movement of the boat around a cataract when William Hoffman dashed up to him with the news, "Sir, Emin Pasha has arrived!"

"Emin Pasha!"

"Yes sir. I have seen him in a canoe. His red flag, like ours [the Egyptian flag], is hoisted up at the stern. It is quite true, sir!"

Everyone made a mad dash for the river. There, instead of Emin, they found a lieutenant of an Arab slaver who, with nine Manyuema, was on a scouting expedition for his master, Ugarrowwa. Stanley was dismayed to find the slavers so far inland on the Aruwimi, for there would be no chance of meeting friendly natives where the slave hunters were at work. Besides, the Zanzibaris had a propensity to desert in the vicinity of Arab encampments.

The next day they came across a native village, deserted except for the bodies of a small boy who had been literally hacked to pieces and a woman who had been speared. They were indeed in slave hunting territory.

Desertion and its concomitant thievery now became an almost daily occurrence. On September 17, the expedition camped opposite Ugarrowwa's fortified settlement and Stanley called on the slaver, securing his promise to send messengers with a letter to Major Barttelot. Ugarrowwa did send men, but the letter was never delivered.

Stanley had now lost sixty-two men through death and desertion and there were still fifty-six men on his sick list. He made arrangements with Ugarrowwa to leave his sick and wounded at his settlement, paying the Arab five dollars a month for each man's board. Before Stanley left, Ugarrowwa turned over to him three deserters his men had captured. Stanley decided that he must make an example of them, for unless the desertions were stopped the expedition would disintegrate and the precious ammunition would never reach Emin Pasha. After explaining the matter to the rest of his men, he determined that the deserters would be hanged, one each day for three successive days.

On the morning of September 20, the expedition was drawn up into a hollow square with the doomed men in the center. Lots were drawn to determine which man should be hanged first. Mabruki, the slave of one of the headmen, drew the unlucky straw. A rope was thrown around his neck, and Stanley asked him if he had anything to say before he died. The man dumbly shook his head and the signal was made to hoist him up. Immediately the branch broke. There was an awkward delay while a new tree was selected. Mabruki was again hauled up by the other two prisoners. After a short interval, Stanley asked, "Is he dead?"

Parke said, "Yes," and the expedition filed out of camp, leaving the body of Mabruki hanging from the tree.

The remaining deserters were not executed. Instead, Stanley arranged a dramatic scene with his chiefs. The stage was set for the execution, the men again in a hollow square. But just as the second deserter was

about to be hoisted up, the chiefs, as arranged, rushed forward to plead
for his life. Stanley now spared both men, but delivered a stern lecture
to all of his men, telling them that "there is only one law in the future
for him who robs us of a rifle, and that is death by the cord."

When he had finished, his men shouted, "Death to him who leaves
Bula Matari! Show the way to the Nyanza!" Stanley was able to impress them and to gain their respect in a way that his officers could
not emulate. They sometimes complained that when all their efforts
could not get their men to obey, a word from Bula Matari would spring
them into action.

On October 5 they were forced to abandon the river altogether and
to try carrying the boat, the canoes, and the loads overland. This
proved an impossible task. There were now only 263 men left and
52 of them were living skeletons, unable to carry loads and barely
able to move themselves. This left only 211 men able to march, and
there were 227 loads. And even the healthy men were much weakened by their hunger. Food had been a problem from the beginning,
but since entering the area infested with the slavers the shortage had
become acute. Officers and men lived on such fungi and wild fruit as
they were able to procure, but this was not enough. The expedition was
starving to death.

On October 6, it was decided to leave Captain Nelson and fifty-two
sick and starving men at a camp by the river. Nelson was suffering
from ulcers on his feet—each step was torture for him. He was left
with his wretched crew on a sandy terrace, surrounded by rocks and
hemmed in by the dark jungle. Stanley remarked that "no more gloomy
spot could have been selected" than this site of what was known as
Starvation Camp No. 1. Leaving Nelson and his men with eighty-one
loads and ten canoes, the rest of the expedition forged on, hoping to
reach an Arab camp they had been told was just ahead of them.

On October 7 they found some corn and beans in a deserted village,
but it was not enough to relieve their hunger. Two days later they made
camp and sent out foraging parties in all directions, but without success. They were now living on grubs, slugs, caterpillars, white ants, and
such fungi as they were able to find. Lack of proper food weakened
them so that they were unable to resist the diseases and fevers that
raged among them. Huge ulcers, sometimes going as deep as the bone,
plagued them. Ticks entered their nostrils and dug tenaciously into the
membrane. They were all covered with vermin.

One of the officers asked Stanley if he had ever known anything as bad as their present sufferings on his previous expeditions. He admitted that this was the worst he had ever experienced. "We have suffered, but not to such an extremity," he confessed.

By October 15 the expedition had lost seventy-one men through deaths and desertions since leaving Ugarrowwa's camp three weeks earlier. Now rough water forced them to abandon the river. Stanley reluctantly decided that the boat would have to be left behind. He discussed the matter with the boat carriers. The faithful Uledi, ex-coxswain of the *Lady Alice* and now the coxswain of the *Advance*, knew very well how much the boat meant to Stanley and to the expedition. He said, "My advice is this. You go on with the caravan and search for the Manyuema, and I and my crew will work at these rapids, and pole, row, or drag her on as we can."

This suggestion was adopted and the remains of the expedition marched on. Stanley's ass, which was on its last legs, was shot, and the meat was divided. Bones, skin, blood, and even the hoofs were eaten.

The next day they struck a Manyuema path. Following it, they arrived at Kilonga-Longa's camp at Ipoto on October 17. Uledi with the boat and crew arrived a few days later. But the Arab camp was not quite the salvation they had hoped for. There was plenty of food, but the Manyuema were reluctant to part with it except for exorbitant sums. They wanted the rifles and ammunition of the expedition. The poor starving Zanzibaris were soon selling everything they could get their hands on, clothes, ammunition, bill-hooks, ramrods, and at last, even the coveted rifles. Stanley feared the expedition would disintegrate. Finally it was necessary to take drastic action, and one man was hanged for stealing a rifle.

Stanley did everything he could think of to win the friendship of the slavers. Kilonga-Longa himself was not in camp at the time, and Stanley was forced to deal with the cruel and crafty Manyuema chiefs. At last he obtained an agreement from them to send out some men with provisions for Nelson and his party and to supply food for the sick men he intended to leave at Ipoto with Dr. Parke.

On October 26, Mounteney-Jephson, with forty Zanzibaris and thirty Manyuema, started back for the relief of Nelson. By exceptionally fast marching he was able to reach Starvation Camp in three days. As he drew near the camp he passed the skeletons of some who had already died while searching for food. Describing his arrival, Jephson said, "As I came down the hill into Nelson's camp, not a sound was heard but the groans of two dying men in a hut close by. The whole place had a deserted and woebegone look. I came quietly round the tent and found Nelson sitting there; we clasped hands, and then, poor fellow! he turned away and sobbed, and muttered something about being very weak."

Of the fifty-two men left with Nelson, only five remained twenty-three days later! Nelson's description of his trials is simply a chronicle of death: "19th, man died; 22nd, two men died; 23rd, man died; 29th, two men died; Jephson arrived." He was so weak from hunger and so ill from ulcers—at one time he had as many as ten open, running sores on one foot—that he had been unable to search for food for himself and had to rely upon his men.

Jephson returned to Kilonga-Longa's camp with the worn and haggard Nelson and the five other survivors on November 3. Stanley, with the main part of the expedition, had already gone on, having left the day after Jephson started out for the relief of Nelson. Parke had been left at Ipoto with twenty-three sick men and three boys. The survivors of Starvation Camp were also to remain here while Jephson and his Zanzibaris marched on to catch up with Stanley and the main column.

Kilonga-Longa's chiefs at Ipoto now refused to give Nelson any food, maintaining that Stanley had not specifically mentioned him in the agreement with them. Only by selling their own clothing could Parke and Nelson eke out a subsistence diet for themselves and their men. The purpose of the Arabs was to starve the white men into parting with the rifles and ammunition that were in the loads left in their charge. These items, particularly the ammunition, were destined for the relief of Emin Pasha. Stanley had so impressed on his men the importance of the rifles that they felt they would rather starve than part with them. They regarded the ammunition as the most valuable thing they possessed. Without it, their mission would be useless as they would be unable to relieve Emin.

Naturally, under such conditions, few of the men showed any improvement. Captain Nelson, who had been on the edge of starvation, was a "mass of ulcers" and Surgeon Parke said, "I could not have believed that such a manly, well-built, athletic form could have been reduced to such a sickly looking, infirm, decrepit skeleton."

While Nelson and Parke were struggling with the Manyuema to obtain food and preserve the loads of ammunition, the main column was forging its slow, hungry way forward. Theft and desertion continued steadily. The sixteen Manyuema who were contracted to guide the expedition behaved as though the Zanzibaris were their slaves. They refused to allow them food from the villages and beat them with sticks while the Zanzibaris cowered before them, too weak to resist.

On November 8, the forest became less dense and they were able to travel more easily. The next day they came to the villages of Ibwiri. There they saw prosperous plantain groves, fields of corn, herds of goats, and other signs of plenty. They were at last out of the region dominated by the slavers. Stanley soon made friends with the natives, and the expedition enjoyed its first full meal since August 31. For seventy-three days they had been hungry, and for thirteen of those days they had tasted no food at all! The Zanzibaris were "hideous to look upon"; they were naked, for they had sold all of their clothes to obtain food from the Manyuema and their slaves at Ugarrowwa's and Ipoto; their flesh was gone, and their tight skin seemed to cover only bones; their color was a "mixture of grimy black and wood ashes" and they were almost all suffering from ulcers and diseases.

The expedition rested at Ibwiri until November 23. Jephson and his men came up on the fourteenth, and five days later a few men who had preferred to risk death on the road to the cruelties of the Manyuema at Ipoto straggled into camp. All told, Stanley now had one hundred and seventy-four officers and men left with him after the five hundred terrible miles they had traveled since leaving Yambuya.

By the time the expedition left Ibwiri, all of the men were fat and sleek once more. Some had gained by as much as a pound a day. Now there was laughter, singing, and storytelling around the camp fire. Hope and spirit had been taken in with each mouthful of food. They were all eager to march again, and on the morning of November 24, when the Sudanese bugler sounded the call to march, everyone was ready.

Four days later they caught a glimpse of the distant grassland from the spur of a ridge. On December 2, they camped in a deserted pygmy village, and the men were as excited as children when they discovered that the roofs of the huts were made of grass. One man, climbing to the top of the conical roof of a hut, saw the grasslands of Equatoria quite plain, and he called out to the others. In a moment, men were scampering up trees and huts to see the view. The next day scouts were sent out, and they returned with handfuls of grass. Some of the men kissed it, while others shook their fists at the dark jungle that had been their prison for so long.

On the morning of December 4, they filed out of camp to the ford that had been located across the Ituri River. Passing through a narrow belt of tall timber they followed an elephant track for about six hundred yards. Quite suddenly they broke out of the forest into a green rolling plain. Shouting like children, white men and black ran across the grass into "broadest, sweetest daylight, and warm and glorious sunshine, to inhale the pure air with an uncontrollable rapture." For the first time in more than five months they looked the sun full in the face and marveled at the soaring birds.

Far in the distance Stanley saw a range of mountains. He felt certain that beyond these they would find the blue waters of Lake Albert and the valiant pasha who was the object of their quest.

# CHAPTER XIII

## *Emin Found*

WITH THE FOREST of darkness behind them, the spirits of every member of the expedition soared. Success seemed close and believable. The men who had survived and were now marching with Stanley were quite different from the disorganized, undisciplined mob who had joined the expedition at Zanzibar. They were even different from the original advance column that had marched out of Yambuya. Now they were veterans—confident, capable, and disciplined. Stanley had every reason to be proud of them.

As they marched across the grassland, they encountered village after village; all were deserted. But on the hills around them were the villagers, silently watching the column. Stanley marched his men straight through each settlement, being careful to see that nothing was touched. He hoped his forbearance would prove his peaceful intentions to the natives, but instead he found that they regarded his policy as a sign of weakness.

On December 8, an increasing number of warriors, their bodies grotesquely painted and adorned, followed the caravan from the hillsides. Late in the afternoon Stanley made camp on top of a small hill. Looking out over the countryside, he could see fifty villages in view and about eight hundred warriors on the slopes of the surrounding hills, shouting lustily for the blood of the strangers.

Although the Zanzibaris were tired from their thirteen-mile march with sixty-pound loads in the hot sun, Stanley selected some of the strongest men and sent them out to meet the savages. Four scouts were in the lead, and the natives also sent out four men who bounded forward, eager for a fight. When the scouts and the foremost natives were within a hundred yards of each other, the Zanzibaris fired. The bullets missed their marks, however, and the Zanzibaris turned and ran, the natives in pursuit with fingers on their bowstrings. Those in camp groaned, and cursed the scouts for their cowardice. The natives on the hillsides took this initial victory as a good omen and screamed in triumph. The rifles of the rest of the skirmishing party soon checked the onslaught and drove the natives back. At sunset, both sides returned to their respective quarters.

Although the expedition was equipped with rifles and was facing men armed only with bows and arrows, there were less than two hundred in the column against nearly a thousand natives. Besides, their ammunition could not last forever, and if they expended it all in trying to reach Emin there would be none left to give him. That night before going to sleep, Stanley picked up his Bible and read Moses' exhortation to Joshua: "Be strong and of a good courage; fear not, nor be afraid of them: for the Lord thy God, He it is that doth go with thee; He will not fail thee, nor forsake thee." Stanley had long been convinced that he was a man of destiny, that God would not permit him to die until his mission was done. Now he fancied he heard a voice repeating Moses' admonition. But Stanley did not want advice—even from angels. He began to argue with the voice: "Why do you adjure me not to abandon the Mission? I cannot run if I would. To retreat would be far more fatal than advance; therefore your encouragement is unnecessary." But the voice said, "Be strong and of a good courage. Advance, and be confident, for I will give this people and this land unto thee. I will not fail thee nor forsake thee; fear not, nor be dismayed."

The next morning, the expedition completed its thorn-bush fence around the camp. War horns, sounding the eerie notes Stanley had heard in Usogo and Uganda in 1875, summoned the tribes while hundreds of war drums boomed from the hills. Yells and cries were heard flying between the valleys, and the little camp was completely surrounded by thousands of natives, ready and eager to do battle with the intruders.

About eleven o'clock, some of them approached close enough for one of the Zanzibaris, named Fetteh, to distinguish what was being said. Fetteh had originally come from Unyoro, and he was soon engaged in a dispute with the natives. As soon as Stanley learned that he understood and could speak the native tongue, he made him his interpreter and turned the conversation into more friendly and profitable channels. Fetteh, under Stanley's direction, now told one of the natives, "We on our side only fight in defense. You assail us while quietly passing through the land. Would it not be better to talk to each other, and try to understand one another first, and then, if we cannot agree, fight?"

"True, those are wise words," the native replied. "Tell us who you are, where you are from, and where you are going."

"We are of Zanzibar, from the sea, and our chief is a white man. We are bound for the Nyanza of Unyoro."

"If you have a white man with you, let us see him, and we shall believe you."

Stairs promptly stepped out into the open and was introduced to the native.

Fetteh now asked the native, "Now tell us who you are. What land is this? Who is your chief? How far is it to the Nyanza?"

"This land is Undussuma, the chief is Mazamboni. We are Wazamboni. The Nyanza is reached in two days. It will take you five days. It lies east. There is only one road, and you cannot miss it."

Peaceful relations were now established. In the afternoon, a present of two yards of red uniform cloth and a dozen brass rods were sent off to Mazamboni, the native chief. Assurances were given that the next day the chief himself would appear to make blood brotherhood with Stanley.

The next morning, Stanley, Mounteney-Jephson, and Stairs stood on the west end of their hill and looked out over the fertile plain. They talked of the day when this land would be turned into homesteads for civilized settlers. Stairs remarked that it reminded him of the scenery in New Zealand, and he began to lay out an imaginary ranch for himself.

Meanwhile, the Wazamboni were collecting on a hill opposite them. Soon they heard a man haranguing the crowd. Fetteh was called to translate. He went down the hill into the valley to hear better, but he was almost killed by arrows and had to retreat. Stanley decided "to teach the savages a lesson." Stairs was sent out with fifty riflemen toward the river; Jephson took thirty men to skirmish up the left slope; and Uledi with twenty men made a demonstration on the right slope. All were soon engaged in hot fighting. When the natives were routed, the villages in the valley were burned and by one o'clock in the afternoon all parties had returned. Only one man was slightly wounded. But in an hour the natives were back, and the fighting started all over again, continuing until night.

At dawn on December 12, the expedition quietly decamped. But it was not long before their movements were noticed, and the hue and cry was taken up by their tormentors. By noon, they were being followed by two separate bands of natives. Stanley now set fire to every village he encountered. This action had "a remarkable sedative influence on their nerves," he observed.

The path they were following led them to a saddle of land between two mountains. As they marched along, they could see every hill black with masses of men, and in the valleys there were long antlike lines of warriors converging at a point ahead of them.

On December 13, the expedition defeated the natives in a pitched battle and then marched on. Reaching the saddle of the hills—or plateau, as it turned out—they soon caught sight of Lake Albert. The Zanzibaris shouted and danced, congratulating Stanley on his having reached the "exact spot." But as Stanley swept the shore line with his telescope, a chill came over him. Now they needed the steel boat they had left at Ipoto. He had hoped he would be able to buy or to make a canoe when he reached the lake, but there was not a tree in sight, and not a single canoe was seen on the smooth surface of the water. Neither was there any sign of the two steamers Emin was known to possess. While his men were rejoicing, Stanley was trying to decide what should be done.

After a halt of twenty minutes, they resumed their march, passing across the plateau and down the steep slope leading to the lake. The Wazamboni continued to hang on their flanks and to harass the rear guard. There was almost continual firing, but aside from a wound received by one Zanzibari little damage was done.

On December 14, they reached the base of the plateau and traveled through a thin acacia forest. Stanley looked in vain for a tree large enough to be made into a canoe. They unexpectedly encountered some natives who, if not exactly friendly, were at least willing to talk to them. They said that many years ago, when they were children, a white man had appeared in a large smoking boat on the lake, but they had not seen such a thing since. The boat they were referring to was probably that of Gessi Pasha, who had circumnavigated the lake in 1876.

A month earlier, Emin had written to a friend in Scotland reporting, "All well; on best of terms with chiefs and people; will be leaving shortly for Kibiro, on east coast of Lake Albert. Have sent reconnoitering party to look out for Stanley, which had to return with no news yet. Stanley expected about December 15th."

Now although the advance party of the expedition actually arrived at the lake on the fourteenth, there was no sign of Emin, and Stanley could find no one who had even heard of him. Wadelai, capital of Equatoria, was twenty-five days' march by land, although Stanley thought the trip could be made by boat in only four days. To get there by marching overland would require more fighting and the expenditure of more ammunition. Since entering the grassland the expedition had already used up five cases of cartridges, and, although they still had forty-seven cases with them, Stanley feared that most of these would be consumed in trying to reach Wadelai, leaving few to turn over to Emin Pasha.

On the evening of December 15, Stanley informed his officers that there was only one "sensible course" left. They would return to Ibwiri (eighteen days away) and there build a strong stockade. A detachment of men could then be sent back to bring up the boat and the men and goods left at Ipoto and at Ugarrowwa's settlement. A fort such as he proposed to build would also serve as a welcome haven for the rear column under Major Barttelot, which, he assumed, must by this time be struggling through the great forest toward them. So, the next morning, they began their retreat to Ibwiri. Three sick men who straggled behind the column were quickly picked off by the natives, and the expedition had to fight its way through the Wazamboni again as it made its way back across the grassland.

On January 6, 1888, the caravan arrived in western Ibwiri, and Stanley selected a site for Fort Bodo, "Peaceful Fort." By January 18, the stockade was constructed, and Lieutenant Stairs was dispatched with ninety-seven men to Ipoto to get Nelson, Parke, the sick men who had been left there, and the boat. During his absence, Stanley set about to make Fort Bodo a snug and comfortable place. With only mud, wood, and vines for building material, this was not an easy task. Nevertheless, barracks, storehouses, and other buildings were erected, plantain groves and fields of maize were planted, and patrols were set up to keep off the pygmies.

In spite of all precautions, the buildings in the fort became infested with rats almost from the moment they were built. They ran over the sleeping bodies of the men at night, and sometimes they even dared to bite men on the nose or cheek. They seemed to prefer the putrid, running ulcers of the Zanzibaris and would eat out great portions of the rotten flesh. Hosts of fleas and tiny mosquitoes bothered them continually, but worst of all were the armies of red ants that would swarm across the ditch, climb over the stockade, and completely overrun the fort. They came in long, thick, unbroken lines, devouring everything in sight. If an unlucky man came in their way they would swarm over him, plunging their shiny, horny mandibles into the flesh, creating painful pustules. Their approach disturbed every living thing. Men screamed at the pain of their bites; beetles, snakes, mice, and other animals and insects fled their coming. For Stanley, they had one virtue; they invaded the rat holes and destroyed the baby rats in their nests.

On February 7, the first contingent of the men from Ipoto arrived. Parke was extremely thin, but well. Nelson, however, was prematurely aged by his sufferings. His features were pinched and drawn, and he walked with bent back and feeble legs. During their last seven weeks at Ipoto the Manyuema chiefs had given them no food whatsoever, and they had been forced to sell almost all of their clothing and even eight rifles. Parke said, "Apart from starvation, the people, their manner and surroundings, were of the lowest order, and, owing to the mounds of fecal matter and decomposing vegetation which were allowed to collect on the paths and close to their dwellings, the place was a hotbed of disease. Captain Nelson was confined to his bed from sickness for over two months, and I got blood poisoning, followed by erysipelas which kept me in bed for five weeks. During our illness the chiefs paid us frequent visits, but always with a view to covet something which they saw in our tents. Their avarice was unbounded, and they made agreements one day only to be broken the next."

A sample of the hardships of life at Ipoto can be gleaned from entries in Parke's diary:

"Dec. 15. Spent the day in bed, as I am unable to walk on account of enlarged glands in the upper part of the front of my left thigh. I developed these decorations from my over-walking and jumping in search of a shot the other day. I calculate that it will lay me up for a month, and that I will have to use the knife on myself. An inspiring anticipation, surely, under my circumstances: Nelson not being able to walk a couple of hundred yards, for a shot—or for anything else. The poor fellow is nothing but skin and bone, and the skin is broken in several places, especially over the back (sacrum) and hips (trochanters), where he has large bedsores.

"Dec. 16. Dreadful news today; our milch goat has been lost; or, to state the fact more correctly, has been stolen. This is a terrible business for us—we will now have but rice and porridge, and I will be confined to bed for a long time to come, as there is very great inflammatory swelling about my left hip and thigh, with a decidedly erysipelatous-looking blush, and an accompanying temperature of 100° F. I am sure

I've got blood poisoning, from the continual handling of the ulcers from which so many of our men are suffering; and the condition is necessarily aggravated by the results of the wretched dieting to which I have been so long obliged to accommodate myself.

"A most lovely sunset this evening! One would like to be able to enjoy it, but the surroundings are rather against the full appreciation of aesthetic effects."

Of the twenty-nine men left with Parke and Nelson, eleven died there and three more fell dead on the march to Fort Bodo. Only fifteen sick, starved men were left.

Stairs, who had remained behind to bring up the steel boat, arrived back at Fort Bodo on February 12. Four days later, he set off on another mission. This time he was to escort messengers, who had volunteered to take maps and instructions to Major Barttelot, as far as Ugarrowwa's settlement and to bring back the sick men who had been left there.

On February 18, Stanley's left arm, which had been paining him for several days, developed a large abscess. The following day, he came down with one of his gastric attacks. These attacks were so severe that he was almost out of his mind from the pain. This was the fourth he had experienced. One, which he had suffered while in his Bond Street flat in London, had persisted for three months. This time, the attack lasted for twenty-three days, during which he had only a confused recollection of "great pain in the arm and stomach, and general useless-ness." Parke took care of him, giving him generous doses of morphine. In spite of this, he slept poorly, sweated profusely and, when he was able to sleep for any length of time, was tortured by horrible dreams. It was not until March 13 that the pain left him, but even then he was so weak that he was unable to move. It was another two weeks before he was capable of walking more than a few hundred yards. During his illness, life went on at Fort Bodo: two men were killed by natives while on patrol and Uledi captured a pygmy woman.

On April 2, Stanley again set out for the lake, this time taking the steel boat. Of the advance column, there were 201 men remaining out of the 389 who had left Yambuya, including those left at Ugarrowwa's. Stanley took 126 men, including Parke and Mounteney-Jephson, with him, leaving Nelson and fifty-nine invalids at Fort Bodo.

As soon as they entered the grassland, the fighting began with the natives, and Fetteh, the sole interpreter of the language of the plains people, was seriously wounded just above the stomach. When they reached the hill where they had been surrounded on their first trip, Stanley again tried making friends with the Wazamboni. This time he succeeded. In explanation for their former hostile behavior, they said they took the expedition to be a raiding party sent out by Kabba Rega, a powerful Unyoro chief who had made himself feared and hated throughout this part of Africa.

When they asked the Wazamboni if they had ever heard of another white man in a boat, they replied that they had seen a bearded man in an iron boat just two moons earlier. The next day, April 14, Stanley was "a martyr to the cause of human brotherhood." From morning until night he sat in the middle of a close circle of native chiefs, their subchiefs, and servants, making blood brotherhood with them and asking and answering questions.

Two days later, the march was resumed. Now, however, they were escorted and befriended by the natives who had attacked them a few months earlier. Stanley's new-found allies even acted as voluntary pagazis, and at each village the people came out to make friends and to stare at them. On April 19, they reached the village of Kavalli where a letter, wrapped in oilcloth, was given to Stanley. It was from Emin Pasha and was dated March 25, 1888. He said he had heard rumors concerning a white man who had made his appearance in this region so he had come down to investigate. He ended the letter by telling Stanley to remain where he was as he would come to him as soon as he heard that he had arrived. Although Stanley did not know it at the time, Emin had written a letter to a German magazine, *Mitteilungen,* on the same date, concluding with the words, "If Stanley does not come soon we are lost."

Stanley replied to Emin's letter by telling him where he was, the purpose of his expedition, and asking Emin to come to him. The letter was given to Jephson and he left Kavalli with fifty men, the *Advance,* and two native guides for the lake on April 20.

On the morning of April 29, Stanley received a message from Jephson saying that he had reached Mswa, one of Emin Pasha's stations, and that the commandant, Shukri Agha, had sent a messenger to tell Emin of Stanley's arrival. Stanley and his people, with a native escort, set out for the shore of the lake at once. At four-thirty in the afternoon they saw Emin's steamer on the lake. Two hours later the ship anchored. With Emin Pasha was Captain Gaetano Casati, an Italian explorer who, when the rebellion broke out in the Sudan, had gone to Equatoria and had become an informal adviser to Emin.

It was about eight o'clock in the evening when Jephson led Emin, Casati, and an Egyptian officer into Stanley's camp. They were greeted by wild shouts of welcome and repeated rifle salutes from the Zanzibaris. Stanley met them just outside his tent. This time Stanley presumed nothing. After shaking hands with each of the strangers, he asked which man was Emin Pasha. The slight little man with the beard and glasses said in excellent English, "I owe you a thousand thanks, Mr. Stanley; I really do not know how to express my thanks to you."

"Ah, you are Emin Pasha. Do not mention thanks, but come in and sit down. It is so dark out here we cannot see one another."

Inside the tent, by the light of a candle, Stanley saw Emin quite clearly. He was unprepared for the sight. He had expected to see a tall man in a faded and worn Egyptian uniform with a worried and haggard expression, as befitted a beleaguered governor cut off from the world in Central Africa. Instead, a dapper little man about five feet seven inches tall stood before him dressed in a perfectly fitted white cotton suit and a well-kept fez. He looked in excellent health, and there was not a trace of anxiety on his face.

To celebrate the occasion, Stanley produced five half-pint bottles of champagne that had been carefully wrapped in some old stockings and saved, despite their hardships and constant near starvation, for this moment. These were uncorked, and the healths of Emin and Casati were duly drunk.

Surgeon Parke, who was present at this meeting, commented on this extraordinary action of Stanley's: "The small incident of his carrying five bottles of champagne all the way to the Albert Nyanza to drink Emin Pasha's health—without letting any one know of their existence but himself, although the use of them for his own case might have been the means of rescuing him from the jaws of death—forms, I think, as good an index to the character of our chief as anything in his history with which I have become acquainted."

The evening was spent in polite and pleasant conversation, and Stanley did not ask why Emin, although he was aware of Stanley's intentions to come to his relief, had not sent word to the natives to expect him and to prepare for his arrival. As it drew late, Emin Pasha and his party returned to their steamer for the night.

The next morning, Stanley turned over to the pasha thirty-one cases of Remington ammunition, and then went on board Emin's steamer, the *Khedive*, where he had an excellent breakfast of millet cake fried in syrup and a glass of fresh milk. On board the boat, in addition to Captain Casati, there were Vita Hasson, a Tunisian apothecary, some Egyptian clerks, an Egyptian officer, and about forty Sudanese soldiers. All looked well fed and well clothed.

The night before, Stanley had delivered to Emin Pasha the firman from the Khedive and the letter from Nubar Pasha. Stanley still did not know what Emin's intentions were—would he remain in his precariously held province or would he elect to come out with him? That evening, Stanley discussed the question with Emin, setting forth in detail the reasons why Egypt had abandoned the Equatorial Provinces.

Emin replied: "I see clearly the difficulty Egypt is in as regards retention of these provinces, but I do not see so clearly my way of returning. The Khedive has written to me that the pay of myself, officers, and men will be settled by the Paymaster General if we return to Egypt, but if we stay here we do so at our own risk and on our own responsibility, and that we cannot expect further aid from Egypt. Nubar Pasha has written me a longer letter, but to the same effect. Now, I do not call these instructions. They do not tell me that I must quit, but they leave me a free agent."

While it was true that the orders were somewhat ambiguously written, to Stanley they seemed perfectly clear. The pasha should quit his province; if he stayed, the Egyptian government could not be held responsible. But Emin had not envisaged relief in the form now presented to him. He had hoped that a route could be opened up to the east coast, enabling him to receive supplies and the scientific books and magazines that he craved. If Egypt would not support him, he hoped that some other government or some company would find a way to maintain him in his viceregal role. His officials were loyal only through expediency, for they feared that Emin's feeble power would actually be backed up by some real force some day. The relief expedition Stanley led was simply a ragged mob of pagazis in the eyes of the Egyptians and Sudanese. They could see no threat to themselves from this quarter. It should have been obvious, the situation being what it was, that Emin had no real course open to him but to get out of Central Africa if he could. He wondered what he would do when he got out of Africa, and perhaps he feared that his fame had reached the little German town where he had deserted his mistress. He may have preferred the possible consequences of falling into the hands of the Mahdi to the almost certain fate awaiting him at the hands of Madame Hakki.

Stanley was nonplused. He urged the pasha to leave and used all of his persuasive powers to convince him that he must come out: "If you stay here during life, what becomes of the provinces afterward? Your men will fight among themselves for supremacy, and involve all in one common ruin. These are grave questions, not to be hastily answered. If your provinces were situated within reasonable reach of the sea, whence you could be furnished with means to maintain your position, I should be the last to advise you to accept the Khedive's offer, and should be most active in assisting you with suggestions as to the means of maintenance; but here, surrounded as this lake is by powerful kings and warlike peoples on all sides, by such a vast forest on the west, and by fanatic followers of the Mahdi on the north, were I in your place, I would not hesitate one moment what to do."

"What you say is quite true," Emin answered, "but we have such a large number of women and children, probably ten thousand people altogether! How can they all be brought out of here? We shall want a great many carriers."

"Carriers for what?"

"For the women and children. You surely would not leave them, and they cannot travel."

"The women must walk; such children as cannot walk will be carried on donkeys, of which you say you have many. Your people cannot travel far during the first month, but little by little they will get accustomed to it. Our women on my second expedition crossed Africa; your women, after a little while, will do quite as well."

"They will require a vast amount of provisions for the road."

"Well, you have a large number of cattle, some hundreds, I believe. Those will furnish beef. The countries through which we pass must furnish grain and vegetable food. And when we come to countries that will accept pay for food, we have means to pay for it, and at Msalala we have another stock of goods ready for the journey to the coast."

"Well, well. We will defer further talk of it until tomorrow."

Stanley's original intention had been to take at least some of Emin's people out through the Congo, but he knew now that he would never be able to get them through the terrible forest. He was determined that if Emin would make up his mind to leave, he would take them all out by way of the east coast, relying on their numbers to protect them from hostile tribes.

The next morning, Stanley and Emin resumed their conversation of the night before. "What you told me last night," Emin began, "has led me to think that it is best we should retire from Africa. The Egyptians are very willing to go, I know. There are about fifty men of them besides women and children. Of those there is no doubt, and even if I stayed here I should be glad to be rid of them, because they undermine my authority, and nullify all my endeavors for retreat. When I informed them that Khartoum had fallen and Gordon Pasha was slain they always told the Nubians that the story was concocted by me, and that some day we should see the steamers ascend the river for their relief. But of the Regulars, who compose two battalions, I am extremely doubtful. They have led such a free and happy life here that they would demur at leaving a country where they enjoy luxuries such as they cannot hope for in Egypt. They are married, and besides, each soldier has his harem; most of the Irregulars would doubtless retire and follow me. Now supposing the Regulars refused to leave, you can imagine my position would be a difficult one. Would I be right in leaving them to their fate? Would it not be consigning them all to ruin? I should have to leave them their arms and ammunition, and on my retiring all recognized authority and discipline would be at an end. There would presently rise disputes and factions would be formed. The more ambitious would aspire to be chiefs by force, and from rivalries would spring hate and mutual slaughter, involving all in one common fate."

This presented quite a different picture of the state of affairs in Equatoria than Stanley had been given when he undertook the expedition. But there was still much that he did not know. Casati, who spoke no English, repeatedly urged Emin to tell Stanley that one battalion had already mutinied and the other was on the verge of doing so, but Emin's peculiar sense of pride made him ashamed to admit this. After discussing the matter for several days, he at last said that he would leave if his people would go with him, but he did not think that they would. Having received this much, Stanley now made two proposals to Emin. If he stayed, King Leopold had offered to support him and to pay his salary if he would keep open communication between the Nile and the Congo and would annex his province to the Congo Free State. This proposition, which had seemed a logical and reasonable one in Europe, must now have seemed absurd to both Emin and Stanley. With corrupt officials and troops of questionable loyalty, Emin's control of his province was hanging by too thin a thread. The forest between the Congo and the Albert Nyanza being what it was, the task of maintaining communications with the Congo was an impossible one. None the less, Stanley dutifully passed on the offer.

If this proposal was unacceptable, there was still another alternative. Stanley knew that Emin had written to Sir John Kirk, offering his services to Great Britain, so he offered to take Emin and his people to Kavirondo in the northeast corner of the Victoria Nyanza and to help them establish a settlement there in the name of the newly formed East African Association. Stanley made this proposal on his own initiative, counting on his friend William MacKinnon to sanction the act after it had been accomplished. This proposition appealed to Emin and he at last decided to adopt this course.

Emin Pasha was most kind, courteous, and generous to the officers and men of the expedition, supplying them with food, clothing, and even items which were luxuries to him. It almost appeared that Emin was the rescuer and Stanley the one who was being relieved! Since Emin did not seem to have any immediate use for the ammunition that had been brought to him at such peril, privation, and cost, and since he appeared to have an abundance of everything he needed, the whole expedition began to take on a ridiculous aspect.

Stanley was perplexed by this strange man who called himself Emin. The whole situation in Equatoria had an unreal quality about it. It was a kind of problem that he had never encountered before. On May 4, Stanley wrote in his diary, "There is something about it all that I cannot fathom."

The mystery of Emin Pasha was to deepen as far as Stanley was concerned. It would be difficult to find two men more different. Stanley was never at a loss for a decision, Emin could never make up his mind; Emin was generous, Stanley was thrifty; it was difficult for Stanley to forgive an offense, Emin forgave too easily; Emin was an intellectual, interested in scientific pursuits, while Stanley was the personification of the man of action; Stanley was pious, Emin was not; Stanley's morals were above reproach; Emin's tended to be lax. These two men could not understand one another.

One day Stanley suggested to Emin that it would be desirable to erect a small station between the expedition's camp and the nearest of Emin's posts. Two days later, Emin spoke to Major Awash Effendi, one of his Egyptian officers, and begged him, "Now promise me before Mr. Stanley that you will give me forty men to build this station which Mr. Stanley so much desires."

Recording this conversation in his notebook, Stanley wrote: "There is something about this that I do not understand. It is certainly not like my ideal Governor, Vice-King, and leader of men to talk in that strain to subordinates."

Emin wanted Stanley to return with him to Wadelai and to make the rounds of Emin's posts in order to persuade the soldiers that he had really been sent by the Khedive. Stanley refused to do this, however, and instead decided to send Mounteney-Jephson with a letter from him which he could read to the troops and officials. It was Emin's secret hope that the appearance of Stanley or one of his officers would induce his soldiers to return to him, but Stanley, although he did not yet fully understand the true state of affairs, had heard enough to know that all was not well in the province of Equatoria. Stanley's letter outlined the state of affairs in the Sudan and urged the troops and clerks to return to Egypt with him and Emin. It concluded with this paragraph:

"I send you one of my officers, Mr. Jephson, and give him my sword, to read this message to you from me. I go back to collect my people and goods, and bring them on to the Nyanza, and after a few months I shall come back here to hear what you have to say. If you say, let us go to Egypt, I will show you a safe road. If you say, we shall not leave this country, then I will bid you farewell and return to Egypt with my own people."

Mounteney-Jephson was perplexed by his assignment. In his diary he wrote: "If by going round and addressing the people, I can induce them to come out with us, I shall do good work. At the same time it seems so strange to us who have come out to help these people, that it is necessary first to explain who we are. I think there must be a screw loose somewhere."

On May 24, Stanley and Parke set off for Fort Bodo, leaving Jephson and four men to go with the pasha. More and more, as time passed by, Stanley worried about the rear column under Major Barttelot. Not a sign, not a word, not even a rumor concerning them had reached him since he left Yambuya eleven months before. Stanley concluded that if the rear guard had not reached Fort Bodo by the time he got there he would have to go back along the trail, through the great forest, and find them. It was not a pleasant prospect. Parke and Barttelot had been good friends, but Parke wrote in his diary: "It is too awful to think of going back all that way for Barttelot."

Now that Stanley had made friends with the tribes of the grassland, the 126-mile trip back to Fort Bodo was no longer dangerous. The party consisted of Stanley, Parke, 122 Zanzibaris, and 130 men from the docile Madi tribe (not to be confused with the Mahdists) lent by Emin. They had not gone two miles before twenty of the Madis deserted; six miles farther on the entire lot deserted en masse. Most of these were recaptured with the help of some of Emin's Sudanese soldiers and the column moved on.

It was during this march to Fort Bodo that Stanley made an astonishing discovery. Previously, on April 20, Jephson and Parke had reported seeing a white mountain, but Stanley had told them they must be mistaken. On May 24, however, Stanley saw mountains himself. It seemed incredible. There on the equator, in the heart of tropical Africa, stood a towering, snow-topped mountain range! It dawned on him that this must be the fabled Ruwenzori, the "Mountains of the Moon," which form the ultimate source of the Nile! Many men had surmised that such mountains must exist and many men had tried to find them, but it was not until Stanley and his men—passing through the country as it were—actually saw them and plotted them that their existence became factual knowledge. It was an important geographical discovery and, knowing Emin's scientific interest, Stanley dispatched a messenger to announce the discovery to him. Emin sent back a letter of congratulation, writing:

"I shall try hard to get a glimpse of the new snow mountain, as well from here as from some other points I propose to visit. It is wonderful to think how, wherever you go, you distance your predecessors by your discoveries.

"And now since this, for some time at least, is probably the last word I will be able to address you, let me another time thank you for the generous exertions you have made, and are to make for us. Let me another time thank you for the kindness and forbearance you have shown me in our mutual relations. If I cannot find adequate words to express what moves me in this instant you will forgive me. I lived too long in Africa for not becoming somewhat negrofied."

On June 8, Stanley arrived at Fort Bodo. Lieutenant Stairs was the first person to greet him, and Stanley was very pleased to see him. When Stairs had been sent back to Ugarrowwa's to bring up the men and supplies left there and to dispatch messengers to Major Barttelot, Stanley had estimated that the trip would take him thirty-nine days. He now learned that it had taken the young officer seventy-one days because of sickness and bad weather. Of the fifty-six sick men who had been left at Ugarrowwa's settlement, only fourteen survived.

Stanley eagerly asked Stairs if he had heard from Major Barttelot;

he had not. What had happened to the rear column? Fear for them oppressed Stanley. He knew that someone must make the trip back through the great forest and find them. He could have dispatched Stairs or one of the other officers, but instead he decided to go himself. On June 16, he selected a hundred and nineteen Zanzibaris and a hundred of Emin's Madis and left to find Major Barttelot and the rear column. Parke with a detail of fourteen men accompanied him as far as Ipoto to bring up the remainder of the supplies that had been left there. Nelson and Stairs were left at Fort Bodo. Stanley even tried to spare his faithful fox terrier, Randy, the march. The little dog had been by his side throughout the entire trip, but Stanley decided to leave him with Stairs while he made the long, dangerous trip. But the dog, of course, could not understand his master's intentions, and when Stanley left he refused to eat and died three days later.

The great forest was as terrible as before, but traveling was not quite as difficult as it had been on their first trip through it. The Zanzibaris were now more disciplined and experienced, they did not have the extra loads of ammunition to carry, and the route was known. At Ipoto, Kilonga-Longa, fearing a reprisal for his treatment of Nelson, Parke, and the men his chiefs had starved, attempted to make amends by returning nineteen of the expedition's rifles and fifty rounds of ammunition and making Stanley a gift of a goat and some rice.

On the afternoon of June 28, Stanley reached the site of Starvation Camp No. 1, where Captain Nelson had waited so many anxious, wretched days, suffering from ulcers and starvation and helplessly watching his men die. Stanley covered the same ground in four marching days that it had taken them thirteen days to cover the previous October. Here they found their cache of ammunition and some other stores that Jephson and his relief party had been unable to carry away. Stanley distributed a thousand rounds among his men, made up eight loads of additional material, and buried the rest. On making camp that night, it was discovered that four Madis had deserted, taking the personal kits of some of the Zanzibaris with them. Had they known the horrors of the forest, they certainly would have preferred to take their chances with the expedition.

The Madi pagazis still had much to learn. Provisions were issued to each man sufficient to last for twenty-five days, but the Madis, in order to lighten their loads, deliberately scattered their corn meal along the path. Consequently, on June 29, after only thirteen days, there were already about a dozen who were faltering from hunger. On July 6, they came upon a small plantain grove, and the famished Madis rushed on it, quickly devouring every plantain. Three of them paid for their haste by having the soles of their feet punctured by skewers set in the ground by the natives to protect their groves. The following day, when the expedition was hit by a shower, the cold rain on their bare backs pelted the remaining vitality from the weak and hungry Madis, and three of them fell dead within a few paces of each other.

On July 13, they reached the site of Ugarrowwa's camp, but they found the settlement abandoned. The next day they ate the last of their food, but luckily some foraging Madis found a large plantain grove with food enough for everyone. The Zanzibaris wisely dried the plantains over a fire and then converted the fruit into a flour that could be carried with them to be made into bread or cakes. But the Madis refused to learn this method, and, as they marched on, they died by twos and threes.

On July 20, Stanley found three canoes big enough to carry the seriously ill. Lack of food had now affected all of them, however. Of July 25, 1888, Stanley wrote, "I was never so sensible of the evils of forest marching as on this day. My own condition of body was so reduced, owing to the mean and miserable diet of vegetables on which I was forced to subsist, that I was more than usually sympathetic. At this time there were about thirty naked Madis in the last stages of life; their former ebon black was changed to an ashy grey hue, and all their bones stood out so fearfully prominent as to create a feeling of wonder how such skeletons were animated with the power of locomotion. Almost every individual among them was the victim of some hideous disease, and tumours, scorched backs, foetid ulcers, were common; while others were afflicted with chronic dysentery and a wretched debility caused by insufficient food. A mere glance at them, with the malodour generated by ailments, caused me to gasp from a spasm of stomach sickness. With all this, the ground was rank with vegetable corruption, the atmosphere heated, stifling, dark, and pregnant with the seeds of decay of myriads of insects, leaves, plants, twigs, and branches. At every pace my head, neck, arms, or clothes was caught by a tough creeper, calamus thorn, coarse briar, or a giant thistle-like plant, scratching and rending whatever portion they hooked on. Insects of numberless species lent their aid to increase my misery, especially the polished black ant, which affects the trumpet tree. As we marched under the leaves these ants contrived to drop on the person, and the bite was more vexatious than a wasp's or red ant's; the part bitten soon swelled largely, and became white and blistery. I need not name the other species, black, yellow, and red, which crossed the path in armies or clung to almost every plant and fed on every tree. These offensive sights and odours we met day after day, and each step taken was fraught with its own particular evil and annoyance, but with my present fading strength and drooping spirits, they had become almost unbearable. My mind suffered under a constant state of anxiety respecting the fate of my twenty choice men which were despatched as couriers to the rear column under Major Barttelot, as well as of the rear column itself. I had had no meat of any kind, of bird or beast, for nearly a month, subsisting entirely on bananas or plantains, which, however varied in their treatment by the cook, failed to satisfy the jaded stomach. My muscles had become thin and flabby, and were mere cords and sinews, every limb was in a tremor while travelling, and the vitals seemed to groan in anguish for a small morsel of meat."

On July 30, they reached the spot where Stanley had waited with the sick and wounded while the main column of the expedition was lost. This had been more than a year ago. On the last day of July they reached Avisibba, where Stairs had received the arrow in the chest in a fight with natives. The arrowhead, incidentally, was still embedded in his ribs.

On August 11, Stanley caught up with Ugarrowwa and his people, who had been moving slowly ahead of them. In the Arab's camp they discovered the couriers who had been sent to find the Major six months before. The couriers had tried to get through, but they were too few to fend off the natives and had been forced to return to Ugarrowwa's. Four had been killed, and fifteen out of the remaining sixteen had wounds. Two men were still in serious condition, and one of them soon died. Besides the couriers, Stanley found three deserters in Ugarrowwa's camp. All of these men helped to make up for the losses they had suffered. The expedition under Stanley now consisted of a hundred and thirty men. Ugarrowwa, who was out of gunpowder, was more kind than usual, providing Stanley with food and three canoes, which, with the canoes he had acquired along the way, enabled him to make his entire party waterborne. But Ugarrowwa could not give Stanley what he wanted most desperately: news of the rear guard. The Arab had heard nothing of them.

By August 16, they were only about ninety miles from Yambuya, and they had not found a trace or heard a word of the rear column. To Stanley it seemed certain that Major Barttelot and his men had met with some disaster. Over and over in his mind he revolved the possible tragedies that might have occurred. At sunset, he went down by the river and watched the African sun sink behind the river and jungle. The buoyant feeling of confidence that had always upheld him now was gone. He walked slowly back to his tent in the dark. Throwing himself down, he begged God to give him back his followers and ease the heartache that was killing him.

The next morning, August 17, they embarked in their canoes. It was a somber morning, rendered more depressing by the devastated villages they encountered along the river banks, apparently the work of Manyuema slave raiders. About nine o'clock, near the village of Banalya, Stanley saw a stockade beside the river. Through his telescope he saw a red flag hanging from a pole. A puff of wind unfurled it for an instant, and he saw the white crescent and star of the Egyptian flag. Springing to his feet he cried, "It's the Major! Pull away!"

# CHAPTER XIV

## Epic Deterioration

As the canoes raced toward the shore, Stanley saw a group of men standing by the riverside. Calling out to them, he asked who they were. "We are Stanley's men," they replied in Swahili.

On landing, Stanley was met by William Bonny, the middle-aged ex-sergeant. Shaking hands, Stanley asked, "Well, Bonny, how are you? Where is the Major? Sick, I suppose."

"The Major is dead, sir," Bonny answered.

"Dead? Good God! How dead? Fever?"

"No, sir. He was shot."

"By whom?"

"By the Manyuema—Tippu-Tib's people."

"Good heavens! Well, where is Jameson?"

"At Stanley Falls."

"What is he doing there, in the name of goodness?"

"He went to obtain more carriers."

"Well, then, where is Mr. Ward, or Mr. Troup?"

"Mr. Ward is at Bangala."

"Bangala! Bangala! What can he be doing there?"

"Yes, sir. He is at Bangala, and Mr. Troup has been invalided home some months ago."

This rapid exchange of questions and answers was Stanley's introduction to the story of the epic deterioration of the rear guard, a tale of a prolonged nightmare acted out in the heart of equatorial Africa. For Stanley, it was "as deplorable a story as could be rendered of one of the most remarkable series of derangements that an organized body of men could possibly be plunged into."

The catastrophe of the rear column and its aftereffects were to reflect

249

little credit upon anyone concerned with it. Stanley, the officers of the
rear guard, and the entire expedition—all were to be tarnished by the
tragic misfortunes that had occurred on the banks of the Aruwimi.

When on June 28, 1887, Stanley had marched out of Yambuya, his
parting words had been something to the effect that he would be seeing
Barttelot sometime in November, five months hence. Neither Stanley
nor anyone else had anticipated that he would be gone for fourteen
months. Stanley had presumed that the rear guard would follow him
as soon as the pagazis to be provided by Tippu-Tib arrived, or that,
failing the arrival of the carriers, Major Barttelot would move his men
and supplies forward by slow stages, making the same march several
times over to bring up the supplies.

Trouble had started as soon as Stanley left. All of the officers were
brave, energetic, and determined to succeed, but they were still unfamiliar with African life, and they did not know how to deal with the
natives, the Manyuema, their own men, or the Arabs.

The first difficulties were with the natives, who refused to sell them
food. To bring them around, the Zanzibaris, with the permission of
their officers, captured several native women and held them for ransom. The natives retaliated by capturing some of the Zanzibaris. There
was never actual warfare since, strange as it may seem, the whole
purpose of these captures, as far as the men in the rear column were
concerned, was to force the natives to be friendly, but this game of
human pawns for food continued for some time. Jameson kept score,
recording at one point: "They have got one woman and the baby back.
We have got Omari back, still have one woman, one kid, eight or nine
fowls, and some fish; so I think the balance is now in our favour."

In his diary, Jameson also noted, "It is wonderful what they will
pay to get back their women."

When the *Stanley* arrived on August 14, bringing up Ward, Troup,
Bonny, and the men who had been left at Bolobo, together with the
remainder of the loads, the rear guard consisted of Major Barttelot,
four other white officers, forty-four Sudanese, two Somalis, and two
hundred Zanzibaris—a total of two hundred and fifty-one (seven had
died since Stanley's departure). With them at Yambuya they had over
six hundred loads. Now was the time when Stanley had authorized
Barttelot to start forward, but, excluding the whites and the Sudanese
soldiers (who refused to carry loads), there were not enough men to
carry the loads without making three trips. To make matters worse the
men who had been left with the rear guard were not the best; they

consisted of the lazy, the weak, the sick, and the recalcitrants. Barttelot and the other officers agreed that it would be impossible to make these men move the loads. Besides, there was always the hope that Tippu-Tib would supply the promised Manyuema pagazis.

Pending the arrival of Tippu-Tib's men or the return of Stanley, the twenty-eight-year-old major set about fortifying his camp and establishing strict discipline among his men. In this he succeeded admirably. The camp at Yambuya was made into a very defensible fort, and the men were kept fairly well in hand by an iron discipline. Flogging became almost a daily occurrence at Yambuya. As time went on, the punishments became more and more severe, a hundred to two hundred lashes being common; the customary punishment for stealing food from the officers being a hundred and fifty lashes. Jameson, sickened by the continual floggings, once suggested that the men be put in chains instead, but he was voted down by the other officers. Barttelot, who made no secret of his hatred for the Negro, felt that such severe punishment was essential for discipline.

Some of the unfortunate men bore the beatings bravely enough. Jameson, describing one flogging, wrote in his diary: "The Soudanese are wonderfully plucky in bearing pain, for although he received 150 strokes, which cut him up very much, he never uttered a sound." Others did not bear up so well. One man—given three hundred lashes! —died two days later as a result.

Most punishments were dealt out for stealing. A Sudanese who attempted to desert with a rifle was shot. The men said they stole because they were hungry, although there were fields of manioc around them and plenty of fish in the river. While this was not sumptuous fare, it should have kept them alive and healthy. It did not. On December 3 Jameson wrote in his diary: "Several of the men in camp are only walking skeletons, and the marvel is how they exist or move at all. One man, who walks with rather an active upright motion, is a horrible sight, having nothing but loose folds of skin over his bones."

Barttelot recorded similar impressions in his diary: "Some of our men have faded away to nothing. It is surprising to me how uprightly and well they walk, though mere skeletons." Although concerned by the loss of their men, none of the officers seems to have attempted to seek an explanation for their wretched condition.

Every effort was made by Barttelot and Jameson to make Tippu-Tib live up to his agreement with Stanley. In August there was a rumor of a band of Arabs and Manyuema on their way toward Yambuya. Some Arabs with their Manyuema followers did appear, but they only raided the village on the opposite shore of the river. The same Arabs, who were led by a nephew of Tippu-Tib, camped nearby and complicated their situation by trying to corner all of the available food in the area and attempting to restrain the natives from selling food to the rear guard.

On August 22, Jameson and Ward set out for Stanley Falls to learn from Tippu-Tib himself why the promised pagazis had not been sent. Like everyone who met Tippu-Tib, Jameson and Ward were impressed by the gracious but wily old slaver. They returned to Yambuya on September 12 with the good news that Tippu-Tib had promised without fail that the six hundred men would shortly be on their way. But the hopeful young officers waited in vain. On October 4, Barttelot and Troup set out for Stanley Falls to try their luck with the Arab. Arriving eight days later, they found that Tippu-Tib was not there, and they had to wait ten days for him. When he did arrive, he said that it would be necessary for him to get his men from Kasongo, nearly four hundred miles farther up the Congo. Discouraged, Barttelot and Troup returned to Yambuya to wait, but they were now sure that Tippu-Tib would not be able to obtain the men before Stanley returned.

To a young lady in England, Barttelot wrote: "I have done all I can now until Stanley puts in his appearance, and, failing that, I shall not take any decided step till February; it will be weary waiting, but it must be gone through with."

All through November, December, and January they watched the river, expecting the arrival of Stanley any day. In a letter to a friend, Barttelot wrote: "I had no means of moving, for my men were dying fast from want of proper food and medicine; they have nothing but makago or manioc. Our number of loads trebled the men who were fit to carry. Deserters had come in and stated that Stanley had had trouble on the road; so I expected he would be late, but not so late as this. In the meantime, on November 15, Tippu had gone to Kasongo, and was expected back on February 1, 1888. But on February 1 we heard that men were scarce, and that Tippu would not return for several months."

Barttelot now proposed to take a handful of the best men and go look for Stanley, leaving the loads behind. Some of the officers agreed with him, but Troup argued with Barttelot: "Suppose you go up without the loads and should happen to meet Stanley, his first question would be 'Well, Major, where are my loads?' What would you reply? When you informed him that you had left them behind and had come up in search of him, I can well imagine the warm conversation that would ensue."

This seemed unanswerable. But Barttelot wanted to do something —anything—for he knew Stanley's criticism would be bitter. In his diary he wrote, "Stanley and I were never on good terms. He could not threaten me, and threats are his chief mode of punishment."

In a letter to Major Harry Sclater, his brother-in-law, Barttelot said, "This has been a doleful letter, but I write to you because I think one of the family should know how we are situated. I have never been on such a mournful, cheerless trip as this. The harder we worked, the glummer Stanley looked. After a long march, no smile from him or word of any sort, except to say 'You have lost a box,' or some sneer of that sort.

"Bonny told me, by way of a refresher, that Ward had told him that Stanley had told him (Ward) that he (Stanley) had left me behind because I was of no use to him. Certainly, I don't think I am much, but, then, it is because Stanley does not attempt to utilize me, and hates me like poison."

Feeling that he would be blamed, Barttelot wrote to his father: "Stanley, if he gets home, will no doubt twist events so as to make it appear that all the failure was due to me; but if I come back too, I can show him up in his true light."

Barttelot even thought that Stanley, being "such a peculiar fellow," might even have rescued Emin and be in England by now, leaving him and his men stranded at Yambuya. Stanley had awed all of his officers and had impressed them as a strange, extraordinary man. Many years later, Ward wrote: "There are two Stanleys: Stanley the African traveller and Stanley himself. I claim to have known only Stanley the African traveller."

The officers of the rear guard, confused with doubts, apprehensions, and irresolution, were not always in harmony. They were a strange group to be sharing a common fate: an officer, an adventurer, a naturalist, an artist, and a soldier. A close friendship developed between Barttelot, the army officer, and his second in command, Jameson the naturalist. Barttelot and Troup disliked each other and quarreled. Jameson did not care for Ward. The oddest man was Bonny, the senior in years and the junior in rank, a man Stanley later referred to as "the inferior officer." While not actually disliked, he had no close friends among the others. They were gentlemen; he was not. He was a talebearer, a complainer, a resenter of his inferior position among the young officers. Yet everyone grudgingly admitted that he did his work satisfactorily. He was destined to be the only officer of the rear guard to complete the expedition.

By January 18 forty-four men had died, and Jameson wrote in his diary: "This life is becoming tedious and monotonous beyond measure, and God knows when and how it will end."

As the days dragged on, the nature of the officers seemed to change. They were no longer shocked by brutality, and their finer feelings became more and more submerged. They almost lost sight of their real purpose and looked forward only to Stanley's return. If he would only arrive, they would be delivered and all would be well. The desire became an obsession with them. One night Barttelot, Jameson, and Troup each dreamed of Stanley's return. Troup dreamed of Stanley returning alone. When asked about the others, he did not seem to know or care, and remarked that they had each taken their own road and he knew nothing about them.

Barttelot dreamed that Stanley arrived in camp looking jolly and well. William Hoffman, Stanley's servant, came inside the Major's hut and he had to order him out. Barttelot then went to Stanley's tent where he found him with a lawyer. Seeing this, Barttelot heard himself say, "Oh, you are for the crown, I won't say anything." Here Barttelot's dream ended.

Jameson dreamed that he saw a long line of canoes coming down the river, and in one of them was Stanley sitting under a large white umbrella. As soon as he recognized Stanley, Jameson awoke. This was very close to the scene that actually took place when he finally did arrive, but on that day Jameson was not at Yambuya. He was at Bangala, and it was the day of his death.

The rear column was not alone in its concern for Stanley. Back in Europe, public curiosity was aroused. Was he dead? Had he been taken prisoner? What had happened to him? All messengers from the Congo reported "No news of Stanley." There was talk of a relief expedition to go to his rescue, but nothing ever came of it. There was also discussion as to whether another expedition ought not to be sent out for the relief of Emin.

Noted African travelers were asked for their opinions. Dr. Junker said, "The expedition is exposed to no risk on the part of the natives." Dr. Schweinfurth's verdict was that "there is no reason to be uneasy respecting Stanley's fate." But these statements failed to quell the growing anxiety. The leading article in the *North American Review* for December, 1888, was a symposium on the question "Is Stanley Dead?" Four noted men, including Lord Wolseley and Charles P. Daly, President of the American Geographical Society, gave their opinions.

On June 17, 1888, a Paris paper reported that official news of Stanley's death had reached Brussels. The report was denied, but it was said that the families of the pagazis were wearing mourning in Zanzibar. Tippu-Tib was denounced as the cause of the disaster.

The London *Times,* under a dateline of Suakin, June 20, 1888, announced: "According to intelligence received by military authorities from Berber and Khartoum, and confirmed by deserters from Osman Digna's camp, a white pasha has appeared in the Bahr-el-Ghazal district, and is advancing victoriously. The Khalifa Abdulla, the Mahdi's successor, is said to be much alarmed. This white pasha is probably Stanley."

The reports of a "white pasha" rampant in the Sudan continued to come in and were reported and commented on by the papers. Some said the man was Emin, but most believed he was Stanley. A seeming confirmation of this theory was the report that the white pasha's men were said to be armed with Remington rifles, which Stanley was known to be carrying.

Some English papers reported that Major Barttelot had sent scouts along Stanley's track and had found the path littered with skulls and bones. The London *Standard* put out a story detailing the death of Captain Casati. Three weeks later, *L'Echo du Nord,* published in Lille, stated that the president of the Geographical Institute had received word that Stanley and all of his followers except two pagazis had been killed.

In the House of Commons on December 14, 1888, the First Lord of the Treasury, in reply to a question, confirmed the report that Osman Digna had written the governor of Suakin detailing the capture of Emin and Stanley. For the next few days, the report of this disaster was the most prominent news in the papers. Then suddenly, just one week later, a member of Parliament asked leave to read a telegram just received by Reuters. As silence crept over the House, the message was read reporting the arrival of Stanley at Banalya and his intention of taking the rear column up to Emin. Stanley was safe! The entire House of Commons rose to its feet and cheered.

But evil news was to follow. The world had yet to learn of the events that were taking place at Yambuya and Banalya—events that were to create so much controversy in the next few years.

By February, 1888, there was still no sign of Stanley at Yambuya. On February 14 Barttelot and Jameson went to Stanley Falls to see if Tippu-Tib had sent any men from Kasongo. Arriving after their six-day trip, they were told that Tippu-Tib himself would be there within ten days. When he did not show up, they were told that a large caravan of men for them would soon arrive. On March 14, a caravan of three hundred men did appear, but it turned out that only fifty men with smallpox were destined for the rear column. The young officers were sick and disheartened. Barttelot and Jameson then decided that Jameson should go to Kasongo to hunt out Tippu-Tib and make a proposal to him: They would offer the Arab ten thousand pounds out of their own pockets if he would supply six hundred pagazis and four hundred askaris. Jameson left Stanley Falls on March 18, reaching Kasongo on April 11. When Tippu-Tib heard the proposition of Jameson, he readily agreed to provide the men and told them to be ready to leave Yambuya by not later than June 1.

From Kasongo, Jameson wrote a letter to his wife in which he said: "The Major and I have been thrown more together than any of the others, having been left alone at the camp for a long time, and we have kept up the same sort of intimacy ever since the others arrived. He is a real honest gentleman, and I cannot say more. We both have come to one another for advice at any moment, and he has been placed in a hard and difficult position with Mr. Stanley, who, no matter what you do, is sure to say it is wrong. We shall both be blamed, I know, for the long delay at Yambuya Camp, but God knows we have done everything in our power to prevent it. Out of the whole force in our camp, we could only muster eighty sound men, and of what use would it be to go after Mr. Stanley with this force, when he, with 400 men, sixty of whom (besides officers) were armed with Winchester rifles, a Maxim gun, and all the rest armed with Remingtons, has evidently met with opposition which prevents him from either returning to us, or from sending us any message? Twice Barttelot and I have been going to start with the few men we could scrape together, and go after him, but wiser counsels have prevailed, and we at last decided not to go until we had a force sufficient to be of real aid to him. I cannot believe that Mr. Stanley would have gone out by any other route, either with or without Emin Pasha, and not have ensured a message getting back to us. If he has done such a thing, he will be wasting a large sum

of money, and risking the lives of all the men, for no earthly purpose. . . . How I wish that I could kiss little Gladys, and the small
baby that I have never seen! I pray for you all so earnestly every
night!"

Jameson, the only married man on the expedition, had paid a thousand pounds for the privilege of helping to rescue Emin because he was
ambitious to "do something good in this world"; he now lamented
that "there were a thousand other things I might have done which
would never have called me away so far."

Tippu-Tib was very courteous to Jameson and convinced him that
"he really does want to see us go and is trying to get the men." On
April 27, Jameson left Kasongo with Tippu-Tib and some of his men.
They did not go far, however, before Tippu-Tib found some pretext
for delaying their trip, and it was May 5 before they were actually on
their way.

It was while Jameson was on his way back from Kasongo that an
incident occurred which was later to be most damaging to his reputation. Tippu-Tib was talking about cannibals, and he remarked that
they were now among cannibalistic tribes. Jameson told him that he
had heard many tales of cannibals but could not bring himself to
believe they were true. Here is the story as it was recorded in Jameson's
diary:

"He [Tippu-Tib] then said something to an Arab named Ali, seated
next to him, who turned round to me and said, 'Give me a bit of cloth
and see.' I sent my boy for six handkerchiefs, thinking it was all a
joke, and that they were not in earnest, but presently a man appeared,
leading a young girl of about ten years old by the hand, and I then
witnessed the most horribly sickening sight I am ever likely to see in
life. He plunged a knife into her breast twice, and she fell on her face,
turning over on her side. Three men then ran forward, and began to
cut up the body of the girl; finally her head was cut off, and not a
particle remained, each man taking his piece away down to the river
to wash it. The most extraordinary thing was that the girl never uttered a sound, nor struggled, until she fell. Until the last moment,
I could not believe that they were in earnest. I have heard many stories
of this kind since I have been in this country, but never could believe
them, and I never would have been such a beast as to witness this,
but I could not bring myself to believe that it was anything but a
ruse to get money out of me, until the last moment.

"The girl was a slave captured from a village close to this town, and the cannibals were Wacusu slaves, and natives of this place, called Mculusi. When I went home I tried to make some small sketches of the scene while still fresh in my memory, not that it is ever likely to fade from it. No one here seemed to be in the least astonished at it."

Jameson's interpreter, Assad Farran, was shocked, though. Later 'he made formal complaint to the Congo Free State government, charging Jameson with buying a slave girl and having her murdered in order to sketch the scene.

On May 22, Jameson and Tippu-Tib arrived at Stanley Falls where they were met by Barttelot and M. Van Kerckhoven, the Free State chief of Bangala station. Tippu-Tib now informed them that he could supply only four hundred men instead of the promised thousand and that Barttelot and Jameson would have to pay an additional thousand pounds for Muni Somai, an Arab chief who would lead the Manyuema. Forced to be content with this, Barttelot and Jameson went back to Yambuya, arriving on May 31.

All of the officers had suffered from fever, but so far there had been no serious accidents. Troup was the first casualty. He had fallen and injured himself so badly that he was now unable to move. He had apparently injured his testicles, but, being Victorians, none of the officers mentioned the exact nature of his injury—not even Bonny in his official medical certificate that sent Troup home.

On March 24, while Jameson was still at Kasongo, Ward was sent fifteen hundred miles down the Congo to Banana in order to send a telegram to the relief committee in London telling them they intended getting six hundred carriers and four hundred fighting men and that they expected to start about June 1, leaving all loads not absolutely necessary at Stanley Falls. The telegram ended with: "Wire advice and opinion. Officers all well. Ward awaits reply." That Barttelot should send a man so far to send such a telegram reflects his own loss of confidence in his actions.

The committee's reply would not have helped him very much if he had received it—which he did not:

*To Major Barttelot, Care Ward, Congo.*

Committee refer you to Stanley's orders of the 24th June, 1887. If you still cannot march in accordance with these orders, then stay where you are, awaiting his arrival or until you receive fresh instructions from Stanley. Committee do not authorize the engagement of fighting men. News has been received from Emin Pasha via Zanzibar, dated Wadelai, November 2nd. Stanley was not then heard of. Emin Pasha is well and in no immediate want of supplies, and goes to south-west of lake to watch for Stanley. Letters have been posted regularly via East Coast.

*Chairman of Committee*

Even after Tippu-Tib, Muni Somai, and the four hundred and thirty men who were to act as carriers had assembled at Yambuya, Tippu-Tib continued to procrastinate. The loads were too heavy, he insisted; they must be reduced from the normal sixty pounds to forty. Barttelot and the other officers tried to argue the matter, but in the end they complied. When the loads had all been reduced, Tippu-Tib still took exception to some that were a few pounds overweight. After a great deal of wrangling, the matter was finally settled to Tippu-Tib's satisfaction.

On June 4, two Free State steamers, the *Stanley* and the *A.I.A.*, arrived at Yambuya. The loads considered not absolutely necessary were put on board these boats to be taken downriver to Bangala, and a letter was sent to Ward instructing him to remain with these goods when he returned from the coast after sending the telegram to the committee. Included among the "unnecessary items" were parts of Stanley's kit, including medicine and provisions that could have been put to good use by the men at Yambuya, but Barttelot, afraid of being accused of robbing his chief, was determined that nothing of Stanley's should be touched.

The steamers left with the excess baggage, the seriously ill (including Troup), and Assad Farran, the talebearing interpreter. At last, on June 11, 1888, the rear column started out along the path Stanley had taken eleven months earlier. The rear column now consisted of 115 Zanzibaris, 22 Sudanese, 1 Somali, 3 white officers, and 430 Manyuema and Wacusu: a total of 571 people.

Trouble started immediately. There were wholesale desertions by Tippu-Tib's people, and even Muni Somai was unable to control them. Most of these men had never served as pagazis before, and they did not like the job. The march was confusion itself. Men became separated, lost their way, made different camps, and tried to jettison their loads. There were delays while the officers attempted to find lost baggage and hunt for deserters. There was a shortage of food, and the entire caravan was not far from mutiny. Barttelot became distrustful of his own men, ordering the Zanzibaris disarmed and their rifles carried as loads.

Surrounded by the black men he hated, bitter that he had been placed by Stanley in such a complicated and, to him, impossible situation, Barttelot's sense of values was fast crumbling. In the disorder of the march, frustration piled on frustration until his intelligence was overwhelmed by confused masses of conflicting emotions. Still, he retained his will to keep the expedition together and to press on at whatever cost. Muni Sumai was almost useless; he was unable to make the Manyuema obey him or even to move when they did not feel like it, and they burned and looted every village they encountered.

Disciplinary efforts only incited greater rebellion, until the leaders of the rear guard lived in constant dread of the next uprising. Jameson, who had stayed four days behind Barttelot and Bonny, encountered the first threat of personal danger from his unruly men. In a letter to his brother he described what happened: "One night, after Mr. Bonny had left, I had gone to bed, and out of pure devilment they fired off about 100 guns in a minute close to my tent, I suppose to frighten me. Some of the guns were fired off right beside the tent, lighting it up with the flash. I jumped out of bed, and ran out, catching one man in the act of firing off his gun at the back of the tent. I ran at him, when he flung his gun to another man, and I caught him by the arm, and shouted out to the head Arab in charge (Muni Somai) to come to me. He had run into his tent in a funk. The man was a big fellow, and it was all that I could do to hold him. I sent a Soudanese for Muni Somai, when another Manyuema came up, and put his gun at full cock right up close to my breast, when Muni Somai arrived, and then there was a devil of a row. I told them all that I would shoot the very next man that fired off his gun beside my tent, and not another gun was fired whilst they remained in that camp. I did not think much of it at the time, but since then I have."

Taking fourteen Zanzibaris and three Sudanese soldiers, Barttelot went back to Stanley Falls once more to ask Tippu-Tib for additional men to replace those who had deserted and to try to find some of the stolen loads and rifles.

Tippu-Tib was tired of the whole business. He would not, probably could not, give Barttelot any more men. In desperation, Barttelot even tried to buy slaves, but he was unsuccessful. Returning to his expedition, Barttelot found that smallpox had broken out among the Manyuema. Among the savage, discontented men there were frequent fights, each race and tribe hating the others. Between desertions, diseases, killings, and accidents, it was not long before there were again more loads than there were men to carry them, and it was necessary to backtrack to bring up all the goods.

At last Barttelot, with Bonny and the advance column, reached a place called Banalya, or Unaria, about ninety miles from Yambuya, on the evening of July 17. It had taken them forty-three days to come this far, an average of little more than two miles a day. Here, in an area about twenty-five by one hundred sixty yards, more than a thousand people, counting the villagers, crowded into a camp. About seven hundred of these people were cannibals. There occurred in this setting the climax to the tragedy of the rear guard.

Major Barttelot not only disliked the black men, but he had little use for their customs. The Manyuema had one habit that Barttelot found particularly irritating. Every morning the women began the day by singing to the rhythm of their drums. Barttelot had ordered this practice stopped, but at dawn on the morning of July 19 he heard a woman lustily singing in a high-pitched voice and pounding on her drum. The major sent his servant to stop the noise. In a few minutes he heard loud and angry noises; then, two shots rang out. Barttelot ordered some Sudanese soldiers to find the man who was firing; at the same time, he snatched his pistols and stormed out of his tent shouting, "I'll shoot the first man I catch firing." There was no more shooting, but the Manyuema woman continued to beat her drum.

The Sudanese reported that they could not find the man who had discharged his rifle. Brushing past them and pushing through some Manyuema, Barttelot walked quickly toward the drumming woman. Furiously, he shouted at her to stop. A shot rang out. Major Barttelot fell to the ground with a bullet through his heart.

The drum beats stopped, but a wild tumult now took place. Panic gripped the entire camp. The Manyuema stampeded, screaming. More shots were fired. The Sudanese soldiers ran away. Loads were stolen or torn apart as the expedition quickly disintegrated. Bonny was the only white man left in camp. Catching hold of two men, he made them get the major's body and carry it to his hut. Stepping outside again, he saw one of the Manyuema chiefs with a revolver and a rifle leading about sixty men toward him. Bonny kept his head. Unarmed, he walked slowly toward the chief and calmly asked him if they had come to fight him. The chief, somewhat abashed, said "No."

"Then take your men quietly to their houses," Bonny told him, "and bring all the headmen to me, for I wish to speak to them."

The man did as he was told, and a short time later some of the chiefs appeared. Bonny told them, "The trouble is not mine, but Tippu-Tib's. I want you to bring me all the loads, and tell all your men to do the same. Tippu-Tib knows what each of you has in charge and is responsible for them. This is Tippu-Tib's trouble. Tippu-Tib will have to pay up if the goods are lost, and will punish the headmen who caused him a loss. I shall write to him, and he will come here, and he shall know the name of him who refuses to do what I now wish."

This resulted in the return to the storeroom of about a hundred and fifty loads. Rounding up some of his men, Bonny sent them out to gather up as many of the still missing loads as they could. Goods and supplies were scattered all over the camp and in the surrounding jungle. Some of the bead sacks had been ripped open and some of the ammunition boxes had been broken into, but finally Bonny was able to collect all but forty-seven and a half loads.

He now wrote a note to Jameson, who was about four days back in the forest, and a letter to M. Baert, a Congo Free State officer who was now with Tippu-Tib. He asked Baert that Tippu-Tib be persuaded to send another chief to replace Muni Somai, who was among the missing, and to tell Tippu-Tib what had taken place at Banalya. He also asked Baert to warn Tippu-Tib that "all Europe would blame him" if he did not assist the caravan.

Meanwhile, Major Edmund Barttelot's corpse lay unburied. Bonny now took time to sew the young officer's body in a blanket, carry it to the edge of the forest, and dig a grave. Laying the body on a cushion of leaves, he closed the grave and read the church service from his prayer book.

He next wrote up an official report for Stanley. After describing the events leading up to this point he wrote, "I therefore take command of this second column of the Emin Pasha Relief Expedition until I see Mr. Stanley or return to the coast." This, in spite of the fact that Jameson, the appointed second in command, was but a few days away.

On July 22 Jameson arrived at Banalya, but Bonny said nothing about his assumption of command. There were still one hundred and ninety-three Manyuema camped in the vicinity, and Muni Somai had returned. Three days later, Jameson decided to return to Stanley Falls to solicit Tippu-Tib's aid in locating the murderer of his friend. It had been discovered that the man who had fired the fatal shot was Sanga, husband of the drum-beating woman.

On August 1, Jameson arrived at Stanley Falls. He demanded that Sanga be tried for the death of Barttelot and complained about the inefficiency of Muni Somai. Tippu-Tib promised justice. A week later, Sanga was tried, sentenced, and shot. The execution was a botched affair. Six Housa soldiers, at six paces, fired at Sanga and failed to kill him. They fired again and still did not kill him. Finally, a Free State officer ran up and fired two bullets from his revolver into Sanga's skull.

After seeing this bit of justice carried out, Jameson decided that he should go to Bangala to meet Ward and learn what the London committee had said in reply to their telegram. He also intended to send Ward back down the river with another telegram telling the committee what had happened. Jameson left on August 9 and arrived in Bangala, fatally sick with fever, on the sixteenth. He died the next day in Ward's arms. Had he gone back to Banalya instead of to Bangala he might have died in Stanley's arms, for it was on August 17 that his long-awaited leader returned.

It was not that the officers of the rear guard lacked bravery, willingness, or stamina—they were simply not Stanleys. They were faced with a dilemma that they could not resolve. Had they taken their original force and attempted to go forward by slow stages, making each trip many times over to bring up the loads, they would in all probability have lost both loads and men, for which they would have been blamed. They were unable to obtain pagazis from Tippu-Tib for nearly a year, and for this they were censured for remaining inactive. They could have gained honor only by attempting to move forward and, by some miracle, succeeding.

But Stanley was wrathful. When he left Yambuya there had been two hundred and fifty-eight men in the rear column. Of these, only ninety-eight were now at Banalya, including Bonny, the sole remaining white officer. Stanley was bitter because his kit with medicines, maps, clothing, and other gear had been sent to Bangala; he could not understand why European provisions had been sent downriver when there were thirty-three dying Zanzibaris and Sudanese in camp; he was aghast when he learned that over half of the precious ammunition was missing; he could see no reason for sending Ward all the way to Banana merely to send a telegram; he was baffled by Bonny's statement that he had been put in charge of the rear column while Jameson was still with the expedition; but most of all he was perplexed by the failure of the rear column to move forward.

Only Bonny was left to answer the sharp questions of the expedition's angry chief.

"Were you not all anxious to be at work?" Stanley demanded.

"Yes, sir."

"Were you not burning to be off from Yambuya?"

"Yes, sir."

"Were you all equally desirous to be on the road?"

"I believe so. Yes, sir."

"Well, Mr. Bonny, tell me—if it be true that you were all burning, eager and anxious to be off, why did you not devise some plan better than traveling backwards and forwards between Yambuya and Stanley Falls?"

"I am sure I don't know, sir. I was not the chief, and, if you will observe, in the letter of instructions you did not even mention my name."

"That is very true. I ask your pardon. But you surely did not remain silent because I omitted to mention your name, did you—a salaried official of the expedition?"

"No, sir, I did speak often."

"Did the others?"

"I don't know, sir."

The catastrophe that had overtaken his rear column remained a mystery to Stanley. He could understand it only in terms of the failure of his officers. He threw the weight of his anger, his disappointment, and his grief into a condemnation of the officers of the rear column. Writing of his impressions at the end of his expedition, he said:

"My first fear was that I had become insane. When I alone of all men attempt to reconcile these inexplicable contrarinesses with what I know animated each and every officer of the rear column, I find that all the wise editors of London differ with me. In the wonderful logbook entries I read noble zeal, indefatigable labour, marches and countermarches, and a limitless patience. In the Major's official report, in Jameson's last sad letter, I discern a singleness of purpose, inflexible resolve, and the true fibre of loyalty, tireless energy, and faith, and a devotion which disdains all calculation of cost. When I came to compare these things one with another, my conclusion was that the officers at Yambuya had manifestly been indifferent to the letter of instructions, and had forgotten their promises. When Mr. Bonny told me that one of them had risen at a mess meeting to propose that my instructions should be cancelled, and that the ideas of Major Barttelot should be carried out in the future—it did appear to me that the most charitable construction that could be placed upon such conduct was that they were indifferent to any suggestions which had been drawn out purposely to satisfy their own oft-repeated desire of 'moving on.'

"But how I wish I had been there for just one hour only on that August 17, 1887, when the five officers were assembled—adrift and away, finally, from all touch with civilization—to discuss what they should do . . . to remind them that

" 'The path of duty is the way to glory.' "

Bonny, worn down by the chain of events and fearful of Stanley's wrath, threw honesty to the winds in order to clear himself. It is doubtful that the meeting he described to Stanley ever took place. The diaries of the other officers make no mention of it. On the contrary, the officers pored over the letter of instructions and attempted to obey it to the letter.

Bonny stooped to another bit of deception when he showed Stanley the letter appointing him as commander during Barttelot's absence. The letter had been given to him just before Barttelot left for Stanley Falls when Jameson was at Kasongo, Ward was on his way to Banana with the telegram, and Troup was too ill to move. It was intended to be effective only until one of the other officers returned. Most of the confusion regarding the events at Yambuya, and most of the disgraceful attempts to shift or evade responsibility for the failure of the rear guard that occurred later, can be blamed directly or indirectly upon the strange Mr. Bonny.

In Stanley's first attempts to fathom the mystery of the tragedy, there arose from the depth of his Celtic soul a conviction that "a supernatural malignant influence or agency" had been at work. At the end of his expedition, when he was comparing dates, he discovered that on the day he arrived at Banalya, to learn of the death of Major Barttelot and the ruin of his rear guard, Jameson died five hundred miles west of him, and the following day, six hundred miles east of him, Mounteney-Jephson and Emin Pasha walked into the hands of the rebellious soldiers of Equatoria and were taken prisoner. Considering this, Stanley said, "This is all very uncanny if you think of it. There is a supernatural *diablerie* operating which surpasses the conception and attainment of a mortal man."

Speaking of his first impressions he said, "I scarcely know how I endured the first few hours. The ceaseless story of calamity vexed my ears. A deadly stench of disaster hung in the air, and the most repellent sights moved and surged before my eyes. I heard of murder and death, of sickness and sorrow, anguish and grief, and wherever I looked the hollow eyes of dying men met mine with such trusting pleading regard, such far-away yearning looks that it seemed to me if but one sob were uttered, my heart would break."

But Stanley lost little time in moaning and complaining. He intended to bring up the rear column—or what was left of it. His first step was to listen to the complaints of the demoralized Zanzibaris. They poured out their hearts to Bula Matari in a gush of words. Stanley said to them, "Well sit down, children, and let us talk this matter quietly."

The men of the rear column sat in a semicircle in front of him while those he had brought back with him stood behind them. He talked to them as their father and deliverer:

"Ah, my poor men, the days of weeping and grieving are over. Dry your tears and be glad. See those stout fellows behind you. They have seen the white pasha; they have shared his bounties of meat and milk and millet and have heard him praise their manliness. . . . We came back from the Nyanza to seek you who were so long lost to us. We have found you, thanks be to God! Now, let bygones be bygones. I cannot restore the dead, but I can rejoice the hearts of the living. Think no more of your sufferings, but live in hope of a brighter future. It was necessary for us to go before you, to clear the road and assist the white man before he perished. We told you all this before we departed from you. You should have remembered our promise that as soon as we had found him whom we sought we should come back with the good news to you. . . .

"Aye, I see well what has happened to you. You lay on your backs rotting in camp, and have been brooding and thinking until the jiggers have burrowed into your brains, and Shaitan has caused you to dream of evil and death. You became hardened in mind, and cruel to your own bodies. Instead of going to the little masters and telling them of your griefs and fears, you have said Mambu Kwa Mungu—it is God's trouble—our masters don't care for us and we don't care for them.

"Now, Ferajji, you are a headman, tell me what cause of complaint you have."

Ferajji, as spokesman for the men, poured forth the story of how they had been beaten and how thieves stole everything in sight. He told how Zanzibaris accused Sudanese and Sudanese accused Somalis and Somalis accused Zanzibaris. Stanley asked why the men stole.

"Hunger made them steal," Ferajji said. "Hunger killed the strong lion in the fable, and hunger will kill the best man."

"Hunger! What are you talking of. Hunger, with all those fields of manioc near here?"

"Manioc, master! Manioc will do for a time, but manioc with sauce is better. . . ."

"After all, Ferajji, though manioc by itself is very dry eating, it is very good food. Think of it, all the blacks from Banana to Stanley Falls live on it. Why should not Zanzibaris of this expedition live on it as they lived during six years on the Congo with me. I cannot see any reason for manioc to kill a hundred men in eleven months. Tell me, when did the men begin to sicken?"

"There were about a dozen sick when you left, sick of ulcers, bowel, and chest complaints. A few recovered. Then in about four weeks many got very feeble, and some sank lower and thinner until they died, and we buried them. When our friends came up from Bolobo, we thought they looked very different from us at Yambuya. They were stout and strong; we were thin and dying. Then in another month, the men from Bolobo began to sicken and die, and every few days we buried one or two or even three at a time. There was no difference after a while between the Yambuya and the Bolobo men."

"Had you any cholera, smallpox, fever, or dysentery among you?"

"No, the men did not die of any of those things. Perhaps the Somalis and Sudanese did not take kindly to the climate, but it was not the climate that killed the Zanzibaris. . . ."

"Now in the name of the Prophet Mohammed, throw your eyesight on these forty men here who sit apart. Look at those big eyes, hollow cheeks, thin necks, and every rib bare to view. You see them? What has caused those men to be thus?"

"God knows!"

"Yet they are wasting away, man, and they will die."

"It is true."

"Well then, give me some idea of what is killing them."

"I cannot tell you, master. May be it is their fate to be thus."

"Bah! God has done His best for you. He has given you eyes to see, hands to feel, feet to walk, a good stomach to digest your food, and a sense to pilot your path through the world. Don't say that God made strong men to wither them away in this manner. I must and will find the reason for this. Now, you Salim, the son of Rashid, speak to me. The son of a wise father should know a few wise things. There is death among you, and I want to find out why. Say how you and your comrades, living in camp for a year, lose more lives than we did during all our journey through this big forest, despite all the hunger and hard work we met?"

Salim stepped forward and replied: "I am not wise, and all the world knows it. I am but a youth, and a pagazi who for a little wage has come to gather a little money by carrying my load through pagan lands. What strength I have I give freely to the owner of the caravan. Bitter things have happened to us while you were away. I have lost a brother since I came here. You must know, sir, that dry manioc and water is not good for a son of Adam. If our friends and relatives have sickened and died, it must surely be that the manioc has had something to do with it. Thank God I am well and still strong, but I have seen the days when I would willingly have sold my freedom for a full meal. Whatsoever tended to fill the void of the stomach I have sought out and have continued to live on day after day until—praise be to God and the prophet—you have come back to us. . . ."

"Ahee, Salim has the gift of speech," the men murmured.

Thus encouraged, Salim cleared his throat and continued:

"There is no doubt that the main fault lies with the manioc. It is a most bitter kind, and the effects of eating it we all know. We know the sickness, the retching, the quaking of the legs, the softening of the muscles, the pain in the head as if it were bound with iron, and the earth swimming round the place whereon we stand, and then falling into a deadly faint. I say we have felt all this and seen it in others. Some of us have picked up the knack of making it eatable, but there are others who are already too feeble or too lazy to try. . . .

"We knew that in a few weeks we were to leave here for Stanley Falls or for up the river and we had made up our minds to leave the white man's service—every one of us. There has been death among us, it is here still, and no one knows what is the cause of it. I myself don't quite believe that it is because we are working for white men, but there are some of us who do. But we all agreed until you came that we had seen enough of it. There is another thing I wish to say, and that is: we have wondered why we who belong to the continent should die and white men, who are strangers to it, should live. When we were on the Congo and on other journeys, it was the white men who died and not we. Now it is we who die, a hundred blacks for one white. No, master, the cause of death is in the food. The white men had meat of goat, and fowls, and fish; we have had nothing but manioc and therefore died. I have spoken my say."

"Well, it is my turn to talk. I have been listening and thinking, and everything seems clear to me. You say that manioc was your food at Yambuya and that it made you sick and your men died?"

"Yes."

"And you say that the men of Bolobo when they came to Yambuya were in good condition?"

"Yes."

"But that afterwards they became sick and died also?"

"Yes."

"What did the men of Bolobo eat when there?"

"Chickwanga."

"Well, what is chickwanga but bread made out of manioc?"

"That is true."

"Did you make it into bread?"

"Some of us."

"And some of you have lived. Now the truth of the matter is this. You went into the fields, and gathered the manioc tubers, the finest and best. And you cut some leaves of manioc and brought them in, to bruise them and make greens. This manioc is of the bitter kind. This bitterness which you taste in it is poison. It would not only kill a few hundreds. It would kill a whole race. As you peeled the tubers, you cut raw slices and ate them. You pounded your greens and as *kitowêo* you ate them also. These are two instances in which you took poison.

"Now the men from Bolobo had bought the manioc bread from the native women. They had steeped the tubers in the river for four or five or six days until the poison had all washed away. They had then picked the fibers out, dried the mush, and when dry they had made it into good bread. That was what fed the Bolobo men and fattened them. But the men of Yambuya had scraped their manioc, and cut the roots for drying in the sun, and as they did so they ate many a piece raw, and before the slices were well dried they had eaten some, because they had no reserve of food and hunger forced them. . . . That is the reason why there are a hundred graves at Yambuya, and that is what ails these sick men here. . . .

"What you should have done was to have sent two or three daily out of each mess to gather in the manioc in sufficient quantities and steep it in the river, and have always plenty of prepared flour on hand to make porridge or dumplings when hungry. Had you done so, I should have about two hundred sleek and strong men ready for travel with me to Zanzibar.

"Now follow what I have to say to you. Eat as little of this manioc as you can. Go, gather plenty of it, put it in the river to steep, and while it is soaking eat your fill of plantains and bananas. In a day or two I will move away from here. The sick shall be carried to a big island a few hours distant, and there you will prepare twenty days' provisions of flour. . . . Tomorrow, all of you come back again to me, and you will throw those filthy rags of clothing into the river, and I shall clothe you anew. Meantime, rejoice, and thank God that we have come to save you from the grave."

All thoughts of desertion were now banished. The men of the rear column had new hope. Added to the effect of Stanley's speech was the talk of the men who had returned with him. Taking their cue from their chief, they painted an idyllic picture of the grasslands and the lake.

"Inshallah!" said the men who had seen the blue waters of the Nyanza, "we shall feast on beef once again, then you will laugh at the days you fed on manioc roots and greens."

As for Stanley: "I listened to the artless prattle of these adult children, sympathized with their enthusiasm, and pitied them with all my soul."

They stayed at Banalya only three days, then Stanley moved his force to an island in the middle of the Aruwimi River for a thorough reorganization before leading it back through the great forest for the last time.

# CHAPTER XV

# Last Great Effort

IN ALL OF HIS EXPERIENCE Stanley had never seen a jungle to compare with the great rain forest of Ituri, yet he was now to march through it for the third time. The trek through this wet mass of vegetation would have been difficult enough for an exploring expedition with only its own provisions and goods, but for a relief expedition, carrying an additional four tons of gunpowder and ammunition, it was a herculean accomplishment.

Before reorganizing his expedition, Stanley totaled up the numbers and kinds of people who now remained to go with him:

| | |
|---|---:|
| Zanzibaris capable of carrying loads .... | 165 |
| Madi pagazis ........................ | 57 |
| Manyuema pagazis ................... | 61 |
| Total pagazis ... | 283 |
| Sudanese soldiers ..................... | 21 |
| Sick and wounded Zanzibaris .......... | 45 |
| Somali .............................. | 1 |
| Emin Pasha's soldiers ................. | 4 |
| Manyuema chiefs, women, and followers .. | 108 |
| White men ......................... | 3 |
| Total .......... | 465 |

He reconverted all of the goods to normal sixty-pound loads; he also reduced his baggage and at the same time improved the morale of his men by giving them all new clothing and issuing brass rods for purchasing food.

Stanley started back through the great forest on August 31, 1888, just two weeks after his arrival at Banalya. In this last march through the jungle the caravan experienced much the same horrors and priva-

tions as on the previous trip, but there were also new hardships. The
smallpox, which had broken out among the Manyuema, spread to the
Madis and reached epidemic proportions. Most of the Zanzibaris and
Sudanese, who had been vaccinated by Surgeon Parke on the ship from
Zanzibar to the Congo, were immune, but the death toll among the
others was frightful.

A shortage of food combined with the careless failure of the men to
conserve their rations caused many to drop by the path from weakness.
In their hunger, men would forage far afield for something to eat, and
when they came upon a plantain grove, they would rush upon it madly
with little thought of the consequences. Many were crippled by the
skewers hidden in the leaves, and others were perforated by the poison
darts and arrows of the groves' owners. Ferajji, the headman who had
explained the discontent of the men of the rear column to Stanley, was
one of these victims.

The natives of the forest were bolder now than they had been in the
past, and they would lie in wait for the caravan, picking off individual
men with their poisoned darts. Stragglers were invariably found and
killed. One day a lurking native sprang into the middle of the path and
seized a little Manyuema girl. Before anyone could stop him, he drove
his double-edged dagger through her from breast to back. Then, holding the bloody knife over his head, he gave a furious, chilling scream.

In the first forty-nine days of their trip, fifty-four people were killed
by the natives or died of diseases and accidents. One sick man, unable
to bear his suffering any longer, leaped into the river and committed
suicide. But in spite of all these difficulties, Stanley had the consolation
that this was the last time he would have to pass through this region
of horrors and that every step took them closer to the grasslands.

On October 25 he wrote in his journal: "I desire to render most
hearty thanks that our laborious travels through the forest are drawing
to a close. We are about 160 miles tonight from the grassland; but we
shall reduce this figure quickly enough, I hope. Meantime we live in
anticipation. We bear the rainy season without a murmur, for after the
rain the harvest will be ready for us in the grassland. We do not curse
the mud and reek of this humid land now, though we crossed thirty-
two streams yesterday, and the mud banks and flats were sorely trying
to the patience. . . . A little more patience and then merrier times.
. . . Relief also from the constant suspicion, provoked by an animal
instinct, that a savage with a sheaf of poisoned arrows is lurking within
a few feet of one will be something to be grateful for. The ceaseless

anxiety, the tension of watchfulness, to provide food, and guard the people from the dangers that meet their frolics, will be relaxed; and I shall be able to think better of the world and its inhabitants than the doubtful love I entertain for mankind in the forest."

But there were to be many dark days before Stanley emerged from the forest. Starvation walked with them constantly.

While camped near a plantain grove, at a place known as Ngwetza, Stanley sent criers through the camp telling the people to prepare five days' supply of food. The fifth of December was devoted to the preparation of flour, and the next day they resumed the march. In the afternoon they stumbled upon a family of pygmies who were taken captive for use as guides. But the independent pygmies refused to guide the white man, so Stanley sent them to the rear. Two days later, he saw a young pagazi staggering under his load. To his surprise, he learned that the man was weak from hunger. "Have you eaten all your five days' rations already?" Stanley asked incredulously.

No, the man replied, he had thrown it all away when the wily pygmies told them they would soon reach a large plantain grove! On questioning the rest of the men, Stanley found that at least a hundred and fifty others had done the same thing and were now starving. There was only one thing to do—send all of the able-bodied people back to Ngwetza to get more plantains while he, with the sick and weak, remained in camp.

On the morning of December 9, about two hundred people set out for Ngwetza. While they were gone, those remaining in camp searched in ever-widening circles for berries, grubs, and edible fungi. Stanley made a thin broth of some tinned butter and milk and fed it to his people. He expected it would take those who had gone back to Ngwetza about four days to make their trip and return. When at the end of the sixth day they still had not come back, Stanley was tortured with anxieties. He estimated that if they did not return within the next three days all those in camp would be dead of starvation. Already there were forty-three people who probably could not live another twenty-four hours without food.

He made a heavy-hearted entry in his journal. "How will all this end? So many have died today, it will be the turn of a few more tomorrow, and a few others the next day, and so on. We shall continue moving on, searching for berries, fungi, wild beans, and edible roots, while the scouts strike far inland to right and left; but by and by, if we fail to find substantial food, even the scouts must cease their search and will presently pass away. Then the white men, no longer supplied by the share of their pickings, which the brave fellows laid at their tent doors, must begin the quest of food for themselves; and each will ask, as he picks a berry here and a mushroom there, how it will all end, and when. And while he repeats this dumb self-questioning, little side shows of familiar scenes will be glanced at. One moment, a friend's face, pink and contented, will loom before him; or a well known house, or a street astir with busy life, or a church with its congregation, or a theatre and its bright-faced audience; a tea table will be remembered, or a drawing room animate with beauty and happiness—at least something, out of the full life beyond the distant sea. After a while, exhausted nature will compel him to seek a leafy alcove where he may rest, and where many a vision will come to him of things that have been, until a profound darkness will settle on his senses. Before he is cold, a 'scout' will come, and then two, then a score, and finally myriads of fierce yellow-bodied scavengers, their heads clad in shining horn-mail; and, in a few days, there will only remain a flat layer of rags, at one end of which will be a glistening, white skull. Upon this will fall leaves and twigs, and a rain of powder from the bores in the red wood above, and the tornado will wrench a branch down and shower more leaves, and the gusty blast will sweep fine humus over it, and there that curious compost begun of the earthly in me will lie to all eternity."

In these desperate straits, Stanley took as many as were able to walk and started back along the trail to look for those who had gone for the plantains. That night he could not sleep. "Out of the black-pall darkness came the eerie shapes that haunt the fever-land, that jibe and mock the lonely man, and weave figures of flame, and draw fiery forms in the mantle of the night; and whispers breathed through the heavy air of graves and worms and forgetfulness."

When dawn broke, Stanley jumped up and called out, "Up, boys, up! To the plantains! Up! Please God, we shall have plantains today!"

His simulated cheeriness roused his men, and they started on their way. In a few hours they heard noises ahead of them on the path, and the foragers came into view, loaded with plantains. They were saved!

The plantains were rushed back to Starvation Camp where "all that afternoon young and old, Zanzibari and Manyuema and Madi, forgot their sorrows of the past in the pleasures of the present, and each vowed to be more provident in the future—until the next time."

A few days later, on December 20, 1888, the rear guard at last arrived at Fort Bodo. All was well, but the stay of the men at the fort had not been without incident, and Stanley was told the news. The arrowhead was at last removed from Stairs' chest where it had been lodged for fifteen months; he had marched more than a thousand miles with the two-inch arrowhead between his ribs. Several men had been wounded and a few killed by the poisoned darts of the pygmies. Many of the crops they had planted—beans, rice, peas, pumpkins, maize, and plantains—were stolen by the pygmies or destroyed by elephants. In spite of everything there had been enough to eat, although the officers complained of a lack of meat. To supply this deficiency in their diet they killed and ate the donkeys Emin Pasha had given them and fixed messes of fried ants. Sickness plagued them, and at one time thirty out of the force of fifty-five men were incapacitated. Rats continued to be a problem, and Surgeon Parke noted in his diary that "almost every morning some of the men come to me with a bit of toe, or a bit of leg, or a bit of nose nibbled by rats."

But here at least, the officers got along well with each other and with their men. Punishments were infrequent and were not overly severe, a dozen lashes being the common punishment for such crimes as theft and sleeping on guard duty. While the camp at Fort Bodo was similar in many respects to the camp at Yambuya, the atmosphere and mode of life were entirely different. As the rear guard had waited for Stanley, so did the men at Fort Bodo await the arrival of Mounteney-Jephson. After Jephson had made the rounds of Emin's stations in Equatoria, he was to have returned to the fort with pagazis to bring up the men and supplies to Lake Albert, but as weeks and months passed and no word was received from either Jephson or the pasha, the officers at Fort Bodo united in condemning Jephson's delay. By the time Stanley arrived they still had received no word from him. Here then was a new source of anxiety for Stanley.

On December 22, Stanley mustered his men. On the trip back from Banalya, 106 had lost their lives. Thirty-eight of these had been from the rear column. Of the hundred Madis who had accompanied Stanley, only twenty-six remained alive. The largest losses were among the Zanzibaris. There were now only 209 Zanzibaris left out of the 623 who had begun the expedition! One lone Somali was left out of the original contingent of thirteen. Of the 400 Manyuema supplied by Tippu-Tib, 151 remained. In spite of these terrible losses, he was still able to muster 412 people, and with this force, he marched out of Fort Bodo the following day.

After only nineteen days on the road the expedition again became overburdened with sick and wounded. There were now 124 men, more than a quarter of the whole, who were barely able to walk. Much as Stanley wanted to keep this expedition together, his anxiety over the fate of Jephson and Emin Pasha made him eager to push on to the lake. At a place called Kandekore he left Stairs and Surgeon Parke with the invalids and pressed on.

Five days later, the expedition arrived at Kavalli, a country ruled by a friendly chief who was also called Kavalli. Meat and other food was plentiful here, and it seemed as if it would be but a short time before they would be able to "deliver the ammunition into the Pasha's hands and escort a few Egyptians home." But the next day Stanley received letters from Emin and Jephson that put him in a rage. "As I read them a creeping feeling came over me which was a complete mental paralysis for the time, and deadened all the sensations except that of unmitigated surprise. When I recovered myself the ears of Jephson and the Pasha must certainly have tingled."

There were three short letters from Emin Pasha and one long letter with two postscripts from Jephson. Emin's first letter spoke of "very trying circumstances" and mentioned the helpfulness of Jephson who, he suggested, would be able to give Stanley "the benefit of his experience and some suggestions," should Stanley decide to come to them.

Mounteney-Jephson's letter, written two months later, was somewhat more enlightening:

Dufflé, 7th November, 1888

Dear Sir,

I am writing to tell you of the position of affairs in this country, and I trust Shukri Aga will be able by some means to deliver this letter to Kavalli in time to warn you to be careful.

On August 18 a rebellion broke out here, and the Pasha and I were made prisoners. The Pasha is a complete prisoner, but I am allowed to go about the station, though my movements are watched. The rebellion has been got up by some half dozen officers and clerks, chiefly Egyptians. . . . The two prime promoters of the rebellion were two Egyptians, who we heard afterwards had gone and complained to you at Nsabé. . . . These two and some others, when the Pasha and I were on our way to Rejaf, went about and told the people they had seen you, and that you were only an adventurer, and had not come from Egypt; that the letters you had brought from the Khedive and Nubar Pasha were forgeries; that it was untrue that Khartoum had fallen, and that the Pasha and you had made a plot to take them, their wives and children out of the country, and hand them over as slaves to the English. Such words, in an ignorant and fanatical country like this, acted like fire amongst the people, and the result was a general rebellion, and we were made prisoners. . . .

The Pasha was deposed, and those officers who were suspected of being friendly to him were removed from their posts, and those friendly to the rebels were put in their places. It was decided to take the Pasha away as a prisoner to Rejaf, and some of the worst rebels were even for putting him in irons, but the officers were afraid to put these plans into execution, as the soldiers said they would never permit anyone to lay a hand on him. Plans were also made to entrap you when you returned, and strip you of all you had.

Things were in this condition when we were startled by the news that the Mahdi's people had arrived at Lado with three steamers and nine sandles and nuggers, and had established themselves on the site of the old station. . . .

Our position here is extremely unpleasant, for since this rebellion all is chaos and confusion; there is no head, and half a dozen conflicting orders are given every day, and no one obeys; the rebel officers are wholly unable to control the soldiers, we are daily expecting some catastrophe to happen, for the Baris [natives of Equatoria] have joined the Donagla and if they come down here with a rush nothing can save us. . . .

The officers are all very much frightened at what has happened, and we are now anxiously awaiting your arrival, and desire to leave the country with you, for they are now really persuaded that Khartoum has fallen, and that you have come from the Khedive. The greater part of the officers and all the soldiers wish to reinstate the Pasha in his place, but the Egyptians are afraid that if he is reinstated vengeance will fall on their heads, so they have persuaded the Soudanese officers not to do so. The soldiers refuse to act with their officers, so everything is at a standstill, and nothing is being done for the safety of the station, either in the way of fortifying or provisioning it. We are like rats in a trap; they will neither let us act nor retire, and I fear unless you come very soon you will be too late, and our fate will be like that of the rest of the garrisons of the Soudan. Had this rebellion not happened, the Pasha could have kept the Donagla in check for some time, but as it is he is powerless to act.

I would make the following suggestions concerning your movements when you arrive at Kavalli's, which, of course, you will only adopt if you think fit.

On your arrival at Kavalli's if you have a sufficient force with you, leave all unnecessary loads in charge of some officers and men there, and you yourself come to Nsabé, bringing with you as many men as you can; bring the Soudanese officers, but not the soldiers, with you. . . .

On no account have anything to do with people who come to you unaccompanied by either the Pasha or myself, whoever they are, or however fair their words may be. Neither the Pasha or I think there is the slightest danger now of any attempt to capture you being made, for the people are now fully persuaded you come from Egypt, and they look to you to get them our of their difficulties; still it would be well for you to make your camp strong.

If we are not able to get out of the country, please remember me to my friends. With kindest wishes to yourself and all with you,

I am,

Yours faithfully

A. J. Mounteney-Jephson

To H. M. Stanley, Esq.
Commander of the Relief Expedition.

This letter was followed by two long postscripts, the first dated November 24, the second December 18. They told of further fighting between the pasha's soldiers and the Donagla, a Sudanese tribe fighting for the Mahdi. It was a tale of confusion and panic; Emin and Jephson caught between the fury of the dervishes and the rebellion of the pasha's troops. The second postscript was written from Tunguru. It told how Jephson had been forced to destroy the steel boat to prevent its falling into the hands of the Donagla. The pasha, Jephson said, was "unable to move hand or foot," but he himself was able to move about freely. The postscript ended with a last piece of advice to Stanley:

"Do not on any account come down to Nsabé, but make your camp at Kavalli's; send a letter directly you arrive, and as soon as we hear of your arrival I will come down to you. I will not disguise the fact from you that you will have a difficult and dangerous task before you in dealing with the Pasha's people. I trust you will arrive before the Donagla return, or our case will be desperate."

There were many things in these letters that were maddening to Stanley. Emin's letters were vague; Jephson's letter with its postscripts was fairly detailed, but it was not the sort of report Stanley wanted or expected from the young man he had thought to be most like himself. The reports of tales describing him as an adventurer, a liar, and a forger must have been unpleasantly reminiscent of the names he had been called in England following the Livingstone expedition; certainly it was not politic of Jephson to offer suggestions to a man who never asked for or seemed to need advice from others; the destruction of the precious boat, which had been brought up at such sacrifice and hard labor, seemed the height of folly and waste to Stanley; but worst of all, as far as he was concerned, was the failure of Jephson and Emin Pasha to extricate themselves from their position. The revolt of the natives, the attacks of the dervishes, the mutiny of the officers, and the unpredictability of the fickle and disorderly troops did not seem insurmountable obstacles to Stanley. He fired off an angry letter to Jephson. After bitterly noting that Emin had failed to keep his promises to go to Fort Bodo and to establish provision depots, Stanley gave a précis of his recent experiences, describing his hardships and labors in bringing up the remnants of the rear guard. Then:

> The difficulties I met at Banalya, are repeated today, near the Albert Lake and nothing can save us now from being overwhelmed by them but a calm and clear decision. If I had hesitated at Banalya very likely I should still be there waiting for Jameson and Ward, with my own men dying by dozens.
>
> Are the Pasha, Casati and yourself to share the same fate? If you are still victims of indecision, then a long good-night to you all. But, while I retain my senses, I must save my Expedition; you may be saved also if you are wise. . . .
>
> And now I address myself to you personally. If you consider yourself still a member of the Expedition subject to my orders, then, upon receipt of this letter, you will at once leave for Kavalli's with such of my men—Binza and the Soudanese—as are willing to obey you, and bring to me the final decision of Emin Pasha and Signor Casati respecting their personal intentions. . . .
>
> I understand that the Pasha has been deposed and is a prisoner. Who, then, is to communicate with me respecting what is to be done? I have no authority to receive communication from the officers—mutineers. It was Emin Pasha and his people I was supposed to relieve. If Emin Pasha was dead, then to his lawful successor in authority. Emin Pasha being alive prevents my receiving a communication from any other person, unless he be designated by the Pasha. Therefore the Pasha, if he be unable to come in person to me at Kavalli's with a sufficient escort of faithful men, or be unable to appoint some person authorized to receive this relief, it will remain for me to destroy the ammunition so laboriously brought here, and return home.
>
> Finally, if the Pasha's people are desirous of leaving this part of

Africa, and settle in some country not far removed from here, or anywhere bordering the Nyanza [Victoria], or along the route to Zanzibar, I am perfectly willing to assist, besides escorting those willing to go home to Cairo safely; but I must have clear and definite assertions, followed by prompt action, according to such orders as I shall give for effecting this purpose, or a clear and definite refusal, as we cannot stay here all our lives awaiting people who seem to be not very clear as to what they wish.

The next day, his anger having abated slightly, Stanley added the following "private postscript":

Kavalli, January 18th, 1889, 3 P.M.

My Dear Jephson,—

I now send thirty rifles and three of Kavalli's men down to the Lake with my letters, with urgent instructions that a canoe should set off and the bearers be rewarded. . . .

Be wise, be quick, and waste no hour of time, and bring Binza and your own Soudanese with you. I have read your letters half-a-dozen times over, but I fail to grasp the situation thoroughly, because in some important details one letter seems to contradict the other. In one you say the Pasha is a close prisoner, while you are allowed a certain amount of liberty; in the other you say that you will come to me as soon as you hear of our arrival here, and "I trust," you say, "the Pasha will be able to accompany me." Being prisoners, I fail to see how you could leave Tunguru at all. All this is not very clear to us who are fresh from the bush.

If the Pasha can come, send a courier on your arrival at our old camp on the Lake below here to announce the fact, and I will send a strong detachment to escort him up to the plateau, even to carry him, if he needs it. I feel too exhausted, after my thirteen hundred miles of travel since I parted from you last May, to go down to the Lake again. The Pasha must have some pity on me.

Don't be alarmed or uneasy on our account; nothing hostile can approach us within twelve miles without my knowing it. I am in the midst of a friendly population, and if I sound the war-note, within four hours I can have two thousand warriors to assist to repel any force disposed to violence. And if it is to be a war of wits, why then I am ready for the cunningest Arab alive.

I wrote above that I read your letters half-a-dozen times, and my opinion of you varies with each reading. Sometimes I fancy you are half Mahdist or Arabist, and then Eminist. I shall be wiser when I see you.

Now don't you be perverse, but obey; and let my order to you be as a frontlet between your eyes, and all, with God's gracious help, will end well.

I want to help the Pasha somehow, but he must also help me and credit me. If he wishes to get out of this trouble, I am his most devoted servant and friend; but if he hesitates again, I shall be plunged in wonder and perplexity. I could save a dozen pashas if they were willing to be saved. I would go on my knees to implore the Pasha to be sensible in his own case. He is wise enough in all things else, except in his own interest. Be kind and good to him for many virtues, but do not you be drawn into that fatal fascination which Soudan territory seems to have on all Europeans in late years. As soon as they touch its ground, they seem to be drawn into a whirlpool, which sucks them in and covers them with its waves. The only way to avoid it is to obey blindly, devotedly, and unquestioningly, all orders from the outside.

The Committee said, "Relieve Emin Pasha with this ammunition. If he wishes to come out, the ammunition will enable him to do so; if he elects to stay, it will be of service to him." The Khedive said the same thing, and added, "But if the Pasha and his officers wish to stay, they do so on their own responsibility." Sir Evelyn Baring said the same thing, in clear and decided words; and here I am, after 4,100 miles of travel, with the last instalment of relief. Let him who is authorized to take it, take it. Come; I am ready to lend him all my strength and wit to assist him. But this time there must be no hesitation, but positive yea or nay, and home we go.

Yours very sincerely,<br>Henry M. Stanley

A. J. Mounteney-Jephson

Stanley also wrote a cold, terse letter to Emin in which he said: "Having after great difficulty—greater than was anticipated—brought relief to you, I am constrained to officially demand from you receipts for the above goods and relief (ammunition and gunpowder) brought to you, and also a definite answer to the question if you propose to accept our escort and assistance to reach Zanzibar, or if Signor Casati proposes to do so, or whether there are any officers or men disposed to accept our safe conduct to the sea." Stanley could not understand why Emin—at that moment a prisoner of his own soldiers—was offended by this letter.

Obeying Stanley's orders, Jephson left Emin Pasha and went to the expedition's camp, arriving on February 6. When Stanley questioned him about what Emin planned to do, Jephson told him, "I know no more about Emin Pasha's intentions this minute than you do yourself, and yet we have talked together every day during your absence."

Jephson brought back a letter from Emin Pasha stating that he would like to leave with Stanley but that there were a number of his people who wanted to leave also, and he begged Stanley to help them. In the same letter he added "probably I shall not see you any more."

The next day Stanley sent for Lieutenant Stairs, Surgeon Parke, Captain Nelson, and the sick left in their charge at Kandekore. He also sent off a letter to Emin Pasha telling him to do one of three things: (1) seize a steamer and come to him, (2) march overland to Mswa and send him word when he got there, (3) or to stay at Tunguru and let him know if he wanted to be rescued by force. Should the latter prove necessary, Stanley intended to take three hundred of his own armed men, muster two thousand native auxiliaries, and march on Tunguru. In short, Stanley was willing to do anything the Pasha wanted except sit and wait for him!

In further talks with Jephson, Stanley was able to learn more of the true state of affairs in Equatoria. Emin had been a governor in name only—allowed through sufferance to accept the trimmings and respectful gestures that were the concomitants of governorship without possessing any real authority. The people over whom Emin was now concerned were those who had seen that they were caught between two crossfires and had hastened to grovel before the pasha in order to be able to get out of the country. Emin was not a strong man, he could be hurt and angry over a slight, but he forgave easily on the strength of promises to be good and protestations of loyalty.

On February 17, 1889, the pasha, Captain Casati, a Greek trader named Marco, Vita Hassan, the Tunisian apothecary, and about sixty other people with their goods arrived on two steamers at the lakeside. Stanley's officers, who had limited their personal baggage to two loads each, were appalled by the baggage of the people they were to rescue. Emin Pasha had two hundred loads, Vita Hassan had forty, Marco had sixty, and Casati—who had told Jephson, "Oh, you know I have very few things. All my things were taken by Kabba-Regga"—had eighty loads! Included among the articles were even eighty-pound grinding stones! All of these goods were lugged up from the lake shore to the camp on the plateau by the sweating, grumbling Zanzibaris.

The day after the arrival of Emin and his people, at a meeting, the Egyptian officers told Stanley they wanted to return with him to Egypt, but they begged him to wait until they could bring up their families and friends. Stanley granted their request provided they act promptly. He also told them they must provide for their own baggage, warning them that the only supplies actually needed were arms, ammunition, clothing, cooking pots, and provisions.

While the pasha's people and their goods were pouring into camp, increasing the problems of supplies and camp discipline, Emin himself was busy adding to his natural history collections. Stanley humored him by instructing his Zanzibaris to bring the pasha every insect, bird, and reptile they could find; although he felt that "his love of science borders on fanaticism." Emin also took the measurements of the pygmies and told Stanley he expected to acquire a few skulls of the Wanyoro after the expedition's first fight with them on the way home.

In order to protect his camp and to secure additional pagazis and sufficient supplies of provisions, Stanley had organized a confederacy of all the tribes in the region for miles around. By March 18, no less than fifteen tribes had agreed to supply him with food and men, to let him arbitrate all of their differences, and to be their virtual ruler! In return, he promised to protect them from their aggressive, warlike neighbors. He did, in fact, fight several battles against hostile tribes. In the few months he had been in the area, Stanley was able to acquire more real power and authority than Emin had in all of his years as the appointed governor!

By the middle of March there were 1037 pagazi loads in camp, hauled up the steep slopes from the lake shore by the long-suffering Zanzibaris. Most of the goods consisted of furniture, earthen jars, grinding stones, and other superfluous material that could not possibly be carried the hundreds of miles that lay between them and the Indian Ocean.

The rebel officers and government officials continued to send letters saying they wanted only a little more time and they would join the relief expedition. But they did not show up. At each letter, Emin would be encouraged, and Stanley would become enraged. He did not think they would go with him, and he had reasons for believing that they were plotting to capture the expedition and steal its arms, ammunition, and other goods. Finally, he sent the Egyptian officers and clerks an ultimatum. They must arrive in camp by April 10 or the expedition would leave without them.

All was not well in Stanley's camp at Kavalli. There were rumors that none of the people would follow the pasha and that the Egyptians would seize the camp. Three attempts were made to steal rifles from

Zanzibaris, but Stanley's men had been instructed to sleep with their rifles tied to their waists. Stanley was forced to establish a spy system in his own camp to keep himself informed.

The pasha, meanwhile, was once again trying to make up his mind whether he should go with Stanley or remain in his province. On March 31, he came to Stanley's tent and told him that he thought it was his duty to stay.

"Where, Pasha?" Stanley asked.

"With my people."

"What people, please?"

"Why, with my soldiers."

"Well now, really, I was under the impression that you wrote me some time ago with your own hand . . . that you were a prisoner to your own soldiers, that they had deposed you, that they had threatened to take you in irons, strapped on your bedstead, to Khartoum, and I am sure you know as well as I do what that means."

Emin changed his mind once more and said he would leave with Stanley on the tenth of April. There is little doubt that if Emin had been left alone with Stanley the latter's strong will would have ruled him, but Emin's friend, Captain Casati, continued to advise him that it was his duty to stay with his people. Torn first one way and then the other, the pasha was in an agony of vacillation.

Casati, certainly no great admirer of Stanley's, nevertheless recorded a very accurate and unbiased picture of him: "Stanley is a man remarkable for strength of character, resolution, promptness of thought, and iron will. Jealous of his own authority, he does not tolerate exterior influences, nor ask advice. Difficulties do not deter him, disasters do not dismay him. With an extraordinary readiness of mind he improvises means, and draws himself out of a difficulty; absolute and severe in the execution of his duty, he is not always prudent or free from hasty and erroneous judgments. Irresolution and hesitation irritate him, disturbing his accustomed gravity; his countenance being usually serious. Reserved, laconic, and not very sociable, he does not awaken sympathy; but on closer acquaintance he is found to be very agreeable, from the frankness of his manner, his brilliant conversation, and his gentlemanly courtesy."

Casati had occasion to witness the indomitable man in action. On April 5, Stanley decided to end the "pitiable irresolution" of Emin and the mutinous behavior of his guests. Going to Emin's hut, he presented him with two alternatives: he must summon his men and learn how many were willing to leave with him at once, or he must start out himself with an escort to a place three miles away, letting those follow who wanted to leave Equatoria with him. Neither of these proposals suited Emin, however, and he began to argue the matter. But Stanley's control snapped; he could stand this vacillation and uncertainty no longer. Stamping his foot, he told Emin in a convulsed voice, "I leave you to God, and the blood which will now flow must fall upon your own head!"

With this he rushed out of the hut and blew the whistle of alarm. Dashing into his own tent he emerged almost immediately with rifle and cartridge pouch. English officers, Zanzibaris, Sudanese, and Manyuema seized their arms and ran for the square in front of Stanley's tent. The natives in their villages, hearing the alarm, passed the word along and seized their spears and shields, rushing by the hundreds to answer the call of Bula Matari. Each Zanzibari company, under arms, was soon assembled in the square.

Emin Pasha came out, begging the enraged Stanley to listen to him.

"Certainly. What is it?" Stanley demanded.

"Only tell me what I have to do now."

"It is too late, Pasha, to adopt the pacific course I suggested to you. The alarm is general now. . . . Sound the signal, please, for the muster of your Arabs before me."

"Very good," Emin replied and gave the order to his trumpeter.

A few people came out, but most preferred to remain in their huts. Stanley ordered Jephson to take his company and round up the Egyptians and Sudanese. Arming themselves with sticks and clubs, the Zanzibaris fanned out across the camp, driving every male they could find into the square. When they arrived in front of Stanley, officers, soldiers, and clerks were made to line up evenly by the delighted Zanzibaris.

While this was going on, Casati rushed to Emin's side. He found him pale with rage and indignation. In a low, trembling voice Emin said, "We are going. Today, for the first time in my life, I have been covered with insults. Stanley has passed every limit of courtesy."

But Stanley's rage and impatience were growing by the minute. When the Egyptians and Sudanese were at last assembled he shouted at them, "If you have the courage, point your guns at my breast. I am here alone and unarmed."

Blind fury made him forget the Winchester in his hand and the phalanx of armed followers behind him.

"Do you intend to follow your Pasha?" he demanded.

All shouted their intention of going.

"Those who intend following the Pasha form rank on that other side, like soldiers, each in his place!"

They all hastened to obey. Stanley turned to Emin, "Now, Pasha, this business having been satisfactorily ended, will you be good enough to tell these officers that the tricks of Wadelai must absolutely cease here, and that in the future they are under my command. [Stanley was referring to the intrigues of the Egyptian officers and clerks against Emin when Emin's capital was in Wadelai.] If I discover any treacherous tricks I shall be compelled to exterminate them utterly. No Mahdist, Arabist, or rebel can breathe in my camp. Those who behave themselves and are obedient to orders will suffer no harm from their fellows or from us. My duty is to lead them to Egypt, and until they arrive in Cairo I will not leave them. Whatever I can do to make them comfortable I will do, but for sedition and theft of arms there is only death."

Emin Pasha meekly translated Stanley's words into Arabic and the Egyptians bowed their heads in submission. "Good," Stanley said, "and now that I assume command, I want to have a list of your names and exact number of your families, and carriers will be allotted to you according to your number, and on the fifth day we leave."

Exactly five days later, on April 10, 1889, the long column of men, women, and children streamed out of the camp. In round numbers, it consisted of two hundred and thirty members of the expedition, a hundred and thirty Manyuema, five hundred and fifty natives acting as carriers, and six hundred people from Equatoria; a total of over fifteen hundred people. Captain Nelson, in charge of the rear guard, set fire to the straw huts, sending a column of black smoke high in the air that announced to the natives for miles around that Bula Matari and his people were leaving for their homes.

Three days later the long caravan ground to a straggling halt. Stanley was stricken by another attack of "gastritis." For two weeks he was in severe pain. He could not keep solid food on his stomach, and the milk and water he was able to take caused such agony that the pain had to be relieved by injections of morphine. Thoughts of the countries that lay ahead, peopled with savage tribes, worried him, and in his tortured mind he fought imaginary battles with hordes of natives who threatened to exterminate his expedition.

Every morning, day after day, he listened to reports of sedition in his camp and rumors of impending attacks by the rebel soldiers left in Equatoria. Many of Emin's people were panicked by these stories, and some of the Egyptian officers deserted. One deserter, who had stolen some rifles, was captured, tried, and hanged. Stanley had himself carried out of his tent to pronounce the death sentence from his cot.

Intercepted letters between Egyptian officers in the camp and those left in Equatoria revealed a plot to seize the caravan and take the rifles and ammunition of the expedition.

"Worthless" was the word most often applied by Stanley and his officers when referring to the Egyptians they were taking home. Most of them were undesirables who had been "exiled" to the Sudan where they had lived a life of debauchery and comparative luxury, milking the natives for their personal pleasure. Surgeon Parke wrote in his diary: "The Pasha's people are an utterly worthless lot; they are certainly not value for the trouble taken to relieve them. . . . Such perfect human rubbish I have never had an opportunity of observing before."

Many of the clerks used more pagazis than Stanley or his officers. They burdened their own servants with heavy, useless encumbrances which killed some of them. They also tried to keep as their slaves some of the friendly natives who had helped them by serving as pagazis. Stanley said of them that they were "practiced in dissimulation, adept in deceit, and pastured in vice."

Four days after Stanley was prostrated by his illness, Parke and Jephson also took sick. Jephson was close to dying at one point, but Surgeon Parke managed to drag himself from his own bed to nurse both Jephson and Stanley. By May 7 Parke was better and Stanley, although still very weak, was able to march. Jephson had a high fever, but he walked. Every officer in the expedition had, at one time or another, marched with temperatures of over 105°.

Before breaking camp Stanley instructed Lieutenant Stairs to bury thirty-five cases of the precious Remington ammunition. The thirty-five cases turned over to Emin when Stanley arrived with the advance guard had already been seized by the rebels and might even now be used against them.

At first the caravan moved very slowly, making only a mile and a half or two miles a day. Even so, the Egyptian officers complained, and Emin expressed regrets that the marching interfered with his insect and bird collecting. Arriving at the Semliki River, Uledi found a fording place and they started across. Wanyoro tribesmen attempted to prevent the crossing, but were driven back. This was their first fight on the return trip, and it was a small one. They marched on toward Ruwenzori, the Mountains of the Moon, and on June 3 reached the base of the range, where Stanley called a halt to permit Lieutenant Stairs to attempt to climb the highest mountain (now called Mount Stanley), rising 16,795 feet above them. Stairs attained a height of about ten thousand feet before he was forced to return because of lack of food and adequate clothing.

When Stairs returned, the march continued. Emin Pasha at this time submitted his muster roll to Stanley:

> 44 officers, clerks, and heads of families
> 90 married women and concubines
> 107 children
> 223 guards, soldiers, orderlies, and servants
> 91 followers
> ———
> 555

Up to this point, Stanley and the pasha had kept their relations cordial, though strained; but when Stanley told Emin that he wanted to form an extra company using the pasha's men, Emin protested, and they had a violent argument. It ended with Emin saying, "You had better leave me where I am, Mr. Stanley."

"You can do as you like, Pasha. You are a thankless, ungrateful man!"

Emin later apologized and the incident was closed. Neither Emin nor Stanley mentioned the proposal that had originally been most pleasing to Emin: founding a new country near the Victoria Nyanza. To Stanley, at least, it was evident that Emin Pasha was not an empire builder; besides, he had neither faithful followers nor loyal soldiers.

Early in July they reached the country of Ankori where Stanley had expected to meet stiff resistance to the caravan's advance. Instead, the native chief was eager to make friends with such a large and powerful force, and he helped them on their way. This was a good start, and their luck was to continue. Although they fought several skirmishes, the march to the coast was made with very little fighting. In fact, Stanley was able to make many treaties with the natives that were later useful to the British East African Company.

Slowly but steadily the caravan moved southeastward. There were no major difficulties, but the march was not without incident. On June 16, they discovered a new lake, the Albert Edward Nyanza; on July 31, a Zanzibari inexplicably deserted, leaving his box and rifle on the path and forgoing thirty months' pay due him in Zanzibar; on August 10, two more boxes of the once precious, now useless, Remington ammunition were discarded by being tossed into Lake Albert Edward. At last, on August 27, they reached the mission station of Reverend A. M. Mackay in Usambiro. Mackay had been in Africa for twelve years, and Stanley described him as "the best missionary since Livingstone."

The expedition stayed at the mission station from August 28 to September 17. Four days after leaving they were forced to fight with the inhabitants of Usukuma, but this was the only major battle of the return trip and the expedition was never seriously threatened.

Late in October they came to the German military station at Mpwapwa, commanded by Lieutenant Rochus Schmidt. The German officer treated them hospitably and gave them an escort. There were no more troubles. From now on they met with missionary stations and German outposts (tangible evidence of Germany's growing colonial empire in East Africa). Four days from Bagamoyo they were met by a caravan headed by Major Hermann von Wissman, the Imperial German Commissioner in East Africa, and shortly thereafter another caravan sent out by Sir William MacKinnon loaded with provisions and clothes for Stanley and his people.

Accompanying Wissman were two reporters, Edmund Vizetelly of the New York *Herald* and Thomas Stevens of the New York *World*. Stevens was the first to meet the returning hero, and Stanley questioned him about the news of the world during his absence as, seventeen years earlier, Livingstone had questioned him. Stevens told him how Montana and the Dakotas had been admitted to the Union, of the growth of the Western cities and the proposed World's Exposition of 1892, of the Paris Exposition and the Eiffel Tower, of the marriage of the eldest daughter of the Prince of Wales to the Duke of Fife, of the death of the King of Portugal, and the state of affairs in Zanzibar. Then it was Stanley's turn to give some of the highlights of his ordeal.

For the first time, he had been able to return with some of his white companions, but the over-all losses, both in numbers and percentages were the highest they had ever been. The exact number of deaths directly attributable to the expedition cannot be calculated exactly, but here is a table of the losses from the original expedition:

|          | *Started* | *Returned* | *Loss* |
|----------|-----------|------------|--------|
| Whites   | 10        | 5          | 5      |
| Zanzibaris | 623     | 178        | 445    |
| Sudanese | 62        | 12         | 50     |
| Somalis  | 13        | 1          | 12     |
|          | 708       | 196        | 512    |

Thus, of those who left with the expedition from Zanzibar, scarcely one man in four returned! Of course, desertions accounted for part of this loss, but most of the missing were dead. Besides these, nearly two thirds of Emin Pasha's people fell by the wayside. Then there were the eighty Madi pagazis who had died on the trip back through the great forest to bring up the rear column, the losses of the Manyuema and, of course, the natives who were killed fighting the expedition. It would be a conservative estimate to say that at least seven hundred people lost their lives in the rescue of Emin Pasha.

But at least Stanley had not failed; Emin was safe, and now the trip was almost ended. On the morning of December 4, 1889, Stanley, Emin, and Major Wissman rode out on their donkeys ahead of the caravan and were soon in Bagamoyo. Rounding a corner of a street, they came to the square in front of Major Wissman's headquarters. On their left, close by, was the Indian Ocean. Stanley turned to Emin and said, "There, Pasha, we are home!"

"Yes, thank God," he replied.

The guns of the German warships in the harbor boomed out a salute, announcing to all who were interested that Emin Pasha, ex-governor of Equatoria, had arrived at Bagamoyo.

# CHAPTER XVI

# *Aftermath*

THE LONG, terrible trip was over. Jason had returned. Never mind if the golden fleece turned out to be ordinary wool, the mission had been accomplished. Now was the time to rest, let taut nerves relax, regain lost strength and health, and bask in the praise of an admiring world.

But that Fate which seemed always to follow Stanley was to give a cruel twist to the final hours of the Emin Pasha Relief Expedition. If God watched over Stanley in his hours of trial, hardship, and danger in the jungles, surely it was the devil who waited to claim his due when he returned to civilization.

But in the first few hours after his arrival in Bagamoyo, Stanley could revel in the pleasure of knowing that his job was over and indulge in the satisfaction of a difficult task successfully completed. Major Wissman and the German officers had planned a banquet in honor of Emin Pasha and his rescuers. On the second floor of the German officers' mess was a broad veranda, gaily decorated with palm branches and German flags. In the central room, tables were laid out for the thirty-four Europeans: the English, Italian, and German consuls, the captains of the English and German warships in the harbor, the German officers, French and German missionaries, Emin, Stanley, and the officers of the relief expedition were all there in the best clothes they could find. The band from the German warship *Schwalbe*, anchored in the harbor, provided European music inside while the tireless Zanzibaris celebrated the end of their long trip in a less sedate manner outside in the streets.

Major Wissman, a noted African explorer in his own right, knew very well how to please weary African travelers. The food was superb and the wines choice. Any kind of European food would have been welcomed by the white men, but Major Wissman had outdone himself to provide delicacies. The wine flowed freely, and Stanley found it necessary to dilute his champagne with Sauerbrunn water to keep himself reasonably sober.

About nine o'clock, the music stopped and Major Wissman stood up to deliver a congratulatory speech and propose the health of Emin, Casati, Stanley, and the officers of the expedition. This was followed by a speech from Stanley which he concluded by saying, "Emin is here, Casati is here, I and my friends are all here. Wherefore, we confess that we have a perfect and wholesome joy in knowing that, for a season at least, the daily march and its fatigues are at an end."

Then Emin Pasha stood up and delivered a polished speech. He thanked the English people who had thought of him and had sent the relief expedition, his German countrymen for their kind reception, and His Imperial Majesty Wilhelm II for his message of welcome and congratulation.

The banquet was a gay affair, and it seemed a most fitting end to the years of hardship, pain, and trouble. Emin Pasha seemed the happiest of all. He went from one end of the table to the other, talking and laughing with each guest in turn. Then, to catch a breath of fresh air, or perhaps to watch the celebrations of the Zanzibaris, Emin strolled out on the veranda. No one saw him go. Stanley was talking with Major Wissman, listening with interest to his accounts of the German war on the Arabs. When his boy, Sali, came up and whispered in his ear that Emin had fallen down, Stanley paid little attention, thinking that perhaps the pasha had stumbled over a chair or tripped on a rug. Seeing that his master did not take the matter seriously, Sali again whispered in his ear. The pasha, he said, had fallen over the veranda wall into the street; he was dangerously hurt.

For fourteen years Emin had lived only in one-story buildings. His eyesight was not good, and he had drunk a good deal of wine. One or all of these may account for Emin's fall. He had wandered out on the veranda, toppled over the railing, and fallen on his head in the street twenty feet below.

The singing and dancing Zanzibaris and natives below paid little attention. Bloody accidents were no novelty to them; they went on with their festivities. What was Emin Pasha to them? Someone dragged the pasha away and poured water on his head. Lieutenant Schmidt found him still unconscious and had him taken to the German hospital. By

the time Stanley arrived on the scene he found only two small pools
of blood.

He went immediately to the hospital, where he was guided upstairs
and shown to a room filled with an anxious group of doctors, nurses,
and German officers. Stretched out on the bed was the half undressed
body of the pasha, still unconscious. Stanley looked down in despair
at the man he had endured so much to rescue. A wet bandage passed
over the right side of his head and covered his right eye; blood was
oozing from both ears. Was this to be the end of Emin Pasha?

Surgeon Parke, who had himself just recovered from a severe eye
infection, arrived to assist the German doctors. The faithful Parke
stayed by Emin and nursed him—even after Stanley and the rest of
the expedition had moved on to Zanzibar. Then Parke himself was
stricken with an attack of malaria and was taken to the French hospital.
When Emin finally did recover he spurned both Parke and Stanley.
Not a word of thanks did Stanley, his officers, or the relief committee
ever receive from Emin Pasha.

Stanley felt Emin's ingratitude deeply. He wrote: "Knowing what
my companions and I know, we have this certain satisfaction, that let
envy, malice, and jealousy provoke men to say what they will, the
acutest cross-examination of witnesses in a court of justice would elicit
nothing more, so far as we are concerned, than a fuller recognition and
higher appreciation of the sacrifice and earnestness of the endeavour
which we freely and gratuitously gave to assist Emin Pasha and Captain Casati, and their few hundred of followers. Money, time, years,
strength, health, life, anything and everything—freely, kindly, and
devotedly—without even giving one thought to a reward, which, whatever its character might be, would be utterly inadequate as compensation. To one like me, what are banquets? A crust of bread, a chop, and
a cup of tea, is a feast to one who, for the best part of twenty-three
years, has not had the satisfaction of eating a shilling's worth of food
a day. Receptions! They are the very honours I would wish to fly from,
as I profess myself slow of speech, and nature has not fitted me with
a disposition to enjoy them. Medals! I cannot wear them; the pleasure
of looking at them is even denied me by my continual absence. What
then? Nothing. No honour or reward, however great, can be equal to
the subtle satisfaction that a man feels when he can point to his work
and say, 'See, now, the task I promised you to perform with all loyalty
and honesty, with might and main, to the utmost of my ability, and
God willing, is today finished. Say, is it well and truly done?' And

when the employer shall confess that 'it is well and truly done,' can there be any recompense higher than that to one's inward self?"

When Emin recovered, some three months after his fall, he sought new employment in Africa. The Khedive of Egypt offered him a new but inferior post, placing four hundred pounds to his credit in Zanzibar. Emin was scornful and cabled back, "Since you cannot treat me better than that, I send you my resignation."

For a while he negotiated with the British East African Company. Then, it was announced that he had taken service with the Germans for a thousand pounds a year, a fraction of what he had been offered by the British. The news created shock and resentment in England. The *Evening Standard* editorialized: "We cannot conceal from ourselves that a keen competition exists in Central Africa between Germany and England; and that if Emin is not acting for England he is acting against her. His well-known irresolution can scarcely be held to mitigate a conduct which borders on treason."

For a while it looked as if English fears would be realized. On April 26, 1890, Emin set out for the interior with his own expedition. His purpose was to secure for Germany the territory around Lake Victoria and Lake Albert. Emin marched on to Uganda, but his mission was already wasted. The German and British governments signed an agreement on July 1, 1890, marking their spheres of influence in East Africa. Lake Albert was given to Great Britain. The Germans tried to recall Emin, but he never answered their letters. He pushed on toward his old province, collecting natural history specimens along the way. When he arrived on the outskirts of Equatoria he was greeted by some of his former officers who again assured him of their loyalty. But the province was in disorder and Emin did not have the heart or the energy to set it right. He decided to leave and asked his officers and soldiers to go with him, but they refused. With only thirty-five followers, he wandered in a southwesterly direction, becoming the first man to explore the southern and western shores of Lake Albert Edward. But he was now almost blind from cataracts on his eyes, and his health was broken. In October, 1891, he wrote in his diary: "Would that I had died after my fall on the stones of Bagamoyo."

A year later, death—bizarre and violent—at last caught up with Emin Pasha. Although he did not know it, death had been following him for many months. On the shores of the Victoria Nyanza, Emin had rescued some slaves and captured the Arab slavers. The latter he turned over to the natives, who gleefully tortured them to death. Reports of Emin's action spread among the Arab slavers—and the word went out for revenge.

By October 23, 1892, smallpox had decimated Emin's little expedition, and only a handful of sick men were left. In spite of his miseries, Emin never ceased to collect, preserve, and classify new insects, birds, and plants. He was engaged in this occupation when death found him. Camped in a little village of Kinena near the Lilu River about eighty miles from Stanley Falls, he was waiting for a safe-conduct to arrive from the Manyuema chief of the district. Sitting at a table in his tent, Emin bent over a pile of dead insects and birds. Suddenly, several Manyuema men and Arab chiefs strode through the doorway. Two Arabs seized him by his arms and one of them said, "Pasha, you must die."

Emin protested. The Arabs laughed at him. He tried to shake loose his captors and reach his pistol. One of the Arabs snatched it away. While two men held him tight, the chief held the death warrant, written in Arabic, close to Emin's weak eyes. He was still protesting that it was all a mistake when four men threw him to the ground. They held him firmly while the Arab chief knelt down and deftly slit his throat.

When Emin was still in the German hospital at Bagamoyo, Stanley embarked with his expedition for Zanzibar. Here the remains of the Zanzibari contingent were paid off. In addition to their wages they were paid a bonus from a special purse of ten thousand rupees (about thirty-seven hundred dollars)—three thousand from the Khedive of Egypt, three thousand from the Relief Committee, a thousand from the Seyyid Khalifa of Zanzibar, and three thousand from Stanley personally. The Relief Committee also set aside an extra sum of ten thousand rupees for the widows and orphans of the men who had died on the expedition.

While in Zanzibar, Stanley learned that Tippu-Tib's agent held ten thousand pounds of the slaver's money in Zanzibar. He put in a suit against Tippu-Tib for failure to live up to his contract and for offenses against British subjects. Nothing ever came of this, however.

Having completed his business in Zanzibar, Stanley, his officers, and about two hundred and sixty of the refugees from Equatoria set sail for Egypt, arriving in Cairo on January 16, 1890. Putting up at Shepherd's Hotel, Stanley prepared to finish up the last business connected with the Emin Pasha Relief Expedition and to return to a civilized way of life. But for Stanley, the virtues of civilization never seemed so clear as when he was in the jungle, and the wilds of Africa never seemed so pleasant as when he was in the midst of civilization. In Cairo he found himself once more in a cosmopolitan milieu. Civilization rushed in upon him, and he was unprepared for it.

"My pampered habits of solitary musing were outraged," he wrote, "my dreaming temper was shocked, my air-castles were ruthlessly demolished, and my illusions were rudely dispelled. The fashionables of Cairo, in staring at me every time I came out to take the air, made me uncommonly shy; they made me feel as if something was radically wrong about me, and I was too disconcerted to pair with any of them, all at once. They had been sunning without interruption in the full blaze of social life, and I was too fresh from my three years' meditation in the wilds.

"If any of the hundreds I met chanced to think kindly of me at this period, it was certainly not because of any merit of my own, but because of their innate benevolence and ample considerateness. I am inclined to think, however, that I made more enemies than friends, for it could scarcely be otherwise with an irreflective world. . . .

"Indeed, no African traveller ought to be judged during the first year of his return. He is too full of his own reflection; he is too utterly natural; he must speak the truth, if he dies for it; his opinions are too much of his own. Then, again, his vitals are wholly disorganized. He may appear plump enough, but the plumpness is simply the effect of unhealthy digestion; his stomach, after three years famishing, is contracted, and the successive feasts to which he is invited speedily become his bane. His nerves are not uniformly strung, and his mind harks back to the strange scenes he has just left, and cannot be on the instant focussed upon that which interests Society. To expect such a man to act like the unconscious man of the world, is as foolish as to expect a fashionable Londoner to win the confidence of naked Africans. We must give both time to recover themselves, or we shall be unjust."

To escape from polite society and the staring eyes of the curious, Stanley sought a secluded spot where he could write the story of his expedition. He found such a place in the Villa Victoria in Cairo. There he retired to write *In Darkest Africa; or the Quest, Rescue, and Retreat of Emin Governor of Equatoria*. The man who had coolly faced a thousand diseases in Africa gave a curious answer for not returning to London. "An infectious sickness prevailed that season in London, and my friends thought it better that I should wait warmer weather."

On January 25 Stanley sat down to write, but he did not know where to begin. So much had happened. "What to say first, and how to say it, was as disturbing as a pathless forest would be to a man who had never stirred from Whitechapel." Days passed and still he found himself unable to begin. At last he wrote a chapter on the great forest. This seemed to relieve him of some of his more acute feelings, and he began to write of the march from Yambuya. He continued to write now from six o'clock in the morning until midnight. At the end of fifty days he had covered 903 pages of foolscap besides answering four hundred letters and about a hundred telegrams!

With the book completed, Stanley, with Stairs, Parke, Nelson, Bonny, and Jephson, left Cairo on April 7 for Alexandria, boarding a ship that same night for Brindisi, Italy. An enthusiastic crowd was on hand to see them off, and more crowds cheered them as they made their way in triumphal fashion through Europe. From Italy they passed to France, where Sir William MacKinnon met them at Cannes. Stanley took this early opportunity to warn him of "German aggressiveness" in East Africa. From Cannes they went to Paris and then to Belgium, where they received the most enthusiastic reception of all.

In Brussels, soldiers lined the streets from the railroad station to the royal palace, where Stanley was to stay. Behind the troops, crowds of people cheered and shouted, *"Vive* Stanley!" Brussels and Antwerp gave him gold and silver medals; King Leopold presented him with the Grand Cross of the Order of Leopold and the Grand Cross of the Congo.

Every morning from ten-thirty to twelve the King led Stanley into his private room to discuss the problems of Africa—political and economic considerations, the suppression of the slave trade, boundary lines, and the value of various regions, the temperament of the different tribes, transportation, and other problems connected with civilizing the Dark Continent.

On April 26, Stanley and his officers crossed over to Dover, where they were met by a large number of friends and acquaintances who put them on board a special train for London. Again a large crowd was on hand at Victoria Station to cheer them heartily.

The Emin Pasha Expedition—the least rewarding in terms of its accomplishments—brought Stanley to the height of his fame. The *Spectator* commented that "the cultivated and the populous seem alike disposed to make of him the hero of the hour." A cigar company asked the hero to endorse their product. In spite of his writing marathon in

Cairo, the world could not wait to hear his story. Some of the letters he had written from Africa describing his experiences were hastily compiled and published. Edward Marston wrote a magazine article entitled, "How Stanley wrote *In Darkest Africa.*"

Stanley's book was published in England in June, 1890. Soon afterward it appeared in the United States, Italy, France, Germany, Spain, Portugal, Sweden, Norway, Denmark, Holland, and Hungary. One hundred and fifty thousand copies were sold in England and the United States alone. But even Stanley's lengthy two-volume book could not satisfy the curiosity of the public for details of the exploit. Nearly everyone connected with the expedition wrote a book about it. Parke, Mounteney-Jephson, Ward, Troup, and Casati each wrote a book. Jameson's wife and Barttelot's brother put together diaries and letters to make books. Father Augustus Schense, who had accompanied the expedition only during the last few uneventful weeks, also felt compelled to write a book, as did Thomas Stevens, the New York *World* reporter who went out to meet Stanley on his return. A man named J. R. Werner, an engineer on one of the Congo steamboats, wrote a book with the snappy title of *A Visit to Stanley's Rear-Guard at Major Barttelot's Camp on the Aruhwimi.* Even those unconnected with the expedition wrote accounts of it in books like *Stanley's Emin Pasha Expedition,* written by a Belgian geographer named A. J. Wauters, and *The Other Side of the Emin Pasha Relief Expedition,* by H. R. F. Bourne. There was also a fresh rash of spurious biographies of Stanley, collections of Emin Pasha's letters, and new histories of African exploration with emphasis upon Stanley's latest expedition, such as *Heroes of the Dark Continent* and *How Stanley Found Emin Pasha.* A good-natured parody of Stanley's book, *A New Light Thrown Across (The Keep It Quite) Darkest Africa,* by F. C. Barnard, came out. Newspapers and magazines covered every aspect of the story. Never had a single African expedition called forth such a profusion of literature.

At least half of the books and articles written about the expedition were the result of the controversy arising from the tragedy of the rear guard. Everyone united in condemning Tippu-Tib, but a few placed the major blame upon the leader of the expedition. Although Stanley, in his heart, placed all of the blame for its failure upon the officers of the rear guard, he tried to be Olympian at first. He wrote, "My limited knowledge of the actual facts will not permit me to judge who is to blame for the fearful conditions of things." But he could not keep up the pretense for long; he did blame his officers—harshly and publicly in a letter published November 8, 1890, in the London *Times*. But even before this—while he was still in Africa—he had written letters to England censuring the officers of the rear guard. Before making his wholesale condemnation of the rear guard officers he ought to have consulted with Ward and Troup, the two remaining officers, aside from Bonny, who were still alive. He did not. Nevertheless, both young men wrote to him. Ward he halfheartedly excused; Troup he did not. The bulk of the blame, unfortunately, fell upon the two senior officers, Barttelot and Jameson—both now dead and thus unable to defend themselves.

All of the officers were bound by their contracts to withhold publication of their own experiences and impressions until six months after the publication of Stanley's book. This time lag was later reduced to four months. John Rose Troup attempted to publish his book while Stanley was still in Africa, but he was restrained by a court order effected by Sir Francis de Winton on behalf of the Emin Pasha Relief Committee. Troup maintained that this contract had been broken by the failure of Stanley and the relief committee to provide him with a cot, tent, and some other equipment.

Troup and the relatives of Jameson and Barttelot tried hard to restore the honor of the senior officers of the rear guard and place all of the blame on Stanley. The controversy reflected little credit upon anyone—perhaps Stanley least of all. Rather than let the case remain where it was, Stanley, under the pressure created by the publication of the books by Ward, Troup, Barttelot's brother, and Jameson's wife, fought back as hard as he could. He found a dubious ally in Bonny who, to retain his own good name or to gain the favor of his ex-chief, swore that Barttelot intended to poison Assad Ferran; that Barttelot bit a Manyuema woman; that Barttelot stabbed a native chief without provocation; that Barttelot thought Stanley intended to poison him; that Jameson had told him (Bonny) that he had bought a native woman in order to sketch her murder and consumption by cannibals; and other equally improbable charges. Stanley had at first refused to believe these tales, but now he did not hesitate to use them to defame those who would defame him.

Stanley's attack upon the dead officers could not create a good impression. Some journals passed it off as petulance or as simply bad taste, but others were quick to blame him. The *Saturday Review* apologized to its readers for referring to "the disgusting subject of Mr. Stanley's charges against the officers of his Rearguard." There was talk of bringing the case to court or of having it investigated by a special court of inquiry, but nothing ever came of it. Political considerations made it almost impossible for the British public (and the controversy centered in England) to turn its back on Stanley, for a tremendous rivalry was beginning to spring up between England and Germany. The German public, which took little notice of Emin while he was governor of Equatoria, made a hero of him after he entered the German service. In Germany he became "the solitary warrior on the abandoned watchtower in Central Africa." While praising Emin, the German press railed at British incompetence and bitterly denounced Stanley. The German Emperor spoke of the "forcible abduction" of Emin, and in the translations of and references to Stanley's book German editors placed the word "rescue" in quotation marks, indicating, of course, "socalled." With nationalistic lines so drawn—Emin symbolizing Germany in Africa and Stanley representing Great Britain—the British public could hardly help becoming Stanley's champion.

But in addition to—or perhaps as a result of—the controversy over the rear guard, there were other charges leveled at the famous man. It was said that some of the men he hired in Zanzibar were slaves; that he was cruel to his own men and to the natives; that he should not have made the agreement with Tippu-Tib; that the Congo route was a bad mistake; that he should have helped Emin to hold his province. Stanley was stung by these accusations.

But the controversy over the rear guard, with all of its charges and countercharges, came later. In the first weeks following Stanley's arrival in England there was scarcely a voice to be heard that did not have praise for the rescuer of Emin Pasha.

In the first three months after his return, Stanley was busy preparing lectures and attending banquets and receptions. One of the most notable affairs was a reception in his honor given by the Royal Geographical Society at Albert Hall in London. About ten thousand people attended, and Stanley, who was presented with a special gold medal, described it as "by far the grandest assembly I ever saw." Royalty, the peerage, members of Parliament, famous authors, and leading scientists were present to see, hear, and honor the ex-workhouse brat, John Rowlands, alias Henry Morton Stanley. As he looked over this distinguished assemblage who had come to pay tribute to him, he must have remembered that bitter day at Brighton eighteen years earlier; doubtless, he remembered also the coolness shown to him by this same Royal Geographical Society. How different it was now!

Stanley's name was familiar to nearly every man, woman, and child in Europe and in the United States. Londoners in their clubs were saying, "I suppose he's a plucky beggar, confound him." And comedians in the music halls of London were saying that Stanley had gone out to find Emin and instead had found him out. Comedy teams, in the manner of end men in minstrel shows, were asking why Stanley had been unable to find Emin Pasha and were replying, "Because there is no M in Pasha!" A would-be wit referred to Stanley as "the Emin-ent explorer." In a more serious vein were the reams of eulogistic poetry written about the intrepid explorer. The New York *Herald,* always ready to capitalize upon its former employee in spite of the secret enmity of its publisher, offered a hundred dollars for the best poem on Stanley.

In the midst of all this adulation and fame, Stanley was busy with great plans for the political, economic, and cultural improvement of Central Africa. At the home of Miss Dorothy Tennant he contrived to meet England's famous prime minister, William Gladstone, now eighty years old. Stanley wanted to talk to him about a plan for the suppression of the slave trade by building a railroad from Mombassa on the African east coast to the shore of the Victoria Nyanza in Uganda. When Gladstone arrived for "a chat and a cup of tea," Stanley eagerly spread the latest map of Africa before him on a table and began to talk.

"Mr. Gladstone, this is Mombassa, the chief port of British East Africa. It is an old city. It is mentioned in the Lusiads and, no doubt, has been visited by the Phoenicians. It is most remarkable for its twin harbors, in which the whole British Navy might lie safely and—"

"Pardon me," Gladstone interrupted, "did you say it was a harbor?"

"Yes, sir, so large that a thousand vessels could be easily berthed in it."

"Oh, who made the harbor?" Gladstone asked, scowling at Stanley.

"It is a natural harbor," Stanley replied.

"You mean a port or roadstead?"

"It is a port, certainly, but it is also a harbor, that, by straightening the bluffs, you—"

"But pardon me, a harbor is an artificial construction."

"Excuse me, sir, a dock is an artificial construction, but a harbor may be both artificial and natural, and—"

"Well, I never heard the word applied in that sense," Gladstone said, and was off on a discourse on the harbors of Malta and Alexandria.

Stanley began to fear that he would never get a chance to talk about the slave trade. Seizing the first pause, he brought the conversation back to the map. Skipping about the region between Mombassa and Uganda, he landed Gladstone on the shores of the Victoria Nyanza. He asked the old statesman to look at this great inland sea surrounded by large tribes. When Stanley came to Ruwenzori, Gladstone's eye noticed two isolated peaks.

"Excuse me one minute," said Gladstone, "what are those two mountains called?"

"Those, sir, are the Gordon Bennett and the MacKinnon peaks."

"Who called them by those absurd names?" Gladstone demanded, frowning fiercely.

"I called them, sir."

"By what right?"

"By the right of first discovery, and those two gentlemen were the patrons of the expedition."

"How can you say that, when Herodotus spoke of them twenty-six hundred years ago, and called them Crophi and Mophi? It is intolerable that classic names like those should be displaced by modern names, and—"

"I humbly beg your pardon, Mr. Gladstone, but Crophi and Mophi, if they ever existed at all, were situated over a thousand miles to the northward. Herodotus simply wrote from hearsay, and—"

"Oh, I can't stand that."

"Well, Mr. Gladstone," Stanley said, "will you assist me in this project of a railway to Uganda for the suppression of the slave trade if I can arrange that Crophi and Mophi shall be substituted in place of Gordon Bennett and MacKinnon?"

"Oh, that will not do; that is flat bribery and corruption." Smiling, Gladstone rose to his feet, buttoned his coat, and said his good-bys.

"Alas!" Stanley said to himself, "when England is ruled by old men and children! My slave trade discourse must be deferred, I see."

Stanley was continually being astonished by what he regarded as the stupidities of politicians and statesmen when they were talking about Africa or dealing with its problems. The months of May and June were spent lecturing to chambers of commerce and geographical societies in England and Scotland, and urging them to take vigorous action to prevent East Africa from being wholly absorbed by Germany.

Returning from Scotland, Stanley learned that Great Britain had negotiated a treaty with Germany, securing Zanzibar and what is today
Kenya. But he was incensed when he discovered that in the line drawn
from the east coast to Lake Victoria, separating British from German
territory (today the boundary between Kenya and Tanganyika), a
slight jog had been made to give Mount Kilimanjaro to Germany
"because the German Emperor was so interested in the flora and fauna
of that district."

In spite of his frantic activities Stanley, at the age of forty-nine,
found time, less than three months after his return to England, to
marry. His bride was the talented and beautiful Dorothy Tennant,
thirty-six, whose friendship Stanley had cherished for five years.

She later wrote: "On Saturday, July 12, 1890, I was married to
Stanley, at Westminster Abbey. He was very ill at the time, with
gastritis and malaria, but his powerful will enabled him to go through
with the ceremony."

One of the wedding guests remarked that he "looked almost a dying
man." He was forced to sit down during part of the ceremony and
when it was over he tottered out of the abbey leaning on his wife's
arm.

But his illness did not prevent him from writing of his marriage in
his journal that night: "Being very sick from a severe attack of
gastritis, which came on last Thursday evening, I was too weak to experience anything save a calm delight at the fact that I was married,
and that now I shall have a chance to rest. I feel as unimpressed as if
I were a child taking its first view of the world . . . it is all so very
unreal. During my long bachelorhood, I have often wished that I had
but one tiny child to love; but now, unexpectedly as it seems to me,
I possess a wife; my own wife—Dorothy Stanley now, Dorothy Tennant this morning."

Now that he was married he would "have a chance to rest." An
odd view of marriage, surely! But he was right. Thanks to his wife,
Stanley did eventually find rest and, more important, love and real
happiness for the first time in his life.

# CHAPTER XVII

# Retirement and Last Days

Dorothy Tennant was the second daughter of Charles Tennant, onetime Member of Parliament. On her mother's side she was descended from Oliver Cromwell. Although her father was now dead, the Tennant family was wealthy and their home at No. 2 Richmond Terrace, Whitehall, where Dorothy lived with her mother, was described as a "much-to-be-envied house" and "one of the most delectable sites for a private house in London."

Dorothy Tennant was what was known as a "lady artist"; she was an individualist in an age of female conformity. She had studied under Alphonse Legros at the Slade School in London and under Jean Jacques Henner in Paris. Her favorite subjects were nudes and children. Particularly, she liked to make drawings of urchins, and a few months after her marriage she published a book of "ragamuffin drawings" entitled *London Street Arabs*. Her pictures had already been hung in exhibitions at the Royal Academy, the Grosvenor, and the New Gallery.

The wedding caused great excitement in London that summer. It was the social event of the year, and London's best society turned out en masse. The ceremony in Westminster Abbey was performed by the Bishop of Ripon assisted by the Archdeacon of Westminster. Count d'AArche, acting on behalf of King Leopold II, was best man, and he was supported by Stanley's officers: Parke, Stairs, Nelson, Mounteney-Jephson, and Bonny.

Immediately following the wedding, the bride and groom went to a quiet place in the country where Stanley could rest and recover from his attack of gastritis. Surgeon Parke went along on the honeymoon to teach the bride how to care for her disease-ridden, fever-wasted husband.

A month later, Stanley was better, and he took Dorothy to Switzerland for a few "quiet, happy weeks," then on to Lake Como in Italy, back to Geneva, then Paris, Ostend, and London. Dorothy Stanley soon learned that wherever they went they could not escape Africa. In Switzerland they met Sir Richard Burton; in Italy, Casati; in Ostend, King Leopold. Always the talk was of Africa—its past, present, and future.

Back in England they paused only long enough for Stanley to prepare new lectures and to receive honorary degrees from Cambridge and Durham—he had already been given degrees from Edinburgh, Halle, and from Oxford, where he had been disconcerted at the interruption of the doctoral ceremony by an undergraduate who called out, "Dr. Stanley, I presume?"

On October 29, 1890, the Stanleys sailed for the United States to begin a great lecture tour. For Dorothy it was a "tremendous experience" and she thought the welcome they received everywhere was "something very wonderful." But Stanley was tired of crowds and of lecturing. In the bustling, raw American cities civilization overwhelmed him. In New York he complained of the din of bells, wheels, and horses' hoofs; of the unsightliness of the piles of earth, planking, boarding, and stacks of bricks. He thought the man who invented the "hideous Elevated" should be expelled from civilization. From his hotel window he indignantly counted one hundred and seventy-four telephone lines in the air, obstructing his view. He thought it a disgrace that rows of unpainted telephone and telegraph poles should be permitted in the center of New York. It was all very untidy.

Stanley was scheduled to give a hundred and twenty lectures in the United States and Canada. The tour was organized by Major James B. Pond, who was also the booking agent for Mark Twain, Henry George, Bill Nye, and the Ricca Venetian Mandolin Quintette. When Dorothy Stanley met Pond she was already jealous of the demands made on her husband by others. When they were introduced she quietly remarked, "I don't like you, Major Pond."

"I'm very sorry, Mrs. Stanley," Pond said, taken off guard by this cool comment. "I think so much of your husband that it will be sad for me if I cannot have your friendship."

"That's why I'm sure I'll dislike you. Why should you want him more than I do?"

Pond was one of the greatest impresarios in America, and he had made elaborate plans for his lecturer. Stanley and his bride traveled in a special Pullman car that had been named *Henry M. Stanley,* a grand affair equipped with its own kitchen, a dining room, three state bedrooms, a bathroom, and a drawing room complete with a piano. But while engaged in this luxurious and triumphal trip through America, Stanley was at the same time carrying on a furious contest in the English press. It was during the period of this American tour that the mud-slinging battle over responsibility for the tragedies of the rear column was being fought.

In March, 1891, the lecturer and his wife reached New Orleans. Stanley had not been back since he had said good-by to his foster father there more than thirty years before. He tried to find the houses and stores he had known in his youth, but all was changed now. That part of his life seemed so long ago. He was more interested in finding sights that he hoped would please his bride and in treating her to "the best cup of coffee in the world."

Stanley's diary and letters of this period reflect the changed attitude of the man of action. Rest! He wanted rest. The word, like a refrain, is repeated over and over. The old fire was burning out. He was no longer the man who twenty years before had written, "To the devil with a vacation! I don't want it." But he knew that even the completion of his American tour would bring him no peace. Sitting in his private car, he wrote, "I sometimes think with a shiver of what I shall have to endure in London." He did not know which was worse, the adulation or the condemnation; the blame and criminal accusations in the rear guard controversy or the endless rounds of teas, receptions, dinners, and parties that awaited him in England. "This is not freedom!" he wrote despairingly. "To be free is to have no cares at all, no thought of the next hour, or the next day, or the next month."

On April 15, 1891, the Stanleys sailed for Liverpool. Soon Stanley was off on another lecture tour of England, Scotland, and Wales—alone this time. To Dorothy he wrote, "Rest! Ah, my dear! we both need it —I more than you. Absolute stillness, somewhere in remote and inaccessible places, in an island or in the air. . . ." But there were the lecture audiences, the reception committees, and the cheering crowds that waited for him everywhere. In Carnarvon his fellow Welshmen pulled at his clothes, stroked his head, and pounded him on the back until he thought "there were but few thumps between me and death." But at last the tour ended, and in July Stanley was free to take Dorothy to Switzerland for the longed-for vacation.

Since their marriage, Dorothy had chiseled through many of the layers of reserve her husband had placed between his sensitive nature and the world. She was a woman who was as intelligent, thoughtful, perceptive, and loving as she was beautiful.

A month before his last lecture in Great Britain Stanley wrote her: "It is a relief at last to be able to 'speak my mind,' not to be chilled and have to shrink back. Between mother and child, *you* know the confidence and trust that exist; *I* never knew it; and now, by extreme favour of Providence, the last few years of my life shall be given to know this thoroughly. Toward you I begin trustfully to exhibit my thoughts and feelings. . . . Professing belief . . . yet inwardly doubting . . . I shyly reveal this and that, until now, when I give up all, undoubting, perfect in confidence."

Dorothy Stanley had won a great victory. But to many people, the well-bred, artistic lady and the rugged, stern explorer seemed an incongruous pair. One unkind critic remarked that "Dorothy Tennant always said she would marry a lion, and she has certainly married the king of beasts." Ugly stories of their married life began to circulate. It was said that Stanley was treating his wife with the cruelty and harshness he had used with the African savages. When such rumors reached the ears of James Gordon Bennett, Jr., he sent Aubrey Stanhope, then one of the *Herald's* star reporters, to the Tyrolian resort where the Stanleys had gone to rest. Stanhope arrived at a time when Dorothy was ill and Stanley was restless and lonely. The reporter from his old paper was given a warm welcome. For three days Stanley talked with his visitor, scarcely giving Stanhope a chance to say a word. Then, almost contritely, he remarked that he feared he was boring the reporter. Did Stanhope have some particular problem concerning Africa that he wanted to discuss with him? What was his mission?

Stanhope flinched, dreading to frame the question he knew he must ask. "No," he replied, "it isn't Africa this time. It's something quite different." Taking a deep breath, he blurted out: "Do you beat your wife?"

There was a tense silence. Stanley's hand tightened into a fist. "Now kill me," Stanhope said to himself as he braced to receive the explorer's wrath. Then Stanley relaxed and sighed, "God! I used to do that myself."

When Dorothy recovered, she and her husband took long walks, read aloud to each other, and retired early; Stanley could not break his habit of rising at six. His mind had to be occupied every minute—when he was not reading, he was writing or talking of articles he intended to write and things he planned to do. Dorothy tried to teach him to play cards, but he found this a great waste of time, and he thought playing for money discreditable. He had never found time for games or sport of any kind. Even big game hunting in Africa had not appealed to him, and, although a crack shot, he had never hunted game unless it was needed for food.

Stanley had marched across thousands of miles of rugged and treacherous terrain in Africa without ever receiving a serious injury, but, while strolling across a Swiss meadow, he slipped and fell, breaking his left ankle. It was a bad fracture, and it caused him a great deal of pain. Although it eventually healed without shortening his leg, the injury left him lame for many months.

In spite of his broken ankle and an attack of malaria that struck him shortly after the accident, Stanley planned an extensive lecture tour of Australia, New Zealand, and Tasmania. Before leaving, he accepted an invitation from King Leopold to visit him at Ostend. The King approached him on the subject of returning to the Congo, but Stanley only pointed to his cast.

"Not now," the King said, "but when you return from Australia, sound in health and limb."

"We shall see, Your Majesty," was Stanley's only reply.

"I have a big task on hand for you when you are ready," Leopold told him.

Before his marriage he had spoken of his return to Africa as a matter of course. The press and the general public had also assumed that some day he would go back. But he was married now. Many thought Mrs. Stanley would accompany her husband on his next trip, but Stanley knew the dangers of African travel too well, and he loved his wife too dearly. He talked eagerly of the many tasks still to be done in Africa, but he did not commit himself to undertake them. These plans could wait. Now he was with his wife, and they were on a six months' tour of Australia, New Zealand, and Tasmania.

Although Australia did not have great African explorers of its own, there were men who had traveled in Africa and men who had known Livingstone and other African explorers; so, as always, there was talk of Africa. At first, this talk seemed interesting and exciting to Dorothy Stanley; but more and more often the haunting fear possessed her that the Dark Continent would take her husband from her. Her wits, charm, and love seemed pitted against the dark lure of the savage Congo. She knew that however much her husband talked of rest and quiet, he was incapable of enjoying it for any length of time; she knew that although he loved her deeply, he must always have important work to do. She must think of some employment for him that would keep him near her. Her father had been in Parliament; her husband could be, too. It would provide an outlet for his pent-up energy; it would give him an opportunity to forward African interests; and—for Dorothy Stanley, the most important reason of all—it would keep him securely anchored in England.

In the early summer of 1892 the Stanleys returned to London, and Dorothy discussed her ideas with Alexander Bruce, Livingstone's son-in-law and a friend of Stanley. He thought her plan an excellent one; together they urged him to stand as Liberal-Unionist candidate for North Lambeth, London. Reluctantly, he agreed. The question of Stanley's citizenship did not come up since the British government at this time took the position that a man born a Briton always remained one. Stanley entered the battle only ten days before the polling day. Describing the brief campaign, Dorothy said, "I must say we had a dreadful ten days of it."

On the night before election day, Stanley held a great meeting in Lambeth. The Radical opposition imported an organized crowd of toughs for the occasion, turning it into a near-riot. The leader of the rowdies sat in the balcony; from time to time he would wave a folded newspaper as a signal for a storm of abuse. The meeting broke up when the platform was stormed. Stanley fought his way through the mob and put his wife in a brougham. As they tried to drive away, the toughs held on to the carriage door, tearing it off. Stanley was furious and disgusted. African savages, he thought, would have behaved better.

Writing of this evening some months later, he said, "I have been through some stiff scenes in my life, but I never fell so low in my own estimation as I did that day; to stand there being slighted, insulted by venomous tongues every second, and yet to feel how hopeless, nay impossible, retort was! and to realize that I had voluntarily put myself in a position to be bespattered with as much foul reproaches as those ignorant fools chose to fling!"

Stanley lost the election by only one hundred and thirty votes. Perhaps no better example could be given of the power Dorothy Stanley had acquired over her husband than the promise she extracted from him to remain the Liberal-Unionist candidate. He agreed to make speeches, but told her that "*never* will I degrade myself by asking a man for his vote" or to "do any silly personal canvassing." He also warned her that his "forbearance must not be tested too far."

Just three years later, in June, 1895, there was a new election. True to his word, Stanley did not ask men to vote for him—but his wife did. Almost as soon as the first campaign had ended she had begun to make friends among the voters of North Lambeth. During the days of active electioneering, she worked long hours calling on voters and discussing their problems with them. Victory meant a great deal to her—much more than to Stanley. It would give her restless husband a useful, honorable, and worth-while job to do. It also meant that, for a time at least, she would be relieved of the fear that he might return to Africa.

The contest was a bitter one. All of the old accusations and degrading stories concerning Stanley were unearthed by the opposition. On the eve of the election one Liberal newspaper wrote that "Mr. Stanley's course through Africa has been like that of a red-hot poker drawn across a blanket," and that "he nightly sleeps on a pillow of blood."

Dorothy worked long and hard during the period of active campaigning; by election night she was too exhausted to await the counting of the votes. She went to a little club in Lambeth and crept upstairs to the attic. She knew that sometime between eleven and twelve o'clock she would see the signal in the sky: a red flash if Stanley won; a blue flash if his opponent were returned. The attic was dark and empty. As she huddled by a little window looking out over a confused, shadowy mass of roofs and chimneys, she thought of how desperately she had worked for this day and how passionately she wanted her husband to win. When he consented to run again she had vowed that if it were possible to win by human effort, she would put him in Parliament and keep him with her. She had done all that she could; there was nothing left to do now but pray.

The hours passed slowly for her. The muffled roar of London mingled with the pounding of her heart as she watched the sky and prayed that her great husband would not be defeated. What would the verdict be —Parliament or Africa? Suddenly the sky gave the answer. It was red! Red flares tinted the dark roofs and chimneys. Victory! The roar of the cheering crowd rolled toward her as she ran down to join her Stanley.

The crudely lighted club was packed with black masses of men who surged up the street and pressed into the room. The short, stocky, gray-haired man who was now their representative in Parliament stood in their midst looking pale and very stern. They swung him onto their shoulders and carried him to a table at the farther end of the hall. As he passed his wife she caught his hand. It was freezing cold.

"Speech! Speech!" the crowd called out.

Perched on the table, Stanley drew himself up and, with a steady look, said quietly, "Gentlemen, I thank you. And now, good night!"

A few minutes later he and Dorothy stepped into a hansom cab on a back street and rode home. During the ride, neither of them spoke. In the hall of their house, he looked at his wife, smiled, and said, "I think we both need rest. And *now* for a pipe!"

Serving in Parliament was important work, but it was not Stanley's kind of work. He was a man of action, a commander who could lead half-wild men through deadly jungles and massed savages; but he was not a politician who could persuade cultivated Englishmen by elegant logic. Besides, he was unfamiliar with, and distrustful of, democratic procedures. The halls of Parliament seemed a greater labyrinth than the equatorial jungles. He was completely out of his element here.

At the end of his second day in Parliament, Stanley wrote in his journal: "I was so tired, when I came home, that I felt as if I had undergone a long march. The close air of the House I feel is most deleterious to health, for the atmosphere of the small chamber after the confinement of about three hundred and fifty Members for eleven hours, must needs be vitiated. We are herded in the lobbies like so many sheep in a fold; and, among my wonders, has been that such a number of eminent men could consent voluntarily to such a servitude, in which I cannot help seeing a great deal of degradation."

Stanley also felt that the endless talk was a great waste of time. It taxed his patience to listen to long speeches on topics which did not interest him. When Africa was discussed he found it hard to get in a word, and he was forced to listen to less competent but more eloquent men debate subjects they knew little about. It was more than he could stand. He had hoped to persuade Parliament to adopt some of his pet projects, but he accomplished very little in the five years he served. When his term was ended nothing could induce him to stand for office again.

He was able to do much more by his writing than by his speeches in Parliament. Between his political defeat in 1892 and his election to Parliament in 1895, he had contributed a stream of articles on Africa to magazines and newspapers in Great Britain and the United States. He also published three books in this period: *My Dark Companions and Their Strange Stories,* a collection of folk tales he had heard

Africans and Zanzibaris tell around the camp fire, was published in 1893; in the same year he wrote a short book, *Slavery and the Slave Trade in Africa;* and in 1895 he published a two-volume work entitled *My Early Travels and Adventures in America and Asia* in which he described his experiences in the western United States and his trip through the Middle East and Asia Minor just prior to embarking on his Livingstone expedition.

In 1893 he started to write his autobiography, beginning: "There is no reason now for withholding the history of my early years, nothing to prevent my stating every fact about myself. I am now declining in vitality. My hard life in Africa, many fevers, many privations, much physical and mental suffering, bring me close to the period of infirmities. My prospects now cannot be blasted by gibes, nor advancement thwarted by prejudice. I stand in no man's way. Therefore, without fear of consequences, or danger to my pride and reserve, I can lay bare all circumstances which have attended me from the dawn of consciousness to this present period of indifference."

For nine years he worked spasmodically on this autobiography. The man who, with a thousand other claims upon his time and attention, wrote a thousand-page book in fifty days, now complained that he could not find the time to write more than a few pages of his autobiography. He never completed it. His narrative ends just after his discharge from the Union Army in 1862 when he was but twenty years old. The book was eventually completed in a sketchy fashion by his wife and published five years after his death.

In spite of his statement that he now had no reason to hide his past, he found it very difficult to reveal the facts concerning his birth and early years which he had concealed for so long. When a Welshman named Thomas George wrote to him, saying that he believed him to be none other than his old playmate, Howell Jones of Bwlchmelyn, and that he believed it his duty to write a biography of his "birth, boyhood, and younger days," Stanley did not deny or affirm the truth of George's premise but simply acknowledged the letter and told him: "You are at liberty, so far as I am concerned, to do whatever you think your duty prompts you to."

The brief story of his early years that he did write for his autobiography is both truthful and revealing. In the introduction he said: "My inclination, as a young man, was always to find congenial souls to whom I could attach myself in friendship . . . friends on whom I could rely, and to whom I could trustfully turn to for sympathy, and the exchange of thoughts. But, unfortunately, those to whom in my trustful age I ventured to consign the secret hopes and interests of my heart, invariably betrayed me. . . . But when I emerged from childhood, and learned by experience that there was no love for me, born, so to say, fatherless, spurned and disowned by my mother, beaten almost to death by my teacher and guardian, fed on the bread of bitterness, how was I to believe in Love? . . . But I was not sent into the world to be happy, nor to search for happiness. I was sent for a special work."

But Stanley's work was now done, and he knew it. He was free to find happiness, and his wife gave it to him. His marriage needed but one thing to make it complete—a child. In 1896 the Stanleys adopted an infant son, Denzil. Although he was less than one year old, Stanley, like many a new father before and since, bought picture books and toys suitable to a child of four. Not long after the arrival of Denzil, Stanley was stricken with another long and serious gastric illness. During this terrible period he liked nothing better than to have the baby placed on the bed beside him. Once when the child was there, he looked up at his wife and said, "Ah, it is worth while now to get well."

Stanley's attacks of malaria and gastritis frightened his wife. Dorothy would come in from a walk and look for him in the library. Not finding him there, she would run up to his room. There she would find him in bed, covered with blankets, quilts, and heavy coats; his teeth chattering while his violent shivering shook the heavy bed. In a hurried voice he would tell her to pack hot-water bottles around him. When the cold fit passed, the hot spell would begin. His face wet with sweat, he would ask her to prepare twenty to twenty-five grains of quinine. Then he would try to reassure her; it was only "Africa in me," he would say.

But worse than the attacks of malaria were the sudden, sharp pains that warned of an immediate attack of gastritis. These attacks came more and more frequently now, and with greater severity. No doctor was able to relieve the intense pain and the violent spasms that twisted his abdomen and took away his breath.

In June, 1896, Stanley took his wife to Spain. He wanted to show her Madrid, Toledo, and Valencia. On the train, four hours from Madrid, he was suddenly seized by a terrible attack of gastritis. By the time the train arrived, the racking pains were so extreme that he was barely conscious. Dorothy knew no Spanish, but she managed to get her husband to a hotel. The next morning she located a doctor, but there seemed little he could do. The pain continued for days, and

Stanley was unable to keep food on his stomach. In desperation, Dorothy decided to get him back to England. There, with patience and tenderness, she nursed him for three months before he finally recovered.

In spite of his poor health, Stanley, on October 9, 1897, boarded the steamer *Norman* at Southampton and returned to Africa. This time, however, his mission was simply to take part in the ceremonies celebrating the opening of the Bulawayo Railway in Southern Rhodesia. There would be no expedition, no long marches, and no privations. He would be more likely to get indigestion from too many banquets than starve; more likely to be mauled by cheering crowds than attacked by wild natives.

He made the trip alone, and now, for the first time in his life, he became homesick. He missed his wife and his infant son. After four days on board the *Norman* he knew every child on the ship. "A baby cries—there is a child at home, with just such a voice sometimes; and then [Denzil] trots into memory's view, looks up brightly, and is gone."

After visting Rhodesia, Stanley toured some of the other South African states: the Transvaal, Orange Free State, and Natal. South Africa was then disturbed by the differences between the English and the Boers. After an interview with Paul Kruger, President of the Boer Republic, he predicted that only force would make a stubborn man like Kruger come to terms. He was right. Two years later the Boer War started.

In the spring of 1898 Stanley returned to England and wrote up his trip in *Through South Africa,* his last book. That summer he and Dorothy went to southern France. Again he was stricken with a terrible gastric attack. It was with great difficulty that Dorothy managed to get him home. He was in bed for two months and was much longer in regaining his strength.

Since their marriage the Stanleys had been living at Dorothy's home with her mother in London. While convalescing, Stanley decided that he needed more fresh air; they would buy a place in the country.

Stanley tackled house hunting with his old enthusiasm. He made a list of real-estate agents and clipped newspaper advertisements of likely places. Sorting these out according to locality, he went to work. Between November 15 and December 16 he looked at fifty-seven houses in Kent, Buckinghamshire, Berkshire, and Sussex. At last he found a large Tudor mansion known as Furze Hill near Pirbright in Surrey, about thirty miles from London. Dorothy also looked at the place and said "it was delightful, and could be made ideal." Stanley bought it.

The following year, 1899, at the age of fifty-eight, Stanley was knighted. The degree of knighthood was the Grand Cross of the Bath, a lesser order of the type commonly given to minor government officials. The honor came too late to be meaningful. His great works were all behind him now. He would never return to Africa.

Through the summer and spring of 1899, the Stanleys bought furniture and made plans for their new home. Stanley completely remodeled the house. He replaced the wooden window frames with stone; he dipped the gate posts and fence posts in pitch so they would not rot in the ground; he installed an electric light plant and constructed a fire-fighting engine; he planted trees and built bridges. He designed a farm and called the place "the bride," and he and Dorothy competed in decking her out. Stanley gave her a piano; Dorothy gave her an orchard. He gave her a bathhouse and canoes; she gave her rose bushes. For the first time in his life Stanley was working and building for himself. He had a wife, a child, and now a home. He was blissfully happy.

Dorothy named the various parts of their estate after places and persons in Africa. The little lake became "Stanley Pool," a stream was named the "Congo," the fields were called "Wanyamwezi," "Mazamboni," and "Kinchassa." And so Stanley's great African empire was reduced to this little plot of English countryside. It did not matter. This bit of land held more happiness than he had ever known or dreamed of.

One day Stanley announced that he had received a case of books he had ordered. Opening it eagerly, he hauled out translations of Homer, Polybius, Euripides, Xenophon, Herodotus, Caesar, and Thucydides; there were piles of books on architecture, landscape gardening, and decorating; books on ancient ships and modern shipbuilding. When he had finished, Dorothy sadly remarked that there was "not a book for me!" The next week another case of books arrived containing all the best fiction and the latest novels.

By 1900 Furze Hill had been almost rebuilt. But Stanley had been so happy in the doing that he could not stop. He continued to draw up plans for further changes. The hall, drawing room, and other rooms were enlarged. He built a billiard room with upraised seats. Although neither Stanley nor his wife played, he said, "I want those who come to stay here to enjoy themselves."

When he finished a piece of work, he would bring his wife in to admire it. She once said, "Beautiful as everything seemed—it was just

Stanley, he who had conceived and carried out all this for my enjoyment, it was Stanley himself I was all the time admiring."

He thought of everything and planned each little operation with great thoroughness—even the "fancy trifles," as he called them. There were delicate vases, enameled jars and a collection of pictures. For the drawing room, he installed a new marble mantelpiece ornately decorated with sculptured cupids—"because we both love babies," he explained to Dorothy.

When almost every improvement had been made, he stocked his castle with enough stores to withstand a siege. He bought huge canisters of rice, tapicoa, and flour. There were soap, cheeses, and provisions of all sorts. Each box, can, and package was neatly labeled by hand, and lists of all stores were kept in a record book.

At Furze Hill the Stanleys entertained their friends and the visitors who came to see the retired explorer. Strolling through the fields, sitting around a tea table, or lounging in front of a roaring fire in the library, Stanley would talk of Africa. He no longer spoke of the problems, the work that must be done, or his plans for bringing civilization to the savages; now he talked of his past adventures—the strange sights he had seen, the narrow escapes, the brave men, black and white, who had served with him. Uledi, Frederick Barker, the Pocock brothers, Livingstone, Manwa Sera, Parke, Nelson, Stairs, and Bonny —all were dead now. From the Emin Pasha Expedition, only Ward and Mounteney-Jephson were still alive.

Occasionally, though, Stanley's old reserve would come back to him in the presence of visitors, and he could not be coaxed into talking. At such times Dorothy would resort to an ingenious strategem. She would undertake to tell one of his stories herself. Deliberately, she would make mistakes. She knew his love of accuracy; she knew he would be unable to bear listening to her garbled version. Before long he would plunge in, telling the tale in his own vivid and dramatic manner. Dorothy was always his best audience; she never heard him tell a story without experiencing "a racing heart and quickened breath." Richard Harding Davis once remarked, "Never shall I forget one late afternoon when Stanley, in the gathering darkness, told us the story of Gordon."

And so Stanley found his own kind of peace and contentment. It lasted until April 17, 1903. In the middle of the night he awakened his wife with a cry. The left side of his body was paralyzed, his face was drawn, and he was unable to speak. It was a stroke.

Bula Matari, breaker of rocks, was now almost helpless. The following morning, after the doctors had gone, he made signs to Dorothy that he wanted to be propped up. He seemed only half conscious and the doctors had ordered absolute quiet, but Stanley was accustomed to being obeyed. Dorothy raised him. He made more gestures, indicating that he wanted to shave. Throughout his life, even during the most trying days in Africa, he had shaved himself every morning. He felt that it was necessary for "self-discipline and self-respect." Herbert Ward recalled a time when, after working in the jungle for two days and two nights without rest, he appeared unshaven before his chief. Stanley sternly told him, "Dr. Livingstone, you know, used to shave *every* morning." The habit was strongly ingrained. When Dorothy brought him his razor, soap, water, and a mirror, Stanley shaved himself clean.

Spring passed into summer and then autumn. Stanley lay on his bed, helpless. Calm and uncomplaining, he never expressed by a word or a sigh any grief or regret. By late autumn he was able to sit up and even to walk a few steps. His speech had returned, but he was easily tired. He wanted to go to London and was taken there by ambulance-carriage, but he returned to Furze Hill on Easter, 1904.

On April 17, exactly one year from the day of his first attack, he was stricken again, this time with pleurisy. Furze Hill was a wonderful place to work, but he could not just sit in his house. On the twenty-seventh, the ambulance-carriage again pulled up to the door and took him to London. It was the great traveler's last trip.

On May 3, when little Denzil came to visit his father he asked, "Father, are you happy?"

"Always when I see you, dear," Stanley replied.

On the night of May 9 his mind wandered. With passionate longing he cried out, "Oh! I want to be free!—I want to go—into the woods—to be free!"

Dorothy never left her husband's side. When four o'clock sounded, he opened his eyes and asked, "What is that?"

When told, he spoke softly and slowly, "Four o'clock? How strange. So that is time! How strange!"

As Big Ben was striking six on the morning of May 10, 1904, Henry Morton Stanley, Bula Matari, died. He was sixty-three years old.

A few days before, he had discussed his approaching death with his wife. "Where will they put me?" he asked. Seeing that Dorothy did not understand, he added, "When I am—gone?"

"Stanley, I want to be near you," she said, "but they will put your body in Westminster Abbey."

He smiled and said, "Yes, where we were married. They will put me beside Livingstone." A pause, and then he added, "Because it is *right* to do so!"

But burial in Westminster was denied by Joseph A. Robinson, Dean of the Abbey, who did not feel that Stanley's achievements warranted such national recognition. Funeral services, however, were held in front of the altar where he had been married.

Stanley's body was cremated and his ashes were taken back to Pirbright and buried in the village churchyard. Dorothy felt that a conventional headstone would not be appropriate for Stanley. She wanted a great monolith, "a block of granite, fashioned by the ages, and colored by time." She sent a man to search the moors. Soon landowners and tenant farmers became interested and joined the search. At last a suitable boulder was found. It stood twelve feet high, was four feet across, and weighed six tons. On it, in rough letters, Dorothy had inscribed:

HENRY MORTON

STANLEY

BULA MATARI

*1841–1904*

AFRICA

# GLOSSARY OF AFRICAN AND ARABIC WORDS

| | |
|---|---|
| *Askari* | soldier or guard |
| *Bismillah* | in the name of God |
| *Boma* | protective enclosure |
| *Honga* | tribute |
| *Inshallah* | God willing, if Allah wills it |
| *Kabaka* | king |
| *Katekiro* | prime minister |
| *Kirangozi* | guide |
| *Manyapara* | subchief or elder |
| *Meskiti* | native temple, fetish hut |
| *Nyanza* | lake |
| *Pagazi* | carrier, porter, bearer |
| *Shauri* | discussion or council |

## Swahili Prefixes

| | |
|---|---|
| *Ki-* | the language of a country |
| *M-* | a person of a country |
| *U-* | the name of a country |
| *Wa-* | the people of a country |

Names of Africans and Arabs, tribes, and African place names can be spelled in a variety of ways. For the most part, the spellings adopted have been those used by Stanley.

# SELECTED BIBLIOGRAPHY

BOOKS BY HENRY MORTON STANLEY:

*How I Found Livingstone.* Charles Scribner's Sons, New York, 1872.
*Coomassie and Magdala.* Harper and Brothers, New York, 1874.
*My Kalulu.* Charles Scribner's Sons, New York, 1874.
*Through the Dark Continent.* 2 vols. Harper and Brothers, New York, 1878.
*The Congo and the Founding of Its Free State.* 2 vols. Harper and Brothers, New York, 1885.
*In Darkest Africa.* 2 vols. Charles Scribner's Sons, New York, 1890.
*My Dark Companions and Their Strange Stories.* Charles Scribner's Sons, New York, 1893.
*Slavery and the Slave Trade in Africa.* Harper and Brothers, New York, 1893.
*My Early Travels and Adventures in America and Asia.* 2 vols. Charles Scribner's Sons, New York, 1895.
*Africa, Its Partition and Its Future.* (Stanley and others.) Dodd, Mead and Company, New York, 1898.
*Through South Africa: a Visit to Rhodesia, the Transvaal, Cape Colony and Natal.* Charles Scribner's Sons, New York, 1898.
*The Autobiography of Sir Henry Morton Stanley.* Edited by Dorothy Stanley. Houghton Mifflin Company, Boston and New York, 1909.
All of the above except the autobiography and *Africa, Its Partition and Its Future* were also published by Sampson Low, Marston & Co., London.


BOOKS RELATING TO STANLEY:

Anonymous. *Livingstone's Life Work.* Columbian Book Company, Hartford and Chicago, 1875.
Anonymous. *Livingstone's Thirty Years Explorations and the Stanley Expedition.* Hubbard Bros., Philadelphia, Boston and Cincinnati, 1872.
Anstruther, Ian. *I Presume.* Geoffrey Bles, London, 1956.
Barclay, Sir Thomas. *Thirty Years Anglo-French Reminiscences.* Houghton Mifflin, New York and Boston, 1914.

Barttelot, Walter George (Editor). *The Life of Edmund Musgrave Barttelot.* Richard Bentley and Sons, London, 1890.

Benét, Laura. *Stanley, Invincible Explorer.* Dodd, Mead and Company, New York, 1955.

Bourne, H. R. Fox. *The Other Side of the Emin Pasha Relief Expedition.* Chatto and Windus, London, 1891.

Brode, Heinrich. *Tippoo Tib.* Edward Arnold, London, 1907.

Buel, J. W. *Heroes of the Dark Continent and How Stanley Found Emin Pasha.* Desmond Publishing Co., Boston, 1889.

Burnand, F. C. *A New Light Thrown Across (The Keep It Quite) Darkest Africa.* Trischler & Co., London, n.d.

Busoni, Rafaello. *Stanley's Africa.* Viking Press, New York, 1944.

Cameron, Verney Lovett. *Across Africa.* Harper and Brothers, New York, 1877.

Canot, Theodore. *Adventures of an African Slaver.* World Publishing Co., Cleveland, 1928.

Casati, Major Gaetano. *Ten Years in Equatoria and the Return with Emin Pasha.* 2 vols. Frederick Warne & Co., London and New York, 1891.

Clemens, Samuel. *Mark Twain's Speeches.* Harper and Brothers, London and New York, 1923.

Coupland, Sir Reginald. *Livingstone's Last Journey.* William Collins Sons, London, 1947.

Crabitès, Pierre. *Gordon the Sudan and Slavery.* George Routledge, London, 1933.

Davis, Richard Harding. *The Congo and Coasts of Africa.* Charles Scribner's Sons, New York, 1907.

George, Thomas. *The Birth, Boyhood, and Younger Days of Henry M. Stanley.* The Roxburghe Press, London, 1895.

Glave, E. J. (With introduction by H. M. Stanley.) *Six Years of Adventure in Congo-Land.* Sampson Low, Marston & Co., London, 1893.

Godbey, A. H. *Stanley in Africa.* Standard Publishing Co., Chicago, 1889.

Gunther, John. *Inside Africa.* Harper and Brothers, New York, 1955.

Hanson, Lawrence and Elizabeth. *Chinese Gordon: the Story of a Hero.* Funk & Wagnalls Co., New York, 1954.

Headley, J. T. *The Achievements of Stanley.* Hubbard Bros., Philadelphia and Chicago, 1878.

Hinde, Sidney Langford. *The Fall of the Congo Arabs.* Thomas Whittaker, New York, 1897.

Huxley, Elspeth. *East Africa.* Hastings House, New York, n.d.

Ingersoll, L. D. *Explorations in Africa.* Union Publishing Co., 1872.

James, F. L. *The Wild Tribes of the Soudan.* Dodd, Mead and Company, New York, 1883.

Johnston, Sir Harry H. *The Story of My Life.* The Bobbs-Merrill Co., Indianapolis, 1923.

———. *George Grenfell and the Congo.* 2 vols. Hutchinson and Co., London, 1908.

Keltie, J. Scott (Editor). *The Story of Emin's Rescue As Told in Stanley's Letters.* Harper and Brothers, New York, 1890.

Lander, John and Richard. *Journal of an Expedition to Explore the Course and Termination of the Niger.* 2 vols. Harper and Brothers, New York, 1839.

Livingstone, David. *Travels and Researches in South Africa.* J. W. Bradley, Philadelphia, 1858.

———. *The Last Journals of David Livingstone.* Edited by Horace Waller. Harper and Brothers, New York, 1875.

Long, Col. C. Chaillé. *Central Africa.* Harper and Brothers, New York, 1877.

Ludwig, Emil. *Genius and Character.* Translated by Kenneth Burke. Blue Ribbon Books, New York, 1927.

Malte-Brun, M. *Universal Georgraphy,* Volume IV. Wells and Lilly, New York, 1825.

Manning, Olivia. *The Reluctant Rescue.* Doubleday & Co., Garden City, New York, 1947.

Marston, E. *After Work.* William Heinemann, London, 1904.

Maurice, Albert. *Stanley Lettres Inédites.* Office de Publicité, S. A., Bruxelles, 1955.

Mounteney-Jephson, A. J. *Emin Pasha and the Rebellion at the Equator.* Charles Scribner's Sons, New York, 1890.

———. *Stories Told in an African Forest.* Sampson Low, Marston & Co., London, 1893.

Northrop, Henry Davenport. *Wonders of the Tropics or Explorations and Adventures of Henry M. Stanley.* J. C. McCurdy & Co., Philadelphia and St. Louis, 1889.

Ogrizek, Dore (Editor). *South and Central Africa.* McGraw-Hill, New York, 1954.

Park, Mungo. *Travels and Recent Discoveries in the Interior Districts of Africa.* M. M'Farlane, New York, 1801.

Parke, Thomas Heazle. *My Personal Experiences in Equatorial Africa as Medical Officer of the Emin Pasha Relief Expedition.* Sampson Low, Marston & Co., London, 1891.

Perham, M. and Simmons, J. *African Discovery.* Farber and Farber, London, 1942.

Pond, Major J. B. *Eccentricities of Genius.* G. W. Dillingham, New York, 1900.

Schweinfurth, Ratzel; Felkin and Hartlaub (Editors and annotators). *Emin Pasha in Central Africa.* Dodd, Mead and Company, New York, 1889. (A collection of letters and journals.)

Seitz, Don C. *The James Gordon Bennetts.* Bobbs-Merrill Co., Indianapolis, 1928.

Slatin, Rudolf C. *Fire and Sword in the Sudan.* Edward Arnold, London and New York, 1896.

Stanley, Mrs. H. M. (Dorothy Tennant). *London Street Arabs.* Cassell & Co., London, Paris and Melbourne, 1890.

Stevens, Thomas. *Scouting for Stanley in East Africa.* Cassell Publishing Co., New York, 1890.

*The Story of the Life of Mackay of Uganda* (by his sister). Hodder & Stoughton, London, 1907.

Symons, A. J. A. *H. M. Stanley*. The Falcon Press, London, 1950.

Troup, J. Rose. *With Stanley's Rear Column*. Chapman and Hall, London, 1890.

Ward, Herbert. *Five Years with the Congo Cannibals*. Robert Bonner's Sons, New York, 1890.

————. *My Life with Stanley's Rear Guard*. Chatto and Windus, London, 1890.

————. *A Voice from the Congo*. Charles Scribner's Sons, New York, 1910.

Wassermann, Jacob. *Bula Matari*. Liveright, New York, 1933.

Wauters, A. J. *Stanley's Emin Pasha Expedition*. J. B. Lippincott, Philadelphia, 1890.

Werner, J. R. *A Visit to Stanley's Rear-Guard at Major Barttelot's Camp on the Aruhwimi*. William Blackwood and Sons, London, 1889.


PERIODICALS:

"The Achievements of Stanley," *Current Literature*, July, 1904.

Adams, C. C. "What Stanley Lived to See Accomplished in Africa," *Review of Reviews*, June, 1904.

"Africa for the Americans!" *Review of Reviews*, July, 1890.

Carpenter, Frank G. "Fireside Talks with Great Men," *Chautauquan*, July, 1896.

"Character Sketch: Mr. H. M. Stanley," *Review of Reviews*, January, 1890.

Connery, Thomas B. "Reminiscences of Two Modern Heroes," *Cosmopolitan*, June, 1891.

Creel, George. "Bold Pathfinder: Stanley, the Undaunted," *Colliers*, February 27, 1932.

Ferris, G. T. "H. M. Stanley: Sketch," *Harper's Weekly*, May 21, 1904.

"A Forerunner of Missionaries," *Missionary Review of the World*, May, 1910.

Godkin, E. L. "Was the Emin Pasha Expedition Piratical?" *Forum*, February, 1891.

Grant, C. H. B. "Livingstone-Stanley Memorials in Africa," *Geographical Journal*, April, 1932.

Hubbard, James M. "Stanley's Africa Then and Now," *Atlantic Monthly*, May, 1910.

Johnson, H. H. "Where is Stanley?" *Fortnightly Review*, January, 1889.

Keltie, J. Scott. "What Stanley Has Done for the Map of Africa," *Science*, January 24, 1890.

————. "Mr. Stanley's Expedition: Its Conduct and Results," *Fortnightly Review*, July, 1890.

"The Lounger," *Critic*, November 15, 1890.

Marston, Edward. "How Stanley Wrote His Book," *Scribner's*, August, 1890.

Mounteney-Jephson, A. J. "In Camp with Henry Morton Stanley," *Cosmopolitan*, January, 1892.

————. "Reminiscences of Sir Henry Stanley," *Scribner's*, September, 1904.

————. "The Truth About Stanley and Emin Pasha," *Fortnightly Review*, January, 1891.

Mullins, J. D. "Stanley and the African Missions," *Missionary Review of the World*, March, 1905.

"The New-Found World and Its Hero," *Blackwood's Magazine*, August, 1890.

Nicholson, Charles. "Stanley and the Congo," *Month*, September, 1885.

"Obituary," *Bulletin of the American Geographic Society*, May, 1904.

Peters, Carl. "Stanley and Emin Pasha," *Contemporary Review*, November, 1890.

Rawnsley, H. D. "A Welcome to Stanley" (poem), *Murray*, June, 1890.

Review of *In Darkest Africa, Athenaeum*, July 5, 1890.

————. *In Darkest Africa, Edinburgh Review*, October, 1890.

————. *My Dark Companions and Their Strange Stories, Critic*, March 3, 1894.

————. *My Early Travels and Adventures in America and Asia, Critic*, July 27, 1895.

————. *Through South Africa, Nation*, April 21, 1898.

Rideing, W. H. "Two Explorers and a Literary Parson," *McClure*, December, 1909.

Schneider, I. "Stanley and Africa," *Nation*, February 15, 1933.

Skilton, E. A. "Livingstone and Stanley," *Hobbies*, June, 1946.

Springer, Mrs. J. M. "Following Stanley After Fifty Years," *Missionary Review of the World*, June, 1931.

Stanley, H. M. "African Legends," *Outlook*, September 30, 1899.

————. "Anglo-Saxon Responsibilities," *Outlook*, September 30, 1899.

————. "Boer Indictments of British Policy," *19th Century*, April, 1897.

————. "The Emin Pasha Relief Expedition," *Scribner's*, June, 1890.

————. "Great African Lake," *Independent*, April 3, 1902.

————. "How I Acted the Missionary and What Came of It," *Cornhill*, January, 1901.

————. "How I Found Livingstone," *Golden Book*, February, 1935.

————. "Italians in Abyssinia," *Review of Reviews*, May, 1896.

————. "Origin of the Negro Race," *North American Review*, May, 1900.

————. "The Pigmies of the Great African Forest," *Scribner's*, January, 1891.

————. "Splendid Isolation or What?" *19th Century*, June, 1898.

————. "Stanley's Explorations" (letter), *Science*, January 3, 1890.

————. "Story of the Development of Africa," *Century*, February, 1896.

"Mr. and Mrs. Henry M. Stanley," *Harper's Weekly*, November 8, 1890.

"Henry M. Stanley," *Once a Week*, December 17, 1872.

"Henry M. Stanley, A Study in Character," *Eclectic*, July, 1890.

"Mr. Stanley," *Nature*, February 14, 1878.

"Mr. Stanley," *Nature*, November, 1889.

"Mr. Stanley and His Column," *Review of Reviews*, December, 1890.

"Mr. Stanley and the Congo State," *Spectator*, June 6, 1885.

"Mr. Stanley on England," *Spectator*, May 17, 1890.

"Mr. Stanley as an Explorer," *International Review*, September, 1878.

"Mr. Stanley and Dr. Livingstone," *American Bibliopolist*, November, 1872.

"Mr. Stanley and the Rear Column," *Review of Reviews*, December, 1890.

"Mr. Stanley and the Rear Column. What Should the Verdict Be?" *Contemporary Review*, November, 1890.

"Mr. Stanley and His Rearguard," *Saturday Review*, November 1, 1890.

"Mr. Stanley's Book," *Spectator*, July 12, 1890.

"Mr. Stanley's Charges," *Saturday Review*, November 15, 1890.

"Mr. Stanley's Discoveries," *Saturday Review*, November 30, 1889.

"Mr. Stanley's Early Travels," *Saturday Review*, October 5, 1895.

"Mr. Stanley's Expedition," *Saturday Review*, June 23, 1888.

"Mr. Stanley's Letters," under "Notes of Travel and Exploration," *Dublin Review*, July, 1889.

"Mr. Stanley's New Book," *Westminster Review*, August, 1890.

"Mr. Stanley's Reception," *Spectator*, May 30, 1890.

"Sir Henry Morton Stanley," *Scottish Geographical Magazine*, June, 1904.

"Stanley and His Work in Africa," *Dial*, December, 1890.

"Stanley's Emin Pasha Expedition," *Lippincott's Magazine*, April, 1890.

"Stanley's Expedition: A Retrospect," *Fortnightly Review*, January, 1890.

"Stanley's Forest March," *Spectator*, April 6, 1889.

"Stanley's Return," *Spectator*, November 30, 1889.

"Stanley's 'Through the Dark Continent,'" *Nation*, September 19, 1878.

"The Stanley Medal," *Science*, May 23, 1890.

Tennant, Winifred Coombe. "Henry Morton Stanley" (poem), *Scribner's*, September, 1904.

Troup, J. Rose. "Mr. Stanley's Rear-Guard," *Fortnightly Review*, December 1, 1890.

Ward, Herbert. "The Tale of a Tusk of Ivory," *Scribner's*, November, 1890.

"Why Missionaries Went to Uganda," *Missionary Review of the World*, March, 1901.

"With Emin in Equatoria, and the Rear Column Story," *Dial*, June, 1891.

Wolseley, General Viscount, and others. "Is Stanley Dead?" *North American Review*, December, 1888.

Young, John Russell. "Through the Dark Continent," *Harper's*, October, 1878.

# Index

327